As Told by Herself

WISCONSIN STUDIES IN AUTOBIOGRAPHY

William L. Andrews
Series Editor

As Told by Herself

Women's Childhood Autobiography,
1845–1969

Lorna Martens

THE UNIVERSITY OF WISCONSIN PRESS

The University of Wisconsin Press
728 State Street, Suite 443
Madison, Wisconsin 53706
uwpress.wisc.edu

Gray's Inn House, 127 Clerkenwell Road
London EC1R 5DB, United Kingdom
eurospanbookstore.com

Copyright © 2022
The Board of Regents of the University of Wisconsin System
All rights reserved. Except in the case of brief quotations embedded in
critical articles and reviews, no part of this publication may be reproduced,
stored in a retrieval system, transmitted in any format or by any means—
digital, electronic, mechanical, photocopying, recording, or otherwise—
or conveyed via the Internet or a website without written permission
of the University of Wisconsin Press. Rights inquiries should be
directed to rights@uwpress.wisc.edu.

Printed in the United States of America
This book may be available in a digital edition.

Names: Martens, Lorna, 1946– author.
Title: As told by herself : women's childhood autobiography,
1845–1969 / Lorna Martens.
Description: Madison, Wisconsin : The University of Wisconsin Press, [2022] |
Includes bibliographical references and index.
Identifiers: LCCN 2022000577 | ISBN 9780299339104 (hardcover)
Subjects: LCSH: Autobiography—Women authors. | Girls—Biography—
History and criticism. | Women authors—Childhood and youth—
Biography—History and criticism. | Children in literature.
Classification: LCC CT25 .M378 2022 | DDC 920.72—dc23/eng/20220405
LC record available at https://lccn.loc.gov/2022000577

For my
granddaughters

Contents

Acknowledgments	ix
Introduction	3

**1 Beginnings: Women's Childhood Autobiography
Prior to World War I** — 22

Women's Childhood Autobiography in France — 24

*Mother-Daughter Conflict • Remembering • The Self-Portrait •
The Working-Class Woman*

Women's Childhood Autobiography in England, the
United States, Australia, and Ireland — 36

*"We" • The Study • Short Pieces • The Victim • Capturing the
Child's Vision • The Inner Life of the Child • Mixing Genres*

Women's Childhood Autobiography Elsewhere around 1900 — 67

In sum — 74

2 The Interwar Years: Memoirs and Semi-Memoirs — 78

Memoirs — 81

*Memoirs from the Lands of the Victors • Memoirs from the Land of
the Vanquished*

Semi-Memoirs — 92

1935 • "Splendor in the Grass" • Humor • Souvenirs

In sum — 108

viii Contents

3 The Interwar Years: The Golden Age of Psychological
Self-Portraiture 110

Self-Portraits in the 1920s 112

How I Became What I Became • In Your Face

Self-Expression in the 1930s 125

Self-Assertion

The Child's Vision 144

The Study

In sum 162

4 Women's Childhood Autobiography during World War II 166

Semi-Memoirs 167

Self-Focused Works 170

*Self-Assertion • Remembering • The Family Nest and the
Challenges beyond It*

In sum 184

5 Women's Childhood Autobiography from the End of the
Second World War through the 1960s 186

Autobiographies of Abuse 196

Self-Focused Autobiographies 214

Bildungsroman • Relationships

The Child's Perspective 233

A Stylistic Mix

In sum 242

Conclusion 247

Notes 265

Bibliography of Women's Childhood Autobiographies to 1969 281

Index 291

Acknowledgments

After writing my first book on the history of a genre, I swore I would never again do the like. Yet empirical research—the promise of discovering the undiscovered—proved seductive, and somehow, twenty years later, my desire to write what I thought would be a short history of women's childhood autobiographies overcame my wise resolve. Before long, I was swamped with potential examples. I found myself writing the history of the 170-odd works that met my criteria. I never would have been able to accomplish this if it had not been for the generous support of the University of Virginia, which funded two Sesquicentennial Associateships in 2012–13 and 2018–19, a summer grant in 2013, and travel to the Cambridge University Library. I was also greatly aided by the staff of the University of Virginia Library, including Jim Campbell, George Crafts, Miguel Valladares-Llata, Bryson Clevenger, Chris Ruotolo, Anne Benham, and Renee Reighart, who helped me track down and consult materials. I particularly wish to thank my colleague Janette Hudson for reading and critiquing the entire manuscript in its original form. I also wish to thank the one reader for press whose name I know, Kate Douglas, for reading a later version of the manuscript and encouraging publication.

As Told by Herself

Introduction

Childhood, of course, decides what kind of adults we shall be.

—Janet Hitchman, *The King of the Barbareens*

Famous autobiographical narratives of childhood, or childhood and youth, were written by women starting in the late 1960s and 1970s with the advent of second-wave feminism. One could name, in a first two-decade span, Maya Angelou's *I Know Why the Caged Bird Sings* (1969), Kathleen Raine's *Farewell Happy Fields* (1973), Maxine Hong Kingston's *The Woman Warrior* (1976), Christa Wolf's *Patterns of Childhood (Kindheitsmuster*, 1976), Janet Frame's *To the Is-land* (1982), Nathalie Sarraute's *Childhood (Enfance*, 1983), Marguerite Duras's *The Lover (L'Amant*, 1984), Jamaica Kincaid's *Annie John* (1985), and Annie Dillard's *An American Childhood* (1987). In the following decade the phenomenon—autobiographical childhood narratives written by women—was well on its way to becoming global. The genre caught on internationally. Women writers from countries that did not have comparably strong traditions of women's autobiographical writing joined the ranks of those who published books about their girlhood experiences. Some became famous: Moroccan writer Fatima Mernissi (*Dreams of Trespass*, 1994) wrote about her "harem girlhood" for Western audiences; Iranian author Marjane Satrapi's graphic childhood autobiography *Persepolis* (2000–2003) has been translated into many languages and produced as an animated film.

This recent wave of women's self-writing about childhood prompts the question: What is its history? How long have women been writing autobiographical narratives that dwell on their lives up to age ten, age twelve, age eighteen? In order to find this out, I looked back at the unwritten history of women's childhood autobiography. The result is this book.

Women's autobiographies of childhood tell incredibly revealing, moving, and interesting stories about what it is like to grow up female in different places and circumstances. Some of them are, in addition, extraordinarily accomplished literary productions. Many adult women authors not only show an impressive degree of insight into their childhood, and by extension into childhood generally, but sophistication in writing about it. Some focus squarely on women's problems like sex discrimination, disempowerment, or sexual exploitation, whereas in others such "typical issues" are tangential to the author's presentation of her own individual story.

These works have a twofold allure: they open a window on women's childhoods, and they illustrate the ways in which women authors thought best to present themselves to and write about their personal experiences for the public.

Autobiography is one of many sources for historical information, but it above all promises insight into a human being, into another life. This glimpse into another person and her life is filtered through the author's self-reflection and self-representation. Autobiography is unique in its capacity to reveal how a person saw fit to present herself to contemporaries and to posterity. I am interested in the emergence of women's self-writing. Therefore, I focus on works in which women write about themselves as children rather than merely about the circumstances in which they grew up. Since I am further interested in the ways women chose to present their younger selves to the public rather than what they wrote in diaries or for the desk drawer, I confine myself to works that women published or intended for publication. Writing for publication, in contrast to writing for oneself or one's family or friends, testifies to a belief that what one has to say will be of interest to a wider readership, hence to a certain self-confidence, and also to the confidence that one will be able to express oneself about one's own person in a manner worthy of the public sphere. Presenting facts about oneself in public and acknowledging oneself as the author of a self-representation require gumption. Today the barriers are down, but this was not always the case.[1]

The questions I seek to answer are: How did women's public self-performance of their earlier identities as young persons start and progress? What shapes did it take? What kinds of things did women think would interest and engage a wider readership?

In looking for works, I have gratefully used other scholars' bibliographies. In particular, I combed Richard N. Coe's "The Autobiography of Childhood and Adolescence: A Bibliography of Primary Sources in the Major Languages of European Origin," which lists over 650 titles published through 1984,[2] and Jeffrey Long's *Remembered Childhoods*, a book-length reference work that lists autobiographies and memoirs from 1725 to 2007 that were written in or translated into English and contain at least fifty pages on the author's childhood and youth.[3] Additionally, I consulted more specialized bibliographies, such as Joy Hooton's bibliography of Australian women's autobiographies of childhood and youth in her *Stories of Herself When Young: Autobiographies of Childhood by Australian Women*[4] and Gudrun Wedel's lexicon of published autobiographies by women born between 1800 and 1900 in the German-speaking countries, *Autobiographien von Frauen*.[5]

Beyond that, I read what I found. My aim was to be comprehensive—no woman's childhood autobiography left behind—because I believe that empirical evidence, the more of it the better, should ground theory. It is perhaps needless to say that comprehensiveness is an unrealizable dream for archival work. I make no claim to having found all relevant works. Readers will surely think of titles that I do not mention. In particular, there are surely many untranslated works in languages I do not read, such as Russian, Spanish, Italian, Dutch, and the Scandinavian languages. I treat above all the two major traditions: the French, which was undeniably early and trendsetting; and the Anglophone, which, comparably early but very different, came to dominate the field by sheer force of numbers, since writers in England, Ireland, the United States, Canada, and Australia, to name the major areas, all contributed to it. Readers may also wonder why I leave out some titles that other bibliographers include. The reason is that I exclude works in which the author's childhood self receives too little representation: where the childhood years are treated briefly, the self is marginalized, or the author hides her self-representation in a work of creative fiction.[6] More on these borderline types presently.

I did read a great many works that had been completely forgotten and that libraries had relegated to distant stacks. I was more than surprised to find myself gradually discovering a storehouse of treasures. Women, it turned out, had written and published passionately and eloquently on the subject of their own childhood and youth since the middle of the nineteenth century. Consequently, my history ballooned beyond the scope I had initially envisaged. After World War II, the production of childhood autobiographies increased by leaps and bounds, and particularly with second-wave feminism in the late 1960s, publication numbers skyrocketed. Therefore, I decided to stop at 1969—just when the better-known works produced in the era of second-wave feminism started to appear.

This book is written for a multidisciplinary audience. It is meant for anyone who is interested in women's self-writing about their childhood or in the childhoods themselves. I trace the inception and evolution of a genre—childhood autobiography—as it was written by women through the end of the 1960s. The purpose is to show how women came to write childhood autobiography and how their writing changed over the years. The "dark continent" of femininity (as Sigmund Freud described it) is not nearly as dark as it was forty years ago, yet four decades of belated scholarship have not sufficed to put women's history and women's writing on the same footing as events and cultural products that were noticed and documented all along. Thus, this book surveys a century and a quarter of neglected and forgotten works that preceded the renowned contemporary examples—a great many of which are themselves of high quality. I look at the content, form, style, and tone of these works, showing how the authors chose to present themselves to the public, as well as at any pronouncements the authors make about gender issues.

I follow a method known in the social sciences as "grounded theory." Thus, I do not start with a "research question" and look for "examples," but rather look at everything, at all the data at my disposal: 178 works. The alternative, to start with a present-day concern, can illuminate an area of the past that was previously invisible, but it has the obvious side effect of relegating other areas to darkness. Moreover, attempts to generalize on the basis of a few "examples" risk skewing the picture. As E. H. Gombrich wrote in *Norm and Form*, "You can never get more out of your classification than you put into it."[7] So I pursue an inductive method. I let the data suggest the questions. My supposition, which genre studies generally bear out, was that generic models together with the cultural climate at a given moment strongly influence the kind of thing written. But other questions about women's childhood autobiography, and their answers, arise out of the evidence. The more I read, the more I had to correct my own initial conjectures. For example, is there, as I expected, a "mother/daughter plot,"[8] and if so, what does it consist of? Today, women's victimization—in one way or another—is often emphasized. Do historical women portray themselves as victims? Trauma

Introduction

is a fashionable topic today. Is trauma an important motivator in this genre? I let the evidence corroborate or correct these ideas.

I employ some terminology to categorize the different types of works I found. I try to keep it simple. Some of the terms I use correspond to those proposed by other critics—"confession," "memoir," "Bildungsroman," "self-portrait," "relational autobiography," and so forth. But I oriented myself on the primary works rather than on the critical conversations, so the resemblance between my use of these terms and definitions found elsewhere is coincidental rather than deliberate. It does not reflect the discussions that have sometimes built up around them or seek to influence them.[9]

When I started the historical project, having no idea of what I would find, I imagined that women's childhood autobiographies before 1970 would fall into a few patterns. In reality, the historical works turned out to be much more diverse and also vastly better than I had thought. They did not lend themselves to being condensed into a few patterns. I also reflected on my own frustration at reading literary historical work that breaks new ground but emphasizes patterns at the expense of conveying a sense of the individual works. I find myself asking: Dear critic, couldn't you possibly have told me a bit more about the works? So I decided not to overdigest my material, but to give readings of a great many individual works, ranging from very short to rather long depending on what I see to be the work's importance. This procedure, of course, runs the risk of frustrating the reader in a different way. Like Hansel's bread crumbs, themes connect the works, but the reader nevertheless has to make her way through the "trees," or commentaries on the individual works, en route to getting a sense of the woods. For readers who want to see the woods without looking at the trees, my suggestion is to read the chapter summaries and otherwise skip around. This book can be read consecutively, but it is not essential to read it that way. It is meant to serve as a reference work, and as such it lends itself to partial consumption.

Genres arise in tandem with cultural values. It stands to reason that the very existence of a genre of childhood autobiography implies a climate in which childhood is considered important and worth writing about. This was not always the case. Romanticism ushered in an era in which childhood was considered formative. Modern autobiography, which came into being in so-called pre-Romanticism and which more than any other genre testifies to the existence of a concept of the self,

8 Introduction

from its inception with Jean-Jacques Rousseau and then even more strik-ingly with William Wordsworth, signals a new belief in the importance of childhood. The genre of childhood autobiography, which originated as a late Romantic phenomenon, cemented it. If an entire autobiographical work is devoted to childhood, then it is because the author shares with the readership the belief that childhood is interesting and impor-tant, that memories of childhood are worth recovering, that childhood events are worth reconstructing, and that childhood holds the key to future character, convictions, and even career. This era has not come to a close. The advent of psychoanalysis gave new impetus to the belief in the importance of childhood, even though psychoanalysis drastically changed the conceptualization of childhood.

The first and most comprehensive historian of this subgenre of auto-biography, Richard N. Coe, believes that the first genuine childhood autobiography was written by Stendhal in 1835 (it was published much later, in 1890). Coe's criterion for what he calls a "Childhood" is that the work show development and not just paint a sentimentalized or ideal-ized portrait of what it was like to be a child. Subsequently, and espe-cially in the last decades of the nineteenth century, burgeoning interest in education, psychology, and child welfare inspired childhood auto-biographies in increasing numbers.

But when and where did women start to write about their childhoods?

Women came to the genre later than men. No doubt this relative lateness had to do with such issues as literacy, privacy, and above all women's inhibitions about publishing work that focused on themselves. Yet initially, in the nineteenth century, women published accounts of their childhood and youth more readily than autobiographies that ex-tended into their adult lives, a fact I attribute to childhood autobiogra-phy's proximity to family history, its perceived suitability for young audiences, and the relative harmlessness of the subject. In England, women had long kept family histories. In the nineteenth century many women wrote children's books. The first childhood autobiography was published in 1845 by the English children's book author Mary Howitt, best known for her poem "The Spider and the Fly." Her book, entitled *My Own Story, or the Autobiography of a Child*, was destined for young audiences. In France, George Sand, whose real name was Amantine Aurore Lucile Dupin, took her cue from Rousseau and wrote extensively about her childhood in her autobiography *Histoire de ma vie* (*Story of My Life*, 1854–55). In 1866, also in France, Athénaïs Michelet published an autobiography entitled *Mémoires d'une enfant* (Memoirs of a child) that was exclusively devoted to her childhood years. Presently, women elsewhere, in the United States and Australia and in other European countries, began to join the ranks. Before 1900, however, examples were sparse. After the turn of the century, production picked up, and between the world wars, the genre became popular and widespread. Most of these early examples have been forgotten, even if they achieved a broad audience in their day, which most did not. After World War II examples mushroomed. Starting in 1970, with the women's movement, women's autobiographical writing generally, including women's childhood narratives and coming-of-age stories, experienced a boom.

What has motivated women to write about childhood, or childhood and youth, specifically? Writing about one's life for publication is a strange project, no matter who does it. The obvious motivation for writing an autobiography is the desire to create an image of oneself for posterity. Initially at least, this does not appear to have been an important motivation, or at least not the paramount motivation, for women to write about their childhood. The more famous the woman, the more she can be suspected of writing in order to frame herself for posterity. But few women were famous, and while famous women were indeed more likely to write an autobiography or even a childhood autobiography than others, many women who were not famous, some of them professional or aspiring writers but some not, turned to the genre. At this point, a caveat: it is perhaps misleading to use the word "autobiography" here, which suggests the chronological account of a life; "autobiographical narrative" is a more accurate, because a broader and more inclusive, term accommodating the variety of ways in which women have approached their project. But "autobiographical narrative of childhood" is a long and cumbersome designation, and so, agreeing with Susanna Egan's defense of the traditional term "autobiography" as "comprehensive" and "flexible,"[10] I shall continue to speak of "childhood autobiography," it being understood that I mean all types of adult nonfictional self-writing about childhood.

To return to the question of motivation: many women appear to have been motivated to write about their childhood out of a desire to make something, to express themselves creatively: to write a story. One's own childhood lay close at hand. Another motivation was to make something of *oneself* by publishing a book. The professional writers, especially the children's book authors, no doubt also hoped to make money.

Beyond these there were all kinds of different motivations. To judge from the directions the published work took, one predominant motivation for writing was the strong pull the child's mind exercises on the adult imagination. Childhood can seem like the most real time the adult has ever known: a time of flux and transformation, of discoveries and surprises, before life settled into a groove; a time of instability in perspective, of powerful imaginings coupled with uncertainty about what is real and what is imaginary; a time of keen passions, desires, sorrows, and fears. Some women were enticed by the prospect of reconnecting with the lost world of childhood and by the challenge of recapturing the mentality of the child. Others wanted to analyze themselves and the circumstances under which they grew up so as to reach self-understanding—a self-understanding that they thought would be instructive for a broader public as well. Keeping a record for a small group, such as one's family, children, or friends, could initiate an autobiographical project, as in the case of Cornelia Gray Lunt's *Sketches of Childhood and Girlhood* (1925), written for younger members of her family, or Eleanor Margaret Acland's *Good-Bye for the Present: The Story of Two Childhoods* (1935), which Acland wrote for friends. Alas, revenge for bad treatment at the hands of parents or relatives could also be a motivator. Bringing the problems of a disadvantaged social group into the public eye increasingly became a major motivation, especially after World War II. In the case of a famous person around whom misrepresentation swirled, such as Doris Lessing, an important motivation was to set the record straight.

All women experience childhood. But most do not write about their childhood, much less publish a book on the subject. The question of what segment of the female population writes childhood autobiography is easily answered. It has been predominantly professional writers—women of letters—who have written and published childhood autobiographies. Secondarily, famous women have turned to autobiography, including childhood autobiography. Finally, in more recent times, particularly after World War II, women who "had a story to tell"—often a bad one—wrote childhood autobiographies. The demographic of childhood autobiographers is thus skewed toward professional or would-be writers, celebrities, and those whose childhood was somehow remarkable.

What do women's childhood autobiographies look like? How do the authors set up their stories? By this I mean not only whether they organize their material chronologically or by theme or a combination of both, whether they present it retrospectively with abundant authorial commentary or attempt to recreate the perspective of the child. More crucially, I mean what position they opt to occupy on the spectrum from fact to fiction. At one end of the spectrum we can imagine an attempt at historical reconstruction written in a sober factual style, and at the other an autobiographical novel. Most childhood autobiographies—again, the more cautious designation is autobiographical narrative of childhood—fall between the two. As theorists have amply shown, autobiography is not a simple, transparent, unproblematic conduit of the truth. It always gives a constructed image. Even if an autobiographer is committed to the project of telling all, she confronts the fallibility of memory and inevitable distortions in self-perception. Childhood autobiographies are constructed out of especially flimsy fabric, namely, shadowy recollections of a child's fluid, imaginative perceptions. Making something of such material is a challenge. One might object that fiction has no place in life writing, but in reality, fact-fiction blends in various admixtures constitute a vast gray area between autobiography and fiction, between a purely factual account and one that is pure invention. As Maxine Hong Kingston insightfully observed: "I think that having two categories—fiction and nonfiction—is too small. I picture a border between fiction and nonfiction, and I am making that border very wide; fiction is a narrow place on one side and nonfiction is a narrow place on another side, and there's this great big border in the middle, in which real life is taking place and also fantasies and dreams and visions."[11] Another issue is that, while some autobiographers pursue an autobiographical ideal of truth, not all of them *want* to tell all. Discretion and consideration for other people cause autobiographers to omit material. Finally, whereas many works bear a rubric—"autobiography," "fiction"—many do not. Even if they do, the rubrics can be deceptive. As Sidonie Smith and Julia Watson have shown, and as we shall see, authors have many reasons for calling autobiography fiction and also for mixing fiction into autobiography and calling it autobiography.[12]

In this study, I draw the line at novels. As critics affirm, autobiography and novel are fundamentally different,[13] and in ways that transcend fidelity to fact versus invention—a plot, for example, being all but de rigueur in a novel but in obvious conflict with autobiography's pretension to tell the truth. The autobiographical novel, as a large subgenre of the novel, lies beyond the scope of this book. But the line is often hard to draw, and in "the great big border in the middle" I consider quite a few works. It would impoverish investigation, distort the reality of women's autobiographical writing about childhood, and deplete the richness of its variety if one were to confine oneself to those works that adopt a factual style. Many of the best and most revealing works contain a considerable injection of fictionalization. Fictionalization may be a "problem," an impediment to the researcher searching for true stories, but it is actually one of the most interesting theoretical issues that childhood autobiography confronts. I shall pay close attention to authors' claims and practices in this regard.

The genre of childhood autobiography has inspired several previous studies: Werner Brettschneider's *"Kindheitsmuster": Kindheit als Thema autobiographischer Dichtung* (1982), which treats the theme of childhood in German autobiographical literature; Richard N. Coe's foundational book on the genre worldwide, *When the Grass Was Taller: Autobiography and the Experience of Childhood* (1984); the proceedings of a 1987 Nanterre conference led by Philippe Lejeune on *Le récit d'enfance en question*; Roman Reisinger's *Die Autobiographie der Kindheit in der französischen Literatur* (2000); Debbie Pinfold's *The Child's View of the Third Reich in German Literature* (2001); Rocío G. Davis's *Begin Here: Reading Asian North American Autobiographies of Childhood* (2007); Katrin Lange's *Selbstfragmente: Autobiographien der Kindheit* (2008), a study of the genre in Germany; and Kate Douglas's *Contesting Childhood* (2010), a study of the genre since 1990.[14] In 2007 Jeffrey E. Long published *Remembered Childhoods*, a bibliography that has relevance for childhood autobiography. All of these scholars mention childhood autobiographies written by women, but none pay especial attention to gender.

In contrast, Valerie Sanders devotes a chapter of *The Private Lives of Victorian Women: Autobiography in Nineteenth-Century England* (1989) to Victorian women's autobiographical writing about childhood.[15] She gives an excellent analysis of the differences between men's and women's autobiographies in nineteenth-century England. Sanders has also published an extremely useful two-volume anthology of nineteenth-century British women's autobiographical writing about childhood, *Records of Girlhood* (2000, 2012), with commentary.[16] The authors and texts in Sanders's anthologies are selected "primarily because they have something important to say about the experience of growing up as a girl in the nineteenth century" (2012, 2). The selections are mainly excerpted from longer autobiographies, many of which were published posthumously and some of which remained unpublished. Such works form an interesting comparison to the self-published works of the same period

Introduction   13

that I treat, although the two sets of texts add up to many of the same conclusions about women's autobiographical writing about childhood in the Victorian period.

Another work that investigates women's childhood autobiography is Joy Hooton's *Stories of Herself When Young: Autobiographies of Childhood by Australian Women* (1990), the product of extensive archival research on Australian women's autobiographies of childhood and youth from their nineteenth-century beginnings to the time of writing.[17] Noting that only a handful of the Australian nineteenth-century narratives were published before 1900, Hooton, like Sanders, includes unpublished as well as posthumously published work, and she casts a wide net, including not just autobiography and memoirs but also autobiographical fiction. She is above all interested in themes, such as the representation of the parents. For this purpose the difference between autobiography and novel is of less consequence than it is for the issue of public self-performance. Besides bringing the substantial Australian tradition to light, Hooton summarizes and critiques extant autobiography theory and theories of women's autobiography, insisting that research "from below" is needed to correct both—a premise with which I agree. Hooton's work is not a history. Although she discusses narratives about pre-1920 childhoods in a set of initial chapters, thereafter she proceeds thematically.

Beyond Sanders's and Hooton's works, there has been no broader study of women's autobiographical childhood narratives. Nor has women's childhood autobiography been considered in its historical progression, as a genre that has evolved over time. What happens after the nineteenth century in the English-speaking countries? What about the other breeding ground of autobiography, France? What of the other European countries? What happens after World War I, that important turning point for women's rights? Does World War II bring changes? Such questions deserve to be explored, along with the gender issues that arise along the way.

The existence of an *écriture féminine*—a distinctively female way of writing—has been disputed. Early theoreticians of women's autobiography asserted that women wrote differently from men. Later theoreticians found abundant evidence to the contrary. Yet if gender differences manifest themselves in any type of writing, it ought to be in self-writing, including childhood autobiography. Women everywhere have been raised differently from men. They have had different childhoods, their lives have fallen into different patterns, and from the perspective of their lives they have looked back on their childhoods differently. In many cultures they have been taught to speak of themselves differently from men. One can expect, and one finds, differences in content, emphasis, style, and tone. Jill Ker Conway, who looks closely at public self-performance in autobiography, eloquently makes the point that to have "persuasive power," "autobiographies cannot depart too dramatically from popularly accepted stereotypes,"[18] and goes on to assert that autobiographies in the West conform to gender stereotypes at least until the world wars. Conway is absolutely right about the need to conform to current norms if one seeks acceptance of one's work. Like full-length autobiography, childhood autobiography has a gendered aspect. Its gendered characteristics are, however, not identical to the stereotypes that Conway discerns in full-scale autobiography—"the man of action and the suffering or redemptive female"[19]—for here, autobiographers are looking back on childhood, not summing up their lives. To give an example, the nostalgic strain that flourishes in nineteenth- and early twentieth-century men's accounts of their childhood is far less pronounced in works by women written in the same era. This particular disparity was, in fact, what first led me to believe that there might be a separate women's tradition of childhood autobiography. Coe asserts that there is no difference between men's and women's writing in childhood autobiography. I disagree. As will be seen, I find differences right from the start—in fact, especially at the start, in the period before World War I. These differences are traceable to the different socialization of men and women—not to biology—and they change over time.

Conway asks provocatively: "Given that Western language and narrative forms have been developed to record and explicate the male life, how can a woman write an autobiography when to do so requires using a language which denigrates the feminine and using a genre which celebrates the experience of the atomistic Western male hero?"[20] It is a good question, but childhood autobiography offers a ready response to it. Once Romanticism established that childhood was a worthy focus for self-writing, childhood autobiography held a particular appeal for nineteenth- and early twentieth-century women. Society credited women with a particular affinity for children. Maternity—childbearing—fostered the idea that women and children belonged together. In an era of separate spheres, it was women's job to raise the young. Mothers cared for their children or entrusted them to other female caregivers. In the age of large families, almost every woman—mothers, sisters, aunts, grand-mothers, nursemaids—spent a great deal of time looking after children. The female sex was assumed to have, and no doubt had, expertise in childcare-related matters. Thus, if women enjoyed authority in any cor-ner of the world, it was the nursery. A second reason why self-writing about childhood appealed to women has to do with the safety of the topic. In an era when childhood was presumed to be an innocent, asex-ual time of life, making one's own childhood the subject of a book was a relatively uncontroversial thing to do, compared to writing the story of one's adult life.[21]

Does women's writing fall into any patterns? Do traditions form? Are they different in different countries? Are there any cross-cultural pat-terns? The biggest divide comes between the works that tell "the story" —memoirs—and the works that tell "my story"—autobiography. Many women write books—"memoirs"—about the world of their childhood without focusing on themselves as children. Thus, life in a large Victo-rian family, or a childhood spent in the Himalayan jungle, in an orphan-age, in the company of itinerant actor parents, seems itself to justify a book. In such works the girl functions more as a witness than as a sub-ject. But other writers focus on the self: the author's subjectivity, her personality, her development.

Most scholars of childhood autobiography assume that childhood autobiography is self-focused: the centerpiece of childhood autobiog-raphy is the writer's child self. Coe makes self-focus part of his very definition of the "Childhood": the "structure reflects step by step the development of the writer's self."[22] Self-focused autobiography justifi-ably attracts critical attention: it marks a spot where the uniquely human activity of self-reflection meets public norms. It is thus an entic-ing object for analysis. It is one that promises to be revealing for gender as well. Yet if one looks at the history of women's production of child-hood narratives, it is hard to isolate this type of work. As Coe, Davis, and Douglas all agree, the adult creates the child self in the childhood autobiography. But a bottom-up historical approach—the one prac-ticed in this book—shows that it is also the case that the adult chooses how much of that child self to include. The history of women's self-writing about childhood shows that besides self-focused childhood *autobiography* women wrote childhood *memoirs*, in which the author's child self can be all but eclipsed, and between these two ends of the spectrum a populous body of writing exists that encompasses family history, stories of the group of siblings, and "relational" autobiographies whose central focus is not the developing self but the child's relationships to others, or indeed the others themselves, and shadings in between.[23]

Even though G. Thomas Couser in his book *Memoir* assures us that today the word "memoir" has eclipsed other terms in the field of life writing,[24] the older terminology that distinguishes between self- and other-focused work is useful in a historical study because it differentiates between distinct types that were written with different agendas. I use the terms "memoirs" and "autobiography" according to the distinction made, for example, by Bernd Neumann and Sidonie Smith and Julia Watson, who cite Lee Quinby.[25] A fair number of works mix both, but even there, there is generally a preponderance of one focus over the other, so that one can assign a given work to one category or the other. Before the twentieth century, it was mainly French women who focused on the self, whereas English-language writers typically opted for the demure alternative of stories about "us" — the family, the group of siblings. Later two broad avenues are distinguishable, that of memoir and that of autobiography, with women everywhere traveling both. In the interwar and World War II years, memoirs outnumbered autobiographies, comprising approximately 60 percent of women's childhood narratives.

In this period, particularly as of the 1930s, a variant that I call the "semi-memoir" became popular: a memoir to be sure, which justifies itself as the story of the time, place, and/or family, but which builds in a subjective element as well, telling how the protagonist felt about outward events and perhaps also devoting some space to her personal story. In fact, the rise of such hybrids, which became increasingly prevalent in self-writing about childhood and which Couser calls attention to in contemporary life writing generally, may have paved the way for the contemporary displacement of the term "autobiography" by the term "memoir" as *the* popular umbrella term for personal recollections.[26]

In the 1950s and 1960s the percentage of memoirs, which at that point were mainly semi-memoirs, remained at nearly 60 percent. In this era, when the genre could no longer be considered nascent but was established, it is the autobiographies that interest me, not the memoirs. Yet a considerable number of women writers chart a middle route between memoir and autobiography, forging a variety of paths that crisscross between the two types. In this terrain I have found it necessary to make some judgment calls about what to include and what to exclude. Is there considerable autobiographical reflection in the memoir? Alternatively, does a writer adopt the memoir style as a roundabout way of making autobiographical points? In such cases, the memoir or semi-memoir bears discussing. Conversely, if an autobiography is purely an account of outward events, even though it is *this woman's story*, but lacks self-reflection, it is not of great interest.

Are there any surprises? Yes. The main surprise is the high quality of the works that comprise the genre. Until the post–World War II period, one finds few light, trivial, fluffy, or "boilerplate" works. From the earliest examples, nearly every woman writer took her childhood very seriously. Most appear to have thought deeply about it and put their best effort into writing about it. Occasionally one encounters a mediocre writer or a conventional mind. But mainly, the writers are smart and insightful, and their presentation eloquent and carefully wrought.

A final question is, what is understood by childhood? Today we think of childhood as the period of life between birth and puberty. But historical usage has not been so strict. As Rosemary Lloyd observes, many nineteenth-century writers do not explicitly separate adolescence from childhood.[27] Some women autobiographers confine themselves to writing about the years prior to puberty. Others, however, write "autobiographies of childhood and youth" and take their stories beyond childhood, into their teen years, or even into their twenties, up to the point when they leave home for school or work or to get married. Where does one make the cut?

Women's autobiographies that continue their story into young adulthood are fairly prevalent, and I do not exclude them, because precisely these are the most developmentally oriented. Female adolescence and the changes in outlook and upbringing that girls experience when they pass from childhood to adolescence is a topic of interest. It has often been asserted, for example by Simone de Beauvoir, and moreover documented in a 1991 United States study, that girls lose their early confidence in the process of becoming women.[28] So I do look at autobiographies of childhood and youth, although I exclude works that bypass childhood and start with adolescence. I also look at full-length autobiographies if the author's attention to her childhood warrants it. My criteria for inclusion are that the author devote a substantial portion of the work to her childhood years, and moreover that she treat her childhood, and herself as a child, as an important topic.

To further crimp the edges of this study, I have omitted autobiographies that are conceived as autobiographies of the author's life, or a substantial portion of her life, and in which only a brief opening segment is devoted to childhood, such as Harriet Jacobs's *Incidents in the Life of a Slave Girl* (1861), Harriet Martineau's *Autobiography* (1877), Fanny Kemble's *Record of a Girlhood* (1879), or Violette Leduc's *La Bâtarde* (1964), or if they break off before their intended ending because the author died (Henry Handel Richardson, *Myself When Young* [1948]). Obviously, most autobiographers devote at least a little space to their childhood. But most whisk through their childhood years en route to adolescence and adulthood. Sometimes, however, an author will devote a section of a longer autobiography to childhood that is equivalent in length to a typical childhood autobiography, or, like Juliette Adam, Mabel Dodge Luhan, Marie Bonaparte, Simone de Beauvoir, and Clara Malraux, publish an account of her childhood and youth as the first volume of a multi-volume autobiography. I include such works. Sometimes an author will choose to write only about a limited span of childhood years or to write a series of discrete stories about her childhood. I also include such works.

Despite the importance of the topic for social history, this is not primarily a book about women's childhoods. Rather, my principal interest lies in discovering how women represented themselves, the childhood influences on them, and their minds as young persons, in an era when childhood was considered important, its experiences formative, and the child's vision of the world special and worth recovering. It is above all the gender-specific aspects of these works that I wish to pursue: how women wrote about themselves as girls. The self-presentation as well as the self-representation counts: an author's tone and commentary are illuminating as well as her selection of material and her shaping of the subject. If a childhood narrative written by a woman has a special focus, such as handicap, mental illness, or the like, but slights gender issues (Helen Keller's *The Story of My Life* [1902] would be an example), I do not discuss it. Finally, I am interested in the history of the genre—how the genre of childhood autobiography, as written by women, came into being and evolved. It constitutes a long, substantial tradition.

This book is organized in such a way as to show the emergence and evolution of a genre. Like all genres, women's autobiographical writing about childhood evolved historically. A genre comes into being because some work or cluster of works capture the imagination and are imitated; then someone will innovate in an appealing way, create a variant of the model that displaces the generic horizon of expectation, and be imitated in turn.[29] I consider it a given that writing orients itself on previous writing and believe that this determinacy holds the edge over others. In life writing, changes in people's life patterns obviously influence what gets written; autobiography is not a closed system, and genre evolution is not just about books; yet if a woman writes a family story, this is likely because she has read and admired other women's family stories, rather than because, say, as a woman she has a relational self-concept.

The chapters are organized by historical period. These periods may look conventional, but they are not arbitrary. Each one marks a change in the way women wrote. Prior to World War I works were extremely disparate. Works written in the interwar years are more homogeneous—patterns emerge—and overall, they manifest significant changes in content and tone compared to the pre–World War I works. Works written in the World War II years continue developments begun in the interwar years. They have their own separate chapter because, despite the preoccupations of wartime, they start to become astonishingly numerous, presaging the flood of such works that appeared in the 1950s and 1960s. After World War II, writers begin to employ the genre to several new ends.

At the start of each chapter the reader will find, for orientation, a list of the authors to be discussed, organized chronologically by publication date. Within each chapter, subheadings mark transitions between different types of works. The table of contents provides a roadmap. In chapter 1 the reader can expect to find out what works written before World War I looked like, and so on. Readers interested in specific themes should consult the index.

My argument in a nutshell, for which readers will find the evidence in the following chapters, is this:

In the nineteenth century, when women faced publishing hurdles and social constraints inhibited the revelation of their lives to the wider public, childhood autobiography presented an attractive outlet for self-reflection and creativity. Childhood, glorified by Romantic writers such as Wordsworth, had risen in status as a topic worth writing about. Women, immersed in child-rearing, possessed an authority in matters relating to children's experience that was difficult to challenge. Writing about one's childhood offered an opportunity for comparatively free self-expression, a hole in the fence, so to speak. It helped that in the same era childhood was regarded as an innocent, asexual time of life. At this point, as of midcentury, women started to write and publish at length about their childhoods.

From the start, and also as the feminine version of this genre gained traction in the twentieth century, a host of considerations—the changing status and self-consciousness of women, world historical events and the social and political climate, ruling fashions in intellectual ideas, the reception of previous autobiographical writing by women, publishing options—left their mark on women's successive production of this type of work. Especially starting in the 1930s, one sees childhood autobiographies that are buoyed by a belief or worldview, psychoanalysis being the main one. In the autobiographies and the memoirs alike, however, tone is a more pervasive, if more superficial, instigator of patterns than ideological conviction. Authors, with an instinct for mimicry, began to write in a tone—an ironic, nostalgic, or humorous tone—according to their intention and the fashion of the times.

Norms, conditions, and influential works have, of course, affected the history of autobiographies written by both sexes, not just women's. Nevertheless, autobiography counts as a referential genre, and the sex of the referent—the protagonist—as well as that of the author influences the look of the final project. Autobiography is not gender neutral. The differential treatment of women by society has always persisted in some form. A woman's name on the title page creates expectations, which a female author anticipates in her choices of what and how to write. The writer's notion of her envisaged audience inevitably affects her self-presentation. This is not to say that a published autobiography is a smooth mirror of public norms; rather, it incorporates a form of "mirror talk" (to quote the title of Susanna Egan's book) between the author and those norms.[30] As will be seen, the overall trend in women's childhood autobiographies over time was toward increasing outspokenness. However, as will also be seen, a woman would often see fit to dress her story by explaining herself, adopting a certain tone, casting herself in a certain mold, and foregrounding certain kinds of content while suppressing others. Above all, fictionalization tempted women with advantages too serious to be scorned.

Finally, some constants. Even as social norms changed, women's childhoods continued to be different from men's in specific ways. Mothers and female caregivers were typically in charge of girls, and they functioned as role models. Mothers, other women, and the differential upbringing of girls and boys were topics in women's childhood autobiography from the start and remained topics. While many other aspects of women's writing changed, these preoccupations stand out as consistent themes.

CHAPTER ONE

Beginnings: Women's Childhood Autobiography Prior to World War I

1845: Howitt (1799–1888)

1854–55: Sand (1804–1876)

1859: Farnham (1815–1864)

1866: Michelet (1826–1899)

1871: Braun (1815–1886)

1883: Daudet (1844–1940)

1889: Kovalevskaya (1850–1891)

1889: Larcom (1824–1893)

1891: Mrs. F. Hughes

1892: Adelmann (1842–1915)

1892: Campbell

1893: Burnett (1849–1924)

1896–97: Nesbit (1858–1924)

1899: H. Lynch (1859–1904)

1901: Gilder (1849–1916)

1901: L'vova (1854–after 1910)

1901: Schumacher (1848–1931)

1902: Adam (1836–1936)

1902: J. Gautier (1845–1917)

1905: Bischoff (1848–1925)

1906: Ebner-Eschenbach (1830–1916)

1907: Barton (1821–1912)

1909: Popp (1869–1939)

1910: Audoux (1863–1937)

1910: Lenk (1841–1914)

1912: Antin (1881–1949)

1912: Dohm (1831–1919)

1913: Arden (1882–1926)

1914: Hunt (1876–)

1916: Creevey (1843–1920)

1917: Stern (1889–1954)

1918: Cohen (1880–1925)

In Europe and the United States women began to write childhood autobiographies starting in the middle of the nineteenth century. Before the turn of the twentieth century, examples were sparse. The few that were written are very different from one another. There is yet little sign of a genre coming into being, except in the line of children's books, nor of any sort of jelling of theme or approach, or a feminine tradition within the genre. There are, however, some common themes: the mother, memory, reading, dolls, and early vocation. Publication picked up between the beginning of the twentieth century and World War I. Patterns start to be discernable; with ingenuity and energy, women explored the logical possibilities of the genre, which later formed types. The women who wrote childhood autobiographies came from different backgrounds and walks of life, although predictably women who were "somebody" predominate. They came preeminently from France, England, the United States, Ireland, Australia, the German-speaking countries, and Russia.

The French and the English-language works derive from two distinctly different literary traditions: the confessional tradition of autobiography (France) and books for young audiences (England). As befits the confessional tradition, even the earliest French women's childhood autobiographies are self-focused. The first English-language works, in contrast, tell the story of the childhood rather than the story of the little girl herself. Early German works do likewise. Russian works follow the French model.

Self-focused childhood autobiographies by women and men alike appeared earlier and in greater numbers in France than elsewhere. Jean-Jacques Rousseau can be held accountable for this development, inasmuch as his *Confessions* initiated a secular autobiographical and confessional tradition that also led, for example, to the rise of the intimate journal in nineteenth-century France. Women autobiographers in France received an enormous impetus from George Sand's monumental Rousseau-inspired *Histoire de ma vie* (*Story of My Life*), which appeared in 1854–55. Right from the start French women's childhood autobiography had an intimate and confessional element. Although most of the nineteenth-century women explicitly or tacitly, through the very style of their writing, excuse themselves for (or from) taking the bold step of writing about themselves, the French women nevertheless do write about their personal experiences and feelings. So do the Russians.

The origins and early examples of published women's childhood autobiographies in the English-speaking countries were quite different from those in nineteenth-century France. They do not derive directly from an autobiographical tradition, but rather from children's and youth literature. As early as 1845, the British children's book author Mary Howitt published the story of her own childhood, *My Own Story; or, The Autobiography of a Child*, for "young readers."[1] Others, such as Grace Greenwood in her story collection *Recollections of My Childhood* (1852), Mrs. F. Hughes (1891), Ellen Campbell (1892), and Frances Hodgson Burnett (1893), followed suit. These practitioners were more tentative,

24 Beginnings: Women's Childhood Autobiography Prior to World War I

less forthright than their counterparts in France, situating their work in the vicinity of children's literature, writing for young people, or literature about children. They foreground the idea of "childhood" rather than the idea of "self." Characteristically, they opt for pronouns other than "I" (such as "we," "she") to present their childhood experience. In Germany, similarly, children's book authors such as Isabella Braun (1871) and Tony Schumacher (1901) wrote about their childhoods.

Women's Childhood Autobiography in France

Sand's *Histoire de ma vie*, with its copious writing on her childhood, was seminal for French women's childhood autobiography. Sand was close to fifty when she published her autobiography. She was inspired by Rousseau and expresses admiration for him, although she explicitly quarrels with his tell-it-all exhibitionism, which she thinks lacks respect for others. She aligns her own work, instead, with the model of Augustine, who, she says, told the story of his struggles and sufferings for the instruction of all.[2] She warns the reader that her style will be digressive — and it is. Sand's autobiography contains a long, detailed, fascinating section on her childhood that is much more extensive than Rousseau's. Indeed, her section on her childhood is by far the longest of the book. As Sand reaches her notorious adult life, she writes less and less. Childhood experience was relatively uncontroversial; this is presumably why Sand feels free to dilate on hers. Nineteenth-century women generally may well have felt a greater affinity for autobiography that confined itself to childhood than for autobiography that told their adult stories, because it was low-risk. Sand starts with her parents' history, which she records at great length, including, in particular, her father's letters to his mother, and goes on to her earliest memories, which she painstakingly records, including an early physical trauma at age two, her belief that Santa would come down the chimney, songs she knew, a nightmare, a scary episode, and so on. Already a famous writer, Sand provides the reader with an account of the making of the writer, of how and under what circumstances she started daydreaming and making up stories as a child. Her childhood, which took place during the Napoleonic Wars, was eventful, involving a trip to and from Spain, where her father served as a soldier. Particularly the return trip, during which the family crossed battlefields, affords an extraordinary portrait of the times. But Sand focuses on her own experiences during these world historical events, and she often speaks of them as recollections, prefacing what she writes with "in my memory" or "as I remember it." She does not attempt to gloss over holes in her memory, but rather acknowledges and even thematizes the "broken" nature of her memories.

The work's principal plot involves the contest between her mother and her paternal grandmother for her custody and her soul. Her parents, very in love, were mismatched: her father of noble extraction, her mother a Parisian woman of the people. Sand portrays her relationship to her mother as having been very close from the start. Upon their return from Spain to France, the family lived with her paternal grandmother in Nohant. Presently her father died in a riding accident; and when she was age seven or eight, this well-to-do grandmother wanted to be the one to raise her. After a considerable dispute with her mother, who was also a striking personality though a strikingly different one—beautiful, warm, tempestuous, artistic, creative, and easily irritable—Aurore was left with her grandmother in Nohant while her mother went to Paris to make a living. Thus Aurore was separated from the person she loved most—her mother—early on; she missed her actively and could not quite get used to the tutelage of her strict, calm, relatively cold Saxon grandmother. After her grandmother's death when she was age seventeen, however, she found it impossible to get along with her increasingly erratic, volatile mother, with whom she had so desired a reunion. A realistic, vivid, detailed account of a woman's childhood memories, the work already reveals several of the principal affinities that would draw future women to childhood autobiography: an interest in writing about personal experiences and emotions, albeit not about those of their adult lives, and a sharp eye for and interest in the psychology of children.

Mother-Daughter Conflict

Athénaïs Michelet's *Mémoires d'une enfant* (Memoirs of a child, 1866) is the earliest self-focused autobiography written by a woman and devoted exclusively to childhood that I have been able to find. Michelet explains that she wrote it at the instigation of her husband, the historian Jules Michelet. She was just short of forty. A triggering factor was presumably the death of her mother several months earlier—for the text paints a portrait of her mother that would hardly have been possible during the latter's lifetime.[3] Her childhood was not a happy one. She felt oppressed by her mother, neglected and disfavored as the middle child in a family of six children. Her story ends with the death of her adored father when she was age fourteen. Michelet initiates what will turn into an entrenched pattern in women's accounts of their growing up: mother-daughter conflict.

Athénaïs Michelet writes precisely, carefully giving the facts. Although one can certainly not say that the child subject pales into a portrait of her milieu, as will be the case with her American contemporary Lucy Larcom, Michelet does aim to give a portrait of the time, place, and people in Montauban where she grew up. Indeed, she calls her book "memoirs" and not "confessions." She describes the countryside around Montauban as it looked before midcentury. With a historian's attention, she devotes space to the village fair and other festivals, complete with a transcription of songs; she describes work on the farm; she writes about each member of her immediate family and about the people who lived on neighboring farms. Having come into the possession of her father's papers, she also extensively writes up the story of her father's life, of which marriage and family were the final stage. But she herself is at the center of her story, which she tells in chronological order, dwelling on the events that were especially significant for her as a child.

She does not indulge in much emotion or commentary. Yet her factual account lets the reader surmise that strong and stormy emotions, mainly sorrow and jealousy, gripped her as a child. The adult narrator apparently continues to empathize with her child self, since she picks episodes to recount that are emotionally fraught and does nothing to rationalize them or otherwise put them in an adult perspective. The mother is introduced immediately, in the narrator's account of her first memory, which she says dates to age four or five. In this memory Athénaïs is seated next to a young, serious woman with a beautiful, severe face and pale eyes of a very particular shade of blue. This is her mother, an Englishwoman from Louisiana, whom marriage had transported to a large farm in Montauban in the southwest of France. Athénaïs tells us, in a factual and explanatory sort of way, that her mother loved her two older children, a daughter and a son, but that her third child's birth was not wanted. Her mother did not nurse her, but sent her away from the family to board with a peasant nurse for her first four years. When she returned home, two more boys had been born.

Her first memory of being seated next to her mother turns out to represent a habitual state of affairs. From early childhood Athénaïs was taught to sew and knit and spent most of her time doing those things under her mother's eye. Her portrait of her mother is chilling. Athénaïs describes her as controlled, diligent, and exact, quite unlike the lively

Beginnings: Women's Childhood Autobiography Prior to World War I   27

and spontaneous people of the South of France. Athénaïs, who wanted to be loved and to please, encountered only coldness. She characterizes her mother as "rule and order," as a person who liked silent docility. Yet Athénaïs apparently suppressed the worst part of the real story in her memoirs. Athénaïs Michelet is a woman about whom a great deal is known, thanks to her husband's journal, in which he wrote continuously and with great solicitude about his beloved wife. According to the *Journal*, Mme Mialaret beat and whipped her daughter, locked her in dark places, and shut her out of the house for days on end.[4] Athénaïs herself never mentions this type of violence.

Athénaïs got along with none of her siblings and envied all of them for one reason or another. She had become accustomed to the freedom she had enjoyed in the countryside with her nurse, but at home she found herself confined. Whereas her brothers could run free after they had finished their lessons with her father, Athénaïs had to return to her mother. For "girls belong to their mother."[5] Her younger brothers play with her only as long as the older boys won't play with them, but drop her immediately when they can run with the big boys. This is a common tale; Enid Starkie, who grew up in early twentieth-century Ireland, and Doris Lessing, reminiscing about her interwar-years childhood in Southern Rhodesia, similarly complain of their brothers' disloyalty.[6] Mainly, Athénaïs remembers that her brothers play tricks on her; she wants their friendship, but fears their tricks. Her older sister, in contrast, took after her mother in her domestic proclivities, and indeed, the two were companions. She played mistress of the house and had a doll, dresses, friends. Athénaïs yearned for all three. Her obsessive desire for a doll and then the story of the doll she finally got occupy an astonishingly large portion of the narrative.

It is her sex, her birth order, and, above all, her subordination to this particular mother that make her childhood confining, empty, lonely, unhappy, and anomalous. Perhaps because she had a country upbringing, was not part of a group of children, and was too much alone, her child's mind takes strange, obsessive twists. Fed stories of Santa, fairies who bring babies, and sorceresses, she places her hopes for realizing her desires in supernatural creatures. Her world seems small, and even her joys seem petty. She confesses to having been suicidal when she lost her first handmade doll.

Under these circumstances Athénaïs became passionately devoted to her father, who represented the one ray of sunshine in her emotionally deprived life. He called her "princess." Her love and admiration for this very much older, kindly, and in fact universally beloved man is unbounded. It has often been said that Athénaïs Mialaret "married her father" in Jules Michelet, twenty-eight years her senior.[7] Her husband remarks in his journal that Athénaïs remained emotionally frozen at age fourteen, the age of her father's death, and that as an adult she kept relapsing into her childhood.[8] This text with its careful narrator, who seems to have little distance from what she writes, who paints the portrait of herself as an oppressed child but at the same time seems to be biting her tongue in an effort to be seemly and refrains from giving the perpetrators the blame that is due them, tends to corroborate what he says.

Many later women's childhood autobiographies would be driven by the author's problematic relationship with her mother, but this is not because Athénaïs Michelet set the tone. On the contrary, her book was barely read at all until it was reissued in 2004. According to the editor of the 2004 edition Pierre Enckell, the original edition of 1866 did not sell well and was soon forgotten. Neither the reissue of 1888 nor that at the beginning of the twentieth century did well.[9] The 2004 republication had to do with the new contemporary interest in women's lives.

Remembering

Julia Daudet's "L'Enfance d'une Parisienne" (A Parisian's childhood), first published in 1883, is a very different sort of work. The book presents itself as memories and is constructed as a series of remembered spots, where Paris and its surroundings are as much the subject as is childhood. This book is more about Paris as experienced by a little girl of a certain social class than it is about the precise person of its author, who emerges, above all, as a poetically remembering sensibility. This short book, which Daudet wrote in her late thirties and is undeservedly forgotten today, is similar to Walter Benjamin's famous *Berlin Childhood around 1900* both in its conception and form, in the sense that it occupies the threshold between autobiography and the prose poem cycle. Each delicately and carefully crafted piece expounds on some activity, place, or event of her childhood: "Les Fêtes" (The holidays), "Les Poupées" (Dolls), "La Rougeole" (Measles), "L'Émeute" (The riot), "Les Promenades" (Walks), and so forth. The many references to remembering make clear that the narrator is an adult looking back. She even engages in some theorizing about memory — "the very early memories, in their confused limbo, have great flashes of lightning surrounded by night, apparitions of memories much more than real memories"[10]—and sheds doubt on one of her very early memories (that of a riot) in a way that anticipates the memory questioning of later authors writing at the turn of the century like Juliette Adam or Hannah Lynch.

The stellar achievement of the book is the chapter called "Les Livres," where Daudet describes how her early relationship with books and reading experiences engaged with the material qualities of the book such as the pictures and the length of the lines. Her comments on reading in childhood surpass many other treatments of this often-treated subject.

In its conception Daudet's work does not resemble previous childhood autobiographies written by women. Her book does, however, bear some resemblance to a childhood autobiography written by her exact contemporary Anatole France, *Le Livre de mon ami* (My friend's book, 1885), which unites pieces that previously appeared in journals between 1879 and 1884, in form (separate pieces), in tone (idyllic and nostalgic), and in the novel association of this tone, which was habitually reserved for childhoods spent in nature, with a predominantly city childhood.

The Self-Portrait

Just after the turn of the century two French childhood autobiographies appeared that are full-blown self-portraits. Both are written by prominent women. The works are, however, very different: Juliette Adam's *Le Roman de mon enfance et de ma jeunesse* (*The Romance of My Childhood and Youth*, 1902) is the first volume of the author's memoirs and gives the story of this politically important woman's early years, whereas the writer Judith Gautier's *Le Collier des jours* (The necklace of days, 1902) is a true childhood autobiography that cuts off at an unspecified age around nine or ten and presents, with considerable psychological acumen, the picture of a strong personality.

Juliette Adam, born Juliette Lambert in 1836, was the foremost *salonière* of the Third Republic. A beautiful, intelligent, and ambitious woman from an undistinguished provincial background, she became a protégée of Marie d'Agoult and to a lesser degree of George Sand. She married money, power, and politics in the person of Edmond Adam. She was close to many prominent Republican politicians of the age, especially Léon Gambetta. As a widow she used her fortune to enter French political life to an increasing degree. She founded and ran the *Nouvelle*

Revue, a literary and political journal through which she attempted to further her pet project, her overriding and unchanging conviction that only an alliance between France and Russia would enable France to recoup its losses from the Franco-Prussian War and save it from further onslaughts by Prussia-dominated Germany. She knew everyone who was anyone in political, military, journalistic, and artistic circles. As of the 1880s she figured in France and internationally as La Grande Française, the great lady of French politics and patriotism. She wrote novels early, political articles in her editorial days, and finally, starting in her sixties, her monumental memoirs *Mes souvenirs* (My memories), of which *Le Roman de mon enfance et de ma jeunesse* (1902) forms the first volume. A very important woman in her day, she died at the age of ninety-nine.[11]

Of all the early women's childhood autobiographies, this is the one that most follows the dominant masculine tradition of childhood autobiography in presenting the background, character, and formation of a person who became successful and important in later life.[12] It is the portrait of a strong-willed and intelligent personality who came "from nothing" and was the center of her warring family's attention. She designates herself as a peacemaker. Already as a child she shapes up as a heroine, saving her father from arrest by hiding his seditious papers.

She does not write analytically or probe psychologically. Seemingly pro forma, she questions the accuracy of her memory at the outset, but this questioning is not sustained in the text. Rather, she writes novelistically, describing herself from the outside and giving accounts of turns of events that include a lot of dialogue. She does not take the stance of remembering in the autobiography; she simply tells her story.

Although she recounts her "first great sorrow"—her grandmother sold her beloved garden to raise money for her dowry—she certainly does not play the victim. Raised by her grandmother, she threw a tantrum early on so to avoid having to go to school, and her grandmother gave in. Consequently, she figured she had done well and told her grandmother that if she was ever "naughty" again she would behave badly. Adam the author makes the point that this event probably formed her character.

Mother-daughter tension figures in her story: she describes her mother as a cold and jealous personality. In any event her mother did not raise her, and she was married early, at age sixteen, to a first husband who, fortunately for her, left her a widow after fourteen years of marriage.

Beginnings: Women's Childhood Autobiography Prior to World War I

This enabled her to marry her lover, Edmond Adam. She takes her story through the birth of her daughter in 1854 and ends with a glimpse into her future life as a writer.

Judith Gautier's *Le Collier des jours*, published in the same year, 1902, is also a self-portrait, but the portrait of a rebel. Born in 1845, nine years younger than Juliette Adam, Gautier was fifty-seven years old when she published her childhood autobiography. The oldest daughter of the writer Théophile Gautier and the actress Ernesta Grisi, and the niece of the famous dancer Carlotta Grisi, she herself had become a prolific novelist and woman of letters. The immediate impetus for writing her childhood autobiography may have been the death of Carlotta Grisi in 1899, which liberated her to tell her story. Carlotta Grisi, exercising her authority as Judith's godmother, had been responsible for having her put in convent boarding school at the age of seven. Gautier's childhood autobiography is of stellar literary quality, a delight to read. It is particularly memorable for its self-portrait of a strong personality, and it stands out for recording an unusual number of exceptionally clear memories from very early childhood. It is a fascinating study in childhood passions, which only a stint spent in convent school sufficed to calm down.

Most children are passionate beings, and some children experience tempestuous passions beside which the passions of later life pale. Judith Gautier tells of an early self who was just such a creature. The author paints the portrait of an unusual personality: rebellious, wild, spunky, smart, and unsubmissive. Juliette Adam represents herself as a self-assured, strong personality who dominated her family; but the only girl in a prior childhood autobiography who comes close to Judith in her blaze of intelligence and feeling is Irish author Hannah Lynch's Angela (discussed later in this chapter). Angela, however, is a sensitive soul who runs afoul of her brilliant and temperamental mother, and what Lynch stresses above all is her victimization, not her wildness.

Gautier tells us in her childhood autobiography that she had read "all of" George Sand as a child.[13] It is hard to imagine from what woman writer other than Sand she might have derived the idea of writing extensively about her childhood. Yet the picture she draws of her childhood is much more strongly focused on her own person and personality than is Sand's account of her childhood. She is more intent on self-portraiture, on establishing the extraordinary kind of person she was. Gautier would have also known the childhood autobiographies of her male contemporaries Anatole France and Pierre Loti (her close friend), but her work completely lacks their tone of nostalgia.

Gautier claims that her birth set the tone for her life. She cites accounts that she showed such an obstinate negativity in entering the world that the obstetrician called her a monster. Thereafter, in the typical nineteenth-century pattern that we have already seen in Michelet, she was initially raised by a nurse. Gautier explains that her mother, an actress in a famous Milanese acting group, had no time to deal with a child and therefore handed her over to a carpenter's wife who lived in the Paris suburbs. It was a fateful relationship. Judith came to love her nurse, Damon—whom she thought of as "la Chérie" ("the Sweetie")—with an incredible passion. Gautier admits that this nurse adored her and spoiled her, preferring her to her own children, and that she throve on this kind of adoration, reciprocally idolizing her nurse. She avers that the happiest time of her life was when she lived with her nurse, because she was so loved: "She was my strength, my support, the implementer of all my fantasies that wouldn't hurt me. . . . Such a richness of love created a vast and splendid kingdom for me" (44). Gautier thus replicates to an extreme degree the experience of Michelet, who was happy in her early years when living with her nurse. As an adult, Gautier recognizes that her happiness had a great deal to do with the fact that in her nurse's family she was treated like a superior being, indeed like "the infant Jesus" (24). She distinctly remembers the sense of superiority and dominance over the rest of the group that she enjoyed at her nurse's, the sense of being on a pedestal. What is most extraordinary is the fact that at age fifty-seven Gautier remembers her attachment to her nurse and her early afflatus so vividly; adulthood and memory did not overwrite it as an archaic, long-overcome, embarrassing piece of infancy.

The child, Gautier informs us, retained her sense of power when her unfeeling parents tried to terminate her sojourn in paradise. A catastrophe ensued when her parents tried to separate her from her nurse and take their daughter back into their apartment. Judith, who had battened on the exquisite treatment she received from her nurse, sobbed for days and nights on end, while her nurse, who could not stand the separation either, started to be poisoned by her own milk. Her parents were forced to capitulate and put them back together again. So Judith was victorious. The next time her parents tried to separate Judith and her nurse

Beginnings: Women's Childhood Autobiography Prior to World War I   33

they did so slowly, letting Judith stay initially with her grandfather and two aunts in the beautiful countryside of Châtillon.

Gautier claims that she has clear early memories of complex events. She insists explicitly that her earliest memories are her liveliest. She compares them to large clear letters, in contrast to the cramped handwriting of her later memories. These memories "writ in large letters" (20) are predominantly emotionally loaded ones, consonant with the acknowledged finding that emotional events are better remembered. With the exception of a medical trauma and the death of a pet, most of these memories revolve around her love object, her nurse. Memory after memory shows that she ardently desired to protect and defend her beloved nurse. She recalls disliking her parents, whom she is forced to visit, who do not treat her like a goddess and who, she realizes, represent a potential threat to her and her nurse.

The first part of the book is brilliant. The farther Gautier gets from her early passion—when she writes of a child who thinks, is taught, and reads—the autobiography becomes increasingly anecdotal, more of a story, although later memories are also detailed and clear. The narrative turns a first corner when Judith is moved to the country to live with her paternal grandfather and aunts. There, Judith becomes the leader of a band of kids and earns herself the nickname of Ouragan (hurricane). Gautier masters the art of telling events in a way that conveys the passion with which a child engages with every aspect of life. There is the intriguing business of learning to read. There is the obstinate stubbornness with which Judith refuses her grandfather's injunction to learn some of her father's verses. There is her fascination with the curé's wondrous mechanical clock. There is the terrible pain of getting her arm sprained while playing. Yet that night, in all her pain, as she is carried home face upwards, she sees the stars as if for the first time, and her fascination with that unknown world begins. She remains her indomitable self, refusing to be scolded and eluding attempts at punishment.

Convent school represents another turning point. Besides the girl's passion for her nurse, the most interesting part of Gautier's account concerns her years in convent school, to which she is sent at age seven. Over the objections of her father's family, Carlotta Grisi insisted that she attend such an institution. Nearly a third of the book is devoted to an account of her experiences there. The interest is, above all, sociological: convent schools of the era were very particular places. Her father has to insist, when he and her mother visit, that she get a weekly bath. The nuns are not always the best pedagogues. There is corporal punishment. Judith feels imprisoned there and schemes to escape. But it is not all bad. The Mother Superior is kind to Judith, who becomes the best student in her class. Judith makes several friends among the girls. When her parents take her out of the convent after nearly two years, she is sad to be parted from her best friend there. She remarks that the convent does make her change: Ouragan calms down.

Judith starts living with her actual parents for the first time at age nine, and as of this point she portrays herself as relatively contented and docile, eager to become a citizen in her parents' interesting world. She has become a different Judith. We do not hear about any more passions, and the narrative peters out, ending abruptly. Although Gautier hitherto made us acutely aware of how the child felt in the thick of her various adventures—and these amount to passions, not sedate or even tame reflections—in the end she shows us a child who was more reconciled to her life than Athénaïs Michelet. We do not hear of any lasting or obsessive hatred for either her mother or her father. In fact, when she finally returns home at age nine, she immediately becomes very fond of her father. The former blazing egotist turns heliotropically toward the famous, kindly man. All in all, Judith Gautier represents herself as a highly intelligent and willful child who was gradually smoothed into a semi-presentable human being.

The Working-Class Woman

Up to now the French women who wrote childhood autobiographies were "somebody," persons of social standing or professional writers. Marguerite Audoux (1863–1937) is one of the first working-class women to have contributed to the genre with her childhood story. (The working-class Austrian socialist Adelheid Popp published hers anonymously a year earlier.) Audoux was a Paris seamstress. Her lover, the writer Michel Yell (Jules Iehl), introduced her to his Parisian literary circle and encouraged her to write. *Marie-Claire* was her first major work. She wrote it over a period of six years and published it in 1910. It immediately became a bestseller. Arnold Bennett, who introduced her to the English public in 1911, calls her "a little over thirty," and her English translator writes that she was "about thirty-five,"[14] but in fact she was age forty-seven when her book appeared.

Marguerite Audoux has been acclaimed as a "pioneer," as the first proletarian writer "to have created an aesthetic object worthy of critical attention out of her authentic working-class experience."[15] *Marie-Claire* is a "highly autobiographical" first-person novel.[16] It was awarded the Prix Fémina in 1910. It is a sad story, pathetic toward the end, that illustrates how limited possibilities for women were in the era, particularly if they grew up without parents, empty-handed, and uneducated. Fate dealt Marie-Claire all the wrong cards. Her mother dies; presently her father disappears; at age five she is taken along with her sister to an orphanage run by nuns, where the two children are quickly separated. Audoux's story shows what could happen to a girl without family or resources in the nineteenth century. Although Audoux was eighteen years younger than Gautier, she seems to be living in an earlier period, no doubt because her story took place in rural France. She was born in Sancoins (Cher) and sent to work as a shepherdess in the Sologne region in 1877.

Told in the first person, this work appears to be a straightforward and simply written autobiography of childhood and youth. But Audoux did call it a novel. She gave her protagonist a fictitious name, and on closer inspection it is full not only of fictionalizations, departures from biographical fact, as her biographer Bernard-Marie Garreau has shown,[17] but of novelistic techniques. Audoux's outstanding technique is allusion. She has Marie-Claire tell her story strictly from the perspective of the child she was at the time, without authorial interpolations. This renunciation of the backwards look, of hindsight, of narratorial wisdom is a novelty within women's childhood autobiographies to date. Audoux constructs the childhood perspective so as to leave holes, mysteries, loose ends. They tempt the reader to try to fill, solve, and tie them. Frequently the mysteries resist solution, but sometimes they yield readily to adult knowledge. To cite the most glaring case, the reader figures out that the friendship between Sister Marie-Aimée and the priest is a love affair, and that the Sister's period of seclusion, her screams during the night, and the bundle with which the priest leaves the convent amount to a pregnancy and birth.

Audoux beautifully captures the psychology of the child, both in its detail and in the overarching plot. When her mother dies—her biography tells us that Audoux lost her mother at age three—Marie-Claire plainly does not understand what has happened and is quickly distracted by some earthworms. At age thirteen, when she runs away from the farm where she has been placed as a shepherdess, Audoux renders her sense of being pursued as she runs down the road toward town at night by telling how she hears steps behind her, an invisible person seeming to touch her, animals jumping out of the forest at her. Her journey-of-life dream at age eighteen after her lover has abandoned her shows an unconscious understanding of her own life as hardship and oppression and adeptly conveys her state of mind, never transcending the character's perspective, always showing and not commenting. As for the plot, it shows a girl hungry for affection who, after her mother dies, keeps seeking a substitute, a person who loves her. Similar to Félicité in Gustave Flaubert's ironic tale *Un Coeur simple*, Marie-Claire is a working-class woman without prospects in provincial France. Similarly to Félicité, she keeps losing her significant other: she loses her beloved Sister Marie-Aimée in the orphanage; she loses Eugène, the farmer's kind brother; and she loses her lover Henri Delois, her employer's son, in her next home. Whereas Flaubert's fictional protagonist is reduced to progressively lesser love objects culminating in a parrot, Marie-Claire's losses follow a plausible biographical curve.

The dismal stories of the other girls at the convent and of Sister Marie-Aimée fuel the book's unspoken message that girls without means in the era had a tough life in store and that it was above all women who oppressed other women. Marie-Claire's story ends when the Mother Superior turns her out of the orphanage to which she finally returns at age eighteen. Her sister, whom she has not seen in twelve years and who is now married, meets her at the gate of the convent and is "hard," advising her to stay in the town. Feminine solidarity is nowhere to be seen.

Women's Childhood Autobiography in England, the United States, Australia, and Ireland

Rousseau wrote "confessions" and Sand published the "history" of her life. The word "autobiography" did not enter French until mid-nineteenth century, and even then the women who published significant autobiographical works about their childhood used other terms: Michelet published "memoirs," Gautier "recollections," and Adam a "romance." The term "autobiography" came from England, where it was coined in 1797 to describe a "new" genre.[18] Linda H. Peterson describes how the word quickly caught on in tandem with a growing interest in finding and publishing personal documents written in earlier ages.

Within two decades of the advent of the term, British antiquarians, scholars, and critics started to unearth and publish seventeenth-century spiritual memoirs and family memoirs, which they often labeled "autobiographies,"[19] while at the same time Victorian writers, including some women, produced their own "autobiographies." This explains how *Jane Eyre* could appear at midcentury with the subtitle "An Autobiography."

Peterson also shows how nineteenth-century British women autobiographers drew above all on two traditions: the spiritual memoir (which had seventeenth-century women practitioners) and the domestic memoir (in the seventeenth century an upper-class women's genre). Often they appear in combination: Charlotte Elizabeth Tonna's *Personal Recollections* (1841) and Harriet Martineau's *Autobiography* (1877) both draw on both genres, although Martineau retooled the spiritual memoir into the story of a professional. The safest, most "natural" option for women was the most traditional, the domestic memoir. Peterson writes: "The memoir—domestic in its focus, relational in its mode of self-construction—allowed women to write as mothers, daughters, and wives. It allowed them to represent their lives in terms of 'good' feminine plots." She observes that "women felt the pressure of the domestic memoir even when their agenda was to avoid this tradition and reclaim another."[20]

In her two-volume anthology *Records of Girlhood*, Valerie Sanders shows that the nineteenth-century women who wrote full-scale autobiographies devoted attention to their childhood, in contrast to their seventeenth- and eighteenth-century predecessors. Some of these autobiographies were intended to be read only by family, some were meant for posthumous publication, and some, mainly starting in the 1890s, were published by the authors themselves. As a rule, the women wrote discerningly and at some length about their childhood years. Some even wrote in a self-focused, intimate, confessional way, comparable to that of the French, about their childhood, none more so than Martineau in her *Autobiography*, which she planned to have published after her death. But candid childhood reminiscences written by women spottily started to see the light of day considerably before that, with Anna Jameson's self-published "A Revelation of Childhood" (1854), a letter in which she based her thoughts on child-rearing on "some recollections of my own child-life,"[21] and Mary Martha Sherwood's *Life of Mrs Sherwood* (1854), published by her daughter three years after her death in 1854, her mother having declared, "It is not while I live that the world, if I can

38   Beginnings: Women's Childhood Autobiography Prior to World War I

help it, shall ever see these memoranda."[22] The contrast between the recollections of childhood found in the unpublished and posthumously published autobiographical work (anthologized by Sanders) and the childhood autobiographies women wrote for publication (discussed here) is marked. The latter are more polished, more stylized, more calculated, less digressive, and less indiscreet.

The subgenre of childhood autobiography, as it came into being in English in the second half of the nineteenth century, harmonizes with the domestic memoir tradition. In 1845 Mary Howitt published an autobiography of her childhood, *My Own Story, or the Autobiography of a Child*. She was, to my knowledge, the first woman autobiographer to limit her focus to childhood. Previously she had published a successful series of children's books. She wrote for a young audience, reminiscing about her first ten years as if she were telling stories to her grandchildren. Her path-breaking childhood autobiography would find many progeny, especially among later children's book authors. She does not focus on herself, but rather gives a picture of the family, the place, the times, the people, and the customs when she was a child. The customary first-person pronoun used is "we." Howitt explains: "I say *we*, not in any editorial capacity, or because it sounds better, but because, when I write of myself as a child, I must write of my sister also. My sister was a year older than myself, but we were so constantly together, and were so guided by a constant amity of will, that we were something like one soul in two bodies."[23]

Consistent with its intended audience, Howitt's book focuses on aspects of her childhood that were important to the child. The narrator is a distinct personality and comments copiously, guiding the reader's reactions, but she represents events as the children themselves experienced them, such as, for example, the totally unexpected arrival of a baby sister and then a baby brother. We hear quite a lot about the children's feelings: a couple of nice little boys dispel the sisters' initial dislike of boys; the maid scares them with her lurid stories; the grown-ups talk anxiously about Napoleon's conquests, which makes the children anxious as well that he might invade England; meeting and playing with new friends delights them; they and their friends dislike being teased by grown-ups; the prospect of being sent to boarding school fills them with anxiety. Howitt even sometimes records her own personal feelings, notably when her pride is piqued when her father tells her she can't keep a secret. But her work is emphatically not a self-portrait. Nor is it psychologically oriented. Mary and her sister react and feel as any

Beginnings: Women's Childhood Autobiography Prior to World War I 39

child might. Overall, the happiness of childhood is emphasized. Scares and problems are not omitted, but the tone is optimistic. As Howitt tells it, the world is a good place, and problems are not left unsolved. Thus, for example, an underhanded acquaintance is punished by ill fortune, whereas her patient and upright father, who returns good for evil, is universally admired and rewarded in the end.

In her posthumously published *Autobiography* (1889), Howitt again wrote about her childhood, but more briefly and, typically for unpublished autobiographies, more confessionally. She mentions fear, shame, and dissatisfaction with her plain Quaker clothing, and voices some criticism of her parents. All of this was elided in her 1845 work for young readers.[24]

Subsequent children's book authors who wrote their childhood autobiographies followed in Howitt's footsteps in maintaining a predominantly positive tone, as befits writing for young audiences. Their childhoods were not necessarily rosy, but they have the knack of turning upsetting events into moral, humorous, educational, and even identificatory stories, in contrast to autobiographers who did not have their background and focused on telling exactly how they themselves felt, such as Harriet Martineau, whose childhood memories in her *Autobiography* emphasize fear and shame. Mrs. F. Hughes's *My Childhood in Australia: A Story for My Children* (1891), for example, is cast in exactly the same mold as Howitt's. Hughes writes about growing up on a sheep station in South Australia, focusing on aspects of interest to children: the farm animals, the wild animals, the pets, "the natives," and such activities as candle making and sheep shearing. She emphasizes how happy she and her siblings were.

Jane Eyre, a bestselling, universally known novel, which devotes its first part to the tribulations of a ten-year-old orphan girl, had few imitators among women's childhood autobiographies written in English. Fiction copies factual writing easily, but the reverse move encounters more impediments. Jane Eyre's real-life counterparts would have had to be willing and able to tell their stories. Like Charlotte Brontë, numerous women subsequently wrote about childhood fears, and, like Jane, women writers in both England and France complained about their boarding schools. But these facts likelier had to do with the prevalence of childhood fears and the grim experience of boarding schools than with the influence of Charlotte Brontë.

The all-but-orphaned American writer Eliza Farnham (1815–1864) may conceivably have taken some inspiration from Brontë in writing

40 Beginnings: Women's Childhood Autobiography Prior to World War I

My Early Days (1859), though the thematic resemblance may also be coincidental. Farnham's work hovers between autobiography and fiction. On the one hand, Farnham hints in the preface that the work includes "the painful relation of my early sufferings,"[25] and she does keep what Philippe Lejeune termed the "autobiographical pact," by giving her protagonist her own name.[26] On the other, she writes novelistically, preferring to tell her story through scenes with a great deal of dialogue, similarly to *Jane Eyre*. A subsequent publisher says that "there is more truth than fiction" in the narrative,[27] and commentators take it as a source of information about Farnham's life, but the book has also been classified as fiction. Either way, it is a long and serious book, and not just an abuse story, but an account of the feelings, thoughts, and aspirations of the protagonist "Eliza," a highly intelligent, thoughtful, idealistic girl who desires to do good and thirsts for education. Her foster mother, who adopts her at the age of six, scolds, beats, and punishes her, and fails to send her to school. She merely wants to keep her as a servant on her farm. Not until she is fourteen does Eliza find the resolve to appeal to what is left of her geographically distant family and escape her bondage for a better life. Authentic touches include the plethora of episodes and Eliza's constant worry that she is dark complexioned and ugly, hence not lovable.

Besides Farnham, Hannah Lynch, discussed in this chapter, may have had Brontë at the back of her mind when she wrote *Autobiography of a Child* (1899), a work that is also probably at least partly fictional. In 1910 Marguerite Audoux published the sad story of an orphan—but in France. In English-language life writing, Brontë strikes notes that find resonance in women's childhood autobiographies over a century later: the pseudonymous *A Cornish Waif's Story* (1954) concerns a stigmatized and victimized orphan; and Janet Hitchman, a war orphan who lived in a succession of foster homes until adulthood, tells us in *The King of the Barbareens* (1960), in a moving tribute to Brontë, that she changed her given name from Elsie to Janet (Rochester's pet name for Jane) when she read *Jane Eyre* at age sixteen. These two works will be discussed in chapter 5.

"We"

The American Lucy Larcom, born in 1824, was nine years younger than Eliza Farnham and two years older than Athénaïs Michelet. The childhoods of these women—Farnham, Larcom, and Michelet—born in the

1810s and 1820s seem extraordinarily remote from the perspective of the twenty-first century. They grew up in a world we no longer know, a world that has dropped behind the horizon of our cultural understanding. To give an example, both Michelet and Larcom spent a good part of their childhood sewing. The poet Larcom was actually sent to work in the Lowell cotton mill when she was "between eleven and twelve years old,"[28] and it was to recount her experience there that her publisher asked her to write her autobiography, *A New England Girlhood* (1889), the intended audience being young persons.[29]

By the time Lucy Larcom wrote, there was a tradition in the United States of writing about one's childhood for the young, just as Mary Howitt had done in England. This tradition was exemplified by Grace Greenwood's children's stories and Catharine Sedgwick's "Recollections of Childhood," a piece of family history addressed to her grandniece, written in 1853–54 and posthumously published in 1871. Such works take the perspective of an adult looking back. The purpose is to usefully acquaint the younger generation with the history of the family and with the customs and lifestyles of the previous age. They are devoid of confessional intention and eschew an analytical or psychological approach. In fact, they are barely autobiographical at all: they are less about the writer than about her family, friends, and surroundings. They impart such wisdom as the adult has to give and take a positive tone.[30]

Descended from Puritans, Larcom grew up in a family of ten siblings in Beverly, Massachusetts. Religion was an important part of family and community life, and Larcom was deeply religious from early on. Although she had poetic talent and aspired to be a teacher, she went to work at age eleven in the Lowell mills when the family fell on hard times following her father's death, so as to make money for the family. She spent ten years there, working a thirteen-hour day in the spinning room and the dressing room until she was finally transferred to a lighter job. In later life she became a teacher and a published poet. As such, she was a person who set great store by her privacy. She had to be talked into writing her autobiography by her publisher Houghton.[31] Her statement in her book that she never sought fame seems quite candid: "Fame, indeed, never had much attraction for me . . . I could never imagine a girl feeling any pleasure in placing herself 'before the public.' The privilege of seclusion must be the last one a woman can willingly sacrifice" (132). In her preface too she exhibits real hesitation at stepping into the limelight. She writes that her autobiography is "written for the young, at the suggestion of friends" (9). She seemingly needs to justify it thus, because "To many, the word 'autobiography' implies nothing but conceit and egotism" (9). And she adds, seemingly quite torn: "I do not know that I altogether approve of autobiography myself, when the subject is a person of so little importance as in the present instance" (10).

Indeed: To publish under one's own name implies a bid for attention, for a readership; it means stepping before the public as a person, putting one's "name" in circulation. It means committing oneself publicly to one's published statements and bracing oneself to be quoted and misquoted, paraphrased and misparaphrased, talked about, objectified, and stereotyped. A name, and to a greater degree fame, can bring recognition, influence, money, and power; but at the same time a name, and to a greater degree fame, are dearly paid for with a loss of anonymity and seclusion, of potential, of the freedom to change one's mind, of the right to be treated like a living human being instead of "a name." To write one's autobiography for publication requires even more gumption than other types of writing, because it means stepping into the public spotlight as someone who believes that her life is worth writing about. It radiates a sense of self-importance. Unless written by a person of real importance who might be able to stick carefully to the publicly known facts, it displays a willingness to reveal information about oneself, to make what is private and intimate public, to hang out the laundry of one's soul. Few women were of real importance, and going public, calling attention to one's unimportant self, was so little consonant with the meekness and modesty that were regarded as part and parcel of femininity that a woman who made herself a "name" could be seen to have denatured herself by the very act. Jane Marcus has suggested that under these circumstances, women retreated to a discourse of domesticity, "signing themselves into the seemingly insignificant apron pocket of history."[32]

From this point of view, the genre of childhood autobiography actually offers a would-be author a convenient escape route. It affords the option of circumventing the distasteful aspects of autobiography by treating childhood less as an individual and more as a shared, communal experience. This manner of writing about childhood may well have suggested itself naturally to children who grew up in a large nineteenth-century family, where the children of well-off families were raised in "the nursery," and where in any case a child spent most of his or her time in the company of siblings. A number of childhood autobiographies

Beginnings: Women's Childhood Autobiography Prior to World War I   43

written in the era of large families, and not just by women, witness Kenneth Grahame's works, take this route of writing about the lives of children as a group. These books are among those that tend to represent their subject most idyllically and nostalgically. It is the route typically taken by writers who intend their stories for young audiences and leads to the point where childhood autobiography shades off into children's literature.

A New England Girlhood is ostensibly intended for young readers, but it is not a children's book; from the beginning it appeals to adult readers as well. Yet this autobiography is fundamentally grounded in the first person plural. In the first seven chapters, in which she writes about her childhood up to the beginning of her employment in the Lowell mills, Larcom avoids self-profiling and self-revelation by dilating on the times, the place, and the family. Growing up in a family of ten siblings, she credibly disappears into a sea of children. In the next four chapters, she continues in much the same style, bringing in much information about the mill, mill work, and the mill girls, before concluding in a twelfth chapter in which she summarizes her career as a teacher and writer after leaving the mill. To a striking degree, the book is about "we"—first the siblings, then the mill girls—rather than "I." Larcom's writing thus occupies the opposite end of the spectrum from Gautier's. She, the subject, is not perpetually in the center, but tends to fade into a crowd of other people. As Shirley Marchalonis states, in the first seven chapters she makes herself "one player in a larger scene," but also later, "her own story remains a thread through the larger picture."[33] Thus, "the front shop window was especially interesting to us children, for there were in it a few glass jars containing sticks of striped barley-candy, and red and white peppermint-drops . . ." (28). "One of our greatest school pleasures was to watch Aunt Hannah spinning on her flax-wheel . . ." (29). Nonetheless, a portrait of Lucy as a child does emerge: she repeatedly uses herself as her own example in the matter of moral upbringing (e.g., she purloins pennies, and they burn in her hand) and the awakening to religion, and she profiles herself as someone who had a poetic talent, loved poetry, and spontaneously wrote verses. She insists on her gift, thereby individuating herself and underpinning what the reader presumably knows already, that she is a successful poet—a fact that she mentions in an extremely modest, career-deprecating way at the end of her autobiography. But she edges away from giving the impression that she was special by suggesting that she just did what the others did and that others must also have felt the way she did. Thus: "I began to go to school when I was about two years old, as other children about us did" (30). In Wordsworthian tones: "These recollections [of a heavenly life before birth] . . . so distinctly belong to the baby Myself . . . But other grown-up children, in looking back, will doubtless see many a trailing cloud of glory" (32). This style consistently carries forward the considerations she advances in her preface, where she represents herself as being far from unique, but rather a part of a type or trend: "The commonest personal history has its value when it is looked at as a part of the One Infinite Life" (9); "You see that I am nothing remarkable" (10); "Whatever special interest this little narrative may have is due to the social influences under which I was reared" (11). Even her mention of her poetic gift is couched in the phrasing of typicality: "Rich or poor, every child comes into the world with some imperative need of its own, which shapes its individuality. . . . My 'must-have' was poetry" (12). Individuality is explained, one might almost say excused, through typicality; it is something everyone has. Such self-effacement is certainly gender-specific, inasmuch as it reveals the acculturation of women in Larcom's day. It is also genre-specific, informing the "apron-pocket" of autobiography occupied by women in Larcom's day.

Virtually every critic notices that Larcom combines a certain degree of self-profiling with a remarkable degree of other-centeredness and even self-effacement.[34] The bottom line of this discussion is that *A New England Girlhood* does not correspond to generic expectations aroused by the dominant, male tradition of autobiography, but rather weds autobiography to a set of different, historically feminine values. Divergences in the critics' readings reflect above all the fact that women's self-expectations had changed utterly by the late twentieth century. It says a great deal about the mindset of the late twentieth century that the modern critics pay little attention to Larcom's modesty and desire for privacy—values of yesteryear that had long since dead-ended in unprofitability and had hence become incomprehensible.

Larcom's modesty is consistent with her faith. Deeply religious and reflective, she believes that everything is a part of an Infinite Whole, that God is manifest in all things, that His voice speaks through the natural world, and that hymns and poetry alike unite the natural with the spiritual. Jessica Lewis, whose reading stands out for not looking at the text through modern-day frames but rather examines it carefully and sympathetically in order to tease out its own terms, emphasizes how these beliefs contribute to the poetic qualities of the autobiography and also inform its construction. She argues that in the first seven chapters Larcom establishes an identity that is based on her early experiences with nature, language, religion, and poetry, while the second part "portrays a model of existence, of living out that identity."[35] In short, Larcom's identity sustains her in her ten years as a mill girl, allowing her to find the "blessing hidden in the curse" of toil.[36]

A New England Girlhood is an appealing book that presents an interesting life. The reader also quickly discovers in Larcom an attractive narratorial personality. She projects the woman of sixty-five that she was when she published her book: a woman who is wise, modest, cheerful, and accepting of what life has brought her and what she has made of her life. On account of necessity, she devoted her formative years from age eleven on to something that had nothing to do with her talents and aspirations. She made the best of what others might have regarded as adversity: she embraced her fate and ultimately was proud of the Lowell mill and the girls there and their efforts at self-improvement, which included the production of a fortnightly newspaper. For the mill was not just thirteen-hour-a-day drudgery; it was one of the first types of gainful employment open to women in the United States aside from teaching and domestic service. Working in the mill meant economic liberty for the girls and, because the mill girls came from all over New England, was a broadening life experience. Lucy develops a philosophy of life and has wisdom to impart. This wisdom is obviously hard won and fairly come by, so one cannot accuse her of preaching platitudes. She writes to impart her wisdom to young girls. For her the meaning of life is "love, service, the sacrifice of self for others' good" (105). Her view on being a woman is: "God made no mistake in [a girl's] creation. He sent her into the world full of power and will to be a helper; and only He knows how much his world needs help. . . . Nothing can deprive her of her natural instinct to help, of her birthright as helper" (117). And: "Their real power, the divine dowry of womanhood, is that of receiving and giving inspiration" (118). Moreover, she calls for feminine solidarity, observing that it is an unworthy tendency of womankind to indulge in petty estimates of other women. Rather, "It is the first duty of every woman to recognize the mutual bond of universal womanhood" (119). And on her own life: "I had early been saved from a great mistake; for it is the greatest of mistakes to begin life with the expectation that it is going to be easy, or with the wish to have it so"

(146). Her philosophy thus encourages girls to make the best of what seems ineluctably to be the fate of most women. For what woman of Larcom's day did not lead a life that was driven far from her early aspirations by this or that necessity?

The "we" mode did not hold the keys to the future of women's childhood autobiography written in English. Nevertheless, after Larcom certain other childhood autobiographers did cut their works from this template. For example, the Bostonian Laura E. Richards's *When I Was Your Age* (1894), a memoir of family, friends, and place written for children, is so dominated by the pronoun "we" that it cannot be properly considered an autobiography at all. Ida Gandy's *A Wiltshire Childhood* (1929) is a charming, idyllic story of growing up in the secluded Wiltshire village where the author and her siblings spent their "peculiarly happy and unfettered childhood."[37] As much a portrait of Wiltshire as of the children and their pastimes, its successive chapters trace a spatial widening out from the house to the other rural places that the seven minister's children considered their kingdom. M. Vivian Hughes's *A London Child of the Seventies* (1935), the story of life in the author's ordinary middle-class London family, of the pastimes and adventures of herself and her four older brothers, is of this type, as is Eleanor Margaret Acland's story of "Milly" (herself) in *Good-Bye for the Present: The Story of Two Childhoods* (1935). Both authors organize their childhood memoirs by thematic groupings that illustrate the siblings' communal activities. A Canadian childhood autobiography of childhood and youth published the same year, Nellie L. McClung's *Clearing in the West: My Own Story* (1935), is cast in the same mold, even though the author, a noted Canadian feminist and public figure, takes care to profile her own personality, recount her own doings and feelings, and introduce her nascent ideas about women's rights.

Two women from New England backgrounds like Larcom's, one of her vintage and the other a generation younger, subsequently published autobiographies of childhood and youth that resemble Larcom's in salient respects but do not adopt the "we" mode. Clara Barton (1821–1912), famous as the founder of the American Red Cross, was Lucy Larcom's contemporary and like her a Massachusetts Yankee. Like Larcom, she wrote her story, entitled *The Story of My Childhood* (1907), in old age, claims that she did so at the suggestion of others, and addresses it to the young. She even precedes her text with a couple of letters from schoolchildren in which they ask her to tell them about her early life. She dedicates her book to such children, announcing that she will keep it small so they can read it easily. Compared to Larcom's, however, her book is undidactic; she does not include instructive messages. She appears simply to tell what she remembers, without any particular agenda. Finally, hers is not a "we" story. As the youngest of five siblings, "a dozen or so"[38] years younger than her closest sister, she was in fact often alone, except for an interlude when her family lived on a farm with a widow and her children. She simply tells her own story, without analysis, leaving the reader to wonder how it all adds up and how this child became the woman she became. Like Larcom, she observes the maxim that one should say good things about other people or nothing at all, but about herself, quite in contrast to Larcom who credits herself with a cheerful disposition, she emphasizes that she had a personality problem: she was an extremely sensitive child, bashful around people, timid and inordinately afraid of causing offense. Thus, writing eighteen years later than Larcom, she takes a step in the direction of confession. With due modesty, she tells how she was set on the track she would pursue in later life: her older brother fell off the roof of a barn and was severely injured; though only eleven, she voluntarily devoted herself to nursing him for two years. Her main point about herself, however, is that she remained painfully timid, although she was good at school and played intrepidly at boys' sports like skating. Finally her parents, puzzled about what to do with her, took a noted phrenologist's advice to make her a teacher, and so, in her midteens, she was started on a vocation at which she was successful, not least because she could deal with boys. Barton mentions "our sweet poetess, Lucy Larcom" (108) because she too briefly worked in a fabric mill. But she points out that she did this voluntarily, in a mill that belonged to her brothers, and unlike Larcom was far from being a heroine of early American manufacturing. Her family was prosperous, and she did not undergo hardship.

Caroline A. Stickney Creevey (1843–1920) actually had Larcom as her English teacher at Wheaton Seminary. Her *A Daughter of the Puritans: An Autobiography* (1916), written at a twenty-seven-year remove from Larcom's autobiography, paints a similar picture of a New England upbringing, but frames it in an entirely different manner. Creevey neither uses the "we" style nor addresses herself to a young audience. She tells her own story forthrightly and at considerable length and includes many photographs of people and places. Her purpose is to document, not to teach or inspire. She states that she wants to describe, at a distance of two generations, the upbringing of children in a bygone age: religious, strict, and severe. One recognizes many of the elements of Larcom's story: daughters were still expected to sew household linens; children were minimally supervised, but morality was strict (like Larcom, Creevey stole a small sum and felt guilty about it); baked beans and brown bread were still prepared on Saturday so as to avoid cooking on the Sabbath; a thrift ethic ruled. But all of this is told through an entirely different lens from Larcom's: the lens of the time of writing, when most things in America, but especially religious beliefs and practices, had irrevocably changed. Creevey also writes about medical matters that were beneath Lucy Larcom's poetic purview, about the use of leeches and bleeding and a disregard for germs and the possibility of contagion, her point here too being contrastive. She emphasizes that medicine made huge advances since her childhood. She conveys her old-school views on the burning issue of the "woman question." Like Larcom, she believes in "the ideals of true womanhood . . . healing and comforting" and pronounces "that which is termed feminism" "dishonoring to the home."[39]

The differences between Larcom, Barton, and Creevey typify the changes that took place in English-language women's childhood autobiography from the nineteenth to the early twentieth century. Creevey's documentary effort already has much in common with retrospective works that would abound in the interwar years.

The Study

Frances Hodgson Burnett's *The One I Knew the Best of All* (1893) is a first in several respects. There is a new motivation here that will define many subsequent works in the genre: to capture the mind of the child. Burnett turns the life of the child's mind into an extraordinary drama. The work owes a great deal to its ingenious narrative pose. It is written in the third person. The child subject is "she," the narrator "I." The child subject is "the Small Person," while the narrator is someone who remembers the child and looks back at her quizzically. This narrative stance and use of personal pronouns erect a sharp division between the narrator and the child, underscoring that they are not in a relationship of identity. The narrator, however, seems identical to the author Burnett.

The narrator-author's view of the (nonidentical) child is uniquely privileged. Burnett, well-known author of many children's books including *Little Lord Fauntleroy*, writes here about "the one I knew the best of all." Thus the narrator-author garners the advantage of portraying the child she once was without falling into the snare of autobiography, without appearing to "tell her own story" (although the reader realizes it is exactly that). What are the snares of autobiography? One of them, in her era, would have been to incur the accusation of presumptuousness. The author immediately sidesteps that accusation, deftly excusing herself from autobiographical arrogance by claiming that the child she describes could stand in for any other imaginative child. She begins the preface with a sentence reminiscent of Lucy Larcom's demurrals: "I should feel a serious delicacy in presenting to the world a sketch so autobiographical as this if I did not feel myself absolved from any charge of the bad taste of personality by the fact that I believe I might fairly entitle it 'The Story of *any* Child with an Imagination.'"[40]

The third person, the "she," gives the narrator great liberty. It allows her the liberty to maintain her own voice, her wisdom, her wit, her storytelling savoir faire. It sustains the "study" aspect of the book by objectifying the child as a "case" or example. It also facilitates her turning her personal history into a charming and readable story. Burnett writes with a light touch. She has the air of not taking herself too seriously.

One can only admire Burnett for having devised a narrative form that allowed her to write a study, a childhood autobiography, and a delightful story all in one. I say "autobiography" because despite the author's initial protestations to the contrary, the child's singularity and the uniqueness of her story become more and more apparent. The work turns into the story of how the little girl became a writer. In the process it turns from the typical to the culture-historical: it shows by what unlikely stratagems a girl could become a writer in the United States in the 1860s. Frances addresses editors as "Sir," signs "F. Hodgson," and receives replies addressed to "Sir."

Like Daudet, Burnett stresses remembering. In fact, like Daudet's story, Burnett's is told strictly through the lens of memory. Burnett takes a sharper theoretical interest in memory than Daudet: for example, she is interested in the precise age at which memory starts, a question she settles by showing that memory came for her with a sense of self and with thought. "I have no memory of any time so early in her life that she was not a distinct little *individual*. Of the time when she was not old enough to formulate opinions quite clearly to herself I have no recollection, and I can remember distinctly events which happened before she was three years old" (3). Writing in an age where memory was just starting to be studied scientifically, and making her own empirical observations, Burnett comes to some conclusions that appear doubtful today. For instance, she implies that her early memories are accurate: "[Asking questions] is a very clear memory to me." "I see a comfortable English bedroom" (4). She does add, much like Daudet, that her early memories take the form of spots: "Perhaps the interest of such recollections is somewhat added to by the fact that one can only recall them by episodes, and that the episodes seem to appear without any future or any past" (5). Then, while she implies that memories start with a sense of self, she also believes that both thought and memory precede language — a conclusion that would be disputed today. She says she has clear memories from the age of two or three, before she has "the *words*" (8), including a memory of a complex moral matter having to do with how to tell the truth and yet be polite — the issue is whether she likes the unattractive name a family friend gave her daughter. Finally, she touches on the mystery of why she remembers one thing and not another. Thus, she remembers an encounter with a policeman around the age of four, but not her father's contemporaneous death. Sally Shuttleworth sees evidence that Burnett was aware of the child study movement in her reference to the present "Children's Century" in which children are regarded as "embryo intellects, whose growth it is the pleasure and duty of intelligent maturity to foster and protect" (110).[41] If Burnett had child study in mind, it would explain her scientific interest in the order of the advent of a sense of self, thought, memory, and language.

Burnett tells the story of the Small Person more or less in chronological order, but her main organizing principle is theme. Her thematic organization is more pronounced than Larcom's and different from Daudet's in the degree of attention she pays to the psychology of the child. Some of her themes are ones that we have seen in earlier works: early memories (Sand, Gautier), reading (Sand, Daudet), dolls (Sand, Michelet, Daudet), theft (here, "borrowing" — Larcom), response to nature (Larcom), and early vocation (Sand, Larcom). But in addition, she initiates a number of new themes that will become recurrent in later childhood autobiographies. One important such theme, which will occur in the future in works by Séverine, Lucy Sinclair, and Marie Bonaparte, is that of the deceptiveness of adults. Two of Burnett's stories engage this theme. The first involves a nursemaid who practices a seemingly harmless deception when she is a toddler: she wants to hold her mother's newborn baby, and the nurse pretends to let her hold it, all the while supporting it herself. The second is more nefarious: when she is seven,

Beginnings: Women's Childhood Autobiography Prior to World War I 51

an unscrupulous adult plays a cruel practical joke, promising to give the baby-hungry little girl a baby of her very own. Another theme is the socialization of children, that is, their perplexity in learning what the world considers acceptable and what taboo, although Burnett presents it here as a moral issue: how should she answer when asked if she likes the name Eleanor? Another theme is the child's perception that there are different social classes. And finally, she discusses the extreme dullness of certain adults—here, a nursemaid.

Very interesting is Burnett's analysis of how she started playing with dolls. She stresses that reading came first. She was a child who quickly became addicted to books. She read for the plot, for stories. It was only when she knew stories that dolls became interesting; dolls served as heroines in elaborate stories that Frances started making up herself based on books she had read. At age seven she wrote a first poem, and from this point on her narrative starts to track the story of how she became a writer, culminating in the publication of her first stories when she was fifteen. Burnett treats her early passion for stories and storytelling with a great deal of humor, gently mocking her penchant for heroines with violet eyes and flowing tresses. She styles her passion as a voracious appetite rather than a gift, possibly out of Victorian feminine modesty, though that modesty is also satirized: "Being an English little girl she knew the vast superiority of the Male" (40).

The mother in this work is a positive figure. She is represented as gentle, unworldly, and a lady. She is helpless in practical affairs—though always supportive of her children. Certainly, complaint would have disrupted the light tone of this book. But also in more straightforwardly confessional autobiographies, a mother who conforms to this type is generally presented as a beloved figure. Loving, impractical mothers are not hated; severe ones are. Sand and Larcom had impractical mothers as well, and neither condemns her.

Notwithstanding her father's death when she was four and her mother's problems in coping with the financial aspect of things, which led to her family's move to the United States, Burnett gives the impression of having had a wonderful childhood, both in Manchester and in beautiful Tennessee. "She was not a self-conscious, timid child, to whom constant praise was a necessity. She was an extremely healthy and joyous Small Person, and took life with ease and good cheer" (208). She gets along very well with her sisters and tolerably well with her brothers, and she has nothing but kind words for her mother. "Poor gentle

52   Beginnings: Women's Childhood Autobiography Prior to World War I

and guileless little lady, she was all unfit to contend with a harsh, sharp, sordid world" (240). Her mother is nothing if not encouraging, and her encouragement extends to Frances's attempts to write a story for money: "What she thought it would be difficult to say, but she was lovable and sustaining as usual" (299). She describes a cruel incident (of the grown-up who promises her a baby for a laugh), a letdown that rings true (the preparations for a party are more exciting than the party itself), and experiencing a classmate's death, but on the whole she tells of incidents and enjoyments that justify her tone of nostalgia.

Short Pieces

Burnett casually lets herself be called "Frances" at a late stage in her narrative. Another British work that is genuinely autobiographical, in the sense that the author gives the protagonist her own nickname, "Daisy," is E. Nesbit's *My School-Days*, commissioned and published serially in *The Girl's Own Paper* from October 1896 to September 1897.[42] Soon thereafter Nesbit, who thought of herself as a poet but did a lot of writing for money, began to write the many bestselling children's books for which she became famous.[43] In this collection of childhood stories, Nesbit's storytelling style, her adherence to the child protagonist's point of view, and her light tone make palpable that she was writing for a young audience. Nesbit does not write "the story of my life," but discrete, albeit chronologically sequential, pieces about herself from ages seven to ten that are compatible with serial publication. The pieces were republished in 1966 in book form under the title *Long Ago When I Was Young*. Like Burnett, Nesbit justifies publishing her story by asserting that it was typical. She writes by way of introduction to the pieces: "Not because my childhood was different from that of others, not because I have anything strange to relate, anything new to tell, are these words written. For the other reason rather—that I was a child as other children, that my memories are their memories, as my hopes were their hopes, my dreams their dreams, my fears their fears—I open the book of memory to tear out some pages for you others."[44]

Like Burnett, Nesbit states that she remembers well and clearly: "There is nothing here that is not in my most clear and vivid recollection. When I was a little child I used to pray fervently, tearfully, that when I should be grown up I might never forget what I thought and felt and suffered then. Let these pages speak for me, and bear witness that I have not forgotten" (27). Indeed, Nesbit focuses on her joys, sorrows, fears, rages, disillusionments, and hopes, so that despite the light tone, the reader does have the sense that the psychology of children is captured, even though Daisy seems a bit high-strung. For example, one installment, entitled "In the Dark," is devoted to fear. We find out that Daisy was afraid of her father playing at wild beasts with her brothers and roaring, of her sister appearing in a mask and costume to kidnap her in a nursery charade, of noises, of dim night lights, of a stuffed two-headed calf (her father ran an agricultural college), of an emu skin hung on the wall, of bad dreams, and of course of the dark generally.

The outward events of Nesbit's childhood were not at all typical. Daisy's widowed mother changed locations frequently. Consistent with Nesbit's exclusive focalization through the child, the reader does not find out why this was the case. (In reality, she was seeking a cure for Daisy's older sister's tuberculosis.) This constant moving about had consequences for Daisy. She was often placed in boarding schools and on one occasion lodged with another family, between periods of living with her mother and siblings in different places in England and France and traveling with them on the Continent. The initial episode tells how she was bullied at age seven by another girl in her first boarding school. Her unsettled existence and frequent change of regimes had the effect of making the child value her mother greatly: "The world, all upside down, had suddenly righted itself" (43) when her mother rescued her from one boarding school. The constant changes of scenery she was subjected to for a period of many years also made Nesbit cherish familiar objects: "The small material objects that surround one's daily life have always influenced me deeply. . . . I have a cat-like fondness for things I am accustomed to" (94). Everything Nesbit writes about her mother makes her seem a thoroughly positive figure. She is kind, intelligent, and wise enough not to supervise her children too closely. Daisy is the youngest of four siblings, and, typically for Victorian childhood autobiography, the large family appears to be an advantage. In particular, the little girl likes and plays with "the boys," her two older brothers. Yet this is emphatically not a "we"-style autobiography. The focus is Daisy herself, her experiences, and the way she felt about them.

The Victim

Hannah Lynch has been described as an unjustly neglected writer. She was an Irish feminist, novelist, and journalist who ultimately made her home in Paris, where she died an untimely death at age forty-four.

Autobiography of a Child came out when Lynch was just short of forty. It was soon translated into French. The status of the text is cloaked in mystery. It originally appeared anonymously in serials in *Blackwood's Magazine* in 1898–99, where it was already under the copyright of Dodd, Mead, and Co., which brought out a book version under Lynch's name in 1899. An anonymous publication can signal, though inconclusively, an autobiographical story whose author would rather not identify herself. For her own part, Lynch tried to fend off the allegation that the book was "a history," insisting in a letter to *The Bookman* that it was "essentially a work of imagination."[45] But "many suspected that the book was an account of Lynch's own experiences."[46] It is written in a novelistic fashion, but its principal themes suggest that the author was writing about her own life. The protagonist is named "Angela." She tells the story of her childhood up to the age of twelve.

Not enough is known about Hannah Lynch's life to be able to decide to what degree this book is autobiographical. What Lynch tells us about Angela corresponds to certain agreed-on facts about Lynch's biography. For example, we learn that Angela is twelve in the year of the Franco-Prussian War (1871); this dates her birth to 1859, the year in which Lynch was born. Angela attended an English convent school for five years, from ages seven to twelve; Lynch had a convent education in England. The narrator stylizes herself as a wanderer abroad ("I was abroad, a hopeless wanderer");[47] Lynch wandered abroad. The narrator's polemic about Ireland being the worst place for women (196) mirrors the author's known feminist convictions.[48] Angela's mother, like Lynch's, is Scottish. On other matters, however, one finds conflicting information. In *Autobiography of a Child* Angela's father dies several months before she is born, and Lynch gives Angela seven sisters, three older sisters and four younger stepsisters, as well as a five-year-younger stepbrother who died in childhood. The most recent published account of Lynch's life by Faith Binckes and Kathryn Laing corresponds closely to this account, although it does not mention the brother.[49] But other sources claim that Lynch's father died during her childhood and that her mother's two marriages produced eleven daughters.[50] A website devoted to Lynch's mother, Anna Teresa Calderwood Cantwell, gives a considerably different account of her children.[51]

Lynch shows great interest in and insight into early memories, remarking, as Sigmund Freud did in his slightly later essay on screen memories, on their fragmentary, random, and uncertain nature. Her book stands out for its psychological insights generally, above all about children. The narrator comments, for example, on children's love of sensation and drama, on how easy it is to make them happy, and on the way they experience time. Finally, more even than Michelet, the girl experiences a terrific aversion to her mother, whom she paints as an unmotherly woman who has no spontaneous affection for her children, least of all Angela. She neglects, berates, and beats her large brood of daughters. Lynch portrays her like an evil queen in a fairy tale, as a beautiful and cruel woman with "long delicate and cruel nostrils," "thin delicate red lips," and a "cold blue glance" (184–85). "The mother who did not love me was the handsomest creature I had ever beheld" (185). This mother, "a woman of colossal intelligence, of wide knowledge, a brilliant talker . . ." (226), was also a heartless tyrant. One idiosyncratic detail is her penchant for destroying her children's things. Lynch writes:

> If my mother had been an early Christian or a socialist, she could not have shown herself a more inveterate enemy of personal property. Never through infancy, youth, or middle age has she permitted any of her offspring to preserve relics, gifts, or souvenirs. Treasures of every kind she pounced upon, and either destroyed or gave away,—partly from a love of inflicting pain, partly from an iconoclastic temper, but more than anything from a despotic ferocity of self-assertion. The preserving of relics, of the thousand and one little absurdities sentiment and fancy ever cling to, implied something beyond her power, something she could not hope to touch or destroy, implied above all an inner life existing independent of her harsh authority. The outward signs of this mental independence she ever ruthlessly effaced. (110)

This detail, despite its highly subjective interpretation, does not ring invented. In contrast, one wonders if the author did not exaggerate the violence she suffered at the hands of her female relatives. Her mother routinely inflicts violence on her children: "One or the other, for no reason on earth, but for the impertinent or irrational obviousness of her existence, was seized by white maternal hands, dragged by the hair, or banged against the nearest article of furniture. My mother never punished her children for doing wrong; she was simply exasperated by their inconceivable incapacity to efface themselves and 'lie low'" (47). The women in her mother's Scottish family seem generally disposed toward violence. Her maternal grandmother has a similarly sadistic streak: she threatens the child by holding a red-hot knife sharpener to her mouth (104).

Like Michelet, Lynch's Angela was the middle child in a large family and had no friends. "Mine was the loneliest, the most tragic of childhoods" (89–90). The other girls formed two groups of friends, both of which excluded her. An overly sensitive child, she lacked the robustness that would have made it possible for her to negotiate the situation and enter one of the two groups, so she remained a perpetual outsider. One of the narrator's insights concerns large families: "My dislike of large families is born of the conviction that every large family holds a victim. Amid so many, there is always one isolated creature who weeps in frozen secrecy, while the others shout with laughter. . . . The heart that has been broken with pain in childhood is never sound again, whatever sequel the years may offer" (231). Angela ran away—only to be caught and sent, at age seven, to convent school in England. Convent school is represented as an awful place, where the girls are underfed and overpunished and their letters home dictated by the nuns. Here she turns into a rebel. Highly imaginative, she becomes a leader in the group, one destined for trouble and hence for terrible punishment. She describes how a lay sister whipped her with a three-pointed whip until the blood came for an infraction she did not commit.

Angela's account of her childhood broadens into a diatribe about the treatment of girls in Ireland: "Another lamentable little girl born into this improvident dolorous vale of Irish misery. Elsewhere boys are born in plenty. In Ireland,—the very wretchedest land on earth for woman, the one spot of the globe where no provision is made for her, and where parents consider themselves as exempt of all duty, of tenderness, of justice in her regard, where her lot as daughter, wife, and old maid bears to resemblance to the ideal of civilization,—a dozen girls are born for one boy" (196). She goes on to say that the girls are shoved off to the Continent as governesses and teachers, inefficient and illiterate, without education, "incapable of handling a needle or cooking an egg, without the most rudimentary instinct of order or personal tidiness, incompetent, and vague, and careless" (197). Yet the parents expect them to send money home.

Lynch tells the story with passionate intensity. The narrator is not just insightful, but outspoken and witty. She spares no scorn in her condemnation of the circumstances that turned her child self into a martyr.

The intensity of her passion, the originality and quality of her insights, and her interrogation of memory tend to persuade the reader that this is a true account. For what novelist could summon up such feeling, concoct such insights, and bother to doubt her memories in order to create a fictional character? The detail and the attention paid to characters only tangentially involved in the narrator's life (such as her sister's would-be boyfriend) also lend verisimilitude to the story.

Yet the narrator is obviously a skillful storyteller, whose ploys suggest that she did not make a firm commitment to fidelity of fact. Anecdotes are chosen for their dramatic or traumatic quality or because they are quirky or funny. The narrator has a great comic gift. She is not a sober historian, but a rhetorician who pulls all the stops. She combines wit, irony, passion, a sense of drama, and facility with language. There is a lot of dialogue. Dialogue is almost impossible to remember verbatim over the course of the years and is the mark of a novel, not an autobiography. There are the "authentic" and "censored" versions of her letter home from convent school; it seems unlikely that the adult writer would have had these at her disposition. There is the often-employed stylistic device of an appeal to the reader ("picture, if you can . . ." [154], "I leave you to imagine . . ." [159]). She stylizes her reiterated dramatic transformation from a "tiny inarticulate pensive creature of Ireland" into "a turbulent adventurer, . . . a glorified outlaw" (136) in England.

The transformation of a sensitive and highly intelligent child from a wretched martyr into a resolute rebel is itself plausible, but Lynch's stylization of it and the overstated diction with which she emphasizes it are novelistic. Thus on first introduction, "The cowed and suffering baby of Ireland on Saxon shores at once revealed the Irish rebel, the instinctive enemy of law and order" (126). In the same chapter: "The start in Lysterby ends my patient martyrdom. Here I became the active and abominable little fiend unkindness and ill-management made of one of the gentlest and most sensitive of natures" (127). And in the concluding paragraph of that chapter: "Little Angela of Kildare and Dublin, over whose sorrows I have invited the sympathetic reader to weep, was a pallid and pathetic figure. But Angela of Lysterby held her own—more even than her own, for she fought for the others as well as for herself, and gave back (with a great deal more trouble at least) as much pain and affliction as she endured" (128). Much later: "The quaint little booby of Kildare, whom they had bullied to their liking, had grown into a lean, delicate, and resolute fiend, prepared to meet every blow by a buffet, every injustice by passionate revolt" (191). Additionally, Lynch carefully choreographs dramatic scenes, such as one about her siblings' excited and chaotic behavior when she is put on the boat to England, or the children's delight when a Christmas hamper arrives in her board-ing school, or the buildup over the first confession, which ends with her collapse in the confessional.[52]

Autobiography of a Child thus appears to be a fiction-autobiography blend. It often happens that soon after an autobiographical genre ap-pears, fiction springs up to mimic it. The diary novel is a good example; but the same thing holds true for all of the formally mimetic eighteenth-century forms of the novel, such as epistolary and memoir novels. *Jane Eyre* rapidly mimicked autobiography.[53] Conversely, historians avail themselves of fictional techniques. Given this ready merging of the waters, it is not productive to seek a sharp fiction-fact distinction in the style of an autobiographical narrative.

The turn toward storytelling we see in Burnett, Nesbit, and Lynch had certain advantages. A light tone, humorous moments, and fictional retouchings deflected the stigma attached to autobiography—its con-notations of self-importance and of taking oneself too seriously—and en-hanced the palatability of the work. Publishing one's story as a "novel"— or just changing people's names—also allowed a woman writer with living relatives to shelter them by raising the shield of fiction. Other writers adopted these strategies. Ellen Campbell's *An Australian Child-hood* (1892) is a humorous, storified short account of her adventures and misadventures in the Australian bush. The American journalist Jean-nette Gilder published a much more extensive account of her childhood from ages six to around fifteen in *Autobiography of a Tomboy* (1901). Gilder, who grew up in New York State, New Jersey, and Connecticut, does treat serious matters such as the Civil War and her father's death, but she chooses to frame her narrative as the story of a smart, impul-sive, feisty girl's escapades, which enables her to write with humor and irony. Despite the title of her book, she changes her own name—she is "Nell Gilbert"—and the names of others. To return to the French con-text, Lucie Delarue-Mardrus published the story of two years of her childhood as a third-person novel, *Le Roman des six petites filles* (1909), and gave it a page-turning plot that has to do with the girls' father's seduction and abandonment of their English governess. Although we find out plenty about the group dynamics of the horde of six little girls

Beginnings: Women's Childhood Autobiography Prior to World War I   59

who were the children of this well-to-do family, this devilish set ("they," not "we") essentially provides comic relief and gives the novel its light-hearted tone, whereas the littlest, Lili (Delarue-Mardrus herself), is taken dead seriously, as the one whose thoughts, feelings, and passions count.

Capturing the Child's Vision

In the years immediately before World War I, some remarkable English-language childhood autobiographies appeared. In 1913, when she published *A Childhood*, Joan Arden, age thirty-one, was the youngest English-woman to have published a childhood autobiography. Joan Arden is the pen name of the poet Melicent ("Milly") Jourdain.[54] She was born in 1882 and, afflicted with a progressive form of multiple sclerosis,[55] died an untimely death in 1926. She dedicates this short volume to her parents. Professor Gilbert Murray writes a preface in which he recommends it as a work in which "the randomness of childhood is well represented . . .; also its mysterious sense of a mysterious life in lifeless things, its terrors and its heartlessness."[56]

Of all the women's childhood autobiographies written in English up to this point, this one most succeeds in effacing the narrator, making her disappear except as a medium for remembering childhood places, scenes, things, pastimes, and people.[57] In this regard it parallels Marguerite Audoux's *Marie-Claire*, published three years previously in France. But unlike *Marie-Claire*, this childhood autobiography is not full of allusions to a subtext that the reader is invited to piece together. Arden plunges into narrating what she sees before her mind's eye, into the way she saw and felt as a child. As Murray says, there is "no continuous story." The chapters are not arranged in a discernable chronological order, although she is older (at boarding school) near the end; we do not find out in what part of rural England she grows up; names of family members ("my brother Bertrand," "my sister Judith" —neither name corresponds to her siblings' real names), ages, and facts about her family (her father is a clergyman) are mentioned only incidentally; she does not give portraits of other people; she ends abruptly. The work has a certain similarity to Daudet's both in its form and in its focus on, as Murray says, "scattered memories." Neither writer writes "autobiography," both make repeated and explicit allusion to the fact that they are remembering, neither gives facts about her family except casually, neither writes a linear chronological narrative, and both works are written in a poetic style. The difference lies in the degree of narratorial presence. Daudet's narrator has a firm grip on the narrative; she tells her story in the basic tense of narration, the *passé simple*; she feels free to comment, to impart her opinions and her wisdom about childhood; from time to time she adopts a nostalgic tone. Arden writes in the first person past tense—as if she were looking, riveted, into a crystal ball of the past. She writes without self-reflection, commentary, or tone; she effaces herself completely except to say, "I remember." The work's great accomplishment is to step back into the mind of the child and recreate the child's mode of vision. Everything about the narrative contributes to this one goal. The nine chapters group aspects of life that were especially important to the child, such as "Summer and Winter," "Gardeners," and "Animals." Within the chapters, Arden singles out reminiscences that reveal the mind of the child, obsessions that are peculiar to childhood and vanish with adulthood. All in all she shows us an alien who, however, is an extremely familiar creature to the reader once his or her memory has been jogged. Although we may not all have seen and felt exactly like Joan (she calls herself by her pseudonym), of all the little girls we have met thus far, this one is closest to "every child." With its emphasis on recall, its confinement to the child's point of view, and its nonconsecutive presentation, this book most closely resembles among its English predecessors Nesbit's sketches, which Arden arguably could have read when they were serialized in *The Girl's Own Paper* in 1896–97. But Arden does not follow suit in writing for a young audience, nor does she emphasize typicality. She focuses on representing the child's experience of things, and she does not try to persuade us that these are anything other than her own experiences.

Arden emphasizes outdoor and indoor spaces, lavishly describing the places of her childhood. She never does this from a distance or through panoramic overviews, but always in such a way as to reproduce the child's own sense of a space. She focuses on things that captured the child's attention: a pool, stone skulls on the churchyard gates, water rats, the swifts circling in the air, pretending to be a horse while pulling the lawnmower, collecting horse chestnuts. Likewise, she singles out ideas and endeavors unique to childhood, such as trying to understand the language of the starlings and wondering if things are there when she can't see them. She often transmits a child's keen sense perceptions through metaphor ("sharp gray rocks standing out suddenly like the bones of a monster showing through its skin of turf" [12]).

There is a strong emphasis on affect, emotion, and sensation. Fear is a recurrent motif. It is by no means Joan's exclusive emotion, nor does it dominate the narrative, but it does differentiate this childhood story from previous ones, with the exception of Nesbit's. Arden recalls fear of a blacksmith's shop (3), of the space under the fir trees in the wood (3), of a pool (6) and of a canal (93), of being caught in their hunt for plovers' eggs (6), of Black Harry the poacher (20), of her nurse's beetle-like father (21). She writes of the scary lighting of the gas (85), scary children's games (77), scary upstairs rooms (80). Above all there is the fear of drowning, which, she admits, "followed me into my waking life" (39). One entire chapter, "The Dark," centers on fear. The title echoes Nesbit's segment "In the Dark," though the similarity in title could be coincidental, given the prevalence of children's fears of the dark. The terrors the dark brings include the sound of rain, the fear of malevolent creatures like goblins, and bad dreams including a recurrent one of being pushed downstairs. But there are plenty of positive emotions to offset the fear. "A happy wildness filled me when my feet touched the short grass" (4). "The friendly hours spent among the trees" (8). The fresh smell of cut grass "stopped me on the door-step with a sense of happiness all through me" (9–10).

Animals are extremely important to this child. She keeps an imaginary stable of horses. Her interactions with real animals are among her most meaningful experiences. Arden describes her stuffed animals, which she smuggles with her to boarding school, her china animals, and the sugar and chocolate animals she could hardly bring herself to eat.

Although like Larcom Arden grew up in a large family (Milly Jourdain was the youngest of ten children) and spent much time with siblings, the girl herself—her feelings and perceptions—is, as in Burnett's case, definitely at the center of her story. Communal pastimes ("we") are sometimes the focus, but she peels herself out of the group to a noteworthy extent. Arden's distance from Larcom's narrative stance is immense.

This highly original childhood autobiography forms a contrast to previous women's childhood autobiographies in two further respects. First, the mother barely appears at all in the narrative. Second, Arden responds in an unusual way to the typical theme of reading: she writes that she did not like to read. She adds that she did enjoy hearing stories told aloud and looking at picture books, although a certain picture was too scary.

62   Beginnings: Women's Childhood Autobiography Prior to World War I

The Inner Life of the Child

Una Hunt, a painter, published *Una Mary: The Inner Life of a Child* in 1914, an extraordinary work that blends features of Burnett's and Arden's, yet accomplishes something utterly original. In the preface Hunt states, echoing Burnett, that hers is "the story of the life of any imaginative child."[58] Up to a point, *Una Mary* seems to follow in Burnett's footsteps. It is a book of Burnett's length, published by Burnett's publisher, Scribner's. Like Burnett, Hunt begins by scrupulously seeking her earliest memories. She narrates in the first person, not the third, but as in Burnett, the book is told from the narrator's perspective and is organized by subject while following a rough chronological order. Like Burnett, Hunt is sympathetic to her child self. Although the child's ideas are often droll, she narrates with almost no gentle irony. Above all, like Burnett, Hunt seems intent on producing an accurate, even scientific study of her subject. She admits to some fictionalization to conceal the identities of others—she published this book at a relatively young age, when she was in her late thirties—but does not sacrifice details and avoids imposing a story line on them.

Like Arden, on the other hand, whose work she probably did not know given its recent publication date, Hunt sets out to capture the child's vision—or more precisely, her "inner life." Hunt introduces the work with the words, "This is the true story of the inner life of my childhood" (vii). But how different is this child from both Burnett and Arden! The young Burnett was a spinner of stories, and Arden with her fears and delights thought and felt the way many another child might think and feel. Hunt, in contrast, belongs to the small set of children who lead an imaginary life alongside their real life. She makes the imagined second life the central subject of her book. She tells the reader that she had a second self, an alter ego, that was the "deep, inner, real part" of herself "that no one else seemed to know was there" (vii). This second self originated with her perception at the age of two that she had an inner life and by the age of three became a consistent part of herself to whom she gave a name: Una Mary. Dating one's sense of self to the third year of life is very common; becoming aware that one has a *second self* is an unusual variation on the theme of the inception of self-consciousness. Whereas Una is a real-world self, Una Mary is imagination and feeling. Una Mary experiences things that cannot easily be talked about, things for which there are often no words. She is, above all, a private self where inexpressible ideas, emotions, aesthetic appreciations, and cogitations on the meaning of life and religion play out. At the same time, she takes on the features of an ideal self—pretty where Una is plain, attired in fancy dresses where Una has to wear sturdy plain clothes. What is highly unusual about this "other self" is its consistency. Children commonly play roles and fleetingly pretend to be other people, but Una Mary is a stable, long-term presence over twelve years, albeit she changed over time as Una's ideas became more complex. Hunt repeatedly stresses that she thought of Una Mary as her *real* self: "I was always conscious [of this part of my life] with an intensity that at times made my outer life seem a dream and this the only reality" (1). Una Mary only went away when Una was fourteen—when, in Hunt's account, she willed her to merge with Una.

Besides a second self, Una has an imaginary companion: Edward, a boy slightly older than Una Mary. She also has her own country, "My Country," whose makeup changes to suit her fancy but which is always a beautiful, pleasant, enchanted place. This imaginary world is at once a theater for Una's inventive mind and a collection of everything that strikes her as lovely and precious. Una has a magic veil that she can throw around anything so to turn it into part of My Country. Like Una Mary herself, one of My Country's functions is compensatory: "Whenever I had a bad day, . . . I consoled myself with the thought that it did not really matter as the Una in the ordinary world was not the real Una at all, that I only really lived as Una Mary, in My Country" (82). In addition to these congenial inventions, real-world Una also has a malevolent antagonist whose function is to trip her up, to take the wind out of her sails and make her feel bad: the Imp. This Imp sounds a great deal like Walter Benjamin's famous though later Hunchback: "He has been the curse of my life, that Imp, for he is always there, just behind my left ear, a little black demon watching and jeering at everything, and he has a hateful, hunchbacked sort of mind" (25–26).

The real Una was the oldest child of Bostonians, a professor of chemistry and his wife, who had been transplanted to Cincinnati and then, when Una was nine, moved to Washington, DC. Her parents were Unitarians and enlightened Darwinists and not like most other people in the Midwest or in Washington: "My parents had been brought up in Boston among the most unworldly and transcendental set of people, so their point of view was wholly that of 'plain living and high thinking'" (26). Hunt has words of high praise for her parents and particularly her father, who is her "great companion" (58) and teaches her all kinds of important things about the natural world. She notes that in her childhood, "the conflict between Reason and Religion was most acute" (36–37), and her parents were definitely on the side of Reason. She has a mystical streak, however, which demands to be fed by something other than their sensible rationality. In this regard, her Negro nurse in Washington, Mammy, a devout Roman Catholic, introduces her to a kind of church worship that appeals to her emotions. Her other, perhaps keener point of frustration, specifically with her mother, has to do with the latter's conviction that clothing must be sturdy rather than trendy. Like most little girls, Una "longed to be of the vast majority" (222) and in particular to dress like everyone else—a theme that will recur in many other authors. Partly on account of her upbringing, Una is an oddball among other girls. In Cincinnati she has one close friend—a boy. She has no girl friends until at age ten she meets two girls in Washington who are like her. Her close friendship with them brings Una Mary gradually out of wraps and coaxes into being the process by which Una Mary finally merges with Una.

Una is an emotional, intuitive, aesthetically sensitive child. Her religious leanings are a central theme in the book. From an early age she ponders notions of God, whom Santa Claus prefigures. These cogitations are inspired by her early sense of a "beyond," but even more so by death. The prayer "Now I lay me down to sleep" terrifies her by suggesting that Death is always lurking, ready to pounce. "That prayer was the black terror of my childhood" (49). She finally arrives at a conception of death: the soul, which is heavy like a skeleton, is extracted from the body and taken by God. Later she associates cherubim and seraphim with circus animals, and heaven becomes "a glorified Circus World, with all the glamour of the Christmas tree" (52). Una experienced revelation at the sight of her first Christmas tree, and thenceforth Christmas becomes "the great day of the year" (12). Una's final insight, at age fourteen, which leads to Una Mary merging with Una, is that God is Beauty.

But Una's inner life is by no means just about God, life, and death. She has an inquiring mind and wants to get to the bottom of things. Early on, for example, she wonders where babies come from, this being one subject on which her parents maintain silence, and comes to the conclusion that they come from eggs. When her little sister is born she hunts for the shell, but cannot find it. Throughout her childhood she makes creative improvements on her world, tailoring it to suit her. For instance, on the Massachusetts seashore she collects pebbles. Smooth ones become her "cats," while ones with a ring of color around them are her "dogs." She keeps one "dog" for three years, burying him between summers so she can find him again. Then in Washington, given that girls in her generation are still taught to sew, she makes clothes for her dolls—including on Sunday, which prompts Mammy to say that every stitch she sews on Sunday she'll have to rip out with her teeth when she gets to Purgatory. But she outwits the Devil by switching to her mother's sewing machine, whose stitches can be easily ripped out. Finally, from ages ten to thirteen she and her two close friends invent a private language. They find that they have lots of feelings for which there are no words, so they make up words for them and compile a sixty-three-entry dictionary of them. *Una Mary* is a unique book, unlike any other in its revelation of the dimensions of a child's secret inner life.

Mixing Genres

Thus far we have seen self-foregrounding autobiographies (mainly French) and self-effacing ones (mainly English or American). To a degree, these strains are motivated by the divergent impulses of confession and history writing and align with the types distinguished as "autobiography" and "memoir." An author focused on divulging the story of her interior life need not portray the times, whereas, conversely, an author who is intent on transmitting the picture of a remote world to which she was a privileged eyewitness has reason not to include much information about herself.

The two types are combinable, and most authors mix them to some extent. Prior to World War I, no work combines the memoir and the forward-pointing type of autobiography more intrepidly than Mary Antin's bestselling *The Promised Land* (1912). Antin, a Russian Jew who emigrated to the United States and eventually found success there, wrote the book when she was an aspiring writer not yet thirty. Social history justifies the work. Antin states that her life is "illustrative of scores of unwritten lives."[59] It is only marginally about what it means to be female, although Antin notes Judaism's bias against women: boys were taught to say in their morning prayer, "I thank thee, Lord, for not having created me female" (33), and there was no free schooling for girls in the Russian Pale of Settlement, because "a girl was born for no other purpose" than to become a wife (34). Yet the work is noteworthy for the way a family history and memoir segue into a semi-memoir, that is, a memoir that includes some personal perspective, some tracing of the writer's own story, which in turn, once Antin is a teenager, increasingly metamorphoses into a full-fledged autobiography that follows the author's personal career. Once Antin focuses on herself she waxes confessional and includes copious accounts of Mary's (or Maryashe's, her given name) thoughts and feelings at the time. Conceivably, patriotism could be seen to justify the turn to autobiography, for Antin incarnates the American Dream: her story takes her from poverty and oppression in Russia to new life and hope in America (Boston), where free public education is available to her and where, as a gifted child, she rises to the top of her class and goes on to college. Yet the text is curiously marked by tension between self-congratulation at ambition realized and modesty. The modesty seems attributable to the fact that it still behooved women of her era to be modest. In the middle of the later, self-focused part of her account, Antin not only writes ironically of her naïve boldness as a schoolgirl in trying to get a poem published in a Boston newspaper, but recounts how she once embarrassed herself on an occasion when she was reproved for a lack of modesty. She commits a terrible faux pas: at high school graduation, the speaker praises a star pupil whom he does not name, but whom she recognizes as herself. She commits the blunder of rising to thank him. When the principal waves his hand to silence her, she realizes "the enormity of what I had done" (282). Not only is the ceremony ruined for her, but the scene returns to haunt her like a nightmare for years afterwards. The reason: "It was not because I had been bold, but because I had been pronounced bold, that I suffered so monstrously" (283). So—another twist—the text dips its knee at feminine decorum, but then bursts into confession even as it pursues its Horatio Alger–style plot.

Other American Jewish childhood autobiographies followed. Antin's bestselling work may well have inspired Rose Cohen, a Russian-Jewish immigrant to the United States and one year older than Antin, to publish, in 1918, her moving working-class autobiography of childhood and youth *Out of the Shadow*, a more straightforwardly written story of her family's emigration to New York, where from the age of twelve she worked in tailoring sweatshops for up to fourteen hours a day, ultimately ruining her health. E. G. Stern's ardently pro-American *My Mother and I* (1917) strikes notes familiar from Antin, but whether the author was Jewish, much less an immigrant from Russia, has been questioned.[60]

Women's Childhood Autobiography Elsewhere around 1900

If the Western world became increasingly preoccupied with childhood in the course of the nineteenth century, the German-speaking countries were at the cutting edge of this development. At the turn of the eighteenth to the nineteenth century, the Swiss Johann Heinrich Pestalozzi, influenced by Rousseau, revolutionized early education in keeping with Romantic ideas. He aimed to develop a child's natural gifts and emphasized participatory activities. Simultaneously, German Romantic writers such as Jean Paul and Novalis idealized children as innocent and close to nature. Childhood was exalted as a golden age or paradise.[61] Presently, in 1837, the Thuringian Friedrich Wilhelm August Fröbel, influenced by Pestalozzi, founded the first kindergarten. In the late eighteenth and early nineteenth centuries, Prussia started to enact educational reforms; by the 1830s its education system counted as the most progressive in the world.[62] After German unification in 1871 elementary education was made free and compulsory throughout Germany as it had been previously in Prussia. By comparison, elementary education became free and compulsory in Britain and France between 1880 and 1882. In 1870 the German Wilhelm Preyer started his scientific observations of his infant son, resulting in his seminal work *The Mind of the Child* (1882). Preyer is often credited with founding modern developmental psychology.

Given the importance that accrued to childhood and early education in the German-speaking countries, it is not surprising that German women writers started to publish autobiographical accounts of childhood in the last decades of the nineteenth century. As in England, these accounts initially took the form of children's books, family stories, and memoirs rather than self-focused autobiographies. The very titles reflect a lack of self-profiling intention. We see, for example, Isabella Braun's *Aus der Jugendzeit* (From my youth, 1871); Helene Adelmann's *Aus meiner Kinderzeit* (From my childhood, 1892); Tony Schumacher's *Was ich als Kind erlebt* (What I experienced as a child, 1901); Charitas Bischoff's *Augenblicksbilder aus einem Jugendleben* (Snapshots from a youthful life, 1905); and Margarete Lenk's *Aus meiner Kindheit: Jugenderinnerungen* (From my childhood: Youthful memories, 1910). The word "aus" suggests excerpts, hence fragments rather than a definitive or comprehensive account. Combined with words like "Jugendzeit," "Kinderzeit," "Jugendleben," and "Jugenderinnerungen," it leads the reader to expect

68   Beginnings: Women's Childhood Autobiography Prior to World War I

memoirs of childhood and/or youth rather than autobiography. In reality, however, the titles of the works are more uniform than the works themselves.

Thus children's book author Isabella Braun in *Aus der Jugendzeit* (1871) explicitly addresses a young audience. She shapes episodes from her childhood and youth until her school leaving into stories, sometimes written in the "we" style familiar since Howitt, adapting her "memories" to that audience by storifying them and including stated or implied moral messages. Not only does Braun not focus on herself, but there is almost no self-characterization. Yet her stories are full of high emotion as she and her two siblings engage in dramatic, often naughty exploits and suffer the instructive consequences. In one story she dips into her interior life to the point of recounting her fever fantasies. She has good words for both parents and takes care to give each of her stories a happy ending, as befits a children's book. As a narrator, she styles herself as looking back at her childhood across a distance of forty years, and she seizes the occasion to thank many people, such as her teachers, for what they contributed to her development. Her text yields some interesting evidence about gender roles in her youth: as a girl she is obliged to do knitting; it is acceptable for her to be curious because that's the way girls are; and she has less freedom than her brother. She simply states these things and does not formulate them as complaints.

Helene Adelmann's *Aus meiner Kinderzeit* (1892) is a memoir consisting of short pieces. Especially since a number of these pieces deal with naïve childish beliefs, such as about the *Christkind* (the present-bringing Christ Child), the Easter Bunny, and the provenance of babies, the book appears aimed at an adult audience, at readers who can smile along with the author and who, moreover, know who she is. Adelmann was a respected public figure, who in 1876 had founded the Verein Deutscher Lehrerinnen (Association of German Governesses) in England. A teacher, Adelmann had like many German women of her time worked in England as a governess for a number of years. Her own experience there had been good, but she saw how the agents shamelessly exploited many of her compatriots, and she founded her association to help them. Energetic and idealistic, she supported the German women's movement at home. Her memoir reflects her enthusiasm for telling about aspects of her village childhood. She devotes a little piece to each of her topics: Christmas, the goat, the geese, the priest, the harvest, and so on. Some of the pieces concern her own misadventures, but this is not autobiography;

she gives no self-portrait and does not even tell a chronological story. In her brief opening statement she states that she will record her impressions of the uprisings of 1848–49, which would have been of particular interest to readers.

Tony Schumacher's *Was ich als Kind erlebt* (1901) is family history. Schumacher was one of the most famous children's books authors of her day, but this is not a children's book. It is also misleadingly titled. Schumacher explains in her introduction that she considers her own childhood experiences insufficient to capture a wide readership. So in the first half of this lengthy memoir, she tells the history of her important and illustrious family. In the second half, she recounts her own childhood memories; but she follows her great uncle Justinus Kerner's precept, according to which one's own life is merely a thread on which to hang the more important lives of others. So the second part of her book is also primarily family and social history. Indeed, her book is so rich in its references to other people that she furnishes it with an index of persons. What of herself? Schumacher creates a clever blend of memoir and subjective elements, alternating between what she calls the "Hauptereignisse" (the "main events" [189] — the history of her aristocratic military family) and "the personal" (the affairs of "we children," seven siblings of which she was the youngest). She includes some of her own thoughts and feelings and misadventures in which she starred, yet despite an introductory chapter on "first memories" and a closing account of having to undergo medical treatment to correct her adolescent bad posture, the wealth of detail about places, customs, and people vastly outweighs self-representation.

Charitas Bischoff's *Augenblicksbilder aus einem Jugendleben* (1905) is, in contrast to the works by Braun, Adelmann, and Schumacher, a genuine autobiography of childhood and youth. It too is misleadingly titled, for this is no collection of "Augenblicksbilder" or short pieces, but recounts the continuous story of Bischoff's early life. Bischoff's extraordinary story justifies the telling, and she tells it like a story, with the clever touch that she frames the story of her early childhood with a different story, that of a train trip she and her daughter took forty years later in quest of the places and people of her rural childhood in Saxony. Bischoff grew up as the only child of a husband-and-wife team of botanists who made their living by collecting plants, minerals, and insects, which they sold as collections. To her considerable anguish, her parents were wont to leave her with other people for extended periods of time while they

70   Beginnings: Women's Childhood Autobiography Prior to World War I

traveled on business. Finally the family split up for lack of money, and she, a young teenager, was placed with people who worked her hard. Eventually her mother, to whom she was very attached, found a new home in Hamburg and called for her—at this point Bischoff stops the frame story of the train trip—only to place her under the supervision of a wealthy, educated, and benevolent family while she goes on a botanizing trip to Australia for ten years. In this latter part of the book one gets the impression that Charitas is decided over and shunted around without anyone bothering to tell her what the plan is or what is going to happen next. The author does not complain overtly about any of this, but she gives plenty of her own emotions at the time and reconstructs her thoughts, sometimes in free indirect discourse. Although this is autobiography, Bischoff is neither introspective nor self-analytical; she describes her outward appearance but gives no psychological self-portrait.

Margarete Lenk's *Aus meiner Kindheit: Jugenderinnerungen* (1910) likewise qualifies as autobiography. As is characteristic of works published prior to the Great War, Lenk, a teacher, prefaces her book with a short apology: "If in this book I at the wish of friends cast a backwards glance at my childhood years, it is not in order to place my small, very insignificant person in the foreground, but to portray conditions that in many respects are different from those of today."[63] It is the kind of demurral familiar from Lucy Larcom and other English-language writers. The author wants to assure the reader that the book is not autobiography, but merely recollections; she wrote it at the behest of friends; the purpose is to give a picture of the times. Lenk's childhood was far less remarkable than Bischoff's, although she did witness the revolutionary events of 1848 in Dresden at the age of seven. In spite of her apology, she focuses on herself, describing her childhood in a large teacher's family until her school leaving at approximately age fourteen. Her work is somewhat more personal than Bischoff's, for she recalls what she hates and loves, how she was ashamed, and how she was messy. She repeatedly writes that her family considered her useless around the house, which made her despair and even wish to die. But she also, similarly to Lucy Larcom, emphasizes her gift for making verses—a talent of which she, always modest, assures the reader she was not at all proud. She confesses that she hated everything that girls were expected to do, especially needlework and knitting, and had only one practical talent: she was good with small children (75). A children's book author (though this is not a children's book), Lenk writes entertainingly, anecdotally, and nostalgically, painting a rosy the picture of a past that was more idealistic and altogether better than the present. In its mix of autobiography and memoir, its determinedly modest self-presentation, its account of family and social expectations for girls, and its optimistic tone, her short work has certain commonalities with Antin's much longer and more famous *The Promised Land*.

Testifying to the popularity of childhood memoirs in Germany in the early twentieth century, a Leipzig publisher brought out an anthology of male writers' recollections of childhood, entitled *Als unsre großen Dichter noch kleine Jungen waren* (When our great writers were still little boys), in 1911.[64] He followed it in 1912 with a parallel volume devoted to women writers, entitled *Als unsre großen Dichterinnen noch kleine Mädchen waren* (When our great women writers were still little girls). Several of the seven featured women authors write in a remarkably unbuttoned way for the era. In particular Hedwig Dohm (1831–1919), whose piece is the jewel of the collection, declares that she was a "passionately unhappy" child, one of eighteen siblings, whose mother did not love her—a tale similar to that of the Irish author Hannah Lynch.[65]

Knitting is a ubiquitous theme in these German women's childhood accounts published prior to World War I. Girls were taught to knit at age four or five, then sent to knitting schools to perfect their skills. Thereafter, they were obliged to knit socks for their families throughout girlhood. It is hard to find an author born before the 1860s who does not complain about having had to knit, specifically socks, as a young girl. Braun, Adelmann, Schumacher, and Lenk all complain about it, as do certain authors featured in *Als unsre großen Dichterinnen noch kleine Mädchen waren*, namely, Hermine Villinger and Luise Westkirch. Clara Blüthgen, born in 1856 and discussed in chapter 2, devotes a piece to the knitting schools for girls, which by the time of writing (1919) had long since been made obsolete by the advent of knitting machines, including machines for making socks. Yet even some younger German authors join the chorus: Anna Schieber, born in 1867 and discussed in chapter 3, complains about having had to attend knitting school, while Sophie Reuschle, born in 1891 and discussed in chapter 2, observes that she only had to learn knitting on three needles, whereas her mother had had to master seven.[66]

From Austria in the prewar period come two women's childhood autobiographies from opposite ends of the social spectrum. Marie von Ebner-Eschenbach, a member of the Austrian nobility and the most prominent German-language woman author of her day, published her childhood autobiography *Meine Kinderjahre* (My childhood years) in 1906 at the age of seventy-six. Adelheid Popp, an early socialist feminist leader from the Austrian proletariat, published her *Autobiography of a Working Woman* anonymously in 1909 at the age of forty, but then, at the wish of August Bebel, under her own name starting with the third edition. Both women foreground context over self. In both works, issues specific to femininity are both tangential and predictable.

Ebner-Eschenbach's work is above all a memoir. In this slim text, the writer, seventy-five at the time of writing, recalls a succession of maids, governesses, music teachers, and dancing masters as she and her four siblings oscillate between the family's country estate in Moravia in the summer and Vienna in the winter. She admits that she surely does not remember things exactly as they were, but that imagination colors her pictures. She details childhood events that were formative and also recalls some of her childish mindset: around age seven or eight, she disbelieved in the real world and invented a world of her own full of nice children, where she herself plays the role of one after another of these children, and nice adults. She sends letters to that world. She does not give much in the way of a self-portrait, although she persistently returns, self-critically, to her childish overestimation of her genius, to her ambitions, and to her family's disapproval of all this. She actually expresses her thanks to those who obstructed her, for "the harder and more unwilling the ground in which the little tree of my art had to take root, the sturdier it stood."[67] And she records a terrible religious crisis upon being given an astronomy book. She takes the story to the death of her grandmother when she is thirteen, after which, as she is set to cataloguing her library, she reads the biography of Gotthold Ephraim Lessing and realizes she does not have his genius nor, as a girl, his advantage of a classical education.

Popp's even shorter autobiography is a politically motivated work, meant to expose the misery of the working classes in nineteenth-century Austria and to advocate socialism as the solution. Popp chooses episodes to illustrate how hard her childhood was. Her illiterate mother, who gave birth to fifteen children, had to support the five that survived by enlisting their help after her husband died. The family was desperately poor. Adelheid went to school for only three years, though eight years of schooling were mandatory, before she had to help her mother financially by doing various kinds of domestic and piecework and then

Beginnings: Women's Childhood Autobiography Prior to World War I

factory work. An autobiography of childhood and youth, this short work builds up to the moment when the author discovers socialism and leaves the factory in order to work for the socialist cause, particularly for the betterment of working-class women. Popp continues her story through her marriage and the death of her like-minded husband.

In Russia, in the estimation of one scholar of Russian literature, Leo Tolstoy's "pseudo-autobiography" *A Childhood* (1852) inspired a wave of late nineteenth-century childhood autobiographies, written mostly by the middle gentry.[68] The authors of such works include two women whose autobiographies have been translated into English. The mathematician and writer Sofya Kovalevskaya (1850–1891) published her childhood autobiography *Memories of Childhood*, which has been translated as *A Russian Childhood*, in 1889. She had first published it the previous year in Swedish (she had been appointed Professor of Mathematics in Stockholm) as a third-person novel entitled *The Rajevski Sisters*, for the sake of decorum, so as to disguise the autobiographical nature of the work.[69] Princess Elizaveta L'vova (1854–after 1910) was a minor writer who published her short "From the Distant Past: Fragments from Childhood Memories" in 1901. Unlike the German and Austrian works, both Russian childhood autobiographies are highly personal, very much like the French. Moreover, both of them record childhoods that were unhappy. According to Andrew Baruch Wachtel, this was not the norm for Russian childhood autobiographies of their era.[70] Kovalevskaya came from a prominent landowning family, but was born in a generation when young people in Russia rebelled against their parents. She and her older sister were both rebellious and schemed to enter into fake marriages so as to escape from their family; Kovalevskaya succeeded in doing this. Her childhood autobiography is very much her personal story. She starts with her earliest memories, speculating on her capacity and incapacity for remembering in a manner that recalls Burnett (albeit Kovalevskaya published her work four years prior to Burnett), inasmuch as she links memory to her sense of self and records her distinct memory of the start of her self-awareness at age two to three, when her nanny prompted her to say her first and last names. She takes her story to the point where she meets Fyodor Dostoevsky, which took place when she was fifteen.[71] Kovalevskaya openly confesses that she, the middle of three children, did not feel loved by her parents and especially her mother, quite in contrast to her sister and brother: "In general, the conviction that I was not loved in my family wound through my memories

74 Beginnings: Women's Childhood Autobiography Prior to World War I

like a black thread."[72] Consequently, she yearned throughout her childhood and early teen years for love and attention. She confesses an extremely painful memory: when a little friend of hers sat in her beloved uncle's lap, thereby usurping her special relationship with her uncle, she bites her arm until the blood comes. She would have been around age nine at the time. In degree of frankness, this childhood autobiography goes beyond even the French women's childhood autobiographies written comparably early in time.

L'vova is similarly candid. In a loose string of recollections whose order is apparently dictated by memory, she focuses on her mental life—her emotions, fantasies, and childish understanding of things—up to approximately the age of seven. Some details are highly idiosyncratic. For instance, she creates—similarly to Hunt and Ebner-Eschenbach—an imaginary world for herself. But her imaginary world is hardly compensatory: she takes on the identity of a poor widow with six children! L'vova was the youngest child and frequently left alone, which may have fostered such imaginings. Additionally, while she confesses to intense feelings, above all her love of her nurse and wet nurse, she also confesses that she "could never bear to show [her] feelings, the deeper and stronger they were, the more carefully [she] concealed them."[73]

In sum: Given that prior to World War I women throughout Europe were encouraged to cultivate modesty and discretion, it is unsurprising that they lagged behind men in publishing autobiographies, even autobiographies of childhood, although disclosures about this "innocent" time of life were relatively compatible with the feminine virtues. Initially, one sees two distinct strains: a Rousseau-inspired confessional tradition in France and an outgrowth of the domestic memoir tradition in England, meaning that writers focus on family and circumstances more than on self. Within the framework of these two contexts, diverse types of writing spottily emerged. French authors for the most part wrote retrospective first-person autobiographies, but we also see a poetic collection of memories (Daudet's). Russian works (Kovalevskaya, L'vova) follow the self-focused, confessional French type. In the English-speaking countries, stories by children's book authors, sometimes for young audiences, dominate until the turn of the century. These and subsequent works involve various novelistic shapings of autobiographical material, including third-person narrative with a humoristic tone (Burnett), a bitter and seemingly partly fictionalized account of early martyrdom (Lynch), and a poetic recreation of the child's vision of the world (Arden). German works follow comparable patterns: authors, who are often children's book authors or educators, initially write memoirs rather than self-focused autobiographies. More personal accounts start to emerge after the turn of the century.

For a woman, writing about oneself smacked of pretentiousness. Women adopted various strategies for making their stories acceptable. Many involve some form of fictionalization. Howitt, Burnett, Nesbit, Hughes, Campbell, Gilder, and Bischoff took the route of turning their lives into engaging stories. Publishing one's work as a "novel" (Kovalevskaya, Delarue-Mardrus) was one way of deflecting criticism; adopting fictional trappings while leaving the work's status unclear (Farnham, Lynch) was another. Some women—Lynch, Gilder, and Arden—changed proper names. Labels cannot be trusted: the bold word "autobiography" in a title did not mean much more than "a life story told in the first person" and did not necessarily signify that the book contained the true life of the author—witness *Jane Eyre* and Lynch's *Autobiography of a Child*. A "novel," however, could lay claim to the prestige enjoyed by artistic work in that era (Audoux).

Fictionalization was not the only strategy: others included emphasizing that the work had been written at the behest of others (Larcom, Barton, Lenk) and the widespread habit of avoiding or diminishing self-presentation in favor of dilating on family, other people, places, and customs.

Inasmuch as the women do engage in self-presentation, most characterize themselves as unique individuals, though there is a tendency among English-language writers (Larcom, Burnett, Nesbit) to self-deprecatingly pay lip service to the notion that they were just ordinary children. Generally, writers do not style themselves as typical of a social group, or as a spokesperson for a social group, or as reaching out to a particular group. The exception is Popp, who wrote a politically motivated autobiography. Among the authors, professional writers and women of letters dominate. Most authors came from middle- or upper-class backgrounds. Being obliged to perform manual labor and having the ability and opportunity to write a book was an infrequent combination, though Larcom, Audoux, and Popp all managed to do it. None of the writers have a feminist agenda, although many chafe at the restrictions imposed on them as girls. Lynch is the author who comes closest by articulating the idea that the entire female sex is disadvantaged (at least in Ireland). Audoux reveals a women's world where women feel no solidarity and little sympathy with each other. Larcom stands out for calling for feminine solidarity—albeit in what are by today's standards unfeminist terms.

A topic that is absent from pre–World War I women's childhood autobiography is sexual abuse. No doubt this is not because such abuse did not take place, but because there were strong taboos against writing about it. Sexuality, mentionable in the eighteenth century even by women, underwent suppression in the nineteenth in both England and France.[74]

Gender differences between autobiographical writing by women and men are more marked in the pre–World War I era than in any subsequent period. In effect, ladies in this era were not supposed to sound like men. Thus, with few exceptions, women did not write the Bildungsroman type of autobiography ("how I became what I became") preferred by their male counterparts. The obvious reason is that women generally did not become public figures in that era, and if they did, they believed that it behooved them to be modest and deemphasize their career success. Also with few exceptions, women do not adopt the nostalgic tone that male childhood autobiographers picked up on following Rousseau's representation of early childhood as a lost paradise and Wordsworth's stylization of early childhood as an almost divine but forever lost state of being.

The early women's childhood autobiographies stand out for their originality—if not also for their bravery. Nobody obliged these women to write their stories. Women wrote voluntarily and, because of the lack of feminine precedents, creatively. The interest in the mind of the child, in the "inner life of childhood," as Una Hunt calls it, in recovering that lost inner life and in doing so even to the point of relinquishing the authorial perspective in order to recreate the way the child saw the world, as in Joan Arden's *A Childhood*, is a stellar innovation that I believe is specific to women's writing around the turn of the nineteenth to the twentieth century.

Another difference between women's and men's self-writing about childhood is the amount of attention women writers pay to mothers and other female figures. Male writers such as William Wordsworth, Pierre Loti, and Marcel Proust do write lovingly of their mothers, and an occasional man, like Jules Vallès, writes about his mother negatively. Nevertheless, mothers and maternal substitutes like nurses, grandmothers, and nuns receive more attention in women's childhood autobiographies than they do in men's. This difference between women's and men's childhood autobiographies continues beyond the pre–World War I period and will mark women's childhood autobiography generally. A related thread that runs through women's but not men's childhood autobiographies in this era and beyond is attention to the implications of being a girl and the differences between one's upbringing, education, privileges, freedoms, and so forth, and boys'. Girls, aware of being relatively restricted, are watchful. They readily compare their lot to that of boys, whereas boys pay scant attention to that of girls.

There is always strong pressure on people to say certain things and to say them in certain ways, today as much as when these women were writing. This is something children painfully learn. Adults may have internalized the demands and taboos that shape their speech to the point where they are no longer aware of them. The farther away an era lies from our own, the more the norms of speech have had time to change, and, by consequence, the more noticeable these pressures become. From today's perspective, women writing about themselves before the First World War seem extraordinarily discreet. Yet in reading their childhood autobiographies, beneath the cobwebs of discretion, we find out a great deal about how girls were raised and what the issues were for them—even though the authors perhaps did not write for posterity with this particular agenda in mind. We find out that girls were raised in gender-specific ways. As a rule, they were under the control and tutelage of women: mothers, nuns. These relationships were frequently not good. Being a girl meant, compared to today, freedom from parental pressure to become somebody in the world. Correspondingly, their education was generally quite basic, with emphasis on the mastery of household arts. The nineteenth-century German knitting schools are an outstanding example of how girls were trained at an early age to perform specific domestic duties. Besides the differential upbringing of the sexes, there were huge differences between the lives of girls from wealthy families, which had servants and nannies, and those from poor backgrounds, who were destined to be servants themselves or work at a limited number of jobs.

CHAPTER TWO

The Interwar Years:
Memoirs and Semi-Memoirs

1919: Blüthgen (1856–1934)

1921: Icus-Rothe (1875–1947)

1921: Marie zu Erbach-Schönberg
    (1852–1923)

1921: Reuschle (1891–1982)

1921: Soskice (1880–1943)

1922: Colette (1873–1954)

1922: Lagerlöf (1858–1940)

1924: MacCarthy (1882–1953)

1925: Bixby-Smith (1871–1935)

1925: Lunt (1843–1934)

1926: Orpen (1855–1927)

1927: Harder (1864–1939)

1928: K. Woodward (1896–1961)

1929: Gandy (1885–1977)

1931: McHugh (1900–1980)

1931: Thirkell (1890–1961)

1932: Jackson (1870–1944)

1934: M. V. Hughes (1866–1956)

1934: Skariatina (1898–1962)

1935: Acland (1878–1933)

1935: Farjeon (1881–1965)

1935: McClung (1873–1951)

1935: Seidel (1885–1974)

1935: H. Woodward (1882–1969)

1936: Abbott (1872 –1958)

1936: Pagés (1863–1944)

1937: Uttley (1884–1976)

1937: Weiss (1893–1983)

1938: Damon (1881–1975)

1938: Ross (1864–1956)

1939: Lubbock (1879–1943)

The twenty-year timespan between the two world wars witnessed an upheaval in Western social structures and cultural values and brought enormous changes to women's lives. Especially in Britain, World War I had given women a taste of paid labor in jobs that had formerly belonged to men. Although these gains did not prove solid, women started to claim personal freedoms that would not have been admissible before the war. Women's fashions marked the changing conception of femininity: skirts went up; hair was bobbed. In England, the United States, Germany, and many other countries, women finally got the right to vote. In France, in contrast, the interwar years were not a progressive era: the French government pursued a natalist, anti-abortion and anti-contraception policy, and in 1922 the Senate refused to give women the right to vote; suffrage was not granted until 1944.

Emancipation apparently encouraged self-expression, for it was above all in the English-speaking countries, and not in France, that the interwar years saw an upsurge in women's childhood narratives along with major changes in the way such works were written. Particularly as of the 1930s, certain English-language authors started writing about their early lives with unprecedented candor. In contrast, not many French women published childhood autobiographies in this period, and inasmuch as they did, nothing comparable to the English-language authors' breakthrough in style and candidness distinguishes their work. French women's autobiographical writing actually appeared to regress. Jennifer E. Milligan cites the repressive French climate in analyzing why there was relatively little women's self-writing in France in the inter-war years. She believes that one of the "strategies for self-protection" of women who did engage in self-writing was a "concentration on a relatively unincriminating period of their lives" (i.e., childhood).[1] This would be consonant with women's turn to childhood prior to World War I. Nevertheless, Jean-Philippe Vauchel states in his extensive study of the representation of childhood in France in the period that writing about childhood remained an "affaire d'hommes."[2]

Meanwhile, women from other parts of Europe, such as Germany, the Scandinavian countries, and Russia, published childhood autobiographies. Statistics derived from Richard Coe's bibliography show that in the interwar years women published more than one in three childhood autobiographies, in contrast to approximately one in six before World War I, and that the percentage of female to male authors rose steadily throughout the twenty-year period.

In the interwar years, women's childhood autobiographies start to crystallize into distinct types: memoirs and semi-memoirs; self-portraits, including some developmental stories or Bildungsroman-style works; and works that capture the child's perspective.

The women who took up the pen in the interwar years were, as previously, mainly professional writers. There were extreme differences in age among them: the oldest, Cornelia Gray Lunt, was born in 1843, and the youngest, Francesca Allinson, in 1902. The authors thus span three generations. Nevertheless, all of the women writing between the two wars received a significant part of their upbringing before the Great War. Changes in child-rearing had taken place prior to the war. In particular, an increasing acceptance of Darwin's theory of evolution had attenuated the religious instruction of children. After the war, much more changed. The older authors recall that in their youth parents were respected and obeyed with very little questioning. Even Mary Butts, born in 1890 and looking back from the post–World War I era of transformed child-rearing, writes: "My parents were in authority over me; I curtsied when I spoke to an older person. I really was supposed to look up to my parents."[3] The older authors also recall the days when girls were taught housewifely arts, in particular sewing and knitting. These arts were taken seriously. Germany even had schools for them. Ina Seidel, born to a doctor's family in 1885, underwent strict formal training in household arts, in particular cooking, for six months after finishing girls' school. Louise Weiss, born in 1893, was sent at age seventeen by her French parents to a German housekeeping school, which she profoundly detested.

Most childhood autobiographies written by women in the interwar years fall into two types: memoirs that commemorate the past and autobiographies which, mirroring a new, psychologically oriented understanding of childhood and a new feminine self-conception, foreground the subjectivity of the girl. The first type tells "the story"; the second type tells "my story." Over time, memoirs tend to include more subjective elements. On the whole, however, the commemorative type, the memoir, dominates until the 1930s. The middle years of the 1930s are a turning point: women increasingly started to tell their own stories, to write autobiographies rather than self-effacing memoirs. Interest in psychology, particularly the psychology of children, picked up. Consonant with the intensified interest in psychology, some authors pondered the workings of memory. Additionally, some writers pursued a third type of autobiographical writing about childhood, a type that sought, like Joan Arden in *A Childhood* and Una Hunt in *Una Mary*, to recapture the child's vision of the world.

Most of the childhood autobiographies written in the first postwar decade, the 1920s, commemorate yesteryear. With the lifestyle of the Victorian era irrevocably receding into the past, presenting an eyewitness account of what life had been like before what Stefan Zweig called "the great divide" seemed like a worthwhile enterprise. In the decade following World War I, nostalgia for the good old days, for a sense of

The Interwar Years: Memoirs and Semi-Memoirs 81

stability, a simpler lifestyle, and clearer rules, had an audience. These are the years when tones of nostalgia, which had been common in childhood autobiographies written by men from William Wordsworth onward, become most audible in women's childhood autobiographies. Frequently the nostalgia is mixed with irony: how quaint were the customs then, how different the expectations for women, how little the youth of today is interested in hearing about any of this. In contrast to prewar authors, women are no longer shy to write. Apologies for writing disappear or take an ironic tone. If rationales for writing are given, an appeal to the importance of childhood suffices. The works that celebrate the past are not primarily about self-becoming or the psychology of the autobiographical subject. Some border on family history. Especially if family history is within the scope of the author's intentions, the work may brim with photographs.

The interest in commemorating yesteryear in memoirs of childhood was not confined to Britain. American and Canadian women told stories of nineteenth-century pioneer childhoods. German women published memoirs about the better days before the war. The Swedish author Selma Lagerlöf's *Marbacka* (1922) is an extreme example of the memoir style: Lagerlöf writes about her childhood in the third person, and "Selma" is just one of the children. Irina Skariatina's *Little Era in Old Russia* (1934), also written in the third person, tells what childhood was like in an aristocratic family in pre-Revolutionary Russia; there is not much autobiography here.

The interwar years and especially the 1930s were pivotal in the history of women's childhood autobiography. Many of the works written in that period deserve scrutiny, regardless of type.

Memoirs

The 1920s and early 1930s saw a plethora of memoirs. Such works held cultural and historical interest. They attracted a readership, the more so if they opened windows on high society, famous families, or interesting places. They were more likely to flatter than offend family members. Therefore, it took some energy, but not particular daring to write one. As will be seen, however, as the years went by, women increasingly put something of themselves, some personal thread, into their memoirs, and some tried to combine the memoir and the confessional autobiography, starting with the one and switching to the other or otherwise mixing the two.

Memoirs from the Lands of the Victors

In England, two women from illustrious families wrote childhood memoirs: Juliet Soskice in *Chapters from Childhood* (1921) produced a satiric account of what it was like to grow up in an artistic family (she was Ford Madox Brown's granddaughter, Ford Madox Ford's sister, and the niece of Christina Rossetti), including an exceptionally positive portrait of her mother Catherine Madox Brown; and Edward Burne-Jones's granddaughter Angela Thirkell wrote *Three Houses* (1931), a book of reminiscences about the way things were when she was a child, much of it in the "we" style. Mary MacCarthy's *A Nineteenth-Century Childhood* (1924), discussed below, and Ida Gandy's *A Wiltshire Childhood* (1929), a carefully crafted "we"-style evocation of her and her siblings' idyllic childhood in a Wiltshire vicarage, likewise commemorate life in bygone days. All of these women published their books when they were in their early forties. There was no reason not to publish such a memoir when one was relatively young, since such works were uncontroversial, observed the proprieties, and offended no one.

Of these works, Mary MacCarthy's Victorian-era retrospective deserves a closer look because of the way the author twists the prewar trope of feminine modesty and also because of its description of a girl's education in an era of compulsory elementary schooling. The daughter of the vice-provost of Eton and a novelist, MacCarthy, born in 1882, writes a nostalgic, but also ironic and witty, account of growing up in a large upper-middle-class, comfortable but not wealthy Victorian family in the 1880s. Eton's proximity to Windsor Castle gives her a good excuse to evoke Queen Victoria, and the book ends, appropriately for its subject, with an account of Victoria's funeral in 1901.

MacCarthy carries the apology tradition forward, but not in a spirit of humility. She apologizes wittily for the "egotism" of writing an autobiography: "Well, a memoir is a trap for egotism: I have nibbled the cheese, I am snapped in; a wretched mouse quivering with self-importance and destined for immediate drowning."[4] In fact, while this slim memoir is not devoid of subjectivity, the child "I" here has predictable reactions to events and thus seems more like a device to link anecdotes and descriptions together than a genuinely psychological subject. The account is conventionally structured in chronological order; MacCarthy begins with her ancestors and family and ends when she reaches age eighteen.

MacCarthy's memoir addresses the issue of women's education in the last decade of the nineteenth century. Mary's parents are attentive to her education: she is sent away to a large Church of England girls' boarding school for a few years, where she likens existence to that of Rudyard Kipling's "Bandarlog" (48), then is homeschooled until, when older, she is sent to a "dignified school" (82). But girls' education was very different from boys'. MacCarthy makes the point that not much was expected of the girls when she was growing up: "Our parents seemed to have no other wish for us but that we should flit for ever about their house and sit at the round dining-room table day after day in contentment with home. They have no idea of giving us any particular training to any professional end" (83). Growing up in the shadow of Eton, Mary and her sisters adored the Eton boys, but could not take "any real part in the life of the school" (65–66) or use Eton facilities.

Annabel Huth Jackson's somewhat deceptively titled *A Victorian Childhood*, published in 1932, eight years after MacCarthy's memoir, is, in keeping with the turn toward subjectivity characteristic of the 1930s, a more personal work. In fact, Jackson, who was one of the eight children of Sir Mountstuart Grant Duff, Scottish politician and Governor of Madras from 1881 to 1886, and was a high society hostess at the time of writing, tells us little about life in Victorian days, although she transmits a sense of what it was like to be a girl in a large Victorian family of her social class. She was raised by nurses and governesses and tormented by her older brothers when they were home from boarding school. Born before elementary education became compulsory in 1880, she herself was not sent to school (but then also to boarding school) until age twelve. Jackson ostensibly writes for her children, grandchildren, and great grandchildren—her excuse for including a lot of details about visits and family friends. But the outspoken writer, in her sixties at the time of writing, writes a more daring work than MacCarthy's or any of the other memoirs that appeared in the previous decade. It is a sign of changing times that she includes a surprising confessional element, not only telling her dreams (with reference to Freud and Jung), but recalling her emotions at every turn: how she disliked her brothers, adored India, and, most surprising of all, fell in love with and was loved in return by a British army captain when she was a mere eleven-year-old. She stresses that it was "passion undisturbed by the faintest lust," yet he "held me in his arms and kissed me blind."[5] She writes affirmatively about this relationship, which led to the officer being told to change regiments, saying she was lucky to have had the experience of being in love and being loved at such an early age. She emphasizes, however, that she was raised strictly. She negatively contrasts the upbringing of children at the time of writing with the much stricter standards of her youth. Although she tells how she was initially miserable at boarding school, she sent her own daughter to the same one. She claims that as a schoolgirl she was a "violent feminist" (161).

In contrast to MacCarthy's and Jackson's, Kathleen Woodward's *Jipping Street* (1928) is a working-class memoir and as such is an anomaly among British women childhood autobiographers of the day. Woodward writes a slim, depressing account of her childhood in a London slum starting when she was age eleven, focusing mainly on her mother and the other women around her. She published her work when she was in her early thirties. It is unclear to what extent she fictionalizes (there is no "Jipping Street" in London).

Further commemorative works of the 1920s and early 1930s come from different places. Mary Frances McHugh's *Thalassa: A Story of Childhood by the Western Wave* (1931), another work of nostalgic reminiscences, initiates what would become a steady stream of Anglo-Irish women's writing about their childhood after Ireland gained its independence from Britain in 1922. The Anglo-Irish, the erstwhile ruling class in Ireland, lost their privileged status and many emigrated. McHugh's work is primarily social history in the form of a personal memoir, a poetic and nostalgic evocation of the places and above all of the people the author knew in her childhood in County Clare, Ireland, and hardly an autobiography at all. McHugh, born in 1900, had moved to London. She writes that in her childhood, her part of Ireland was "still an eighteenth-century region, little troubled by the commercial civilization of the big world."[6] But by the date of writing, "all that world, the beautiful simple world of my childhood, has vanished into the past" (213).

From the United States and Canada come pioneer stories. Two American works from the 1920s, both of which include enough of a personal thread to be considered semi-memoirs, are Sarah Bixby-Smith's *Adobe Days: A Book of California Memories* (1925), which tells of her family's pioneering sheep farming in California, and Adela Orpen's *Memories of the Old Emigrant Days in Kansas* (1926), an account of her boyish life with her father on the Kansas frontier in perilous Civil War days when she was between the ages of seven and ten. A fascinating piece of history, this latter work is of particular interest because of the argument the seventy-year-old author makes about gender. Her father raised her, the sole surviving child, like a boy—to ride, round up cattle, and use

The Interwar Years: Memoirs and Semi-Memoirs

tools—despite the efforts of her despairing "Auntie" to raise her like a girl. She took to this boy's education like a duck to water: "I hated being a little girl. All a girl's duties were irksome to me. . . . A boy's work exactly suited me."[7] Her upbringing turned her into an adept, confident "cowboy," devoid of feminine meekness—a phenomenon that, as Orpen proudly states, a professor at Antioch thought worthy of study when her father, she, and "Auntie" returned to "civilization." In the following decade, the American Marie Marchand Ross published *Child of Icaria* (1938), a pioneer story about her French immigrant family and the utopian community of Icarians in Iowa in which she grew up, while in Canada, Nellie McClung published *Clearing in the West* (1935), an important semi-memoir of pioneer times that will be discussed below as one of a cluster of semi-memoirs that appeared in 1935.

In the interwar years, a number of women who were not professional writers wrote their memoirs for the sake of family or friends. One such memoir is Cornelia Gray Lunt's *Sketches of Childhood and Girlhood: Chicago, 1847–1864* (1925), privately printed and addressed to young relatives. Lunt carefully explains that her niece gave her a blank book, asking her to tell about her memories of her life. The result is a work somewhat like E. Nesbit's, since Lunt writes separate pieces about her "memories," albeit, unlike Nesbit, at great length. Annabel Jackson also wrote with an eye to younger family members, while Eleanor Acland, discussed under "1935" below, wrote *Good-Bye for the Present* for friends. It is a sign of the new feminine self-consciousness that these women believed their work to be of sufficient interest to posterity and the public to warrant publication.

An unusual story has always justified a memoir. In 1929 a young Californian actress named Joan Lowell capitalized on that insight and published an outrageous hoax about growing up on a ship with her father and an all-male crew (*Cradle of the Deep*, 1929). The book enjoyed success for a month. It was made a Book-of-the-Month Club selection and Lowell sold movie rights before her neighbors exposed her to the press.

Far better known than any of these, and the most nostalgic memoir of all, is the French author Colette's *La Maison de Claudine* (*My Mother's House and Sido*, 1922). This engaging short work is not the story of Colette's childhood, nor does it give a portrait of her as a child, but consists of short pieces set in her childhood years, somewhat like Nesbit's *My School Days*. The protagonist is a child between the ages of six or seven and sixteen. With its pronouncedly nostalgic tone, and also because of its idyllic country setting, her work recalls Pierre Loti's *Roman d'un enfant* (*Romance of a Child*). With its evocation of a French country childhood—its flowers, cats, dogs, and village people—it even faintly echoes Marcel Proust's *Combray*. Colette, born in 1873, was two years Proust's junior. Although Colette does not focus on her child self, her book manages to be an intensely personal account. The adult narrator is a strong presence who riddles her stories of childhood innocence and happiness with allusions to her later knowledge and troubles. It adds poignancy that the child subject is often seen as anticipating the future, imagining what she will be when she is grown up, how she might be abducted by a lover as her mother had been, and what childbirth will be like. The plot that simmers up out of this plotless book is the dialectic between innocence and experience, and Colette intensifies the effect by doubling her cast of characters: we see her as a girl with her mother and also as the mother of a girl.

Above all, *La Maison de Claudine* is a loving memorial to Colette's mother Sido. Ten years after Sido's death, Colette wrote this book at the instigation of her young lover and stepson Bertrand, who noticed that Colette kept talking nostalgically about her childhood. They visited her childhood house in Saint-Saveur-en-Puisaye (Yonne) together.[8] In the book, Sido is made out to be a figure who loves and cares for her children, not just when they are under her wing, but eternally. Colette shows how this gentle and protective woman, who had been unhappily married to a man who fancied her and took her away from her family when she was eighteen, mitigates the future for her daughter, first by not allowing a woman's life to usurp that of the child too soon, and secondly by reassuring her that the fate that awaits her as a woman will not be a bad one. The favorable maternal image that arises out of this book is not foreign to previous French women's autobiographical writing— George Sand loved her mother—yet this feature too recalls Loti and Proust. Colette constantly implies that life lived in her mother's sphere contrasts with the less positive things that will happen to her later. Her decision to call herself "Claudine" is an allusion to her later life. Between 1900 and 1903, at the command of her first husband Willy, she wrote her notorious (because salacious) "Claudine" series of novels, in which Claudine is the name of Colette's fictional alter ego.

In the 1930s nostalgia for the antebellum world of childhood retreated. Authors' interest shifted to presenting an accurate historical picture of

The Interwar Years: Memoirs and Semi-Memoirs

it. By the mid-1930s the style of memoirs started to change in another way as well: personal stories started to be included routinely. One work that turns sharply toward factuality without, however, giving much of the author's personal story is Mary Vivian Hughes's *A London Child of the Seventies* (1934), a goldmine of social history that includes many photographs. Hughes, an educator, the wife of a lawyer, and a mother of four, was in her late sixties when she published this first volume of her three-volume autobiographical memoir. Born in 1866, she was considerably older than previous authors of Victorian childhood retrospectives. She looked back on a childhood in the 1870s. This meant that she grew up before the Elementary Education Act of 1880 mandated schooling to age ten. So, like Annabel Jackson, she was of the generation of women who were raised in the family and escaped early schooling. Her first volume extends from her first memories in 1870 until 1879, when, as she writes, "my happy childhood was abruptly ended" by her father's death when she was twelve.[9] She writes in her preface: "We were just an ordinary, suburban, Victorian family, undistinguished ourselves and unacquainted with distinguished people. It occurred to me to record our doings only because, on looking back, and comparing our lot with that of the children of to-day, we seemed to have been so *lucky*."

Unlike the aristocratic Jackson, Hughes grew up in a middle-class family. She strikes an upbeat, affirmative note throughout her account. At the start of her first chapter she writes, "I hope to show that Victorian children did not have such a dull time as is usually supposed" (3). Molly was the youngest of five children; she had four older brothers and considered herself, therefore, "born under a lucky star" (3). Hughes stresses that the group of siblings made for a happy childhood. Her attitude toward having older brothers contrasts markedly with Jackson's, who blames her brothers' bullying behavior on boarding school.

Hughes writes a "we"-style memoir. We find out virtually nothing about little Molly's subjectivity or her distinctiveness as a person. Instead, we find out how childhood was lived in her family, by the group of children. Hughes focuses outward, giving an unusual wealth of detail. The reader is truly transported back into a different time, a time when so little happened in the course of a day that the girl recorded the fact of going to bed in her daily diary; when London was a quiet place; when baths were taken in collected rainwater; when Sundays were boringly observed. Overall, we understand that her family enjoyed life and had a wonderful time. Nostalgia peeks through the factual account.

The family members appear extraordinarily cohesive and of one mind about things. To the author's mind it was perfectly fine, as well, that Molly as a girl was raised differently from her brothers. Mainly, Molly was kept at home under the wing of her mother, who was delighted to have given birth to a little girl after four boys. She was special, different, and in some ways the darling of the family. Unlike the boys, she was not sent to school until she was eleven. "My father's slogan was that boys should go everywhere and know everything, and that a girl should stay at home and know nothing" (33). But this is not framed as a complaint. Molly's mother homeschools her and also teaches her housekeeping. She is almost always exempt from the routine corporal punishment that is meted out to the boys. She was quite content to receive this different upbringing when she was a girl, and, unlike the critical and judgmental Annabel Jackson, Hughes the narrator does not critique it either.

In the preface, Hughes states, "None of the characters in this book are fictitious. The incidents, if not dramatic, are at least genuine memories." Readers who appreciate the factuality of the account should, however, be aware that, according to Adam Gopnik, who wrote the preface for a 2008 reedition of the book, Hughes falsified an important fact: she substituted a traffic accident for the true cause of her father's death. In reality, Gopnik writes, her father, who was on the Stock Exchange, committed suicide on account of having been caught in a financial scandal.[10] Gopnik does not cite a source. If the suicide story is true, telling it would surely have compromised the cheery tone that Hughes is intent on maintaining.

Memoirs from the Land of the Vanquished

In Germany, a spate of childhood memoirs appeared in the wake of World War I. Like their English counterparts, the German women memoirists are intent on memorializing bygone days. These postwar German works continue a pattern established in prewar German works: they typically consist of a compilation of short pieces such as we saw, for example, in Helene Adelmann's *Aus meiner Kinderzeit* (1892). The sentiment that old times were better than modern times is overwhelming in these memoirs. Germany had fought and lost the war. Compared to the recent dark days, the nineteenth-century days of childhood appear in a gilded light. As Wanda Icus-Rothe puts it in her 1921 memoir:

"Childhood is over, life is bloody earnest, and those who once so merrily told us told us stories of Seventy long since lie beneath the greensward."[11] "Seventy" alludes to the Franco-Prussian War of 1870, which Prussia won and which led to the unification of Germany. Yes, once upon a time Germany won wars and was prosperous! Authors elevate their childhood into a sheer paradise. Noteworthy in these memoirs is a preference for country over city life. Authors aim to create a picture of the homogeneous society and customs in the particular rural region of Germany that they claim as their *Heimat*. The dislike and distrust of big cities, a hallmark of German Expressionist poetry starting around 1910, echo in these childhood autobiographies that extoll the joys of simple country village life.

Thus Clara Blüthgen's memoir *Aus der Jugendzeit . . . Frühe Erinnerungen* (From the youthful years . . . early memories, 1919) is a short collection of pretty, sometimes entertaining pieces about this and that in the rural Huy region of Germany where she grew up. An artist and writer, Blüthgen describes the places and things of her childhood in sensuous detail. Her pieces are mainly not about her, although she recalls and conveys how she used to feel about things and people. A self-portrait of her as a child emerges only obliquely: we learn that she was imaginative and loved to draw and model in wax. Blüthgen's motivation for writing seems to be above all to hold onto and make more permanent some pieces of her past. This motivation appears to have more to do with her temperament and her advancing age than with the war, which she does not mention, although the war could be understood to shadow her theme of loss. She describes her childhood dismay at seeing things erased on the blackboard, at seeing the product of a person's efforts vanish. At the end of the book she turns this image of erasure into a grim metaphor for how human life ends, namely, in forgottenness. In its quality, this work resembles McHugh's *Thalassa*, though it lacks the nostalgia of *Thalassa*. Rather, the narrator describes what was quirky and "of then" — as well as "of there" — pointing out how life has changed since her childhood.

Three childhood memoirs appearing in 1921 all allude to the war. In that year Sophie Reuschle, a children's book author who had had the good fortune to be fostered by a wealthy lawyer's family, published a memoir of her small-town childhood entitled *Kinderzeit* (Childhood time). Her book consists of short pieces on various topics ("The Sun

House," "Mother," "Grandmother's Garden," and the like). The author gives no dates, ages, place names, or self-portrait, but constantly reiterates her main point: childhood is happiness; her own childhood was a fountain of good things; a happy childhood gives a person the foundation to weather the rough times to come; she wants to share the bounty of her delightful memories with people who were less fortunate than she. This is a determinedly idealizing work, steeped in nostalgia for the past, in which the delights of childhood are contrasted with the current "time with no light"[12] and small-town life is praised over life in cities.

The title of Wanda Icus-Rothe's *Sonne der Heimat: Meine Jugend auf den Höhen des Hunsrücks* (Sun of the homeland: My youth on the heights of the Hunsrück, 1921), a work with attractive illustrations, reveals its regional focus. It is a memoir whose entire emphasis is on setting forth "the way things were" in the author's childhood village in the late 1870s and 1880s. There is next to nothing in her book about her. She tells of some exploits of "we children" (she was one of a pastor's five children) but barely gives personal information, much less a self-portrait. Icus-Rothe writes more soberly and meticulously than Reuschle, with satisfying informative detail, but these are nevertheless gilded memories. She gives idyllic descriptions of the hilly countryside where she grew up, making the place, and her childhood, seem like paradise. Like Reuschle, she emphasizes the superiority of the country over the city. She periodically pauses to lament the contrast between then and now and the loss of her hilly countryside.

A German princess, Fürstin Marie zu Erbach-Schönberg, Prinzessin von Battenberg, the oldest child of Prince Alexander von Hessen und bei Rhein and his morganatic wife Julie von Battenberg, made haste to publish the first volume of her memoirs in 1921, when she was nearly seventy. Under the title *Entscheidende Jahre: 1859—1866—1870: Aus meiner Kindheit und Mädchenzeit* (Decisive years: 1859—1866—1870: From my childhood and girlhood), the princess's memoir encompasses her life to her marriage at age eighteen. In response to people close to her who urged her to write about her event-filled adult life, she comments crisply: "Yes. I'd have a lot to tell, and even more to keep silent about."[13] Nevertheless, soon thereafter she published two further volumes of memoirs about her later life. She insists that she is writing the "story of my childhood" (260), even though her teen years dominate, no doubt because starting with her adolescence she can rely heavily on her diary, from which she cites extensively. Justifying her enterprise, she states that she wants to portray "the awakening of the child's soul" (3). She makes an occasional gesture in that direction, writing of her first memories, emphasizing her introverted and conservative nature, and noting her love of animals and teen aversion to worldly amusements. Yet this is a memoir that largely tells about how things were in her childhood and teen years, when she and her siblings led the charmed life of children of the European aristocracy. The wars of 1859, 1866, and 1870 affected the family particularly because of its blood ties to European royalty and because her father was a general. She repeatedly contrasts her "sunny childhood" (64) with the sad events of her later life and the terrible recent war.

Appearing in 1927, Agnes Harder's *Die kleine Stadt: Aus meinen Kindertagen* (The small city: From my childhood days, 1927) is another commemorative work. It spans the years when the author lived with her family in a "small city" in East Prussia where her father was a judge, from her eighth year until she entered a nearby boarding school, and consists of her recollections about the way things were in society and in her family. Fascinating in the abundance and precision of its detail, it is somewhat tendentious in its message. Harder spells out her motivation in writing: to paint a picture, for moral reasons, of the simple, excellent German life of yesteryear. She writes: "I tell this here in such detail because it gives a picture of life at that time, when Germany hadn't yet gotten rich, but was calm and satisfied in itself."[14] Like other German women childhood memoirists of the immediate postwar period she praises country life. Harder was known to have *völkisch* leanings. When Hitler came to power she was among the writers who in 1933 pledged loyalty to him. In this childhood memoir she expresses pro-German and anti-Polish sentiments, but, interestingly, is well disposed toward Jews. Speaking of her Jewish school friends, she remarks, "In those days people were not yet antisemitic" (21). At the end she tells a personal story about a crushing yet formative moral lesson she received from her parents, which involved harsh punishment for what could be considered the pardonable disobedience of visiting home during her boarding school term. Her mother refused to welcome her and sent her straight back to the school. But this personal story is part and parcel of the picture she wants to convey of the wholesome, morally sound East Prussian society in the 1870s. She admiringly cites Immanuel Kant's categorical imperative and considers herself heir to it.

Semi-Memoirs

1935

By the mid-1930s, accompanying the swing toward psychology and the greater assertiveness that one sees in self-focused autobiographies, women memoirists tend to include more of themselves. They publish works that could be described as "semi-memoirs." Such works implicitly justify themselves as pictures of the time, place, people, or family, but feature a considerable subjective component alongside. The author brings in her subjective reactions and also, perhaps, mentions her early memories, personality, education, and personal development. The year 1935 brought a crop of such semi-memoirs. Five such works appeared in 1935, one by the German author Ina Seidel, two by English authors Eleanor Acland and Eleanor Farjeon, one by Canadian author Nellie McClung, and one by American author Helen Woodward. These writers tread in the family history/social history footsteps of Molly Hughes, but in contrast to Hughes, they include self-portraits. The authors were seven to nineteen years younger than Hughes.

Seidel, Acland, and Farjeon had deeply personal, family-related motivations for writing, whereas McClung had a great family pioneer story to tell, and Woodward a Jewish immigrant story. None of them address themselves to a family audience, however, as did Lunt; all envisage a broader reading public. All of them go to considerable pains to produce a work likely to interest the public, and they all, spontaneously and independently of each other, hit on the recipe of interweaving social and family history with a personal story. Subsequently, this "semi-memoir" formula would catch on and supplant the "mere memoir" model. Apart from their semi-memoir characteristic—the fact that each author lets herself emerge as a distinct personality in the context of social and family history—the works are serious, solid, and substantial, in short, conservative. That is, they are not psychoanalytical, formally innovative, or otherwise "modern." They incorporate humorous touches, but their main goal is not entertainment.

The youngest of the four authors, the poet and novelist Ina Seidel, wrote the shortest work. She adopts a traditional chronological form for *Meine Kindheit und Jugend* (My childhood and youth, 1935), starting with her ancestors and parents and taking her own story to age twenty, when it became clear whom she would marry. A principal motivation for the book is to give posterity a memorial to her father, a doctor who was driven to suicide when she was ten years old by the calumny of jealous colleagues. She gives some subjective details about herself, for example, that her father's death instilled in her an unshakeable fear of impending catastrophe, and she emphasizes that she loved poetry, wrote it herself, and was an avid reader of literature. But mainly she engages the reader with a rich picture of the times and places where she lived: the stolid bourgeois town of Braunschweig where she grew up, the fast-paced university town Marburg, and the artists' colony Schwabing in Munich where she spent her teens. Like many other authors who grew up in the late nineteenth century and look back on their upbringing from the vantage point of the interwar years, Seidel addresses the topic of religion, which for children of her generation had become problematic. She notes that the world of her childhood was steeped in a religious atmosphere and that her parents were religious, though they did not belong to a church. In this relaxed home atmosphere, she thought of God as a woman for many years. Later, as a student in a private girls' school, she was obliged to go to church and, unused to the services, found them boring. In 1933 Seidel was one of the German writers who signed the vow of loyalty to Hitler.

Eleanor Margaret Acland's *Good-Bye for the Present: The Story of Two Childhoods* was published posthumously. The introduction by G. M. Trevelyan tells readers that Eleanor Acland was "a woman primarily of public and domestic interests."[15] Acland came from an upper-class English family and married into another. Born Eleanor Cropper, she was the granddaughter of a Liberal member of parliament and married a noted Liberal politician. She tells two separate stories, the story of her daughter's childhood in Devon and the story of her own childhood in Westmorland. The "Ellen" part, a work of mourning, was written soon after her eleven-year-old daughter Ellen's untimely accidental death and printed privately for friends nine years before its actual publication. Eleanor's story, entitled "Milly," as the author calls her child self, appeared here for the first time. The author intended it for publication and wrote it just before her expected death.

The "Milly" story spans the years 1878–88, from the author's birth to age ten. It follows two prototypes. The first is familiar from Frances Hodgson Burnett's *The One I Knew the Best of All*. Acland follows Burnett in her distinctive use of the third person (the narrator here is "I,"

94 The Interwar Years: Memoirs and Semi-Memoirs

the child "Milly" is "she"). Like Burnett, she maintains distance between the knowledgeable adult narrator and the naïve child subject and adopts a somewhat arch and patronizing tone toward her child self. Like Burnett, she organizes the book by theme, takes a close interest in and pays attention to early memories, expostulates over the mental dullness of her nursemaid, and comments on social class. She takes up certain themes familiar from Burnett, themes that had become established topoi of the genre: toys, reading, and moral education. She represents herself as an inquiring and inventive mind and an early reader. Acland's autobiography contains less of herself than Burnett's, however, and is less psychologically probing. Instead, it expands in the direction of giving a picture of the times (i.e., the Victorian period) and of what it was like to grow up in the upper class in Westmorland in those days. The second prototype is the "we" narrative that had deep roots in English and American childhood autobiography. Most often Acland talks about "Milly" in the company of her two younger siblings. In its effort to give a picture of life in the olden days, this childhood autobiography is similar to Larcom's and Gandy's "we"-style works.

Acland's attention to memory shows how thinking on that subject had progressed since the prewar period. "Camera obscura"—meaning both "dark room" and pinhole image—is her metaphor for it. Whereas Burnett stresses what she *can* remember, Acland emphasizes that we remember randomly and capriciously: "Nor can one guess why that subconscious factor in one's being that controls the shutter in the roof of the past, and lets in the beam of memory, admits that beam to play on just a few of those long-ago doings and thinkings and leaves the rest, by far the greatest number, in total darkness as if they had never been" (15–16). There is as yet no sign of psychoanalytic influence in these remarks on memory. Acland does not assert that memory falsifies nor that memories change over time. She is closer to Marcel Proust (*In Search of Lost Time*, 1913–27) than to Sigmund Freud. She touches on the notion of the cue, made famous by Proust, asserting that she experiences present sense impressions such as snowdrops or the blackbird's note "with a double sense" (23), seeing them both now and as she once perceived them with her "child-mind." Like Proust, too, Acland follows the Romantic tradition of ascribing especial value, crucial emotional value, to childhood memories specifically. She asserts that her childhood memories, inasmuch as she can recover them, are more authentic than her adolescent memories, which, to her mind, self-consciousness distorted.

Like Seidel, Acland discusses her relationship with religion. Religion had been an important topic for the 1824-born Lucy Larcom. It continued to be one for the 1843-born Caroline Creevey, who like Larcom was a New England "daughter of the Puritans," but piety had started to decline: Cornelia Gray Lunt, born in the same year as Creevey but raised in Chicago, groans in the diary she kept as a twelve-year-old about the boring Sunday church sermons in the New England boarding school where she was eventually sent. In England, according to John Burnett, church attendance declined throughout the nineteenth century, yet at midcentury approximately half of the adult population attended church. This meant that nearly every Victorian child had some connection with organized religion.[16] Acland's chapters on religion are framed to show how the religious education of children had atrophied since her parents' day. For her parents, Acland writes, religion was still a "governing factor in their lives" (161). Thus she was raised in the Church of England. She was obliged to learn prayers and to go to church. But she grew up in an age when modern thought and discoveries questioned the foundations of religion. Prayers and religious teaching did not remain a living body of doctrine. Tellingly, the religious children's books on the creation of the universe she was given had been written two generations earlier. Like Hughes and Seidel, Acland experienced church as boring and the prayers as confusing.

Acland, who was not a professional writer, makes the impression of packing everything she wanted to say into her semi-memoir, borrowing styles and techniques of presentation from previous models as they suit her purposes. Other nonprofessional authors of the interwar years, like Lunt, produced works that were similarly baggy—but so did some professional writers. One of these is the children's book author Eleanor Farjeon. Farjeon writes in a consistent, distinctive, lively style, and she has an enormous amount to say. Her semi-memoir *A Nursery in the Nineties* (1935) is a family history, which, like Hughes's work, is heavily supplemented with photographs. Farjeon notes in 1959 that she wrote it "in order to preserve for myself and my brothers as full a record as possible of our childhood."[17] The reader expecting a "we"-style autobiography will not be disappointed, but this is by far not the whole story. Eleanor ("Nellie") does not recede as a personality. Particularly in the second section of the work, entitled "Foreground," the author paints her self-portrait as a child and an adolescent in a compelling and candid fashion. Of the five semi-memoirs that appeared in 1935, Farjeon's comes the closest to being confessional, as well as being by far the most emotional, indeed nostalgic. She writes the family history in a novelistic fashion and uses various personal pronouns to talk about herself—"I," "you," and "she"—besides, of course, "we" when she is talking about the close-knit group of four siblings.

Farjeon's decision to write family history serves as its own excuse, since she came from an exceptionally interesting family. Her maternal grandfather was the famous American actor Joe Jefferson; her English father, Benjamin Farjeon, was a novelist, who launched his writing career in Dunedin after running off to Australia to mine for gold; her older brother Harry became a composer; and her two younger brothers, Joe and Bertie, became writers. Farjeon devotes the first 222 pages, or slightly under half the book, to "Background": to her ancestors' and her parents' stories up to the point when she herself was a small child. Thus, the focus of the book overall is not "Nellie"; this is not an autobiography. But the second half of the book contains ample material about her. Moreover, Farjeon makes no claims for typicality. Her talented, well-traveled family was a thoroughly atypical Victorian family—she devotes a chapter to portraying each family member—and she herself was an unusually precocious, imaginative, and literarily gifted child. Her self-portrait begins: "I cannot remember being without a headache; I cannot remember one night of restful sleep" (258). She goes on to contrast a picture that someone else draws of her with her own recollection of herself. The other person recalls "a most attractive and graceful child of extraordinary intelligence, a little Pandora. Your writings, and especially your poems, were wonderful for a child" (258). The reader goes on to discover that Nellie is indeed a precocious literary talent, a voracious early reader, and an early writer of poetry, thus, a child who knows her vocation is writing. But Farjeon continues: "But when I try to make a picture of myself, it seems to me that I was a dreamy, timid, sickly, lachrymose, painfully shy, sensitive, greedy, ill-regulated little girl; not selfish on the whole, very affectionate and desirous of affection, almost as unwilling to inflict pain as to suffer it (I was a coward in most respects), and intensely absorbed in my writing, my reading, my family, and my imaginative life. I never wanted to venture outside my home-door; everything that mattered to me lay behind it" (258–59). This self-description expresses in a nutshell what she will unfold about herself later in the book.

Nellie does appear to be a truly dreamy and imaginative child. The way she describes her experience of the world, all is aswim. In a chapter called "A Bad Day for Nellie," she begins her day by fearing that she is an adopted child. Then she finds a mouse in the trap, which she is forbidden to save. After some meaningless lessons with a governess, she takes it into her head to spend all her and her siblings' pocket money on flowers so as to turn the nursery into a bower—and is forced by her father to take the flowers back to the florist. At a party that day, she asks for ice cream where there is none, thereby embarrassing herself. Later she takes it into her head that her youngest brother should see a real fairy when he wakes up and gets her second-youngest brother to dress up as a fairy. But her youngest brother is terrified by the apparition and shrieks and shrieks.

Her family is her world. All her family members are highly intelligent, imaginative kindred spirits, and the wonderful world they create at home is more important and more real than the outside world. In particular, she is inseparable from infancy from her older brother. Whereas her parents impose no rules, her older brother is the representative of law and order in the nursery, to the point where Nellie lets him dictate her bedtime and send her off to bed every night until she is sixteen years old. When she is five, the two of them invent a game called TAR, in which they become completely absorbed. They remain absorbed in it for an astonishing twenty years. In time they are joined by the two younger boys. The game consists of pretending to be other people, mainly literary characters. Her older brother starts it any time he pleases by specifying the characters they will play and stops it by telling them they are themselves again. She insists that this game "influenced my development more radically than anything else in my life" (206). In short, Nellie is very frequently "not herself," not living in the real world, but inventing new personalities for herself in a world of fantasy, albeit in dialogue with her brother. Nellie's relationship to her older brother, as well as their respective personalities, has a remarkable resemblance to that of Tom and Maggie Tulliver in George Eliot's *The Mill on the Floss*.

Finally, her attachment to her family makes her socially inept—shy and self-conscious—and it also interferes with her achieving discipline and independence. She states flatly, "Possessive experience was less to me than shared experience" (259). At age eighteen she thinks it is time for her to realize her talents as a writer and produce substantial work. But she somehow cannot discipline herself, cannot get down to work. By consequence, "Doubts of myself, of my power, *ever*, to stand on my own feet" (502). "The fault lay in me, in my idle, procrastinating, greedy, self-indulgent, undisciplined nature" (503). Her lack of discipline apparently carries over into adulthood, since "the glow comes and fades, comes and fades as it has always done since I was a little girl. Writing gets done in queer irregular ways at queer irregular times" (512). This sounds like an honest confession. Farjeon takes her family story through her father's death in 1903, when she was in her early twenties. In a coda, she imagines the four siblings reunited on Judgment Day by the "nursery call," for which she gives the musical notes.

The third English-language semi-memoir published in 1935, Nellie L. McClung's *Clearing in the West: My Own Story*, is a Canadian classic. McClung (1873–1951) was a prominent Canadian feminist, prohibitionist, and suffragist. Her accomplishments were many: she was a bestselling novelist, the mother of five, a delegate to the Alberta Assembly from 1921 to 1926, and a delegate to the League of Nations in 1938.[18] Largely through her efforts, women got the right to vote in Manitoba in 1916. In *Clearing in the West*, which she published in her early fifties, she tells the story of her life from her birth in 1878 (an event she recounts in the third person) until her marriage at age twenty-three. Over 150 pages of this 378-page work are devoted to her preadolescent years. Ten years later she published a second volume of her autobiography, *The Stream Runs Fast*.

Written by an important public figure, her semi-memoir is an iconic account of Canadian pioneer life in the late nineteenth century. Composed in a highly readable style with a novelist's skill, it makes for enjoyable, informative, inspirational reading. The reader is treated to history in the form of a story as well as to insight into the background of a courageous woman leader. It is not surprising that the work continues to be republished: after the first edition of 1935, it went into ten subsequent editions through 2009.

What does it take to write a classic? McClung's is the most polished, the most carefully constructed of the 1935 semi-memoirs; despite its length, it is not baggy. In many respects, this work bears close resemblance to the American and British women's childhood autobiographies written up to this point in the "we" style epitomized by Larcom and the Victorian retrospectives written by such writers as Gandy and Acland. It gives a picture of the times rather than focusing on the author herself. First and foremost, the reader finds out what life was like for a late nineteenth-century pioneer family in Canada, first in Ontario but very soon and mainly in Manitoba.

The Interwar Years: Memoirs and Semi-Memoirs   99

McClung had a happy, rural (farm) childhood in a rather large family, so the makings of a "we"-style childhood autobiography are there. She includes plenty of adventures and vivid, scenic descriptions of farm life. Farm life in the 1870s through the mid-1890s is represented as extraordinarily tough, but people were optimistic and had a sense of accomplishment. Her chapters are replete with sensuous details about the landscape, animals, social events, and clothes. She gives mouth-watering descriptions of food. We hear of major political events (the Louis Riel Rebellion), curiosities like women revivalists, and pastimes like spiritist séances and mesmerism. Because her story spans twenty-three years, we get a sense of how Manitoba farming changed. The advent of machines, in particular the threshing machine, caused specialized wheat farming to displace the old self-sufficient farms and also brought a seven-day work week for the men.

In presenting the story of her childhood and youth the narrator adopts a modest, cheerful tone. She is never self-pitying despite her difficult pioneer life. She writes with a humorous touch. As a narrator, she above all poses as a storyteller, one who shapes the past into an exciting story. She plentifully uses fictional techniques, including dialogue and free indirect discourse. All of these features—tone, humor, storytelling—mark a narratorial stance, and precisely this narratorial stance, which maintains distance in giving an account of the past, is similar to that of many of her English-language predecessors, starting with Frances Hodgson Burnett and including Gandy, MacCarthy, Orpen, Acland, M. Hughes, and Farjeon. Finally, like all of these writers, McClung does not hold back with her own present-day insights. For example: "People who write about their own family usually tell much of family tyranny and misunderstanding, and in the minds of many, parents and children are natural enemies, but I have not much to say about parental oppression. My people were hard-working folk."[19] Or, "Looking back on it, I wonder what power nineteenth century parents had over their children and how did they hold it. I was not a particularly meek young person, but I could not stand up to my mother, even knowing that she was wrong" (176).

Similarly to previous works in the "we" style, this story does not foreground, as its central plot line, how Nellie became what she became. Despite attention to memory and accounts of early memories, psychological probing is also not its style. It is untouched by psychoanalysis. Yet if this work does not revolve around Nellie, this seems to be less out of a self-effacing impulse than because this author is in possession of a genuinely great story to tell, the story of her family's pioneer life. That story justifies the work. As for the role assigned to the autobiographical subject, within the framework of the storytelling and the "we" modes, McClung does keep returning to her own perspective: "I often wished we could all slow down a bit" (27); "I wondered what we would do with the dogs" (35); "I remember trailing my hand in the cold water" (46). She also tells some of her personal stories, such as lying so as to save the life of her cattle-tail-biting dog Nap. She sometimes gives her own feelings and reactions: "My heart turned cold with terror!" (113); "there were times when I hated the cows" (117). A self-portrait emerges: Nellie is a distinct character in the farm context, a "lazy" person not suited for farm work or sewing, but an independent thinker who can be outspoken and determined. Even though she attended school late and only learned to read at age ten, she wants, starting at age fifteen, to leave the farm so as to be on her own. Her idea, which she acts on, is that she will go to Normal School and become a teacher. She tells how she read Charles Dickens and how he became her model: "I wanted to write; to do for the people around me what Dickens had done for his people. I wanted to be a voice for the voiceless as he had been a defender of the weak" (281). "I wanted to reveal humanity; to make people understand each other; to make the commonplace things divine, and when I sat on the flat stone on my way home from school, I thought of these things until my head swam and my eyes ran with tears" (282).

Finally, similarly to the way Larcom and Burnett start personal threads in their autobiographies of childhood that show the coming-into-being of their respective vocations (Larcom's love of poetry, Burnett's love of stories), McClung also starts a thread of the development of her feminist ideas, albeit only after 150 pages. The trigger, when she is around age eleven, is her mother's remarks about women's place. After she spontaneously jumps up at a stopping house to pour tea for the guests, her mother reproaches her for being "forward" and instructs her that "it's women's place to help the men and keep out of public matters" (151). Starting at this point in the narrative, women's rights become a theme. Nevertheless, there is no sharp mother criticism in this autobiography. The girl respects her parents. In the context of the feminist thread, however, her mother becomes the mouthpiece of the traditional views on women that meet with her growing criticism. But at the end

The Interwar Years: Memoirs and Semi-Memoirs 101

of the book she makes it up to her mother by reserving special praise for her: "Fearless, self-reliant, undaunted, who never turned away from the sick or needy; for whom no night was too dark or cold, or road too dangerous to go out and help a neighbor in distress, who, for all her bluntness had a gracious spirit, and knew the healing word for souls in distress; who scorned pretense or affectation, and loved the sweet and simple virtues" (375).

The final 1935 semi-memoir under discussion, Helen Woodward's *Three Flights Up*, is a family story, but one that is remarkably analytical. Woodward, an American who had a long career in advertising, tells the story of her working-class immigrant German Jewish family, consisting of her parents and their four children, and what their life was like in New York in the 1880s and 1890s. She takes her story through the depression of 1893, when to make a living the family had to move to Little Rock, up to her thirteenth year when they move to Boston. In writing an American Jewish childhood autobiography, Woodward was following a tradition established by her contemporaries Mary Antin and Rose Cohen. Her story is less dramatic than either of theirs: she herself was not an immigrant but was born in the US; her family was poor but did not have to make sacrifices comparable to theirs; in particular, she and her siblings were not obliged to work. But her writing is more carefully crafted than theirs and, above all, is more psychological. Like other authors of the mid-1930s, she is at pains to give her work some literary flair. She starts in medias res with a scene when she is eight that typifies life in her family and then goes back to the story of her parents, her coming to a sense of self, school, relatives, and friends. She takes care to intersperse short chapters on cultural history, on the way things used to be, such as the way holidays were celebrated in their neighborhood and the types of stores found there, with short chapters devoted to particular people including herself and short chapters that chronicle her family's history. The core of the work is a "we" story. As she states, "I seldom thought of myself as an individual, as a person by myself, but always as part of the family."[20] Yet from the beginning she includes quite a lot about herself when young, painting a portrait of herself as a not-pretty child with ugly eyes who felt inferior to other children. Then she discovered she excelled at school, whereupon she began to adore school. She includes psychological details such as her phobia of broken dolls, which she ingeniously suggests might have to do with her infantile jealousy of her younger sister Dolly. She interprets heavily, so that as a narrator she figures as a distinct personality. One of her techniques particularly stands out: she repeatedly tells the reader that family attitudes and customs influenced the way she became as an adult. She thus gives the impression that her story of the way things were is highly relevant to a developmental story that she does not explicitly tell. This technique in particular makes the work straddle the boundary between childhood memoir and childhood autobiography. Woodward's psychologizing extends to other people: for instance, she insists on the tension between her very different mother and father and analyzes both of them. Her father, a Polish-born cigar maker, loved two things: betting on the races and socialism. Her mother hated both and paid no attention to anything political, but lived in her little world of housework and children ("Most women are like that," the career woman Woodward comments [147]). *Three Flights Up* is a reflective work in which the author tries to impart some of the conclusions she has reached about life. It is not overtly feminist, but the author, who "became someone," cannot resist commenting ironically on the mindset of women in her milieu in the 1880s and 1890s. All the girls know that they will become wives and mothers, unless they are too ugly to find a husband, such as a certain Millie, whose parents send her to Normal School: "It would be her awful fate to earn her own living" (170).

In the second half of the 1930s authors who wrote family or social history or told entertainingly of the old days continued to venture in the direction of the newer style of work with a psychological focus. In Germany, in 1936, Helene Pagés published a semi-memoir, *Die klingende Kette* (The sounding chain), similar to McClung's in several respects: it is a lively, polished, informative, and entertaining childhood retrospective of considerable length that justifies itself as a memoir of the people and places in the Hunsrück region of Germany during the author's childhood and youth in the 1860s and 1870s, but also includes her personal story to age twenty-one, when she finishes teacher's training seminary and starts work as a teacher. It paints a positive, sometimes lyrical picture of life in those rural hills, but does not shy away from sad stories and is therefore more rounded, less nostalgic, and seemingly more objective than Icus-Rothe's 1921 memoir about the same region. Unlike McClung and like Icus-Rothe, Pagés's work is oriented on the notion of *Heimat* prominent in German writers of the era. Unlike either McClung or Icus-Rothe, her thinking is informed by a distinctive sense of connectedness and continuity. The author states in her epigraph that she is a link in a chain, connected to people in the past and future; her rich memories indissolubly connect her to her *Heimat*, where she and her eight siblings felt that the world was theirs although the family was not wealthy; old, inherited objects talk to her of the past. Raised as a Catholic, she inevitably refers to dying as "going home." She devotes a considerable part of her book to writing empathetically of the lives, stories, and sufferings of other people in her village, from her parents to the washwomen to a mad bookbinder to faith healers.

Several writers in England and in the United States published semi-memoirs in the later 1930s that, like those that appeared in 1935, incorporate a subjective element. To this group belong Alison Uttley's *Ambush of Young Days* (1937) and Sybil Marjorie Lubbock's *The Child in the Crystal* (1939) in England, and Eleanor Hallowell Abbott's *Being Little in Cambridge When Everyone Else Was Big* (1936) and Bertha Damon's *Grandma Called It Carnal* (1938) in the United States. Uttley and Abbott bear a closer look—Uttley because her work is the first instance of a minor trend, and Abbott because she pursued the popular American tradition of the humorous memoir with interesting results.

"Splendor in the Grass"

Alison Uttley, author of many books and a well-known children's book author, adopts in her childhood memoir *Ambush of Young Days* (1937) a tone inherited from Romanticism that casts childhood as "splendor in the grass," or, in other words, in an idealizing Wordsworthian light. Her work is a particularly skillful non-self-focused childhood memoir. Like Ida Gandy's *A Wiltshire Childhood*, it is about a happy childhood in rural England. Uttley, who grew up on the family farm in Derbyshire, invokes "the home of my childhood, eternal and green."[21] By casting childhood in Romantic splendor, Uttley invokes the trope of childhood as a lost paradise familiar from male authors such as Rousseau, Wordsworth, Goltz, Loti, and Proust, but which women autobiographers for the most part, aside from German women writing in the wake of World War I, did not latch onto. In later years, it is found mainly in certain Anglo-Irish memoirs such as those by Mary Hamilton and Elizabeth Hamilton.

Uttley writes in the first person and calls herself Alison. The work hovers between a memoir about the time and place and an account of herself, though not in the sense of "what I became," but rather of "the way children feel, as exemplified by me." Uttley's purpose is give a complete picture of the family farm, the village and villagers, and her life there as a child, yet she recaptures "the way things were" in an exceptionally artful way, always imparting information in the form of the child's specific experiences and emphasizing aspects of her rural world that correlated with what she sets forth as the specific nature and proclivities of a child. She insists above all on the importance of the senses and of material objects for children. "The senses of many children are often as acute as those of the wild animals in the fields, until they are dulled by school, or changed by their environment" (53). Regarding herself, "My mind carries such a cargo of smells and sensations" (29). She underpins this statement with copious testimonies to her acute sense of smell. She writes of her desire to touch things: "My fingers itched to hold these fragile treasures, and I am sure the longing to touch things is an intense and aching desire in many children" (111). Like previous childhood autobiographies by Larcom, Burnett, Arden, Gandy, Acland, and M. Hughes, the chapters are organized by topic, such as "The Farm," "Shadows and Night," "Scents and Sensations," or "Tree Friends." The ages Uttley mentions range from two to nine. Many memories come from her at age six, but she also has many early memories from ages two and three.

Alison had a younger brother, and so Uttley sometimes writes in the first person plural. But this is not really a "we" text. It is an outwardly oriented memoir, in which "I" is much more prominent than "we." We find out some things about Alison specifically: she could read before she was five; she went to school at seven; she learned to play the concertina; she had favorite books. In contrast to many children of her day, the Sunday rituals succeeded with her. She even describes herself as devout.

The book is particularly joyous in its tone. Written in a polished style, it successfully transmits in glowing colors the joy of being a child. Its agenda is to recapture what is delightful if not magical about childhood, to make childhood seem a glorious era of life. Not everything that happens is happy—there is an animal death, the long walk to school through the woods is scary, and her piano teacher raps her fingers with a knitting needle if she makes mistakes—but Uttley is uninterested in exploring the effects of such things on the child's psyche, and so they merely add a touch of realism to an otherwise upbeat, happy account. Besides Wordsworth, Uttley seems specifically indebted to another writer who famously glorified his childhood: Marcel Proust. Proust was an obvious model for autobiographers who strongly believed in the integrity of their childhood memories. Like Acland before her and M. St. Clare Byrne and Bea Howe after her, Uttley writes about memory in a way that echoes Proust. Her account of how she retrieves her memories is Proustian: "Remembrances . . . spring to life with such startling vividness that I experience a shock" (29). Chance sensations—a scent, a sound, seeing a slant of sunlight—pull up whole past scenes for her, just as they did for Proust.

Humor

The American Eleanor Hallowell Abbott's *Being Little in Cambridge When Everyone Else Was Big* (1936) adopts an entirely different tone, one that is indebted to the American tradition of the humorous family memoir. Clarence Day's bestselling *Life with Father*, a 1936 compilation of the comic tales that had appeared in the *New Yorker* and other American magazines in the early 1930s, inspired similar humorous memoirs about the life of yesteryear. Day is usually mentioned in one breath with Bertha Damon's bestselling *Grandma Called It Carnal* (1938), an entertaining story of growing up with her grandmother in a small town in Connecticut in the last decade of the nineteenth century. Grandma, who was born in 1829, is, according to the narrator, not really typical for her time, but a throwback to the eighteenth century. She is a devotee of Henry David Thoreau who practiced a life of thrift, rigor, and moral uprightness and shunned all modern conveniences. In the next decade, Alyene Porter's *Papa Was a Preacher* (1944) would continue this type of the humorous childhood memoir. Eleanor Hallowell Abbott's *Being Little in Cambridge When Everyone Else Was Big* is an earlier title of the same type. It is a curious mix of humorous memoir, traditional "we" story, and autobiography. Abbott (1872–1958), a fiction writer, published her memoir of childhood when she was in her sixties. Her excuse for writing is Cambridge. Her Cambridge of the 1870s was not just the site of Harvard College, but home to such luminaries as James Russell Lowell, Henry Wadsworth Longfellow, Oliver Wendell Holmes, Thomas Wentworth Higginson, and William Dean Howells. Her father was a respected minister, and so his family, including his three children, was accepted in this intellectually vibrant society. A fair amount of the book is devoted to the way things were in Cambridge when Eleanor was a child. Although

Abbott's story takes place nearly twenty years prior to Damon's, we seem to enter a privileged and much more advanced world as we move from the glum, joyless, hardworking Connecticut town that Damon calls North Stonefield to Cambridge, Massachusetts.

Abbott uses the child's naïve point of view to achieve a humorous effect. Childish doings are prominent, and since Eleanor mainly did them together with her two older siblings, they are often recounted in the first person plural. Any self-representation that occurs tends to be humorous rather than confessional, nostalgic, or psychologically profound. Eleanor's perfectly normal childish attitudes, comments, and exploits are frequently styled as ones that cause ripples in the enlightened, kindly, deeply moral and religious adult circles around her. She notes tartly, "Such a thing as child psychology was apparently unknown."[22] Topics include religion—prominent in a minister's household—and the quaint upbringing of girls in the day. Girls, says Abbott, were constantly exhorted to be modest, because men allegedly turned into wild beasts upon a female's slightest departure from a "mien or deportment of modesty" (104). The girls are allowed to play freely with boys, but her father ferociously refuses to let any boy pay one of his daughters "an attention." A close family friend teaches her and her sister how to crochet and sew, preparing them for a "worthy and industrious womanhood" (114).

In light of all this, Abbott's book ends in a most surprising fashion. In her two final chapters, where she tells of her mother's death, her father's remarriage, the family's relocation to her stepmother's house, and her resulting unhappiness, she drops her humorous tone. When a doctor enjoins her to tell him everything she thinks, it triggers an incoherent, unstoppable outpouring on her part, parts of which she reproduces. Remarkably, she then goes on to say that her book is like this outpouring: perhaps too much about herself, but not nearly as much as she planned to include, and even if she had included all, what she wrote would have been but a fragment of "the things which I have suffered, enjoyed, tried to analyze" (278). In fact, however, Abbott's book does not at all live up to her characterization of it. It is not a confession. By French standards, or compared with the autobiography Mabel Dodge Luhan had published previously or the one Mary Butts was writing contemporaneously (both discussed in chapter 3), it cannot be called deep or psychological. Why Abbott changes her tone and claims at the end that her humorous book is confessional remains a puzzle.

Souvenirs

Such mixed works also appeared in France. One will be mentioned here, since it is poised at the tipping point between the semi-memoir and the autobiography of childhood and youth, which is the topic of the next chapter. In 1937 Louise Weiss, a prominent journalist and advocate for women's suffrage, published *Souvenirs d'une enfance républicaine* (Memories of a republican childhood). "Souvenirs" (memories), common in French titles, is judiciously chosen for this work, because it accommodates a wide range of types of content. On the one hand, Weiss memorializes whatever she feels like memorializing. She paints lively portraits of important relatives—her grandfather the blind oculist, her wealthy German great-grandmother, her strict, childless chatelaine of a great-aunt in the Gironde who upholds the values of a bygone age (and whose mind she reads). She describes in vivid detail the trips she took to Jerusalem, England, Alsace, and Spain. She describes her schools and the teachers who influenced her. Separate chapters are devoted to different subjects. The overall flow of the narrative is chronological, but Weiss does not give a continuous account. Rather, she writes anecdotally, with humor, and with a novelistic touch (she renders her great-aunt's thoughts in free indirect style). But there is an important thread in this work devoted to herself, in particular to her ardent desire, starting around the age of seventeen or eighteen, to have a career, which she believes will make her a free agent; to her pursuit of an education and a degree (*agrégation*) that will qualify her as a teacher in the public education system; and to her love of writing that will finally lead to a career in journalism. In short, Louise does not just react; she acts. She tells how she was inspired by the original vision and the tenacity of the painter J. M. W. Turner, whose paintings swept her off her feet in the Tate Gallery. Retrospectively, her anecdotes and portraits could be construed as an account of the influences on her when she was growing up.

Weiss's story, as that of the oldest child in a well-to-do upper-middle-class French family, anticipates Simone de Beauvoir's far better known account of her childhood and youth in *Mémoires d'une jeune fille rangée* (*Memoirs of a Dutiful Daughter*), published in 1958 and discussed in chapter 5. Suffice it to say here that each woman's experiences corroborate the other's and that both testify to the repressive conditions that young middle-class French women faced in the early twentieth century. Weiss and Beauvoir, who was fifteen years her junior, had similar ambitions and confronted similar hurdles. The disapproval Weiss encounters from the bourgeois society she belongs to is even more extreme than what Beauvoir had to contend with. Weiss portrays the hindrances a young woman encounters in pursuing a goal other than marriage and maternity as enough to crush all but the most determined—Louise, like Simone, being one of these exceptionally determined women. Like Beauvoir, Weiss finds that excellence in school brings negative reactions at home (in Weiss's case, her father wishes that his sons rather than his daughter would bring home scholastic laurels).

There are differences between Weiss's and Beauvoir's situations, however. Louise's mother, whom she describes in terms of the warmest admiration, is Jewish and liberal, and, in contrast to her Protestant father, encourages her to pursue education and a career, whereas both of Beauvoir's parents are Catholic traditionalists who embody the values of the upper bourgeoisie. Weiss's family is also well enough off so that she does not have to earn a living. She would merely like to do so for the sake of the independence she thinks it will bring. Since to her a career means agency and empowerment rather than money, she is little inclined to put up with humiliation. Having succeeded in the *agrégation* competition after much hard work, she tenders her resignation when a government official offers her a bad position. This offer had to do with her hat. In an attempt to be elegant, she wore a hat ornamented with roses to her examination. Afterwards, one of her examiners observed that she did not look like a woman professor. This reproof aroused her umbrage—are women professors supposed to look dowdy, ugly? She retorted that this was the first compliment anyone had paid her after her exam. She was caught in a classic feminine double bind, about which women were still complaining in the 1970s and 1980s: the first thing her examiner thought about was her appearance, not her intellectual accomplishment. Furious at her retort, the examiner reported her insolence to the higher-ups, who considered it a fitting punishment to offer her a poorly paid teaching position in the provinces.[23]

In sum: In the interwar years, would-be women memoirists and autobiographers were able to look back on a tradition of women's childhood narratives, with the result that more were emboldened to give this kind of writing a go. They looked back on a variety of models published by women as well as men. By consequence, they borrowed from here and there, and, seeking to realize overfull agendas, sometimes produced long, baggy works that sacrificed focus in subject matter and consistency in tone to earnestness of purpose. The phenomenon is visible not just among amateur writers like Lunt, but in professional writers such as Farjeon, Abbott, and Weiss. Many women opted for some form of memoir. In general, the pure memoir ceded to the hybrid semi-memoir. In the interwar years, however, the semi-memoir had not yet become the smooth, easily produced "cookie-cutter" genre that it became after the Second World War.

In the interwar years, women stopped apologizing. They asserted themselves. They spoke authoritatively. In the 1930s particularly, women produced big, substantial historical memoirs and semi-memoirs. On the whole these memoirists and semi-memoirists presented the past in a positive light. Aside from some nostalgia, which is most pronounced in the German writers who look back at their prewar childhoods, their writing is not emotive, for they are not confessing or seeking catharsis. Overall, they maintain distance from their subject. Confessional tidbits they care to divulge about themselves as children appear to have lost their sting with the passage of time. The narrators sometimes adopt the distancing devices of irony or humor. Although an occasional author— Abbott, Weiss—takes the opportunity to vent her feelings, as a rule, they do not express anger or self-pity, such as we saw it, for example, in Hannah Lynch's turn-of-the-century *Autobiography of a Child*.

The memoirs and semi-memoirs written by women in the interwar years were, on the whole, serious, carefully written works—works on which their authors had expended considerable effort, if not talent, and of which they could be proud. The works are presentable, uncontroversial. Without exception, the authors have positive things to say about their families, especially their parents, and most especially their mothers. The picture changes completely when one turns to the confessional autobiographies written in the same era—the main topic of the next chapter.

CHAPTER THREE

The Interwar Years: The Golden Age of Psychological Self-Portraiture

1921: Reuter (1859–1941)

1921: Séverine (1855–1929)

1925: Beasley (1892–1955)

1927–28: Gyp (1849–1932)

1930: Miegel (1879–1964)

1932: Noailles (1876–1933)

1932: Schieber (1867–1945)

1933: Luhan (1879–1962)

1934: Undset (1882–1949)

1935: Deland (1857–1945)

1936: Ishimoto (1897–2001)

1936: Waser (1878–1939)

1936: Whipple (1893–1966)

1937: Allinson (1902–1945)

1937: Butts (1890–1937)

1938: Ball-Hennings (1885–1948)

1939: Creston [Baynes] (1881–1973)

1939: Salverson (1890–1970)

Amid the autobiographical stories of childhood that women wrote for public consumption during the interwar years, the self-focused autobiographies are the works that most clearly reveal the changing norms of feminine self-presentation. Indeed, a handful of English-language works published in the 1930s give those norms an energetic push—over the fence, as it were—landing them in an exposed spot that, however, became the norm in the course of the 1940s and 1950s. Exploding the conventionally "safe" genre of childhood autobiography, their authors indulge in candor and indiscretion about themselves and others to an unprecedented degree.

In the 1920s Gabriele Reuter in Germany and Séverine and Gyp in France published works of the self-focused "my story" type, although the well-connected, socially conscious Gyp drifts from the confessional to the memoir mode. In 1925 the American Gertrude Beasley published a confessional work, extremely shocking for its day (and banned), which is weighted more heavily toward adolescence than childhood but is nevertheless interesting for its sexually oriented treatment of childhood. A subsequent American work of the "my story" type, Mabel Dodge Luhan's landmark *Intimate Memories: Background*—the title hints at its content—appeared in 1933. In the second half of the 1930s, self-focused, confessional, psychologically oriented autobiographical writing about childhood by women rapidly gained a foothold in the English-speaking countries. The widespread reception of psychoanalysis after World War I promoted such self-writing about childhood. Psychoanalysis not only underwrote the belief, fostered by late nineteenth-century child study, in the formative influence of early childhood and turned it into doctrine, but declared the emotional dramas of the earliest years to be the very substance of the unconscious. It became fashionable to recover memories and to analyze and talk to others about one's childhood.

By the mid-1930s a climate had been created in which more and more women were emboldened to write and publish "my own story," whether they were adherents of any of the various psychoanalytic schools or not. Luhan, who can count as seminal for the confessional English-language childhood autobiography, happened to be a devotee of Freudian psychoanalysis. Starting with the publication of her bold *Intimate Memories: Background*, confessional works started to be written in English that resemble those that were previously written in French. Works that tell "my story" are self-revelatory, frank, often indiscreet, and mainly long. They typically do not end with childhood, but carry the tale into the author's teens or even twenties when an event like career success brings closure. Such works include Mary Butts's *The Crystal Cabinet* (1937) and Laura Goodman Salverson's *Confessions of an Immigrant's Daughter* (1939), followed in the war years by Enid Starkie's *A Lady's Child* (1941) and in the immediate post–World War II period by Phyllis Bottome's *Search for a Soul* (1947) and Leonora Eyles's *The Ram Escapes* (1953). Luhan, Butts, and Salverson will be discussed in this chapter, Starkie in chapter 4, and Bottome and Eyles in chapter 5.

Concurrently in the 1930s, a handful of authors wrote a different sort of work, one that pursued the goal of recapturing the mental world of the child as they recall it. The focus in these works is not so much "me" as "the child." Often the writers downplay or even mildly obfuscate the autobiographical origin of the perceptions, as Joan Arden did in *A Childhood* (1913) by changing her siblings' names. Some works hover more or less explicitly between autobiography and fiction. These works are typically comparatively short. Authors include the English writers

Francesca Allinson (1937) and Dormer Creston (1939) and the German writers Agnes Miegel (1930) and Anna Schieber (1932). The Norwegian Sigrid Undset's *Elleve Aar* (Eleven years old, 1934) belongs to the type in many respects, though Undset writes a more ambitious and much longer work that aims to give the whole history of the young girl. The German Emmy Ball-Hennings also writes a longer autobiography of her childhood and youth, *Blume und Flamme* (Flower and flame, 1938), that relies on recreating the child's perspective.

Other authors insist, in contrast, on the vast distance between their adult self and the child they once were, whose inner life they nevertheless claim to remember sharply. The American author Margaret Deland (1935) sets out to penetrate rather than recapture her psychology as a young child and presents the results with more irony than sympathy. The Swiss author Maria Waser (1936) similarly analyzes her psychologically formative experiences from the perspective of an enlightened older adult. Both writers express great confidence in their powers of memory.

Self-Portraits in the 1920s

In the postwar decade, in France, Séverine and Gyp follow in the French confessional tradition and create self-portraits. In Germany, Gabriele Reuter wrote a confessional autobiography that is, at the same time, a developmental story.

Line (1855–1867) by Séverine (Caroline [Rémy] Guebhard) and *Souvenirs d'une petite fille* (Memories of a little girl) by Gyp (Sibylle Gabrielle Marie Antoinette de Riquetti de Mirabeau, comtesse de Martel de Janville) form an odd pair: both women were only children and both wrote long works about their unusual childhoods in their old age, but they were at opposite ends of the French political spectrum. Séverine (1855–1929), Gyp's junior by six years and the first of the two to publish her *récit d'enfance*, was the most famous French woman journalist of her day and a socialist, whereas Gyp, a prolific author of fiction, was a right-wing aristocrat and a self-proclaimed antisemite. There are nevertheless pronounced similarities between their childhoods, which reflect French customs and prejudices that extended from the aristocracy to the bourgeoisie. Both families initially isolate their daughters from contact with other children; both are at pains to educate them well and above all to teach them the proprieties; each girl's closest childhood attachment was to a loving grandparent (Séverine's to her maternal grandmother,

The Interwar Years: The Golden Age of Psychological Self-Portraiture 113

to whose memory she dedicates her book, Gyp's to her maternal grandfather); both speak the same childish, syllable-swallowing French (reproduced in the texts) and are rebuked for it; and both opt to confess childhood misdeeds by writing a letter to the authority in question instead of speaking directly. But there the similarities end.

Commentators sometimes call *Line (1855–1867)* (1921) an autobiography and sometimes an autobiographical novel. It identifies itself as neither. Line's birth date, 1855, is the author's birth date; Caroline Rémy (the author's birth name) is thinly disguised as Line Myre; Line's parents go by the fictitious names of Exupère and Atala, but otherwise fit the description of Caroline's parents. If judged an autobiography, the presentation is idiosyncratic. It is written in the third person. It transmits, through episodes, the portrait of a little girl who is stifled by her well-meaning bourgeois parents. The parents are intent on respectability and take for granted that they can mold their child to their will. Line, "a wild seed in the kitchen garden,"[1] is a free-thinking, rebellious child. She is also hungry for more affection than she gets. Séverine wrote this book in her midsixties, when both of her parents were long dead.

Why did Séverine not simply narrate in the first person? By 1921 there were only disparate examples of French childhood autobiographies written by women and no entrenched way of writing, though all the works were confessionally oriented. Nothing about this text suggests that Séverine was following any particular model, though her work shares outspokenness and a focus on self-portraiture with Judith Gautier's. But Gautier wrote in the first person. Séverine had a British predecessor in the use of the third person in a childhood autobiography, namely Burnett. But Séverine's work is otherwise very different from Burnett's. Unlike Burnett, Séverine makes no attempt to suggest that Line is a typical child (quite the contrary); although there is plenty of narratorial irony, very little of it is applied to her; and the dominant tone is not one of gentle humor, but rather one of pathos. With very few exceptions the narrator takes sides with her child self, supports her, sympathizes with her, defends her, and if need be, excuses her. She represents Line as a misunderstood child whose parents do not care about who she actually is but insist on making her conform to *their* ideals. In short, she is a victim. By the time she is a young adolescent she feels like a marionette who is told to do this and that. There is no strain of adult reflection here to the effect that some of the educational measures her parents took might have been worth something. Possibly the author chose the third person because such total self-sympathy in a first-person autobiography would have been awkward.

The narrator's typical mode of presentation is to recount "telling" stories—stories that frequently have an unstated point that it is up to the reader to "get." Concomitantly, she uses innuendo: her uncle becomes *too* interested in the milliner next door, and so forth. The episodes are chosen so as to illustrate her character and the clash between her character and her upbringing. A first set of episodes all have the point of showing how an innately candid, trusting, loving child loses innocence and is disappointed. To illustrate her loneliness: she snuggles with a pillow. To illustrate her good character: she nearly strangles a boy who tortures a bird and attacks a woodcutter for chopping down a tree. Yet the narrator also makes a terrible confession: she tortured and killed a toad. But she follows this up by stating that she tried to make amends later by saving many toads. To illustrate disappointment: her parents promise her an animal; it turns out to be a fish. When she finally gets the red balloon she longs for, her parents force her to let it go. Later in her childhood, the clashes grow worse. She wants to study drawing, so—she comments bitterly—her parents oblige her to learn the piano.

There are some lighter moments, where the narrator connives with the reader: Line tries to run away to the saltimbanques, but they say they have quite enough children; she tries to reason with her newborn baby brother, instructing him not to make such messes. But mainly the narrator represents, without levity, and with pathos, the child's point of view at a given moment. Thus, for example, her child self hates her first school, because she is separated from her beloved grandmother; she cries at night and even attempts suicide. But then she suffers tremendously because she changes schools—at which point it is mentioned that she had gotten used to the first school. In the next episode, she is reconciled to the second school because the headmistress recommends that she grow her hair. Her feelings in each case are presented with the utmost sympathy; no narratorial voice intervenes to comment on how quickly or on the basis of how trivial an event her attachments change.

Séverine predominantly employs the technique of characterization through revelatory episodes. But she also sometimes says things about her character directly, or about her parents (namely, that they are bourgeois). Thus, she tells us that she cannot be like everyone else and expects to be loved for what she is. She is proud and timid. She is incapable of

The Interwar Years: The Golden Age of Psychological Self-Portraiture 115

dissimulating, hence too of the arts of eliciting sympathy and affection in others. She is not extroverted like other children. Later she stresses her subversiveness. She is always secretly hoping for something to happen that would horrify her appearance-conscious parents. To illustrate this point, she tells us that she hopes a burglar will steal objects she doesn't like from her home. She truly seems to be the relatively unusual kind of child who questions everything, who never just accepts what others tell her. But consonant with the French autobiographical tradition, she does not present herself as a type, but rather as a unique individual. Her book straightforwardly memorializes her.

This profoundly complaining book shares certain themes with other women's childhood autobiographies. There is the theme of learning to read, of books, and of their importance for her. Like Burnett, she touches on the perfidiousness of grown-ups. For instance, her doll sheds hair, and she finds her with her hair removed. Her father denies the misdeed, and she thinks her parents lied. She expostulates to her grandmother, "Parents—they lie! Papa lied!" (26). Religion is among her topics: she doesn't understand why she should fear God if He is good. Like every Catholic child she is confused on the occasion of her first confession. She is given a printed questionnaire a dozen pages long with seven chapters for the seven capital sins, each described in great detail—a wealth of possible sins that she had never suspected. In the end, she decides to accuse herself of adultery.

Line scarcely reflects on what it means to grow up as a girl specifically, but it does finally dawn on her that she would have more freedom if she were a boy. She compares her "crime" of running away from boarding school (for which she is punished) to her uncle's jumping the wall of his barracks, about which her father used to laugh. The narrator writes: "Such severity compared to so much indulgence—so it's because he was a boy and because she's only a girl? . . . She also guesses, prematurely, at the antagonism of the sexes, the so insanely unequal allotment of rights and duties, freedoms and servitudes, absolutions and excommunications! And it makes her indignant; revolt takes possession of her young spirit" (354).

Séverine barely narrates in the past tense. She writes in the present tense and uses lots of dialogue, apparently so as to make scenes vivid to the reader. Her stories have wit but lack psychological finesse. Because she is intent on making points, she overwrites, overstylizes, overstorifies. Thus, as the story of a life, this one lacks verisimilitude.

Pathos is overdone. For example, Séverine pities her lonely childhood self in the following terms when her parents show affection to another young woman: "So they [her parents] didn't sense how much their own child needed these outward expressions that are like the music, light, and warmth of deep feelings? To be reduced to cuddling her cheek against the backs of armchairs to give herself the illusion of a caress; to murmur to herself, with an altered voice so as better to deceive herself, words that she'd heard used to cajole other kids; to dream day and night of a tender, cheerful intimacy, devoid of formality, stripped of rigor—and to see another girl embraced, cherished, pampered!" (256).

While the narrator of *Line* is somewhat irritating, it is hard not to sympathize with the child. Hers is the paradigmatic story of an intelligent, independently minded only child who is suffocated by possessive, uninsightful parents. Her childhood does seem truly wretched. Her parents read her correspondence. They confiscate and interrogate her about her journal. A scene with her father when she is eleven sums the situation up. In her journal she had written, "What woman would not accept death on condition that she were loved like Juliet?" Her father confronts her with this. She sobs, "I want to live! I want to live! . . . see woods, sunshine, breathe, sing!—I want to live!" (284).

The other French childhood autobiographer of the 1920s, the prolific novelist Gyp, starts her childhood memoirs, *Souvenirs d'une petite fille* (1927–28), which she wrote at age seventy-four, with a classic feminine demurral. Through her dedication to Philippe Barrès she immediately makes known that she is writing her recollections of childhood, which she asserts are probably of little interest to anyone but herself, at the request of someone else, namely Barrès's father, Maurice Barrès. Other initial narrative moves are similarly classic. She engages the topic of memory in a manner that shows no acquaintance with the new psychoanalytical ideas: she avers that she remembers events incredibly well, though out of order. She begins her story with "I was born." She was born, she says, on August 15, 1849, in Brittany (where she was apparently placed with a nurse in her infancy, as was the custom). In reality, according to her birth certificate she was born on August 16, 1849, but she nevertheless claims here and throughout her life that she was born on August 15, like her idol Napoleon Bonaparte.[2]

At a later stage of the narrative she tells a great deal about her family, including her parents' divorce when she was one year old. Initially, however, she sticks to her recollections of her infancy and is at pains to

The Interwar Years: The Golden Age of Psychological Self-Portraiture 117

render events exactly as she perceived them then. A major turning point occurred when she was age two and one-half or three: she was relocated from Brittany to the garrison city of Nancy (Lorraine), home to a sizable military colony, where her family (her maternal grandparents and her mother) lived and where she spent the remainder of her childhood. Her first recollections involve her old Breton nurse and another nurse who accompanied her to Lorraine. Gyp tries to give a sense of the fogginess of her infantile recollections and her childish perspective on things. Thus, having been put in a "box," she winds up in the presence of someone with a blonde moustache and a lady with pretty hands (her grandparents), and a personage who insists that she call her "petite mère" instead of "maman," and she is introduced to the agreeable Jeannette, her new maid. The author's attempt to retain her childhood point of view sits oddly with her penchant for rendering her memories as dialogues. Although the rendition of memories as dialogues does not satisfy the reader's sense of plausibility, Gyp nevertheless crafts these dialogues in such a way that they become a tool for preserving a sense of things as the child registered them. Thus, in her own responses, she reproduces her own childish, lazy, syllable-dropping way of speaking. Gyp's other stylistic device is a copious use of the present tense.

At age three, Sibylle does not yet talk, but she does have recollections of her life prior to the age of three, and it becomes clear that she has already internalized language, namely Breton. She would have been capable of speaking, but chooses not to. The narrator's theory is that she realized, vaguely, that to talk would mean lifting the curtain between herself and others. Thus, she represents herself as wary and private from an early age. When she arrives in Nancy, "Bonne maman" (apparently her great-grandmother) literally whips her into speaking. Under the blows, she cries out in Breton, to the horror of her family. The scene epitomizes the principal conflict in her upbringing, a conflict between her own inclinations and others' expectations. As to language, she retained a lasting ambivalence over her fidelity to her first language and the French the others expected her to speak.

Gyp came from an aristocratic family on both sides and even had a famous surname (Mirabeau). These factors made her childhood unusual in a number of respects. For a start, her family wished she had been born a boy. They were disappointed that the illustrious family name of Mirabeau would die out with her. This disappointment is shared by her mother's as well as her father's families, but is mainly conveyed to her by her grandfather, a royalist colonel, her great favorite among her relatives, her constant companion and first teacher, and indeed the person charged with bringing her up according to her parents' divorce settlement. Complicating her self-image, this man whom she so likes and admires gives her lead soldiers to play with, and so it is no wonder that her childish tastes and aspirations run to the military. But her grandfather assures her, disappointedly, that because she is a girl, she will never go to war as she aspires to do. Gyp always vehemently denied being a feminist, but she does convey to the reader the sense of inadequacy that was instilled in her because she was a daughter and not a son. She heard it said over and over that it is too bad she is not a boy.

An only child, she has no friends up to the age of ten. That is the way her family wants it. She spends a lot of her time playing between four mirrors, which multiply her. But for a girl, mirrors are treacherous. People remark in her presence that she is not pretty, in fact more like a frog in appearance, and she herself scrutinizes, criticizes, and dislikes her appearance in these mirrors. Yet she vehemently resists feminization: she suffers under heavy curled hair until a sympathetic boy cousin chops it off for her, and she rebels against getting her ears pierced.

Gyp progresses rapidly in her narrative up to the age of ten, after which her account becomes more like a memoir. Increasingly, she describes her encounters with other people and what they are like. In contrast to her renditions of her early memories, these descriptions are not crafted so as to preserve the child's perspective. As in Louise Weiss's case, the baggy title "Souvenirs" accommodates a memoir as well as a focus on the self—though in Gyp's case, the self-focused part and the memoirs are sequential. Over three-quarters of Gyp's 605-page, two-volume book covers her life between ages ten and fourteen. She takes her story just beyond her first communion, when she is nearly fourteen, and wraps it up with two contrasting final events after her fourteenth birthday: she and an accomplice throw water out of the window onto passers-by (a prank that testifies that she is still a child); and a strange soldier approaches her on the street and asks her to dinner (testifying that she no longer looks like a child).

Before she is sent to a convent day school at age eleven, Gyp's childhood is packed with private lessons in academic subjects and also in ballet, violin, and piano. She does not state it in so many words, but her narrative shows that much of her education consisted in instilling in her the importance of appearance and manners. She absorbs social

The Interwar Years: The Golden Age of Psychological Self-Portraiture 119

instruction and a sense of social taboos without much question. If she worries, it is about not losing face and embarrassing herself or her family by doing the wrong thing or presenting the wrong appearance. She remembers and replicates with relish precise details about people's appearance and clothes.

What about her? The personality she sketches of herself is distinct but also quite ambivalent. Thus, she adores the military, yet, in an astonishing admission, "I'd like other people to lead. I detest decisions, reflections, things I have to be responsible for."[3] This is a facet of her personality she sticks to: of her later self, when she is in convent school, she says, "I would have passionately wished to be a boy, but in this case, I would have confined my ambitions to becoming a soldier—without stripes—in a cavalry regiment. The idea of having to lead frightens me. . . . I like everything that lets me act while I think about other things, without responsibilities, without preoccupations of any sort" (2: 130). Yet she does have strong opinions; if there is one aspect of her personality that she works to bring out through her choice of episodes, it is her independence of mind. She is an imperialist in a family of royalists, digs in her heels when it comes to doing things she doesn't want to do, such as having her ears pierced (though she ultimately gives in), and spontaneously condemns her father for shooting a bird. She dislikes discipline, and she resembles virtually every other female childhood autobiographer sent to convent school in disliking the rigid rules and rote learning practiced there. She plays one significant childhood prank, in cahoots with a friend, repeatedly squirting water into a military office. As the protected and cherished only child that she is, she is unafraid of being punished by her family. Her behavior shows that she senses that she can do no wrong and that her family will always forgive her. Being the young aristocrat that she is, she cannot fall very far.

Both Séverine and Gyp recall that very early in life, before adolescence, having been born female caused them to suffer. The disaster that coming of age means for a woman is the story Gabriele Reuter tells in her Bildungsroman-style autobiography *Vom Kinde zum Menschen* (From the child to the person, 1921).

How I Became What I Became

Gabriele Reuter, famous in her day for her novels about the problems of middle-class women, is the first woman writer to frame her autobiography of childhood and youth as the story of how she became a successful writer. Frances Hodgson Burnett told the reader how the "Small Person" got her first stories published, but Reuter's *Vom Kinde zum Menschen: Die Geschichte meiner Jugend* (From the child to the person: The story of my youth) foregrounds her vocation and career much more pointedly. Whereas Burnett writes with a light touch and at third-person distance from herself, Reuter's work is long, serious, detailed, and confessional. With its focus on telling the story of the prominent person she became, her work anticipates by decades the comparable autobiographies of childhood and youth by Leonora Eyles and Simone de Beauvoir (discussed in chapter 5). Looking back at her life from the vantage point of her early sixties, Reuter adopts the "autobiography of a famous person" model—which is essentially a male model—that George Sand introduced into the sphere of women's life writing and that Juliette Adam continued. Reuter combines the recollective and psychological style of Sand with the teleological mode of Adam. "How I became a writer" forms an important theme throughout the narrative, which Reuter chooses to end with the publication of her first successful novel, *Aus guter Familie* (*From a Good Family*, 1895), when she was in her midthirties.

For a woman of Reuter's era, it can well be imagined that progress toward a successful career as a novelist was hardly linear. On the contrary, it was beset by difficulties and ambivalence. From age thirteen, Reuter had to care for her widowed mother. Dreams of romance and later a desire for motherhood distracted her from her ambition to be a writer. This work has its teleological red thread, yet it also covers the broad flow of Reuter's life. Her life is always at the center of the story, but she had a huge extended family, and she pauses to characterize her relatives and tell their stories. She also gives a rich picture of the times and the places where she lived, in particular Egypt, where her father had a business. Although not as digressive as Sand and better organized, Reuter produced an autobiography of childhood and youth of ample proportions, nearly 500 pages long, interspersed with photos and illustrations, and narrated at a leisurely pace.

Like Sand and Adam, Reuter follows a chronological order. The work is divided into two parts, the "Book of the Child" and the slightly longer "Book of the Girl." Each book is divided into titled chapters. Throughout, Reuter carefully gives dates. The "Book of the Child" begins with her ancestors and ends with her father's death when she is thirteen—an event that, as she states explicitly, brought her happy childhood to a close. The red thread in the "Book of the Girl," which ends with the story of her first literary success, is the story of how she became a professional writer. In the usage of the day, an unmarried woman was still a girl or "Mädchen," which explains how Reuter can use that title for a segment of her life that ends in her midthirties.

Stylistically, this autobiography of childhood and youth is all of a piece. Its style does not change as Reuter grows up. The work is narrated retrospectively from the present of writing, and the past is presented as remembered. Yet Reuter "remembers" a lot of passion and feeling and uses novelistic devices to render it. There are brief passages in interior monologue. Most noticeable is the representation of the passions in bodily metaphors, reminiscent of such works as C. M. Wieland's *Agathon*, J. W. von Goethe's *Werther*, and German Romanticism generally (e.g., "a suffocating ring wrapped itself more and more tightly around my chest and pressed my heart until I felt as if I had a red gaping wound in my chest . . ."[4]). The novelist Reuter presses her life into novelistic forms, including that of the Bildungsroman.

Throughout the work, the present-day writer pauses to give her opinions. She is noticeably interested in dark psychic undercurrents. She mentions "psycho-analysis" (255) but in a distanced way, opining that she thinks it encourages people to focus too much on their inner darkness, whereas the Christian confessional offered people more. Another noteworthy excursus concerns the difference between a mother's love for her child and a child's love for her mother.

The "Book of the Child" focuses on the development of an imaginative girl under what Reuter believes were optimal conditions: her parents were understanding, loving, and generous, and the years spent in Egypt as well as foreign travel broadened her worldview, saving her from the fate of the typical cloistered German daughter of her social class: "In the constant, pleasurably chatty exchanges of trivia with the other schoolgirls, I would probably have become the superficial creature that, tastefully dressed, pretty to look at, and molded by conventional books, is called a 'lady'" (93). The narrative here has an enthusiastic tone—she paints her childhood and youth in bright, appreciative colors, despite bad moments. As she says, "My childhood was a fairy tale full of good things" (51). She loves her parents and mainly gets along fine with her four younger brothers. Throughout the book, she emphasizes positive aspects, even though the story of her life goes sorely downhill in "The Book of the Girl." In contrast to Séverine, who was expected to conform to a repressive bourgeois mold from the start, and to Gyp, who was early on made to feel her family's disappointment in her sex and looks, Reuter's problems do not start in childhood, but at age thirteen, when her father died.

Her father's death was a terrible financial blow to the family. Her widowed mother of five failed to recover any capital from her husband's business, and so the well-off family of the "Book of the Child" became an impoverished family in the "Book of the Girl." For this reason along with many others, young womanhood for Reuter seems like a letdown. From the age of fourteen on she was burdened with family responsibilities, including, increasingly, the need to take care of her mother. She writes about how clothes were a constant problem for her, because she had no money to buy any. She complains, "In a woman's life, clothes can decide your fate" (295). The "clothes problem" will become a leitmotif in autobiographies of childhood and youth written by women of slender means, such as those by Enid Starkie (discussed in chapter 4) and Leonora Eyles (discussed in chapter 5).

Gabriele's desire to find a man who loves her—something that does not happen in the course of the book—is an important thread alongside that of writing. She develops a crush on one of her cousins, only to find out that he is in love with someone else. She then becomes fixated on an artist whom she has never met and for years cherishes a secret, unrequited passion for him. She goes through periods of depression and apathy. She writes that at age twenty-three, "I was appalled at the emptiness of my future" (351). When she sees her cousin some years later married and with a baby, her reaction is, "My God! For one of these adorable babies, I would have sacrificed all the novels in the world and certainly my own present and future works" (365). Reuter in fact became the single mother of a daughter two years after publishing *Aus guter Familie*, but she does not mention this in her autobiography.

As a woman, Reuter has a hard time breaking into literary circles. She tells how she is feted at a literary congress—but only because the men mistake her for someone else, for the daughter of the artistic director of the Weimar theater. She recognizes that she has become, by age thirty, "an utterly . . . insignificant old maid" (412). Life seems to be going nowhere. When she submits the novel that will make her famous to her male colleagues in the hope of eliciting a discussion, they think it is just about sex and make obscene remarks. Her decision to write an autobiography in which she tells how she became a famous novelist

The Interwar Years: The Golden Age of Psychological Self-Portraiture   123

must be seen as an expression of triumph. Despite sacrifices and struggles, she can claim success.

As a woman's life, Reuter's anticipates the lives of some much younger women who published their stories after World War II, Leonora Eyles and Simone de Beauvoir. In all three cases, a decline in family fortunes forces an initially well-off middle-class girl to think about a way to earn her own living. In Reuter's case, her well-to-do family, with servants and governesses, suddenly became poor. But on the heels of the realization that her father's death has impoverished them, near the beginning of the "Book of the Girl," follows an epiphany in which Reuter realizes that her vocation is to be a writer:

> In truth—I would not write little stories for the young—I'd write completely different things. I knew that from that moment on, and no misfortune, no laborious years of apprenticeship would ever rob me of this knowledge, of this exquisite confidence in the profession I was made for. . . . It had come over me like a sudden marvelous illumination that, so to speak, bathed my soul in a rainbow gleam and lifted it out of the black clouds of worry that were trying to shroud it into a high heavenly atmosphere of lightness, courage, and divine fire . . . (193)

Even before this moment, Reuter weaves a red thread into the narrative of her life that has to do with writing. It is foretold at her birth that she will write books, and from time to time people praise her storytelling gifts.

Reuter's work is quite an emotional striptease, especially with its story of unrequited love. But then, the psychological conflicts suffered by bourgeois women is the topic of the novels for which Reuter became famous. In her early thirties she had the revelation that her topic should be the sufferings of such women: "And suddenly I knew why I existed—to tell what girls and women silently suffered" (432). She takes pains to clarify that her first successful novel, *Aus guter Familie*, is not her own story, for, as she writes, she grew up under more favorable circumstances than the typical German girl of her time. She insists that her own story is the story of the development of an artist. So she distances herself from her heroine, who falls in love with the wrong man, then fails to marry for lack of a dowry, recoils from a last romantic attachment because she can't accept the double standard, and finally goes mad. Yet

124   The Interwar Years: The Golden Age of Psychological Self-Portraiture

telling the public that she suffered in some of the same ways as her heroines adds to the credibility of her novels, while the public recognition she received for her revelations about the feminine psyche in those novels smooths the way for her personal revelations. Her autobiographical tribulations and those of her heroines mutually validate each other.

In Your Face

Despite the relatively small number of pages she devotes to childhood (approximately one-sixth of the book covers her life from ages four to ten, another sixth takes her to age thirteen), Gertrude Beasley's book *My First Thirty Years* (1925) deserves to be mentioned because it is a radical harbinger of things to come. It is barely comprehensible that a woman, and moreover one who grew up poor in the Texas Bible Belt, should have published such an angry, extraordinarily confessional, family-maligning, sex-drenched memoir at the early date of 1925. From the first sentence Beasley, who was in her early thirties when she wrote the book, means to shock. Her first memory—she was around four at the time—is of her older brothers holding her down while one of them attempts to have sexual intercourse with her. Nowhere in the book does she have anything good to say about the experience of growing up as one of thirteen children in an uneducated family in rural Texas. She writes of her father's drunkenness and brutality, her mother's complaints and suspicions, their divorce, and her entire family's stupidity and coarseness. She was, as she keeps saying, deeply ashamed of them from an early age—even though she came to pity her mother. She tried to help her, agreeing with her that life had given her a raw deal. If such writing about one's family were not shocking enough, Beasley dwells in a rather obsessive way on the indecencies, including incest and bestiality, perpetrated by her siblings from as early as she can remember, sometimes pausing to note her own sexual responsiveness to this or that talk or action. Her themes are sex, fear, and shame. Such an exposé, such an outpouring, and above all such a focus on sexuality comes out of the blue in the history of women's published autobiographical writing about childhood. One confirmed influence on Beasley was the sexologist Havelock Ellis. Beasley mentions him in the narrative, and Bert Almon, who has researched Beasley's "case" extensively, discovered that Ellis read her manuscript and suggested she publish it with a certain avant-garde Paris publishing house.[5]

Beasley, a self-made woman, struggled out of her unpromising background in Texas to become a highly educated, articulate socialist and even more so, feminist. She received a BA from Simmons College and a MA from the University of Chicago. Intelligent and thirsty for education, at age seventeen she was strongly drawn to socialism above all because it called for women's rights. She was delighted by Margaret Sanger and Emma Goldman and organized meetings for the Woman's Party in Chicago in 1916. She mentions reading Bertrand Russell, who helped her when she went to England, and William James. After a stint as a schoolteacher she took off for foreign countries. Both her book and her life ended badly. Scotland Yard confiscated her proofs on grounds of obscenity, so her book could not be distributed in England. US Customs confiscated as many of the copies sent to the United States as it found. Very few people are believed to have read it, since it had been published in a print run of only 500 copies and most of these were destroyed. As for her, letters written in 1927 testify to mental instability,[6] likely paranoia. Thereafter, she disappeared. Only in 2008 did researchers discover that she had been committed to a mental institution in New York State ten days after her ship landed in New York, where she remained institutionalized until her death at age sixty-three.[7]

Self-Expression in the 1930s

By the mid-1930s, childhood autobiography had become a genre in which a woman could publish as a matter of course. In France, where self-focused work had long flourished, it is not surprising to see a prominent society woman with literary pretensions, Anna de Noailles, publish a self-focused account of her glitzy childhood in the first volume of *Le livre de ma vie* (The book of my life) in 1932—further volumes having been cut short by her death in 1933. In the United States, Baroness Shidzué Ishimoto, a Japanese woman with considerable Western experience, acquaints an American readership with a girl's upbringing and a woman's life in Japan's samurai caste in *East Way, West Way: A Modern Japanese Girlhood* (1935) through an account of her own life up to her marriage at age eighteen. In England, Dorothy Whipple's *The Other Day* (1936) illustrates how rapidly women's self-writing about childhood had come to be taken for granted. Despite its title, the work is not a semi-memoir that commemorates the good old days, nor does it take the psychological turn, yet it nonetheless conforms strictly to the concept "autobiography of childhood." Although she is the second child in a large family, Whipple writes not a "we"-style autobiography, but a true autobiography about herself, "Dorothy." Her childhood in Blackburn, Lancashire, was not remarkable, yet she cuts her story off at age twelve with the stated intention of confining herself to childhood. She dispenses with all justification for writing. Thus, Whipple settles into her genre of childhood autobiography as if it were utterly self-understood for a woman to write one without ado.

The implicit justification for *The Other Day* lies in the fact that Whipple, a popular fiction author, can tell a good story. This autobiography, which is written like a novel, is highly entertaining and often comical, even sometimes hilarious. It takes the form of a sequence of noteworthy episodes that successfully incorporate the child's point of view. True, a note of bitterness runs through it. Whipple represents herself as often embarrassed or shamed or hurt. By writing her book, not in old age but in her early forties, she appears to be taking the classic writer's revenge of exposing the people who embarrassed, shamed, or hurt her. Perhaps the worst indignity she suffered is being unjustly accused by her English teacher of having plagiarized a story she had written and felt proud of. Taken together with Eleanor Abbott's work (discussed in chapter 2), which was published in the same year and whose light tone turns serious and confessional in the end, it makes one wonder about the humorous or witty tone that English-language women writers sometimes adopt. Does it function as a safe veneer that authors imagine allows them to bring deeper and less pleasant matters into the light of day? Other aspects of this book also recall Abbott. Whipple, too, mainly gets along well with parents and siblings, but caricatures them somewhat, though her satire is benevolent. As in Abbott, there is plenty of self-irony in this book. For example, she describes how church and Bible class stultify her, yet, when she is sent to a high-class convent school, she embraces Catholic life with gusto, to the point of changing her behavior and her diction, although she is not Catholic. Like Abbott, Whipple brings in gender issues. She is not subjected to a highly gendered upbringing, but where she encounters such a thing, she resists: at one school "they were too anxious to make young ladies of us,"[8] and the unequal division of labor at home makes her fume: "Why should girls always *set tables*?" (196).

Self-Assertion

Women's autobiographies of childhood or childhood and youth that tell "my story" appeared on the English-language scene in the interwar

The Interwar Years: The Golden Age of Psychological Self-Portraiture 127

years and especially starting in the mid-1930s. They form a brilliant, varied collection of foundational major works. The accent in these works falls variously on self-portraiture, confession, child psychology, capturing the child's mode of perception, and the development of the girl into the adult. Some authors envisage more than one of these agendas and combine them to create complex, multifaceted works. How are these postwar works different from the types of childhood autobiography that women wrote before the war? Before World War I, we saw that French works generally adopted a confessional stance (Sand, Michelet, Adam, Gautier) and that some aimed at creating self-portraits (Adam, Gautier). We saw an English work that investigated child psychology and also tracked the author's development into a successful writer (Burnett). We saw another English work that aimed to recreate the child's perception of the world as the adult remembered it (Arden). All of these kinds of agendas persisted in works written in the interwar years. What, then, is new? Above all, women's outspokenness is new. After the war, women became extremely forthright in stating what they thought. They write in a way that reveals a sense of personal importance. Most abandon the habit of self-justification that their elders had established and write the stories of their childhoods without apology. They start to turn up the volume, to express their opinions publicly and emphatically. Confession acquired new depths. If a woman wrote confessionally, she felt free to reveal much more about herself and her relationships with others than women had before the war. At the same time, in a day when the reception of psychoanalysis had become widespread, childhood autobiography was swept up in a tidal wave of interest in psychology. Works that tell the author's childhood story without foregrounding psychological aspects became the exception. Finally, feminist ideas started to make themselves heard. As we have seen, American first-wave feminist Gertrude Beasley splattered sexuality onto the page with her angry, rebellious work *My First Thirty Years*. Promptly banned for obscenity in Britain and the United States, her book is slanted toward adolescence and young adulthood rather than childhood and cannot strictly be considered a childhood autobiography. But with its confessional tone, insistence on childhood sexual experiences, and feminism, it anticipates women's childhood autobiographies of the 1930s and beyond.

The self-focused works written in the 1930s have the earnestness and seriousness of the semi-memoirs of the same era, but they are much more daring. Mabel Dodge Luhan's *Intimate Memories: Background* (1933), Mary Butts's *The Crystal Cabinet* (1937), and Laura Goodman Salverson's

Confessions of an Immigrant's Daughter (1939) are the boldest works of the decade. Written by an American, an English, and a Canadian woman respectively, they veer abruptly away from the norms of English-language women's childhood autobiography and toward confession, the classic preserve of the French. These long, self-centered works are more indiscreet, more self-revelatory, more outspoken, and also more acid than any other such works published to date—with the exception, of course, of Beasley's, but Beasley's was not read. As a general rule, the more a work is intended as a personal, developmental story, the likelier the author is to extend her account beyond childhood. Accordingly, none of these three works end with the end of childhood. All find a later stopping point. Luhan ends this first volume of her autobiography with her coming-out ball at age eighteen; Butts ends hers at the beginning of World War I, when she was in her midtwenties; and Salverson, intent on showing how she realized her ambition to become a writer, carries her story forward until the completion of her first book when she was in her early thirties.

From the mid-1930s onward, women's childhood autobiography recentered itself around psychology. These three works are cases in point. Luhan's psychoanalytically inspired work does so most strikingly. Her *Intimate Memories: Background* (1933) marks a turn toward a new kind of feminine childhood autobiography in English. It is a confessional autobiography such as hitherto encountered only in France and in Gabriele Reuter, but it is more confessional, more outspoken, and more indiscreet than any of its European predecessors. The author writes of her early erotic experiences, which, moreover, are with women; she speaks her mind about her parents, raking her mother, who was still living, over the coals; she writes about her relatives and discloses their intrigues, in particular producing an unforgettable sketch of her domineering rich maternal grandmother Cook; and she gives candid portraits of her friends and teachers. As in the French tradition from Sand onward, her child self is at the center. Hers is a developmental story, which she endows with a plot: she wants to escape the barren middle-class life her parents offered her and live life to the fullest. We have seen this plot before in Séverine's *Line*. Arguably, a work like Luhan's could only be written by someone conversant with the French tradition, which Luhan certainly was; by an adherent of psychoanalysis—she was the leading popularizer of Freud of her time in the United States; and by someone who had little to fear in terms of reprisals. Luhan was a wealthy, well-connected,

The Interwar Years: The Golden Age of Psychological Self-Portraiture

famous, indeed notorious woman who had made a career of trampling on conventions by the time she wrote her autobiography. She had very little to fear. Some said, however, that the publication of her autobiography hastened or even precipitated her mother's death.[9]

Mabel Dodge Luhan, née Mabel Ganson, was a leading symbol of the New Woman. She broke with her rich, respectable background to elope at age twenty-one with a young man of whom her father disapproved. Both before and after her husband's untimely death she had a string of affairs, and after his death she married three more husbands, two of whom she divorced. She established a salon in Florence, consorting with the European avant-garde, and then a famous salon for radicals, progressive reformers, and artists in Greenwich Village from 1913 to 1916 before starting an artists' colony in Taos, New Mexico, in 1919, where she eventually married her fourth husband, a Native American. In her Greenwich Village years, she embarked on psychoanalysis twice, first in 1915 and again in 1916 with A. A. Brill, the head of the psychoanalytic movement in America. Brill explained Freudian concepts to her. In 1917 she became a syndicated advice columnist for the Hearst chain and turned into one of Freud's earliest popularizers. Encouraged in her project by D. H. Lawrence, she decided to write her memoirs as a form of therapy, for the sake of what Freud called "abreaction." She wrote four volumes of them, of which *Background* is the first. She decided to publish them so as to show others with "guilty, intimate childhood memories" that "theirs was a common and almost universal experience." All of the volumes sold well. *Background* sold 2,699 copies, but it was the only volume that reviewers praised.[10]

Background is a brilliant, extraordinarily well-written piece of psychological, social, and self-analysis. Luhan's organization is a familiar one: she organizes her chapters by themes, yet tells her story in rough chronological order, from the time she was a child in the nursery until she came out as a debutante at age eighteen. She devotes three-quarters of this 317-page book to her preadolescent years. In psychoanalytic fashion, she attempts to explain her life through her childhood. We hear about her fantasies, fears, games, indignation at a false accusation, hurt feelings, exaltations, gaffes, her teenage crush on a teacher, and so forth. Supremely confident in her opinions, she writes from the standpoint of one who knows what's what. She is, as she states in the foreword, a grandmother: she was in her fifties when her book was published. A masterly, analytic narrator whose voice is ever-present, she delivers her story precisely as she has come to look on it. She begins in the first chapter by giving a scathing description of the richer, western district of Buffalo, where her childhood home was located, in 1880. According to the opinionated narrator, society there was empty, sterile, and superficial. People gossiped about other people but never talked about their own feelings. Nothing ever happened. "From very earliest days in Buffalo any accidental heightening of feeling was welcome."[11] The way Luhan, an only child, feels about her childhood recalls Line's sentiments about hers. But already in this first chapter an anticipatory psychoanalytic note is struck when Luhan implies that this is a landscape of sheer repression: inside the fine houses somebody hangs himself, "naked except for a pair of white gloves" (14); someone else goes insane and is taken to the insane asylum. In the second chapter she recounts an early erotic experience that excites her greatly and thereby contrasts sharply with the dullness of her everyday life. Having witnessed a servant press milk out of her breast, she lures another servant to sleep with her and fondles, tries to drink from, and pummels her breast in great excitement for a long time while the woman sleeps.

Luhan describes the family home as filled with meaningless expensive things. Its atmosphere, for her, is symbolized by the rigidly arranged flowers in the round front flower bed. She considers both her parents, but especially her father, to have been very unhappy. Her father is a lawyer and the son of a banker but does not work; she believes he mainly reads novels. His terrible temper is fueled by jealousy of his wife. The narrator judges him as a fundamentally kind person who cannot stand his empty life. Her mother is "obstinate, repressed, and unloving" (35), a cold, sphinxlike woman seemingly without an inner life, who runs the household and controls the servants. She sounds a great deal like Athénaïs Michelet's mother. Outwardly Mabel's mother is quite busy. Yet on Sunday mornings, when she has time to think, she cries. On the positive side, she is "courageous, inflexible, and independent, and at times very generous" (35). Her mother's wealthy parents, the Cooks of New York, bought the house for the couple. This rich husband and wife do not love each other. Each has a dog on which he or she dotes. Mabel is the only child. In her "safe" nursery she calculates that her parents won't divorce, because people didn't divorce in those days. But everyone in the family is lonely, and she is no exception.

The book's message is that Mabel the child longs for life, excitement, sensation, and freedom. The adult narrator underwrites these desires as natural human ones that she will retain throughout her life, the difference being that when she is an adult, she will be able to act on them. Money is something she takes for granted and does not value: "Money has never meant anything at all to me" (147). She calls the experiences she desires "real." "Real" is her supreme value, opposed to all she finds phony and lifeless in human existence. Likewise, she finds people "real" (or "not real"), objects "real" (meaning that they have a life-enhancing value) or "not real." As a child she is mainly bored, afraid of having nothing to do all by herself in the nursery.

Luhan examines her everyday childhood occupations with an eye to discovering how they reveal her nature and predict her future. She says little about gender or femininity in this book, yet, influenced by psychoanalytic ideas about the differences between the sexes, she plainly holds girls to be different: she opines, for example, that they are not self-starters, but need someone else to take the initiative. Thus, as a child she pines for excitement and freedom, but she is stuck with a sluggish nursemaid and does not know how to get these things, except, for example, by kicking over the structures she builds out of blocks. The narrator thinks this childhood solution of hers is portentous. Psychoanalytic influence also makes itself felt in her narrative attitude. Whereas she represents herself as stifled, like Séverine, she does not, in contrast to Séverine, become her child self's sympathetic advocate, nor does she construe herself as a victim. To be sure, she deplores the boredom all around her, and she sympathizes with herself as a bored only child. But beyond that, she is cold and unsentimental toward herself, recognizing her destructiveness, will to power, hatreds, and inventive badness. She observes that she likes activities that bring her power. She recalls how she enjoyed dominating one of her little friends, an unhappy girl whose stepmother disfavored her. Certain cruel behaviors were her idea. She goes so far as to push a new nurse whom she dislikes off the cliff at the seaside, intending to murder her, and feels no regret. She blithely and impenitently plays pranks, such as stealing the house numbers off houses. In this analytical and unsentimental stance toward her childhood self, the childhood autobiographers Deland and Butts, who published in the next few years, resemble her. What all of this signifies is that in the era of psychoanalysis, it was no longer permissible to suggest that a child is an innocent angel. Instead, it was becoming de rigueur to deliver a frank image that recognized the child as an egocentric and willful, if not also an already sexual creature.

132   The Interwar Years: The Golden Age of Psychological Self-Portraiture

Luhan is highly attentive to sexuality. Like Sigrid Undset in the same era, whose work will be discussed under "The Child's Vision" below, she notices the sexuality latent in various interchanges. She describes her attraction to women and her sexual encounters with women as a child and teenager. Her consistent focus of interest is the breast. Sent to boarding school at the behest of wealthy Grandma Cook, who thought she needed discipline, she made friends with a girl fresh from France, Mary Shillito, who in turn idolized her older sister Violet as a superior being. Mabel subsequently met Violet in Paris and found her truly to be a superior being: sophisticated, knowing, and understanding, a person who lived exclusively for the soul, the inner life, in a world of art and music. Her relationship with Violet was the most meaningful thing that ever happened to her; it culminated in a brief sensual phase. After the Violet affair Luhan recounts how she fell into depression and was sent to a different boarding school in the United States, where she had another physical relationship with a girl.

Besides shaping her story so as to feature herself as a rebel in the suffocating emptiness of contemporary American society, Luhan narrates as if from a pinnacle of authority, expressing insightful, consistent, and often original opinions on a variety of topics. She has a philosophy of objects worthy of a Rainer Maria Rilke or Walter Benjamin. Her book is full of descriptions of interiors and objects, many of them negative: she scornfully describes rich houses whose accoutrements lack "reality." She contrasts these with things that have an "aura" (156; she uses the term, today familiar from Benjamin, in the same way he does). She repeatedly intrudes on her story with insights about children, some of them surprising. "Children always know whether things are real or not" (20); "Now children are very rational in their first years" (46); "Never again, after one is ten years old, does anything have so wonderful and terrible a meaning as it has when one is little" (80); "Children instinctively know it all" (102); "For a child to be in bed with a grown person is an event— it always has its own kind of colour or feeling, a high or a low vibration" (129); "That swift, treacherous facility of youth for taking sides, any side!" (243). On mother-daughter relationships, she pronounces:

In those days, only the outermost rim of life was given any conscious attention. People, especially children and parents, never spoke together about or even thought of their hearts and souls. . . . My mother naturally had no intimacy with Grandma Cook. One is not intimate about food and clothing and houses, but about the affairs of the heart. All this was left untouched between them, and left untouched by my mother and me in turn. Example is so strong! If only a mother here and there would be herself, act on her own feelings, and break the chain that holds her to the past and makes her emulate her own mother in every way! (72–73)

Luhan styles herself as someone who has uncommon insight into human psychology. She writes that people have always commented on her ability to understand others' situation and feelings: "People have always been grateful to me for my ability, since I was a child, to put myself in their places, to sense, without knowing causes, the multitudinous fluctuations of the human psyche" (223). This observation is certainly borne out by her childhood autobiography; she correctly identifies her great gift. She has a huge collection of extraordinary portraits of people in her book that testify to her ability to figure out what is causing someone else's pain and sympathize with that person. She says she used to be accused of not being "serious" because she did not apply herself to her schoolwork, but, "Right here I will say, once and for all, that is what I have always been—serious to the point of insanity, serious to the exclusion of all other attributes, serious, concentrated, and absorbed by life, by people, by all experience" (253).

Finally, she implicitly substantiates and justifies the extraordinarily confessional and indiscreet nature of her autobiography by insisting that she was always one to talk about herself, to be indiscreet. She traces her propensity to share confidences to a game called Truth that she and her friends used to play, in which they told each other their secrets. Yet even earlier, she was apparently "inoculated with the curious morality or malady of confession" (90). For example, when she is seven or eight she confesses to wrecking another child's doll by filling it with water to make it do "number one," and she is punished for it. She confesses in writing to a teacher that she called her a giraffe behind her back and is punished for that too. Her analysis of that teacher is: "It was as though all the years of her repressed abhorrence of schools, of girls, of life as she knew it, pressed through the too narrow crevices of her soul and escaped to find a new harbour in me" (255). On this same occasion she feels that her budding need for candor and openness has been destroyed. Yet she truly believes that secrets simply cannot be kept, that people

134 The Interwar Years: The Golden Age of Psychological Self-Portraiture

who think they are hidden from observation are deceiving themselves: "There are no secrets in the world. The sooner everybody knows that and admits it, the better" (314).

Luhan's *Background* represents a turning point, a complete break with prewar decorum. A few years later in England, the genre took a similar turn toward the intensely personal and psychological—and also a giant step in the direction of the literary and sophisticated—with Mary Butts's *The Crystal Cabinet*. Butts, a British modernist writer who published novels and stories, was in the middle of revising the text when she died, according to Barbara Wagstaff, "of a perforated ulcer, peritonitis, and an untreated diabetic condition"; her life might have been saved if she had not lived alone in a remote spot in Cornwall.[12] *The Crystal Cabinet* was twice published posthumously, once in 1937 in a cleaned-up version that omitted a sizable amount of the text and then in 1988 in an "unexpurgated version" that included a foreword by her daughter, Camilla Bagg, an afterword by Barbara Wagstaff, and many photos.

The Crystal Cabinet covers Butts's life from her earliest memories to the beginning of World War I, when she was in her midtwenties. Her father's death when she was fourteen marked a turning point in her life. Over one-third of the text is devoted to her childhood and early adolescence when her father was still alive. Butts's later life, which she does not address in *The Crystal Cabinet*, brought two marriages, male and female lovers, a drug habit, and a breakdown. After her second husband left her she finished up several projects, including this autobiography of childhood and youth.

Camilla Bagg's foreword to the 1988 edition clarifies that the first edition was "a much edited version of the manuscript which was finished in 1936."[13] Butts's friend and literary executor Angus Davidson left out about one-quarter the book, including some passages that Mary herself had bracketed. The book met with a tepid reception. It mainly interested people who lived in Dorset. But it managed to shock her mother's family. Her aunts were pained that it included an account of their younger sister Monica's drowning and upset that their mother had been criticized for her treatment of Monica. What Mary wrote about friends and neighbors and the Hydes (her mother's second husband's family) was, they thought, in "such poor taste." They also thought that her account was full of errors. Camilla Bagg comments, "Just as well they did not know about the full manuscript."[14]

A comparison of the two editions shows the difference between what could be published in 1937 and in 1988. The complete edition of 1988 gives the impression that Butts wrote exactly as she pleased about her feelings, her deepest convictions, topics of interest to her, and last but not least, her parents and relatives. The first edition of 1937 above all censors out a large portion of Butts's story of her bad relationship with her mother. Davidson excised her accusations, for example, her suspicion that her mother set her up to be attacked by a family friend who was a notorious lecher, and her belief that her mother suspected her of trying to seduce her stepfather. Davidson also deleted other references to sex. But even the expurgated version of 1937 is extremely personal. Butts foregrounds herself. She tries to recapture her consciousness as a child and as a girl. She quests for her memories and is interested in the manner in which they come back to her. With a restless and inquiring mind, she seeks the truth, the true story of her own development, trying to reconstruct how things happened in her childhood and youth and why. She dwells on certain mystical moments of sudden understanding, but she also tries analytically to piece together the true story of her family members and to discover what made them the people they were. The "crystal cabinet," an image she borrows from the poet William Blake, is her metaphor for her mind, because she conceives of her mind as a cabinet with many drawers, shelves, and cupboards, which she strives to be both inside and outside of simultaneously. As author, she indulges in profuse commentary. She emerges as a distinct narratorial personality with idiosyncratic views and prejudices, which she airs abundantly. She is brilliant, cold, analytical, unsentimental, highly critical, occasionally catty, often caustic, and sometimes profound. Unlike Luhan, who was a "people person" with strong likes and dislikes, Butts makes the impression of being someone who in general does not like people. She considers herself of the generation wounded by World War I, and she lambasts the present age for its loss of values. She frostily analyzes the present-day upbringing of children and especially of girls.[15] She ardently detests "development"—the development that destroyed the Dorset environment in which she grew up. It forms the object of her vituperative polemic. The theme of the destruction of the Dorset landscape is the centerpiece of the book in both of its versions. In particular, she deeply regrets the loss of her childhood home Salterns, which she intimates her mother allowed to be wangled out of her possession after her father died and she remarried. By consequence of all this, a melancholy tone hangs over the book.

Until she was ten years old, that is until her brother was born, Mary was an only child: lonely, observing, willful, and, by the standards of a child who grows up among siblings, spoiled, for her parents were wealthy and owned a magnificent house in a wonderful natural setting. Her elderly father, intelligent, perceptive, and well-read, is the most positive figure in the book. She was not only fond of him but believed herself to be similar to him. In contrast, she feels different from and at odds with her mother, who she feels—the passage was deleted from the first edition—did not like her. Her criticism of her mother is unstopping. Her mother, whom her father married in order to have an heir (she was over thirty years younger than he), is lovely and charming, but not intellectual and strangely puritanical, something Mary continuously faults her for. "Looking across a threshold into a garden, where I saw, not trees as it said in the poem, but the Tree. The Golden Bough growing, the Tree of Knowledge, not yet of good and of evil, but of pure knowledge; and already I saw man, not Heaven, forbidding me its fruit" (50). Sex cannot be talked about with her mother. Her mother tries to make her feel that there is something different about being a girl, without saying what. She instills in her a fear of the woods. Worse, her mother warns her off the books her father ("men") read—books that today are largely considered literary classics, like *Moll Flanders* and *Les Liaisons dangereuses*, Honoré de Balzac, Stendhal, and Gustave Flaubert. Her mother's crowning misdeed is to burn her father's "dreadful books" (110) after his death and to get Mary to participate in the book burning, about which Mary feels ashamed in retrospect. She notes that the books burned slowly. But she does not hold it against her mother that she remarried a year after her husband's death, apparently for the sake of the romance she had never had. Mary is even fond of her good-looking stepfather.

Her maternal grandmother is not spared: "One of the old breed who gave the Victorian age its bad name. . . . Her desire was to live, a mateless queen-bee, surrounded by her workers, her unmated children" (62). Butts describes her stepfather candidly (and largely positively), his sisters negatively. She is even cold and unsentimental toward herself, whom she at one point calls "a very nasty small girl" (65). She also, however, paints a coherent and sympathetic picture of herself as one who quests for knowledge. She states she had a deep desire to learn

The Interwar Years: The Golden Age of Psychological Self-Portraiture   137

things like a boy (i.e., properly). She repeatedly styles herself as one who loves words, who wants to be a poet; she speaks of her "fantastic touchiness about language" (188). The book has a feminist undertone. Her account of the Scottish boarding school where she was sent after her father's death and her years there occupies over one-third of the book. Although she was miserable and friendless there and learned little except from her adored literature teacher, she approves of the relatively recent institution of girls' schools in Britain that aimed to give girls exactly the same education as boys.

Like Reuter before her, and also like Salverson, Allinson, and Creston (writers who wrote around the same time and will be discussed presently), but to a more pronounced degree than they, Butts writes of epiphanic moments. She has mystical tendencies. The epiphanic moments foster her mysticism, and they are philosophically sustained by it in their retelling. The mystical moments most often take place in nature. When Mary is a child, a wonderful tree stump is an ongoing source of animistic interaction; when she is a schoolgirl, she walks into a "focus" on the beach of Fife; as a young adult, a vision at the Badbury Rings shows her her calling. Mentioning William Wordsworth, she emphasizes fear and awe as valuable sensations, as a salutary return to a natural human existence that has seemed even more precious since humanity was denatured by a loss of belief in God, man's greedy devastation of the environment, and the war.

Butts's work resembles Luhan's in its candor, causticity, and ardent belief in spiritual values that, the author believes, present society has buried. But it lacks Luhan's voluptuousness, interest in people, and thirst for new experiences. Unlike Luhan, Butts does not espouse psychoanalysis—in fact, she opposes fashionable psychology[16]—and she transmits a largely negative and discouraged mood. A thread of anger runs through her book about what the world has become.

The third self-focused, confessional work to appear in the 1930s is Laura Goodman Salverson's *Confessions of an Immigrant's Daughter*, first published in 1939. It is often mentioned together with Nellie McClung's *Clearing in the West*, which had appeared four years previously. Like McClung's, Salverson's autobiography gives a picture of growing up in Manitoba at the end of the nineteenth century, albeit a distinctly different picture: Salverson, McClung's junior by twelve years, was the daughter of Icelandic immigrants, and her childhood years in Manitoba were spent mainly in Winnipeg. Salverson met the famous McClung

138   The Interwar Years: The Golden Age of Psychological Self-Portraiture

after World War I, and they became friends. This autobiography of a young woman is even longer than McClung's (523 pages in the original edition), and like McClung she does not stop at the end of childhood, but takes her story to the completion of her first book *The Viking Heart*, published in 1923. Nearly half the book is devoted to her childhood years in Manitoba before her family moved to Duluth, Minnesota, and the chapters on Duluth years that cover ages nine through twelve bring the total up to over 60 percent. Certainly, in Salverson's case as in McClung's, it is the author's extraordinary childhood story that justifies the work. Much of the interest for the reader lies in the picture she draws of life in western Canada. The picture we get, however, is different from McClung's, for Salverson was born not to an energetic farming family that would eventually prosper in rural Manitoba, but to impoverished immigrants. Her parents arrived in Canada with nothing. Two of their four children had died on the voyage. Her poetically inclined father found employment in a Winnipeg sweatshop stitching saddles for fourteen hours a day. He was beset by serious illnesses, as was she throughout her childhood. The family did not have enough to eat, and her mother lost many babies. Thus, hers was a childhood of extraordinary hardship. Canada is portrayed as a profit-oriented country with a dog-eat-dog mentality. The growing population of Icelandic immigrants banded together for solidarity but were mercilessly exploited for their labor.

In its thematic focus and style, this book is very different from McClung's. It can be regarded as part of the turn in the English-language history of the genre. The title—"Confessions"—points to the autobiographical tradition of Jean-Jacques Rousseau and hence to a different kind of work from what had only recently been the norm for women's childhood autobiographies written in English. This is no "we"-style memoir, but the highly subjective story of the girl herself. It is not only psychological, but self-profiling, self-establishing, and self-affirming, like the works of Luhan and Butts. As such, it adds a feminist dimension to a psychological one. The author plentifully tells of family history and even Icelandic history, but she makes it seem as if all this background is relevant to an understanding of her own childhood experience and her own identity. Thus, "So far as my fundamental characteristics were concerned, I was potentially a true Icelander."[17] She links her first chapter on family history to herself through its title, "I Meet the August Ancestors." Other chapter titles insist openly on her own experience ("I Discover My Birthplace," "I Discover Drama") or

The Interwar Years: The Golden Age of Psychological Self-Portraiture 139

imply it ("Subjective Interlude," "Those Child Transgressions"). Whereas in the memoirs and semi-memoirs of the interwar years the author's child self often seems like a mere thread on which to string information about the time, the place, and the family, Salverson gives this type of information from the child's perspective or finds ways to tie it back into the story of the child. She typically adopts the child's point of view in a serious and sympathetic manner. She also pauses again and again to explain and to characterize her child self. Commenting on her refusal to eat an egg when she is tiny: "In which fine frenzy a predestined rebel was born—the rebel who is myself" (12). "I . . . was swaddled in clothes, made to eat when I had no appetite, and, it now seems to me, actually was coddled into the invalidism she [her mother] meant to avoid" (107). "Even as a child I was bored with the familiar and commonplace, and sought to escape into a weird world of fabulous imaginings" (117).

Besides engaging in extensive narratorial commentary about her child self, the narrator liberally imparts her insights and opinions about all kinds of things: her parents, other people, life in general. We get a distinct sense of this autobiographer as a personality: a bold, independent thinker, full of opinions, which she does not hesitate to express in print. She is the antithesis of the self-effacing gentlewoman narrator. There is no evidence that she had read Luhan or Butts, but like them she portrays and judges her parents, especially her mother, with a frankness that betrays little concern for their feelings. Thus, we hear that her parents were temperamentally mismatched. Her father is romantic, impulsive, literary, sociable, sensitive, people-centered, and warmhearted; eminently impractical, he lets his farm in Iceland deteriorate to the point where they arrive in the New World as paupers; he is full of ill-fated schemes for new ventures in North America. Her mother is practical, hardworking, energetic, prudent, reserved, and remembering. She is the one who keeps everything afloat. True to the pattern that emerges out of women's childhood autobiographies generally, the author prefers the sensitive to the sensible parent. She tells story after story of how her mother, though attempting to do her very best by her, completely misreads her childhood sensibilities and thrusts some wrong thing on her—the Bible as a first reader, a doll as a birthday present (she hates dolls), or a handmade red coat that makes the rotund child look, to her mind, even fatter—while her father does the right thing on the same occasions, turning "disappointment into joy" (113). Thus, he gets her a children's book as a first reader; he gives her a boxful of chocolate pigs,

140   The Interwar Years: The Golden Age of Psychological Self-Portraiture

a "delightfully useless present" (113) because she doesn't eat candy, for her birthday. Her mother's uninsightfulness, however, is just a particular instance of what she believes is the blindness of grown-ups generally in dealing with children. Grown-ups are prone to ask children to do things that embarrass and bore them. Thus the seven-year-old Lalla (Laura) is ordered, to her horror, to kiss a boy who gives her a present at her birthday party, and an older girl is told to show Lalla her handkerchief collection, an activity that interests neither child.

Salverson expresses her feminism much more overtly than McClung and more overtly than any author to date, Butts and even Beasley included. Her quarrel is not with what her parents' generation thinks is a woman's place, as is McClung's—her female Icelandic relatives are outspoken, commanding personalities—but with woman's biological destiny, the way women are frequently poorly treated by men, and the social subjugation accompanied by, as she comes to believe, the brainwashing of women. Thus, around age eleven, the realization that her mother is pregnant "meant a cleavage between me and mamma. It set up a kind of quivering horror in my whole being to have suddenly plumbed the alarming possibilities of the female body" (206). Likewise, she is the auditory witness to her midwife aunt delivering a difficult birth and subsequently hears the "seduced and abandoned" horror story of one of her aunt's unwed clients. She avers that "all that fine balderdash about the glory of motherhood could stand a bit of cool dissecting" (291). She observes that a great many women suffer in their marriages. She comments tartly on the philandering husbands she heard about as a child (129). She is scornful of the way a female acquaintance "performs the labours of Martha" (225) so that her lazy husband can focus on "higher things." She pities a Swedish friend who came from a refined background but married a rude, insensitive man. Part of her rebellion is against housework, which she abhors, the type of work women who are not rich are fated to squander their lives doing: "For girls like us the dice were loaded from the start. The ensign of the mop and the dustbin hung over our cradles. No wonder thousands of us married any old fool! Bed and board!" (323). "Everything about housework is a stupid repetition, with the exception of cooking" (330). Her rebellion against the world of women goes hand in hand with her addiction to the world of books and the development of her writerly vocation. She admits that the world of women was "a world I frantically sought to dodge by burying myself in books more deeply than ever" (260). By the time she marries at age twenty-three, she has set views on "the cruel subjection of women" (378) and treats her husband to the following tirade: "It's all women. They are the slaves, every one of them, slaves of convention, of religion, of the house—slaves in their mentality. Even the modern woman, who thinks herself free, has only exchanged the bondage to one man, to make herself the slave of many. Even in art, women reflect men, ape men, say what the smart man expects the smart woman to say" (378).

Another controversial topic on which she has strong opinions is religion. She makes plain that she has no use for it, because she thinks it just sanctifies materialism, patriotism, and war. As for war, she believes that the interests of capital are responsible for it.

Salverson stated that what she calls her "subjective" style was her intention. For the 1949 reissue she wrote in the foreword: "I am further encouraged by the many United Kingdom reviews which, almost without exception, found the book a singular departure from the usual autobiography. This I take to mean that I may have succeeded in what I tried to accomplish: namely to make of a personal chronicle a more subjective and therefore more sensitive record of an age now happily past" (5). K. P. Stich, who wrote the introduction to the 1981 edition, notes that Salverson was not interested in "mere historicity" (xiv), but rather in the "human element." Stich notes that Salverson urged her friend Nellie McClung to "be more personal in your new [autobiography] . . . Break down and tell all! We want to see you and know how your mind was working" (xiv).[18] Stich complains that Salverson in fact "rarely . . . tells all" (xiv). But compared to previous women autobiographers of childhood and youth, she is more candid than any thus far except for Beasley, Luhan, and Butts.

Salverson tells her story in chronological order, though after the fifth chapter she builds in a four-chapter analepsis concerning family history and events before her birth. Nothing else about her style or manner of narrating is cut from a template. She begins in medias res ("the Dakota prairie was an infinity of darkness" [9]) and in the third person, with a scene from the family's wagon trip from Dakota to Winnipeg: it's pitch black, the horses clop, coyotes yap, the wagon lurches, her parents argue. The narrative starts with the confused child's sense perceptions in the wagon and moves to her thoughts about the chaotic departure, her breakfast, their missing cat. It is a sheerly novelistic beginning. To accept it as the first memory it is insinuated to be (the chapter is entitled

"The First Horizon"), the reader would have to naturalize it as flashback-style memory triggered by high emotional content. Otherwise, it seems unlikely that a memory could be so vivid, so long-drawn-out, and so exact, to the point that the narrator remembers exactly what she had for breakfast and exactly what her parents said to each other. Subsequently on that trip, when she acquires a sense of self (as a rebel), Salverson starts to narrate in the first person. McClung likewise started in the third person, with the scene of her birth, then shifted to the first person to tell her first memory. Salverson may have adopted the third-to-first-person shift device from McClung, though she has no comparably compelling reason to do so; she merely hints that the shift signals the birth of her "rebel" personality. But in other respects as well, the book is written to be riveting. From sentence to sentence, Salverson crafts her style with the utmost care. She uses abundant, eye-catching, evocative, and sometimes quite elaborate metaphors, for example, "in wet weather, the road, like an angry sea-serpent looping along, dripped a red, gummy spume, through which horses and men slithered and slipped" (19). Or "Life is a colossus too great for smart declensions. . . . It cares nothing for the canons of art, and pursues its ironic rhythm, piling up anticlimaxes as a tidal wave piles up the wreckage it has made of some once seaworthy ship" (34). Her lyrical nature descriptions betray her literary beginnings as a poet. Besides writing a carefully elaborated, poetic style, she takes care to tell a good story. In fact, she tells so many around-the-fire, once-in-a-lifetime-type stories that one suspects her of stylization (though not necessarily of fictionalization). For instance, she was constantly sick. She nearly died of diphtheria, then caught whooping cough, and so forth. Her mother lost so many babies that she coddled her, keeping her out of school and away from other children's outdoor play.

So intent is Salverson on giving the subjective experience of the child as opposed to just her own history that she leaves many things mysterious. She barely gives dates. In fact, ages are so rarely given that the story defies attempts to reconstruct her biography, especially of her earliest years. Vaguely giving her approximate age for a memorable birthday party, she notes, "Years did not mean so much, nor do they yet" (108). How old was she when the family moved from Dakota back to Winnipeg? What kind of animal is the "intriguing yellow creature" (15)—not a cat, not a dog—that perches on the back of a chair at the Ericsons? Exactly how many babies did her mother lose? What happened with her weak heart? She does not tell us.

The Interwar Years: The Golden Age of Psychological Self-Portraiture   143

On Salverson's agenda, besides writing a subjective autobiography and giving a picture of immigrant life in Canada and the United States, is a how-I-became-a-writer plotline, evident in her decision to end her story with the publication of her first book. This had not previously been a common plot in women's childhood autobiographies. Before Salverson, it occurred most prominently in Frances Hodgson Burnett, who with gentle humor presented a picture of her child self as one addicted to stories and ended with her selling her first story under a male pseudonym. It also occurred in Gabriele Reuter, who emphatically shaped her autobiography of childhood and youth as the story of a writer's development. Salverson purposefully describes a similar trajectory. She paints the picture of an imaginative, sickly child whose sole interest was watching and thinking about people and who spent most of her time reading. Her discovery of the Duluth library when she is perhaps eleven or twelve is a revelation. Standing there, dazzled by the books, and in a way that recalls Gabriele Reuter's similar epiphany, she formulates her vocation to be a writer: "In the light of that consuming fire, I could see that nothing in the world mattered, except the faculty to see and to feel and to understand what went on in the world of men, so that it might be caught up at a centre, and called a book. And then, in a blinding flash of terrifying impertinence, the wild thought leaped to my mind. 'I too, will write a book, to stand on the shelves of a place like this—and I will write it in English, for that is the greatest language in the whole world!'" (237–38).

Salverson is well aware that a Freudian wave overtook North America in the early 1920s; in fact, she complains about it (402). By the time she started writing, she says, it was the fashion to write about sex. She associates Freud with sex. Sex is a topic she does not play up, but her general outspokenness, especially about her parents, reflects a psychoanalytic readjustment of vision.

All in all, this is a very serious book. Salverson makes the impression of having put her all into it. It reads as if she thought she had one shot at telling the world everything she had to say—about the immigrant experience, about children's experience, about the lives of the people she had known, about life generally. She makes the impression of having carefully considered how best to transmit all this wisdom, and done her utmost to execute her project so as to do credit to her ideas and get the world's attention. She tells the reader again and again that Icelanders are a serious, intellectual, literary people, and that she is one of them.

The Child's Vision

In 1913 Joan Arden published a work in which she plunged into the mind of the child she had been and recreated the way the child saw the world. In the 1930s, more authors endeavored to revive their childhood perceptions and render them in prose. In Germany, Agnes Miegel wrote a short piece (1930) and Anna Schieber a book (1932) that followed this route. The Norwegian author Sigrid Undset pursued a similar agenda within the framework of a longer and more complex work *Elleve Aar* (1934), in which she aims to give a picture of her childhood up to age eleven. In the second half of the 1930s two British authors, Francesca Allinson and Dormer Creston, wrote works that similarly seek to recreate the child's vision. Finally, the German author Emmy Ball-Hennings (1939) presents episodes from the child's perspective in the context of a longer autobiography of childhood and youth.

The works by Undset, Allinson, and Creston have three distinctive features in common with Arden's. First, none of them identifies itself as an autobiography. Allinson and Creston in fact explicitly declare that their works are neither autobiography nor fiction, but a mix of both. All these authors—Arden, Undset, Allinson, and Creston—give their protagonists fictitious names, although Undset calls her child Ingvild in a play on her father's real name Ingvald, who died in her eleventh year (hence the title of her book). Second, all these works confine themselves to the childhood years, in contrast to the straightforwardly autobiographical works of the same era, which extend their accounts into the author's youth. Third, these works limit narratorial commentary, at least in comparison to the intrusive, opinionated, conclusion-drawing narrators we find in Luhan, Butts, and Salverson. Arden withholds herself completely. Undset and Allinson assert themselves sparingly. Creston comments more than the others, but knows when not to spoil an immersive moment. Anna Schieber likewise confines herself to childhood—indeed, to her first seven years—and keeps narratorial commentary to a minimum. But like all the German authors, she acknowledges that her work is autobiographical.

Foregrounding femininity is not the point in any of these works, but gender issues do glimmer up in interactions the girls have with grownups and other children, particularly those involving sexuality. What makes these works fascinating and delightful to read is their sheer insightfulness. Undset's masterly *Elleve Aar* will be discussed first, followed by the English and then the German works.

The Norwegian writer Sigrid Undset's masterpiece *Elleve Aar* (1934), translated as *The Longest Years* (1935), takes the turn to psychology contemporaneously with the English-language works of the mid-1930s. Undset, who was born in 1882 and whose major novels had won her the Nobel Prize for Literature in 1928, published this work when she was in her early fifties. It is a particularly insightful, sophisticated, brilliantly rendered psychobiographical account of a little girl. The early childhood years she focuses on—she takes her subject from age one and a half to age eleven—and the chronological developmental story, recording every turn and change, combined with the length of her account (332 pages in the English translation) combine to make her book an unusual, original, and substantial contribution to the genre of childhood autobiography.

On the flyleaf of the English translation the work is called a novel. Undset uses fictitious names, but the story of Ingvild corresponds in every verifiable detail to her own. She writes in the relatively unusual, though by no means unprecedented, third person. Aside from autobiographical works of fiction like Delarue-Mardrus's, Burnett, Séverine, and Lagerlöf (as well as Acland in seeming imitation of Burnett) all wrote their childhood memoirs in the third person, and each of them used the third person differently. To recapitulate: Burnett employed both the first and the third persons. As her title, "The One I Knew the Best of All," foreshadows, an intrusive author-narrator speaks in the first person about her former self, the Small Person, whom she calls "she." The era in which she wrote and the apology she includes in her preface, where she insists on the typicality of the Small Person, lead one to surmise that one of her purposes was to deflect, by this witty maneuver, the accusation of egocentricity she might have incurred if she had published her own story straightforwardly as such. For Burnett the third person is also a distancing device that abets her quizzical psychological study of her object, the Small Person, a typical "child with an imagination." Séverine, in contrast, seems to have found third-person narration a suitable vehicle for the present-tense storytelling that makes Line's story vivid and pathetic. Lagerlöf's work does not have a psychological focus like Burnett's or an individual focus like Séverine's, but is a novelistic account of "the way things were." Undset uses the third person differently from any of these writers. Her book focuses on tracing the psychology of the individual little girl, Ingvild, and she uses the third person to avail herself of the conventions it affords for rendering the mind transparent.

146   The Interwar Years: The Golden Age of Psychological Self-Portraiture

Practiced in the arts of the novel, Undset employed established novelistic techniques for rendering consciousness. Her narrator is privy to Ingvild's conscious and semiconscious thoughts and to her psychic depths alike, and she reveals them through the means Dorrit Cohn describes as techniques of third-person narrative: quoted monologue, narrated monologue, and psycho-narration.[19]

Yet Undset's choice of third-person fiction as a vehicle for publishing her childhood story is puzzling. Why she did not prefer the first person is understandable: although a first-person narrator also has privileged access to his or her earlier states of mind, in the modernist period in which she wrote, the first person in works of fiction had come to be associated with unreliability, an effect which Undset plainly did not desire. It is the fictionalization that is perplexing. Why did she not simply write her autobiography? Why the fictional names? She publishes such intimate details about Ingvild—for example, that she is a child who bites— in a story that is recognizably her own that it seems unlikely that she was shy, hesitant to publish her story as such. Likelier, it was easier for her to write about herself under the guise of fiction, because fiction makes no claims of factual accuracy and thus gives a writer greater freedom of expression than a declared "autobiography."

In a curious twist, Undset makes many references to remembering. An autobiographer who casts her life as a novel need not invoke memory. Autobiography is dependent on memory, and writers who write about the long-gone years of childhood with the intent to recapture the past are particularly apt to foreground the remembering of those years, as well as to comment on or complain about their powers of memory. But if the life story is turned into "fiction," the issue of memory can be sidelined or dropped. In fact, though, Undset does make references to remembering. It is one of the features of the text that, besides its copious detail, gives it some of the typical marks of autobiography. Thus, she starts the book with her first memory, which she carefully analyzes. She observes early on: "The actual memories of this earliest period of childhood lie far apart, like patches of strong sunlight in a land of darkness."[20] She distinguishes between what she remembers on her own and what people told her. And at the end, when her father dies: "Her memories of the time that followed were like images seen in the scattered fragments of a broken mirror" (325). She makes allusions to Ingvild remembering (or not remembering) her childhood: "Looking back in after years it seemed to her . . ." (193); "In almost all of the memories she

The Interwar Years: The Golden Age of Psychological Self-Portraiture 147

retained from that time . . ." (204). Yet amid her focus on psychology generally, remembering does not take on the importance it assumes in certain of her contemporaries who signed the "autobiographical pact," nor are we encouraged to imagine that the narrative itself is a sequence of memories. Rather, it is a story, told with a dramatic flair that is incompatible with the absent-minded, introspective elsewhere-orientation of the first-person rememberer, but can be marshaled by a narrator telling the story of *someone else*.

Another freedom that fictionalization brings is the option, which Undset exercises, of minimizing the intrusions of the narrator. In autobiography, one expects a certain input from the present-time narrating voice (an expectation that autobiographers usually fulfill but also sometimes dodge). Undset's narrator makes her presence felt from time to time with prolepses (forward glimpses in time, beyond the horizon of the protagonist's story, which ends at age eleven). She also jumps in from time to time (though not very often) with astute commentary. For example, she notes that Ingvild's earliest memory is "her becoming for the first time aware that she had opposed her will to that of another person" (6)—an observation that interestingly complements the venerable identification of selfhood with memory and the more recent assertion that autobiographical memories date to the formation of the cognitive self (i.e., to self-consciousness).[21] But more often she seeks to correct received opinion. For instance, she calls the claims for sibling rivalry exaggerated, and asserts, "The delight of bigger brothers and sisters in a new baby is doubtless often due in some degree to their guessing that now the grown-ups will have their hands full with the little one" (15)—and that they themselves will consequently have more freedom. Particularly insightful is the way she corrects the belief, held by many caregivers, that young children play with each other. Until the age of four or five, she asserts, children are busy exploring their own environment and also take interest in the grown-ups on whom they rely for care, protection, and explanations, but they do not take much notice of their contemporaries, although they do try to take things away from them (46–47). But mainly, the story is told from Ingvild's perspective.

Ingvild acquires a younger sister, Marit, and presently another younger sister, Birthe. Yet this is definitely not a "we"-style work, but Ingvild's individual story. The narrative focuses on her, and the narrator is privy only to her psyche, not to anyone else's. Her differences from Marit are emphasized more than their common activities. While

148   The Interwar Years: The Golden Age of Psychological Self-Portraiture

the narrative focuses strictly on Ingvild, however, the emphasis is not on how Ingvild became a writer, though there are hints that point to her early writerly talent: she loves storytelling and reading, and she hates a number of other activities proposed by the grown-ups, such as sewing and embroidery. A great deal of the information Undset gives about Ingvild is gratuitous, pointless: for example, at age two or three she is fascinated with the play of light on the ceiling and obsessed with a poster of a foot, while later on she likes to occupy a secret garden perch. Information that is just there for its own sake is a hallmark of autobiography.

While we gradually form a picture of Ingvild's proclivities and talents, likes, dislikes, and infatuations, a stronger point is that many of these, however intensely felt, are in flux, ready to change, disperse, be overwhelmed, or reverse at any minute. For example, as a tiny child Ingvild loves bees, but the grown-ups discourage this. A shadow enters her close relationship with her dog after a different dog bites her. Her attitude toward swimming undergoes a sudden reversal. Initially, she detests and is afraid of bathing in the ocean; but two summers later she ventures into open sea, actually starts swimming, and falls in love with it. Generally, Undset paints a picture of childhood as a time of fluidity when issues aplenty arise but then disappear rather than ever being resolved.

Undset pursues Ingvild's preverbal, subrational responses to situations, seeking what Nathalie Sarraute will later call "tropisms" and make the basis for her life's work.[22] For example, she describes the sensation of jumping between two mirrors when she is very small. Fear was a dominant topic in Joan Arden, but Undset takes an analytic approach: Ingvild/Undset prides herself in knowing how every fear started. She knows that her fear of the dark started when she fell down the stairs in the dark. She knows that her fear of fire was sparked by a picture of a fire disaster. In a chapter on an exhibitionist and other forms of "sexual instruction," she describes an experience that combines fear with voluptuousness, namely, the experience of losing one's head in a dangerous situation and recklessly doing something even more dangerous. The ladder slips away when she is clambering around a construction site, and, in panic, she makes a terrifying leap to the ground. She comments: "It was a long time before she became clearly conscious of what she had experienced—of the connection between the spasm of fear and the voluptuous feeling and the distraction which may come over one when one's body believes itself threatened with destruction, so that the blood runs wild and one does things of which one is afterwards terrified" (179). Both these insights and the approach are highly original, without precedent within the tradition of women's childhood narratives.

Concurrently, the narrator reveals things about Ingvild that, without her saying so, the reader may well think hold true for many other children too, and some of which in fact come up as themes in later women's childhood narratives. As a very young child, around age two or so, she experiences the world with the "intense physicality" that Doris Lessing in *Under My Skin* (1994) will ascribe to children's perceptions at that age.[23] She notices the skin on the porridge and the egg and biscuit crumbs in the beard of a man who hugs her. When she is a few years older, the narrator notes that Ingvild, if given the choice, would prefer a quick punishment that is over and done with to a long, boring lecture. Ingvild's family is not wealthy, and she is neither isolated nor only together with her siblings, like so many of the other little girls we have heard about. She is repeatedly a newcomer in groups of children, and so she undergoes the typical problems encountered by a new child in children's group dynamics. Other children bait and tease her and mock her clothes and gear, because they are different. She does find her way through these situations and by no means adopts the self-image of a victim. She resents grown-ups who tease her—a fairly common peeve, which M. St. Clare Byrne will also make a point of complaining about. She shies away from suffering people, something we will also see in Francesca Allinson.

Undset makes clear that Ingvild's intellectual, freethinking family is much more of a formative influence on her than any of the various schools she attends. She admires and looks up to both of her parents. Her father is a brilliant, internationally recognized archaeologist; her mother, an intelligent Danish woman with rationalist ideals that offset her headstrong nature. Portraits of her parents' families, her grandparents' homes where her family spends ample time, emerge: her father's generous, well-intentioned, and highly organized Norwegian family in Trondhjem, and her mother's spontaneous and warm Danish family in Kallundborg. Her parents are her first teachers, and they provide a home where she learns a lot, so that no teacher she ever has in school quite lives up to them. In fact, her well-informed and intelligent parents foster in her a lack of respect for school. Her parents shape her moral development. Her mother insists that she should not pick up stupid values from the pack, so that she learns to put up with being dressed differently from other children and being made fun of for having different things. Above all, her parents frown on lying. Considerable reflection is triggered when her father flogs her (an unusual punishment) at age seven for attributing her own misdeed to her younger sister. Ingvild reflects on the nature of lying, which, it seems to her, is not synonymous with untruth, for there is also make-believe. What exactly is lying, and what not? When the older girl who lives next door, and whom Ingvild idolizes, blatantly and shamelessly lies about finding a necklace, this muddies Ingvild's adoration of her, but she reserves her unambivalent hatred for the little girl who tattles on her idol.

Death is a strong presence in this narrative. The book ends with her father's death when she is eleven years old and sketches the beginning of a new, much poorer family life. Up to that point, the narrative does not let us forget that Ingvild's father is headed for an early death. His illness and impending death function as a dark backdrop that offsets the vividness of the child's own story. We see her father becoming weaker from year to year. The family's moves all take place in order to accommodate his increasingly debilitating illness. The theme of death is not just confined to her father. One of Ingvild's earliest memories is that Christmas Eve was sad at her house because her grandmother had died on Christmas Eve. Later, her grandfather dies after a long illness. Not only does the theme of death lend the narrative a serious tone; Undset wants to tell us how a child experiences death. Death does not simply amount to loss for Ingvild. She confronts it as a physical event, initially in an encounter with a dog's rotting carcass. She touches her father's corpse, and we learn how it feels. After her grandfather's death Ingvild has a vision-like insight into the psychology of people who are gravely ill and dying, into their profound aloneness and therefore distance from everyone else, including their loved ones, who despite their distress are fundamentally in a different world, that of life and health. The narrative reinforces this idea by showing how Ingvild's childhood, rich in events and experiences, paralleled her father's long, worsening illness, yet something like an automatic mechanism made her put his illness out of mind, made her shrink from recognizing that her father's health was declining. Ingvild does, however, emerge from her experiences with death with one clear conviction, which is that religious faith helps the dying: her deeply religious grandfather is wholly resigned to dying, believing it to be God's will.

Unlike virtually every other woman childhood autobiographer up to this point except Luhan (and of course Beasley), Undset does not shy away from the topic of sex, but rather seeks it out. The idea of sex enters her life as a form of fear when she is around age seven. She sees a man watching her, and when he sees that she sees him, he asks if she would like to see a "funny thing" (172). Filled with horror, though she is not exactly sure what is so horrifying, she runs away. In her analysis, the episode gives her a sense of disempowerment. "What she had experienced was a raging resentment against one who had imposed on her a loathsome and humiliating memory" (176). The "rude" remarks men and boys sometimes make to her and her friends likewise seem like a power play: sexual innuendo, she writes, is a means by which a man tries to make a helpless girl feel ashamed so that he can then gloat over it. Sex thus translates into the power men have over women. And so she hates it. Tellingly, Undset groups these episodes together with another one that is about gendered power relations but has no overt sexual content: a man buys her a cake and then makes fun of her, whereupon "she *hated* him, mutely and furiously and helplessly. Since the day she had come across the exhibitionist she had been like this, choking with indignation when strange men tried to make fun of her and let her feel how powerless a little girl was" (174). She remarks that these events were "the beginnings of the sexual instruction from which no little girl is safe—in a town, in any case" (176).

There are kind men, too, and one of them, a boy named Olaf, becomes a powerful source of fantasy for her. He approaches her to play with her, even though at that age (approximately eight) boys and girls don't play together. She touches him, and as she seeks an excuse to touch him again, "he found it himself," putting his "warm hand" on her throat and leaving it there as he looks at her coral necklace (219–20). They play together and become friends—something she never mentions at home—for a considerable period of time until he has to leave for school. She meets Olaf once later and finally, when she is age twenty, hears that he died young. The narrator proleptically informs us that her future love affairs are only "a substitute for Olaf" (259).

Ingvild/Sigrid is, expectably, an enthusiastic reader, whom her parents teach to read books that are too difficult and who later discovers easier, exciting ones. Among these books there is a reference to Louisa May Alcott: Undset remarks that she detested her "insufferably mawkish" *Little Women* (292).

Compared to Undset's work, Allinson's and Creston's writings are, like Arden's, much shorter. Francesca Allinson's *A Childhood* (1937) hovers between fiction and autobiography, declining to be classified as one or the other. It is written in the first person about "Charlotte," but the author avers in the foreword that "Unavoidably, Charlotte is more like myself than anyone else: yet . . . many of her contemporaries felt and acted very much as she did."[24] We are told that we will see Charlotte over the course of one year, but Charlotte's age is anywhere from nine to fourteen, depending on the episode. This work, a thoughtfully recalled, carefully written, poetic account of certain aspects of childhood from the perspective of the child, resembles Joan Arden's *A Childhood* in many respects. Its recreations of the child's perceptions are original. As with Arden, fear is one of the child's dominant emotions. Allinson (1902–1945), like Arden, wrote about her childhood when she was relatively young (age thirty-five). She was not a writer by profession but a musicologist and musician, who would end her life by suicide. She recounts the sort of thing that one generally forgets about in later life. The mode of writing is in the general vicinity of Virginia Woolf's, and so it seems appropriate that this book should have been published by the Hogarth Press. High points are the child's perceptual distortions when she has a fever; her fears when her older brother drags her on a scary adventure to a haunted house; her discovery of a strange world in the mirror; and the sense of the special and the magical that the very idea of Christmas arouses in her. Sometimes, unlike Arden, she offsets the child's perspective with implied narratorial irony. Thus, she refuses to eat normal dinners when she gets well, having been pampered with special food as an invalid; but then, in a change of insight, she admires her maid for disciplining her and decides this is better than her mother's easygoing ways. She also builds in an important turning point, a moment of sudden illumination that results in a change in her thinking. Creston will also use this device, as did Gabriele Reuter and Laura Goodman Salverson. In Allinson's case, she overcomes her ongoing fear and dislike of beggars when she gives her pocket money, a tidy sum, to a beggar woman who has a terrible story.

Dormer Creston, author of *Enter a Child* (1939), is the pseudonym of Dorothy Julia Baynes. Better known as a biographer, Baynes is listed in *The Peerage*. Her chapters about the country estate Hilldrop, the estate itself, the gardens tended by gardeners, the portraits of the ancestors, and the servants all point to her upper-class background. In *The Peerage*, Dorothy Baynes (1881–1973) is listed as the second of four children. Yet siblings do not figure in her book. In fact, the first part, "Chinese

Masks," makes the protagonist seem like a lonely only child. Siblings are, in any event, thematically unimportant here, for this book centers on the first-person narrator's unique subjective feelings and experiences as a child.

Like Joan Arden and Francesca Allinson, Dormer Creston transmits intelligent insights in a carefully, beautifully written first-person narrative. She prefaces her book in a way similar to Allinson: "Though these sketches are far truer than not, only a few of the characters appear under their own names."[25] She calls her persona "Dolly." The detail, the precision, the dialogue, the recollection of exact feelings and the way things looked suggest fictionalization. It is hard to believe that a person actually remembered all this.

The memories go from ages three to four to age ten, in unobtrusive chronological order. Creston devotes the first section to London and the last four to Hilldrop. A contemporary reviewer remarks on the discrepancy between the beginning, which "suggests a barren and miserable childhood of complete misunderstanding," and "the gracious Wiltshire home that she describes with such adoration."[26] Dolly's life in London is monotonous, oppressive, and unpleasant, mainly on account of her parents, who train her always to be polite to grown-ups and to dwell on a sense of her own wrongdoing, of sin.

The anomalous first part is by far the most remarkable. "Chinese Masks" is a tale of extraordinary terrorizing and bullying, which the five-year-old underwent at the hands of other children at a nightmarish children's party. In all parts, Creston excels at recreating the consciousness of the child. She manages to give the child's intense, very immature, quintessentially childlike feelings through the gamut from fear to delight and from excitement to boredom. She writes from her adult perspective with astute commentary, like Una Hunt, but also with much free indirect style and dialogue to make scenes vivid and present. Like Allinson and Salverson, she sometimes writes of "moments" when she experiences something special. There is a moment when she thinks, "kill yourself" (63). At another moment, an epiphany, beauty smites her (142).

Creston's work reinforces something that Mary Butts's autobiography had already made evident: at this point in time in Britain the female tongue had been liberated to the point where intimate, even embarrassing feelings could be aired in print and parents could be scathingly criticized. Thus, at the disastrous children's party, she recollects an extraordinary dynamic between her five-year-old self and a somewhat

154   The Interwar Years: The Golden Age of Psychological Self-Portraiture

older, brash boy: just looking at him, she says, made her feel ashamed. It is a revelatory touch worthy of Undset. Like Séverine, Creston declares that her parents brought her up according to the ideas of two generations prior: "Every day I was met with precept, admonition, repression" (38–39). "My father was one of the major problems of my life" (41). Of her education, she says that her intelligence was raped instead of being wooed (47). Admittedly, she published her book a couple of years after her father's death and long after her mother's.

Several German works of the 1930s also experiment with recreating the child's perspective. In the short piece "Die See" (The sea), which appeared in her compilation of otherwise more conventionally narrated pieces *Kinderland: Heimat und Jugenderinnerungen* (Childhood land: Memories of *Heimat* and youth, 1930), Agnes Miegel attempts to recreate her first encounter with the ocean from the perspective of a very young child. In fact, she creates an example of how this should *not* be done. An exuberant writer, Miegel cannot resist interpolating her narrator's vocabulary, hindsight, and explanations into the child's point of view. She "helps" too much and thereby spoils the illusion. Miegel was a well-known, prolific author, another East Prussian who pledged allegiance to Hitler in 1933. In other pieces in her volume she constructs her childhood interiority much more ably through the use of metaphor.

Anna Schieber, a novelist and children's book author, experimented much more successfully with the recreation of a small child's perspective in an autobiography of her earliest childhood years, entitled *Doch immer behalten die Quellen das Wort: Erinnerungen aus dem ersten Jahrsiebent* (Yet the sources will always have the word: Memories from the first seven years, 1932). Schieber sets herself the challenging task of recreating her memories from earliest childhood to age seven only. She accomplishes this project admirably, with never a false note. Schieber "remembers" above all experiences that were exceptionally meaningful to the child Anna. These include the sight of a burning mill, being all alone on a mountain under a nut tree, gazing into a river, a déjà vu experience, and encounters with death. All of these are events which a grown-up would process quite differently. Schieber also recounts her childish misadventures, such as thoughtlessly wandering off to another town without telling her parents, guiltily taking money from her savings that her mother keeps in her desk, and walking all the way to school with her eyes closed. Presumably, these events exercised a formative influence on her and therefore remained fixed in her memory. Schieber was

The Interwar Years: The Golden Age of Psychological Self-Portraiture   155

a child in a large family, and at every turn, this work testifies to the enormous importance of her mother for her and her siblings. Always maintaining sympathy for her child self and never ironic, the narrator employs, besides free indirect discourse, a particularly ingenious technique for conveying her significant experiences: she plunges into the child's perspective so deeply that she presents her fantasies as if the magical events were really happening. Occasionally, she resorts briefly to abstract adult language to explain what is going on: "In mother's vicinity, fear has no place"; "I can only explain what went on inside me [after she smashes a brand new doll] by saying that the Paris doll was not a 'child,' but a pretty toy with no soul."[27]

Emmy Ball-Hennings's *Blume und Flamme* (1938) is a full-scale autobiography of childhood and youth that, like Undset's, relies heavily on the recreation of the child's perspective to present her story—in this case from her first memories to age seventeen. Hennings was an Expressionist poet and Dada performer who, for many years forgotten, was rediscovered in the 1980s. Her autobiographical writings as well as her poetry were reissued, and she has recently been the subject of two biographies. After growing up in a working-class family and until she converted to Catholicism (1911) and met her future husband Hugo Ball, whom she helped found Dada, she led the "wild" life of an itinerant actress, complete with a stint as a prostitute and jail stays. Her biographer Bärbel Reetz states that Hennings, inspired by other women's childhood stories, planned to write her childhood autobiography as of 1930. Her projected title was "Das Reich der Kindheit" (The realm of childhood). Starting in 1935 Hennings worked with the Catholic publishing company Herder, but in 1937 Herder declined to publish the book. The Nazis were firmly in power. Herder claimed that the public's tastes had changed. Hennings nevertheless managed to find a different Catholic publisher, Benzinger in Switzerland, that was willing to bring out the work.[28]

Hennings acknowledged the book as her autobiography, yet for unclear reasons adopts a fictitious name (Helga) and also renames her half-sister, although she gives her parents their real names. *Blume und Flamme* has the status of a confession. In the preface to the continuation of her autobiography that starts at age eighteen, *Das flüchtige Spiel: Wege und Umwege einer Frau* (The fleeting game: A woman's paths and detours, 1940), Hennings uses the words "Bekenntnis" and "Beichte" — both translate as "confession" — to describe her project. She states that for many years she had intended to write a "confession" ("Bekenntnis") of her life[29]—a project she plainly begins in *Blume und Flamme*. Although in the time frame the narrative covers her sins seem insignificant, she makes a point of being self-critical. Thus, she accuses herself of absent-mindedness. On several occasions she makes clear how her spontaneously empathetic nature led to totally wrong imaginings about what other people valued and how they felt. For instance, she constantly reimagined and romanticized her father's early seagoing life. She writes of her childhood greed to be pitied and how she used her acting talent to provoke that response: for instance, she learns to feign St. Vitus's dance convincingly.

As narrator, Ball-Hennings adopts a humble stance, which appropriately complements her confessional motivation. But she also confesses that, as a narrator, she lacks authority. She says immediately that she has compunctions and doubts about her project; there are things she keeps looking at from a different angle; she's not sure she has understood her life. Things seem like a dream, she writes, but she wants to capture them before she forgets them. Despite her confessional impulse, she seems hesitant to take definitive ownership of her past. But she does believe firmly in the prophetic nature of childhood, likening it to the preliminary sketch of the final work of art that a person becomes. At the end of her narrative she reiterates her self-doubts, once again stating that there are things she does not understand. She also confesses that she hasn't changed since age seventeen; she is still not a person who is goal oriented or makes plans. She adds, as an aside, that wherever she landed, she was thrown out. She makes the impression of a soulful drifter who was not at all the captain of her fate.

Hennings avoids characterizing herself directly, though she reiterates that she was a child with mystical and idealistic yearnings. These gradually beckoned her toward religion. She mentions almost immediately, in the first chapter, "I could not live without venerating and admiring."[30] As a personality type, she recalls Lucy Larcom and Una Hunt. Like Una Hunt, she was raised as a Protestant but was strongly drawn to the beauty and emotional power of Catholicism. When she first encounters Catholic children—a girl and her brother—and listens to them talk about their religion, she steps forward as a narrator and declares: "I consider this acquaintance the most precious of my life. All of a sudden a light flamed up in me, as if one perceives a light approaching through fog and night, which then for some reason again can't be seen" (111–12). She adds that this little human flower (the Catholic girl) made her flame for the first time—thus giving meaning to the title of her book. "She was the messenger who suggested the meaning of life to me. Our life wants to be nothing but a little proof of divine love, and this needs to shine out of people, otherwise all is in vain" (114). Bärbel Reetz, who is skeptical about the authenticity of the entire Catholic thread, believes that this episode is invented. She thinks that Hennings probably made it up because her intended publisher, Herder, had told her she had to write "a Catholic book."[31] Be this as it may, it does lend focus to Hennings's persistent self-characterization as a naïve, dreamy person with religious leanings.

Beyond the budding religiosity that the narrator acknowledges, the child's personality emerges especially in the free indirect discourse that Hennings favors as a stylistic technique. Free indirect discourse serves to recreate her child's perspective in whatever scene she is narrating. Unusually for that style, Hennings uses it with irony. Childhood autobiographies that adopt the perspective of the child are typically not ironic. Here, however, we are always meant to catch the child's naïveté. Hennings's other dominant technique is to tell the story of her life in episodes. After an initial account of her parents and first memories, she delivers her story predominantly through extensive scenes, which she arranges in approximate chronological order. Therefore, not summary carries the narrative forward, but rather an evolving self-portrait afforded by scenic testimonies to her behavior and above all by the first-person free indirect discourse in which these scenes abound.

Unlike the stories written by most earlier German women child-hood autobiographers, Hennings's episodes are not "good stories" with a point or moral, but inconclusive stories about bizarre doings. This makes them seem lifelike. In the chapters that follow her school leaving, an enormous discrepancy yawns between her character, abilities, and desires—she wants to be an actress and longs to travel—and the first few servant-type jobs she lands. She ends her book by saying that in the aftermath, her life went sharply downhill, but in the end she prayed to the saints for help and they showed her the way. Perhaps in order to preserve her work's identity as a "Catholic book" in uncertain political times, she is no more precise than this about the downward path her life took in young adulthood.

The Study

Alongside these psychologically oriented works of the mid- to late 1930s there are two that present themselves as engagements with memory: the American Margaret Wade Deland's *If This Be I, As I Suppose It Be* (1935) and the Swiss Maria Waser's *Sinnbild des Lebens* (Symbol of life, 1936). Each author has her own idiosyncratic idea of how memory serves her.

Deland, born in 1857, is the oldest of the English-language writers to publish a childhood autobiography between the two wars. Her unusual and innovative work is unlike any other written in that period. It is the product of Deland's longstanding interest in psychology. In certain ways, it harks back to Burnett's study of the Small Person. With its focus on language, it anticipates works from the last decades of the twentieth century, such as Maxine Hong Kingston's *The Woman Warrior* (1974).

The Boston author Deland, an established writer of novels, short stories, and poetry, turned to her childhood autobiography in her seventies. Though she does not make this explicit, she evidently had a particular agenda in mind: to explore the psychology of the child on the basis of her own case and, most particularly, to investigate the connections between early experience, memory, and language. To suit this agenda, she devises a particular presentation and organization. She publishes a photo of Maggie at age six as the frontispiece and starts her narrative by talking about photos of herself as a girl. Through her description of her photo album she also introduces her immediate ancestors. This opening gambit does not just introduce her subject, but serves to emphasize the distance of her subject from the present. She avers that she, Margaret, does not know the girl Maggie except through stories she has heard about her. She does not identify with her. Hence the title of the book. But how then is she able to tell us anything about Maggie? The answer is this: Maggie's picture causes memories to come "bubbling up from that well of Truth, my own Unconscious."[32] With her insistence on the existence of mental depths and on the issue of self-identity, Deland signals her psychological focus. Like Burnett, her narrator Margaret adopts the pose of the detached researcher. She writes about Maggie in the third person for some of the same reasons that Burnett writes in the third person about the Small Person: to underscore how different Maggie is from herself and to put Maggie's psychology under the magnifying glass. Like Luhan, Deland is conversant with psychoanalytic terms like

The Interwar Years: The Golden Age of Psychological Self-Portraiture 159

"Unconscious" (a term she insists on throughout the book) and "inferiority complex." Any hint of an egotistical attachment to her six-year-old self is dispelled: "I admit she is selfish, cold-hearted, joyfully cruel, with no love in her, and without a particle of humor. I can sum her up in three words: she isn't lovable. . . . What interests me in her most is that she is usually logical" (7). Her representation of herself (and by implication of all children) as a savage devoid of all better nature and higher purpose that one acquires through civilizing influences is consistent with psychoanalytic ideas.

Although Deland's focus is preeminently psychological, and although she uses the occasional psychoanalytic term, she does not approach her subject in a psychoanalytically orthodox manner. She belabors the topic of memory to an unprecedented degree, but she theorizes memory in a manner inconsistent with psychoanalysis. Margaret has memories, but the six-year-old Maggie also has memories, which she "gives" to her elderly biographer (e.g., 10). Maggie also seems to have memories of things she did not take in consciously, unconscious memories that Margaret can tap into. Deland was a member of two psychical societies and was interested in the occult. Her concept of the unconscious may derive at least in part from such circles.[33]

An even greater preoccupation of Deland's than the workings of memory is the interplay of early experience and language acquisition. This focus is apparent in her innovative narrative organization. The chapters are organized by concepts. The five chapters are entitled "War, Patriotism and Love"; "Law, Justice and Compassion"; "Honor, Death and Truth"; "Fear, Gossip and Savagery"; and "God, Vanity and Nature." Deland tells how Maggie heard, understood, and reacted to these concepts and how they determined her thinking and her behavior. Maggie's mental drama of language versus experience took place between the ages of four and ten, and the narrative oscillates between these endpoints, ages six and seven being the most important. Thus, "love"—a word everyone uses a lot—is one Maggie also uses a lot, even though she's a coldhearted creature who really does not love anyone. "War" sounds very positive to the child, since everyone praises her when she acts like a "patriotic little girl," until a cousin's husband is actually killed. "Compassion" inspires her to establish a hospital where she briefly treats two caterpillars. "Death" is a concept that comes closer and closer, beginning with her grandfather's death when she is four and ending at age

160 · The Interwar Years: The Golden Age of Psychological Self-Portraiture

ten when she gets inflammatory rheumatism and realizes that she too could die. The idea that words shape the child's understanding of the world sounds eerily like the "prison house of language" theories that would later dominate structuralism and poststructuralism and were known in Deland's day through the theories of Edward Sapir and Benjamin Lee Whorf. But Deland explores the relationship between words and thought empirically and seemingly without prejudging the issue of which comes first. She observes that Maggie had her first experience of Nature independently of the word, showing that she is not dogmatically committed to the idea that words come before feeling.

If Deland's work is sui generis, so is Maria Waser's. The Swiss writer tells us that she will gaze inward, not at the outward facts of her life. Waser was exceptionally well educated for a woman of her day. The third and youngest daughter of a professional family—both parents were doctors—and homeschooled in a Swiss village until age eleven, she went on to earn a PhD in history and literature in Bern in 1902 and later became the editor of a cultural magazine and a writer. Her stated presumption, which she expounds both at the beginning and the end of her long book, is that now in her old age, in anticipation of the death that would in fact soon claim her, she is able to survey her past much as she can survey the surrounding landscape from her possibly metaphoric current home, an "attic room." Moreover, the "floodlight of memory"[34] seeks out and illuminates precisely those moments, events, and situations of her life that in retrospect proved the most meaningful. She believes that her memory brings back what is important to her personally. The memories she writes about are mainly emotional ones. All this is consonant with modern memory theory—present concerns dictate what and how we remember, emotional events are better remembered—although the clarity and accuracy that Waser imputes to her memory would be questioned today. Waser consistently refers to her memory as illuminating the past with a bright light. Beyond this, however, Waser announces that her memories will yield the meaning of life. The images that the "floodlight of memory" makes vivid, she believes, are *Sinnbilder* (literally, pictures full of meaning). These important events initiated patterns of similar experiences that were repeated throughout her entire life and hence are the keys to its comprehension. She calls life a "spiral staircase" (170) on which we keep coming back to the same spot one turn higher. Since she believes that human lives resemble one another

The Interwar Years: The Golden Age of Psychological Self-Portraiture   161

to a degree, she hopes that her *Sinnbilder* will also give others the key to the meaning of *their* lives.

Thus, Waser recounts her significant memories, each of which leaves its mark on her, initiates a pattern, and reveals some truth. Her earliest childhood memories are among the most moving. The first involves awakening to sunlight and experiencing joy. She says that for the rest of her life, light, joy, and awakening will be linked. In a subsequent memory, she is sitting on her mother's lap, nestled on her breast. Then suddenly somebody bursts in, interrupting. For her, this experience too is paradigmatic for many subsequent ones: happiness and security are suddenly brutally interrupted by someone or something intruding. In a further memory, a yellow bird—a canary—alights on her bed. Her family says that since it flew to her, it now belongs to her. But it turns out to belong to a neighbor, so she has to give it back. But—surprise— the owner makes a present of it to her. This shows her that evil can turn into good—something she has always continued to believe. Next, the canary falls ill and dies, even though she attempts to save its life by performing a courageous deed. This misfortune instills in her the message that sorrow does not always turn into joy; there is a power we cannot do anything about. After this, the family's move to a new house represents a setting out into freedom—an experience she will often repeat. Having to watch out for her mercurial father, exhausted and overworked from his doctor's practice and prone to wild, angry behavior, during a vacation trip they take together, instills motherliness in her and forever makes her unafraid of men—important in her later life, because her career will take her into exclusively male circles.

Waser continues to maintain throughout her work that the "floodlight of memory" leads her here and there, and from chapter to chapter she continues to identify many *Sinnbilder*. As the autobiography progresses, however, her work comes more and more to resemble a conventional self-focused autobiography, albeit one of the most psychologically insightful ever written. Waser moves through the years of her childhood and youth to approximately age eighteen in chronological order and composes many portraits of family members, teachers, and friends, similarly to—for example—Mabel Dodge Luhan. These portraits show great psychological acumen. They are mainly compassionate. In contrast to Luhan, Waser is rarely scathing. One exception stands out: she heaps scorn on the teacher training institution for women she attended before

162   The Interwar Years: The Golden Age of Psychological Self-Portraiture

switching to a boy's *Gymnasium*. In her opinion, women in all-female institutions can become petty and conformist, just as boys in all-male institutions can become rough. She argues for mixed-sex education.

In sum: In the interwar years, a fraught period of tremendous upheaval, postwar disillusionment, and economic crisis, with the rise of fascism presaging another war, important changes affected women's lives. The efforts of prewar feminism had been partially realized in women's suffrage. A new, emancipated image of women was afloat. Norah Burke, a British author born in 1907, exults in 1955 about the years when she was growing up: "For us, daylight dawned. Chains were falling off women all over the world. My generation were the first women to earn their own living. The freedom and independence which now we take for granted were won only in this very century. I was probably one of the last to watch my skirts go down at each birthday."[35] It is, of course, not true that no woman earned her own living before the 1920s, but before World War I it was much more unusual for a girl born to a middle-class family to do so. Starting in the interwar years, women had less hesitation than previously about writing and publishing their work, including work about their own lives. The rebels from the middle class who had gotten themselves a living and a career joined the women from privileged backgrounds who had the leisure and inclination to write about their lives. In this two-decade period, the number of childhood autobiographies published by women rose sharply, and the percentage of female compared to male authors shot up.

It has been suggested that in France a repressive political climate inhibited women's autobiographical writing. But Anglophone works flourished. Indicative is the very fact that an increasing number of women, above all in the English-speaking countries, felt free to write autobiographical works intended for publication. Their writing took a variety of forms, ranging from conventional memoirs to bold personal statements. Works in the German-speaking countries followed similar patterns. Memoirs dominate in the immediate postwar years, but by the 1930s authors wrote more personally and psychologically, like their English counterparts. Hitler's advent to power in 1933 brought a crackdown on what could be published. Depending on who she was, even the author of a childhood autobiography could encounter publishing resistance, witness Emmy Ball-Hennings.

The Interwar Years: The Golden Age of Psychological Self-Portraiture   163

Whereas before World War I examples of women's childhood auto-biographies were isolated and diverse, and every woman seemed to be an innovator, after the war distinct types emerged. Multiple authors opted for each type. The main types were memoirs and semi-memoirs, self-focused autobiographies, and attempts to recapture the child's vision. In general, and logically, although there is no hard-and-fast rule, authors who explored the child's vision confined themselves to their childhood years, whereas women who wanted to show how their childhood laid the groundwork for what they later became, whether they acquiesced in it or rebelled against it, extended their stories to youth and young adulthood. Authors created hybrid types: semi-memoirs, which wove a personal thread into memoirs (e.g., Seidel, Acland, Farjeon, McClung, Helen Woodward, and Pagés), and autobiographies grounded in the retrospective telling of "my story" that also opened windows into the child's perspective (in particular, Undset). The autobiographers came from all walks of life. Although celebrated novelists like Colette, Reuter, and Undset wrote outstanding works, many of the authors (Soskice, Thirkell, Woodward, McHugh, Hughes, Acland, Luhan, Allinson, Lubbock, Icus-Rothe, and Marie zu Erbach-Schönberg) were not professional writers. Gandy and Baynes were nonfiction writers. Of the prewar modes, the French confessional mode proved the most forward-pointing. It spread from France to the English-speaking countries and elsewhere in Europe.

From a present-day perspective, women's autobiographical writing in this period seems motivated by a woman's desire to write about herself, her experiences, and her family, rather than to appeal to and capture a broad readership. The works are not slick. They are often long and baggy. Many have rough edges. A hesitancy about tone is noticeable. The modest, self-deprecating tone that characterized women's writing before the war ceded to a spectrum of new tones. The explicit apology quickly vanished. One can almost hear women wondering, "How do I package this?" In the English-speaking countries, the ironic tone was a favorite; some adopted a jocular, humorous tone; one writer seized on the idealizing, Wordsworthian tone. The most polished works, the literarily most perfect ones, are those that follow the earlier feminine model of exploring the mind of the child. But an interest in psychology is a hallmark of works in this period across the board. Child study, which dates to 1870, marked an increase of interest in childhood. Child

164   The Interwar Years: The Golden Age of Psychological Self-Portraiture

welfare laws and compulsory elementary school education followed in the 1870s and 1880s. The advent of psychoanalysis then gave childhood a new boost. Freud published his view that infantile memories are both formative and indestructible in *The Interpretation of Dreams* (1900). His *Three Essays on the Theory of Sexuality* (1905) followed with the shocking thesis that infants are already sexual beings. Psychoanalysis began to be widely received in the interwar years, and as of that point no one could doubt that childhood was a very important period of life. It was an insight that spurred the production of childhood autobiographies and influenced what writers wrote.

The autobiographies written in the confessional mode are, historically speaking, the most innovative, since they break convention with their self-assertiveness, willingness to air sexual themes, and disregard for parents' feelings. The autobiographers felt, in one way or another, that the world was out of joint, and, through an analysis of their early experiences, they set out to find the causes, sometimes employing the new "truths" of psychoanalysis or socialism. Some of their works express considerable anger. In the wake of the recent political upheavals, the quest for meaning uprooted the value of adhering to conventions. Writing about oneself may still have been considered daring, but some women took the plunge. Speaking out became the order of the day. Fictionalization persisted, but as a strategy for self-protection it retreated. Séverine and Creston appear to use fictionalized names as a buffer, but Undset seemingly turned her story into a "novel" for different reasons, because fiction offered a palette of more sophisticated narrative techniques and the advantage of greater artistic liberty.

The most interesting development in the interwar years is the new boldness that emerged in the 1930s, presaged by Gertrude Beasley's swiftly banned 1925 publication. To be sure, the interwar years also saw the emergence of a new boldness in autobiography written by men. Taboos started to fall. As the historian of French autobiography Philippe Lejeune puts it, from the beginnings of modern autobiography until 1926, not a single autobiographer was homosexual—at least to judge from their writings.[36] The date 1926 refers to the publication of André Gide's *Si le grain ne meurt*. Lejeune speaks of a "triumph of Puritanism" in French autobiography from the end of the eighteenth century to the end of World War I. He considers Freud to be a kind of Christopher Columbus who discovered the body. Commenting on a similar phenomenon in women's autobiography, Jill Ker Conway finds that what

The Interwar Years: The Golden Age of Psychological Self-Portraiture 165

she calls the "romantic pattern" for women had been superimposed even on slave stories by the middle of the nineteenth century. She writes that "the dictates of sexual propriety and of romanticism did not permit women to speak about physical experience."[37] Conway does not mention the Freudian revolution. She sees the world wars as a turning point that leveled the differences between men's and women's writing, specifically in their writing about the wars. Like Lejeune, I consider the Freudian revolution to have had a strong influence on autobiography. Moreover, whereas Conway speaks of the downfall of the Romantic image of women in the 1960s, I find that the edifice of decorum that had sheltered women's self-writing for so long had already started to crumble in the interwar years, especially from the mid-1930s on.

At issue in the confessional type of childhood autobiography is not just writing about sexuality, though writing about sexuality is one mark of the turn. The contrast between women's diffidence before World War I and the way certain women wrote in the interwar years is astonishing. A discontent-with-one's-lot and desire-for-freedom plot takes shape. Beasley, Luhan, Butts, and Salverson come from very different walks of life. Beasley and Luhan detest the very milieu they come from—rural Texas and wealthy Buffalo respectively. But all four writers hate the life that was prepared for them as girls, the life family and society expected them to lead. Their disrespect for their parents is striking. They have unkind words for their mothers, rejecting for themselves what their mothers, their role models, embody. They hate the constrictions that entangle them—constrictions that have to do both with their social milieu, whether bourgeois or working-class, and with their sex. They, as well as Séverine earlier, long for life—a life that seems to be withheld from women. They unleash anger, resentment, sarcasm—"unfeminine" tones. They present themselves as subjects of desire—truly a new, shocking development. All these writers take their stories into young adulthood, when they start to act decisively on their rebelliousness. Their works implicitly vindicate the paths they choose.

CHAPTER FOUR

Women's Childhood Autobiography during World War II

1940: Flexner (1871–1956)
1940: Posse-Brázdová (1884–1957)
1940: McBride (1899–1976)
1941: Bernstein (1881?–1955)
1941: Starkie (1897–1970)
1941: Neilson (1882–1968)
1941: Carbery (1867–1949)
1941: Crowell (1899–1960)
1942: Adams (1909–1982)

1942: Bowen (1899–1973)
1942: Byrne (1895–1983)
1942: Weinhandl (1880–1975)
1942: Carr (1871–1945)
1943: Coyle (1886–1952)
1943: Phillips (1906–1987)
1944: Treneer (1891–1966)
1944: Porter (1903–1997)
1945: Cannell (1891–1974)

Given the preoccupations of people in wartime, remarkably many English-language women's childhood autobiographies appeared between 1940 and 1945. Granted, some of them came from North America, remote from the theaters of war. Nevertheless, some women who lived in Europe stated that they wrote their childhood memoirs precisely in order to immerse themselves in the recollection of a happier time. The Swedish writer Amelie Posse-Brázdová writes in the preface to her childhood autobiography *In the Beginning Was the Light* (1940) that after what happened in February and March of 1938 (the Anschluss) she saw what was coming: "I suddenly saw with visionary clearness towards what destinies the human race was inexorably rushing."[1] She states that she could not write for almost two years. But then a friend told her to continue her project "to remind people how innocently happy life once could be" (12). Kathleen Cannell, a Paris-based American dance and fashion correspondent for US newspapers, fumes in *Jam Yesterday* (1945): "I was finding life in Paris blacker, gloomier, and more of a survival-of-the-fittest even than a year ago. . . . In order to maintain a minimum of normality it was necessary to remember that there had once, somewhere, been another kind of life. . . . I had to write about it."[2]

The works that appeared during the war years largely follow types established during the 1930s. This is no wonder, for most of the women who published in these years were born during the same decades, from the 1870s until the end of the century. The same generations speak here. Had these women read their predecessors? There are so many echoes in format and strategies of presentation of the memoirs and semi-memoirs of the 1930s in similar works published in the 1940s that it seems safe to say that the later writers were well aware of the memoir tradition. The connections between those who wrote self-focused works and their predecessors are less clear. Whether or not they were aware of following earlier patterns, however, writers who published during the war years made notable contributions to the self-focused type of autobiography of childhood and youth.

Semi-Memoirs

In the war years the older women in the group, those born before the mid-1880s—Mary Carbery, Emily Carr, Helen Flexner, Elisabeth Neilson, Amelie Posse-Brázdová, Margarete Weinhandl—mainly turned to the semi-memoir genre. Carbery, the oldest, contributed to the list of Victorian retrospectives with *Happy World: The Story of a Victorian Childhood*, a book that she began as a diary at the age of twelve and reworked in her seventies. Neilson, daughter of the founder of the Democratic Party in Germany and wife of the president of Smith College, published a memoir of her childhood in Germany, entitled *The House I Knew: Memories of Youth* (1941). In Austria, Margarete Weinhandl published her semi-memoir *Und deine Wälder rauschen fort: Kindheit in Untersteier* (And your forests rustle on: Childhood in Styria, 1942), a work that after the war was placed on restricted lists in the Soviet Occupation Zone, the GDR, and Austria, presumably because the author, a member of the National Socialist German Workers' Party (NSDAP), expresses German-supremacist views.

Some younger women adopted the semi-memoir template as well. In 1940 Mary Margaret McBride, an American radio interview host, published *How Dear to My Heart*, a family memoir of Missouri farm life that has a considerable personal component. Kathleen Cannell manages to turn her chaotic family life into an entertaining family memoir

168   Women's Childhood Autobiography during World War II

of childhood and youth in *Jam Yesterday* (1945); she includes plenty of her own reactions to things. A younger woman who was much less of a somebody, the schoolteacher Anne Treneer, wrote a charming work about growing up in Cornwall. Her *School House in the Wind* (1944) recalls Alison Uttley with its focus on a rural childhood in an interesting place and its unique pleasures, as well as in its careful, beautiful style. What there is of herself in it is not presented as typical to the extent that Uttley implies typicality ("the way I felt which is typical of children"), but is specific to her. The even younger Evelyn Crowell published a sequence of carefully crafted, Nesbit-like pieces in *Texas Childhood* (1941). She too blends stories about place and family with a strong subjective element.

As the years went by and more and more childhood autobiographies were published, women generally put more of themselves, of their individuality, into their childhood memoirs. The evolution toward personal stories proceeded quickly. Authors presented their memoirs about a particular place and a particular time, or about their families, as stories of *their* experiences (e.g., Cannell). Once this type was in place, many women felt encouraged to jump on the bandwagon. The semi-memoir had the advantage of rounding out factual information with the appeal of a human emotional touch. Conversely, some writers padded "their stories" with copious descriptions of time, place, customs, and portraits of other people (e.g., Posse). Posse is a particularly interesting case. She writes an extraordinarily full work of over 400 pages, seemingly in order to preserve a record of the way things were during her exceptionally happy childhood until age thirteen, when her father (a count) died and the family home was lost. She seems almost to be writing for herself. On the other hand, the story becomes extremely personal toward the end, when she describes a sequence of revelations she had in the course of her childhood. From her account one gets the impression that the "revelation" or "turning point" is more than just a literary trope. One of her revelations, at age seven or eight, is that she is *not* the center of the universe! She also admits to having had an imaginary companion, a boy, who accompanies her from an unspecified age (but older than six) and disappears around age eleven—similarly to Una Hunt before her and Mary Lutyens later. Unlike Hunt and Lutyens, she also imagined a girl playmate.

The jewel among the semi-memoirs is the American Helen Thomas Flexner's *A Quaker Childhood* (1940), because of her fascinating representation of the functioning of a Quaker family as well as the implications for girls of being Quaker. Born in 1871, Flexner was the youngest daughter of a leading Quaker family in Baltimore. Her memoir, written late in life, resembles Eleanor Farjeon's inasmuch she tells the story of her prominent and unusual family, which in her case as well as in Farjeon's constituted her world. In contrast to Farjeon, however, Flexner writes in a predominantly historical rather than novelistic style. She writes the history of her family, of her parents, their eight children, and herself up to her seventeenth year, when her mother died. If this book has a plot, it concerns her great love for her mother. From the beginning and throughout, until her mother's death from cancer, it is clear that her mother, "whose love was [her] refuge" is the most important person in her life, her great attachment.[3] Flexner makes a point of showing what being a Quaker meant for women in her era. Quakers considered men and women equal, but there was little real equality for women. Her parents, pillars of the community, conferred and agreed on the raising of children. Yet there were conflicts. These included disagreement over the emancipation of women. Helen's mother, the daughter of a prominent Philadelphia Quaker family, a leader in the church and the Women's Christian Temperance Union, and "the president of nine societies" (107), wanted to see her daughters get an education. Her own education had stopped at age sixteen for lack of a women's college. She had married at seventeen and borne ten children. Helen's father, a physician and pastor, had sexist attitudes about women's education and "divorced women," which stemmed from his belief that women lack men's powers of mind but are (or should be) spiritually and morally superior to men. Helen's mother won out. Helen's older sister, who later became president of Bryn Mawr, insisted on getting an education, and the younger girls all went to college as well. We find out little about Flexner herself, except that she was "a very good little girl" (10) and wanted to be a poet or writer. (In fact, she became an English professor at Bryn Mawr.) She also became a feminist: "So by early emotion was the soil of my mind prepared for passionate interest in righting the wrongs of society to my mother's sex and my own" (82).

The Canadian painter Emily Carr's childhood memoirs *The Book of Small* (1942) is of interest mainly because Carr wrote a completely different account of her childhood a few years later in her posthumously published autobiography *Growing Pains* (1946). The first half of *The Book of Small* is a collection of stories about Carr's childhood in Victoria, British Columbia. These poetic, original, and imaginative pieces, which concern such topics as Sundays and the family cow, are told from the perspective of the child, whose age ranges from four to nine or so. We hear about the child's feelings—her disappointments, longings, joys, and imaginings—many of which, such as her desire for a dog and her animistic vision of nature, are familiar from other childhoods. In contrast, the few pages Carr devotes to her childhood in her autobiography *Growing Pains* (1946) paint a dark, brutal picture that *The Book of Small* does not even hint at. She tells us that her father was a dictatorial disciplinarian who acted as if he were God. Her mother did not challenge him. According to Carr, her father made one after the other of his children his pet precisely when the child was in the man-adoring phase; when the child got out of that phase, he moved on to the next youngest child. Her mother died when she was twelve, her father two years later. Her older sister, twenty years older than the youngest of them, took over the family and ruled the two less docile ones, Emily and her brother, with the whip. At sixteen Emily "escaped" to San Francisco to study art. The contrast between the charming *The Book of Small* and the terrible account in *Growing Pains* shows how malleable the topic of childhood is. Many factors can intervene between a childhood and an autobiography of childhood. Not only can a person think about her childhood in more than one way, but the desire to write a certain kind of book can exert a strong influence on the final product. Carr's case makes one wonder how authentic some of the earlier happy childhood memoirs were.

Self-Focused Works

Some of the younger women, those born from the 1880s on, wrote a spectrum of psychological autobiographies. Six of these are remarkable. Two, discussed in detail below, contributed significantly to larger trends: Enid Starkie's *A Lady's Child* (1941) and M. St. Clare Byrne's *Common or Garden Child: A Not-unfaithful Record* (1942). Starkie wrote a confessional autobiography similar to Mabel Dodge Luhan's and Mary Butts's that is perhaps the outstanding work of this type to date. M. St. Clare Byrne recaptured the child's perspective similarly to Francesca Allinson and Dormer Creston, but intensively investigates the workings of memory in a most original fashion. Both of these works address the problems of growing up female. Two more, also discussed below, are harbingers of *later* trends and deserve a closer look: Aline Bernstein's *An Actor's Daughter* (1941), an example of the relational autobiography that became prominent after World War II, and Elizabeth Adams's *Dark Symphony*

(1940), whose theme is racial inequality. The other two remarkable works, Kathleen Coyle's *The Magical Realm* (1943) and Margaret Mann Phillips's *Within the City Wall* (1943), are one-of-a-kind innovations that neither resemble anything written previously nor are copied by later writers. Coyle has the unusual agenda of showing that ancestry forms us. Written from the child's perspective, her book tells how the child gradually penetrates the mysteries of hereditary destiny. Margaret Phillips writes an unusual, highly original piece about what her twelve-year-old self was up to mentally during the year in which World War I ended. Since these works are anomalous, I shall not discuss them further.

Self-Assertion

The Irish literary critic Enid Starkie was born in 1897. Known for her biographical works on Charles Baudelaire, Arthur Rimbaud, André Gide, and Gustave Flaubert, she became a lecturer in French Literature at Somerville College, Oxford, then fellow of Somerville, and finally university reader in French Literature at Oxford. She wrote *A Lady's Child* in 1939. It was accepted by Faber in May of 1940[4] and appeared in 1941.

In the preface, Starkie writes: "In August 1939, with a further tornado gathering strength, I wished to recapture, while there still was time, what was left of that early life before it was completely buried in the debris of a second World War."[5] She thereby sets the tracks for another retrospective of the pre–World War I period. She grew up in Ireland as one of the five children of the last resident commissioner of education for Ireland under British rule. She emphasizes that this Ireland is already a thing of the past: with the establishment of the Free State, Ireland changed completely. Starkie thus creates the impression of intending to write a social history memoir of the type encountered in the previous decade. Like Molly Hughes, she invokes the justification of typicality: "It is the life of middle-class children in those distant days which I wish to recapture" (14). Moreover, she says that she is not writing autobiography, but family history: "It is not a picture of myself that I am trying to achieve, but a picture of the family" (14). After the fashion of the family memoirs of the previous decade, the book contains many photographs of Enid and her family. She makes apologies for her memory: "I have never kept a diary and I have no letters from my childhood—or indeed any family letters at all—and so as I write I plunge my hands into the rag bag of memory and fish up the various scraps" (13). Starkie thus rehearses a number of traditional moves in her preface: she wants to preserve the past; her childhood is typical; her memories are scraps; she does not aim to write about herself, but to paint a picture of her family.

What she actually does in *A Lady's Child* is something completely different. She writes a true autobiography. Enid's troubled story, from her first memories through young adulthood, is at its center. She paints portraits of other family members and other people who were important in her and her family's life, such as their cook and her first governess, but these portraits are intensely subjective. Her protestations to the contrary, her memory seems excellent and vivid. Her account seems detailed and complete. Although she gives us some memories, such as the poetically beautiful memory of watching the "slight shiver and the flash of light" (88) when the venetian blind slats are shifted from down to up, she does not write in the manner of one who is recollecting, but rather like someone who has long carried her account in her head and thought it over many times. Her claim to typicality lies in her being a "lady's child," a term used in the Ireland of her childhood to denote the child of a family of a certain social standing. She gives the reader a clear picture of her family, but, apart from the constant party-giving and party-going that she says is typical of prewar life in and around Dublin, it never becomes clear whether anyone else's family in Ireland at the time resembled hers.

A Lady's Child is, in fact, alongside Luhan's *Intimate Memories: Background* and Butts's *The Crystal Cabinet*, one of the first serious childhood autobiographies written in English that does not resort to a novelistic style (like DorothyWhipple) or a humorous presentation (like Bertha Damon and Eleanor Hallowell Abbott) despite touches of humor. Starkie also does not adopt a nostalgic tone or take an ironic or condescending attitude toward her child self as do so many previous English-language childhood memoirs. There is no significant break in tone here between the child subject and the author-narrator. If the latter distances herself from her child subject, it is to sum up sympathetically how she felt as a child. The person writing the story seems to be essentially the same person she was as a child.

This work has another feature in common with Luhan and Butts: indiscretion. Butts's worst indiscretions were deleted out of the first edition of *The Crystal Cabinet*. But no editorial hand intervened in the publication of *A Lady's Child*. In the preface Starkie announces that she has exercised discretion (though in suggestive, if not to say indiscreet terms): "My task would have been easier, too, if I could have had a thorough wash of the family soiled linen in public, if I could have spilt out the whole laundry basket, but all I could attempt was a rinsing out of the less dirty articles" (14). She apologizes for hurting anyone's feelings: "I ask forgiveness of all those whose feelings I may unwillingly have wounded, and I beg them to remember that these are the memories of a child and a very young girl—an intolerant and obstinate girl—subjective memories coloured by my clashes with those in authority over me during the developing years of my youth, when I resented any restraint on my personal liberty" (15). Well might she apologize! She changes the names of teachers at her Dublin school, but she writes extensively and candidly about her relatives under their real names. Many of them were still alive. Like Luhan and Butts, she writes a great many things that many people were very unhappy to see in print. According to Starkie's biographer Joanna Richardson, contemporary reviewers agreed that the book had a bitter tone. Elizabeth Bowen, for one, who would soon publish a slim book of her own childhood memoirs (*Seven Winters*, 1942), was among the early reviewers who noticed this tone. The book was badly received in Dublin as "an unpardonable piece of disloyalty" (*The Irish Times*) and prohibited. This increased interest in it, so that it was republished. "Her relatives resented it fiercely," Richardson writes.[6]

Starkie's account is chronological. She takes her family sequentially through three moves, albeit giving few dates and punctuating her tale with portraits of her family members and other key figures. Like Luhan, Butts, and Salverson, she takes her story beyond childhood into adolescence and young adulthood until she reaches a logical stopping point. That point, like Farjeon's, is her father's death and the aftermath, which brings a final disagreement between her and her mother over whether it is more important to spend money on keeping up their "outworn gentility" (336) or to realize her dreams. In the end, she decides to leave home and pursue a doctorate at the Sorbonne.

Starkie's father was an important man, and her parents led quite a luxurious life, though, as it proved, a life that was beyond their means. They gave constant parties. They had many servants: a cook, maids, gardeners, and nurses and governesses for the children. Yet one gets the overall impression that Enid had an unhappy childhood; she paints the self-portrait of a victim. She emphasizes that Ireland in her youth was more old-fashioned than England. The children grew up under the charge of a nanny or a governess and saw little of their parents. Except for once a week, they ate separately from the adults. Her family did not

174   Women's Childhood Autobiography during World War II

show emotions, and her mother never played with her children. Starkie writes that she longed for an animal warmth that she did not get: "As a small child I often longed for the animal warmth of simple maternal love. I longed for some one to take me in her arms, to kiss me and to hug me, to rock me to sleep in her lap" (45).

An undercurrent of feminism runs through this book. Starkie articulates it mainly through her description of the patriarchal conditions in her family and the different treatment of the one son and the five daughters. Thus, for example, she cites her brother Walter, who informs her when they were growing up that "girls only learned to read with great difficulty and that they could in any case never do difficult lessons" (33). Even though she states that she loves her father best, one senses that she disapproved of the way her mother, who married young, believed that her life and the life of all the women in the house should revolve around him, the important man. Her mother supported the Anti-Suffrage League, a fact that, Enid says, outraged her when she was young. Her mother, whose true calling seems to have been as a *salonière*, is an old-style woman, and this is enough to create tension between the two of them. Starkie emphasizes that her mother set great store by appearances, including the personal appearance of her daughters. One bizarre detail is that, in an effort to ensure that her children were beautiful, she kept the girls' noses pinched with hairpins half an hour each morning to keep their noses from spreading (44–45). Even after her father's bankruptcy, her mother continued to insist that it is of paramount importance to keep up appearances. The mother is a conservative in every respect: opposed not only to women's suffrage, but also to every new fashion including bobbed hair, short skirts, sleeveless and backless dresses, slacks, and shorts, and, of course, drinking and smoking for women. Sounding like Séverine, Starkie most resents the way her mother wants to withhold experience from girls: "I did not want to miss any experience, to be kept away from the realities of life merely because I was a girl" (232).

Starkie paints portraits of each member of the older generation early on and of her own siblings toward the end of the book. She portrays her father favorably, as a great scholar, a brilliant speaker, just and fair, and fond of his children, despite his distance from them. Her initial portrait of her mother is not unfavorable, though it emphasizes her mother's preoccupation with appearances. As the story unfolds, however, and particularly when Enid reaches adolescence, Starkie writes that constant clashes marked her relationship with her mother. She candidly passes

Women's Childhood Autobiography during World War II 175

judgment on her aunts and uncles. In her view, her aunts and uncles on her father's side are humorless people who took themselves seriously and "were afraid of lapses from conventionality" (58). Her mother's sisters (unlike her correct and dignified mother) were "fast, pleasure-loving, and self-indulgent. They smoked expensive cigarettes at the rate of fifty or more a day, and trays of drinks were always very visible whenever one went to their houses, and, moreover, they gambled at poker and at the race-courses" (62). Auntie Elsie is "lazy and self-indulgent" (62). Auntie Ida is cynical, witty, and ribald: "Nothing was sacred from the fire of her wit. When I was young the coarseness of her language used often to embarrass me because I never heard anything like it at home" (63). Auntie Helen, however, is her favorite aunt, with whom she has a special relationship. When Enid was small, this beautiful aunt appeared to her as the Fairy Queen one day in the woods and promised to remain the Fairy Queen for her forever. Starkie does, however, feel free to comment on this (now deceased) aunt's sexuality: "Auntie Helen had the reputation of being very fast. I do not know whether this was true, but I know that my mother believed it. Certainly wherever she went she was always surrounded by a bevy of admiring young men, and she had, right up to the day of her death, a very great attraction for them" (71). As for her younger sisters, all of whom are alive at the time of writing, Muriel is inscrutable, Chou-Chou has "a jealous regard for her own rights and interests" (288), Nancy is "lazy" (292). Overall, these portraits of her sisters, despite their candor, are not negative, but quite affectionate. Mainly she tries to account for the fact that none of her sisters ever amounted to anything, despite their considerable talents. How did Starkie have the nerve to publish comments such as these? Seemingly, starting with Luhan, women's childhood autobiography jumped its track. More and more writers, Starkie included, abandoned the constraints of decorum and spoke their mind freely.

Aside from Mabel Dodge Luhan's startling *Background* and to a lesser degree Sigrid Undset's *Elleve Aar*, sex had up to this point been a non-topic in women's childhood autobiographies. Mary Butts talked about sexuality as an issue between herself and her mother, but her editor had excised this out in the first edition. Starkie, though her treatment of sex is tame by today's standards, shows that she is a well-informed product of the Freudian revolution by commenting on or speculating about the sexuality of various women. She suspects Aunt Ida of having been disappointed in sex; she notices that her French governess was attracted to her older brother; Chou-Chou is attractive to older men; Nancy has sex appeal (289). She underscores that she herself was very innocent and childlike for a long time—thus, she believed in fairies until the family was about to move to Dublin, when she was thirteen or fourteen. Yet she is capable of saying casually about herself that a childhood episode involving a boy who pushed her away from her brother lit in her a "masochistic attraction" for "scornful, condescending young men" (27).

Of herself Starkie writes confessionally and seemingly without restraint. Her autobiography makes it seems as if she had imbibed the French confessional tradition, which, in fact, she probably had. From childhood she had been steeped in French literature. She had learned French as a child at the hands of a French governess, read French literature when she was growing up, studied modern foreign languages at Oxford, and then pursued a doctorate at the Sorbonne. Her tastes inclined to writers who were social rebels and controversial figures like herself;[7] these included the confessionally inclined André Gide, whose work she admired immensely. She writes in *A Lady's Child* that reading Gide's *Nourritures terrestres* at the age of fifteen marked a turning point for her, one that gave her courage in her adolescent revolt.

Starkie makes the impression of pouring out bottled-up feelings in *A Lady's Child*. From very early on she believed that grown-ups are cruel and that childhood is equal to suffering. This idea was implanted in her by an early punishment—her wet knickers were hung around her neck all day—and reinforced by subsequent experiences. The word "humiliation" is one that occurs with noticeable frequency to describe the way she was treated. Enid suffers humiliation in myriad ways: because her brother deserts her when another boy comes over to play (a theme we have seen in Athénaïs Michelet), because her mother dresses them differently from other children, by her French governess's punishments, by a spanking she gets from her father, by upsetting water at lunch, by punishments at Alexandra School in Dublin, by not having clothes to lend her friends at Oxford, by having to accept second-best in anything.

Like so many girls of her era, Starkie was initially homeschooled by a sequence of governesses, because "my father had always . . . professed to disapprove of school for girls" (165). She describes her life under her French governess up to nearly age ten as utterly miserable. In the opinion of the governess, she is a devilish child who insists on being different and talking back. The governess, Starkie recalls, is determined to get the better of her. Life, in Starkie's recollection, consists of continual punishments. She cannot remember her own misdeeds, only the punishments. Some of the punishments are standard ones, like copying out lines such as "je n'aurais pas dû raisonner" (111) and going to bed without supper, but Mademoiselle is inventive, too: "I feel acute nausea, even after all these years, when I think of some of her punishments, when I remember that she used to make me kiss the ground beneath her feet to wear down my pride" (108). Starkie tells the pathetic story of how she believed that the Wishing Gift would be bestowed on her on Easter and for six months derived strength from this belief. When it did not happen, she realized that she would not get free of her governess for years, and it drove her to contemplate and finally attempt suicide. She writes of this terrible period under her French governess:

> I no longer recollect what I was myself at that age. I can only remember the desolation and the bitterness of heart which I felt. I can recall my sensation of utter loneliness with no one to protect me or to sympathise with me. I can remember the tears which I used to stifle under the bedclothes at night so that Muriel, from her bed near by, should not hear me. I can remember how I longed to die. I think that the desolation which I felt during these years was greater than any which I experienced later in my life. (121)

It did not occur to her that she could complain to her father or her mother about this governess.

Rounding out the picture of the life of her mind, Starkie states that reading was one of her few joys. Her first desire, she recalls, was to learn to read. She loved stories, especially the *Arabian Nights* and fairy tales. Like Eleanor Farjeon, she soon lived in a world of fairy tales more than in the real world. She remained a child who loved to read, ruining her eyes by reading by dim light or even moonlight at night when reading was forbidden to her (another punishment).

Starkie makes a persuasive case for her personal misery as a child, and it is hard not to sympathize with her. As a narrator, she makes the impression of passionate honesty, and this makes it easy to excuse her indiscretion about her relatives. Starkie takes candor to heights that will be equaled but not surpassed in the next twenty-five years.

Remembering

Like Enid Starkie, Muriel St. Clare Byrne was a graduate of Oxford's Somerville College, albeit her field was English. She overlapped with Starkie there, pursuing her MA during Starkie's undergraduate years. In later life she held various academic positions as lecturer and wrote or edited several books about sixteenth-century England. Her book *Common or Garden Child: A Not-unfaithful Record* (1942) continues the tradition of the psychological childhood autobiography. It aims to recapture the child's sensibility, ideas, and point of view. The tone of Byrne's authorial commentary is serious and investigative. The book is very short on information about names, places, and dates, but what little there is corresponds to known facts about Byrne's life. Though Byrne does not name herself, she sometimes calls herself "Toby," the nickname her grandfather gave her. Liverpool is not named, but its Empire Theatre is. This book offers the most thoroughgoing, original—and from the present-day reader's point of view—prescient exploration of memory seen to date. Byrne counts as the Marcel Proust of women childhood autobiographers. All the material in the book is presented as the stuff of recollection. She treats the period from her earliest recollections prior to age three to age fourteen or fifteen, when she enters the local high school.

Byrne's ideas on memory evince Proust's positive faith in the mind's ability to recapture the past. Her ideas bear some resemblance to his, but are not precisely the same. Like Proust, she distinguishes between two kinds of memory, one of which is worthless, and the other of which is precious. But in place of his "voluntary memory" and "involuntary memory" she distinguishes between memory that has been influenced by others' accounts and what she calls "sense-vision," or the uninfluenced recapture of a past scene.[8] She writes: "It is difficult to carry back the senses. It is so easy for memory, with its treacherous deposit from other minds, to silt up the channel in its leisurely flow. But the sense-vision is instant and piercing, and for the moment that it endures the water is crystal-clear, the experience is seen and felt, not remembered, but timeless. At first the stream is troubled, thick with the sediment of other people's recollections. I remember much: but I see nothing" (7). Throughout the book, she speaks of memory using metaphors of water. By "sense-vision" she means that a past scene comes back to her as if it were sensuously present, similarly to the wonder wrought by Proust's involuntary memory. Unlike Proust, she does not explain by what mechanism the past comes back to her, other than to imply that sensations have their own long and mysterious life (105). But a first memory comes from the age of five, and one memory leads to another. The early memories are disconnected, fragmentary, and vivid. They are so vivid that they seem not to be memories at all: she uses the device of present-tense narration to present these fragmentary scenes exactly as the child experienced them. In subsequently narrated isolated memories Byrne embeds first-person present-tense free indirect discourse in her present-tense account to indicate that she remembers not just the occasion but exactly how she thought about it at the time. Thus, for example, she writes: "I chew desperately; and the cake-stand is again passed around. My pink cake has gone! The blood pounds in my ears ..." (12).

As author, Byrne intrudes to wonder about the nature of these early memories, to analyze why she remembers some things but not others, and to hypothesize about the nature of memory. She goes beyond Proust in several ways. First, she specifically addresses the subject of yet earlier memories that were induced by other people's stories. Second, and even more striking, is her hunch that "there is ... a half-world of remembrance that is, I think, not directly apprehended, but only through the intermediary that is oneself at a later-earlier age" (18). Thus, she remembers a number of events that took place in the period of childhood amnesia. For example, she remembers herself watching an infant lying in a cot (i.e., crib). She knows that at the time she watched the infant she remembered her own days of sleeping in a crib. Thus she can remember sleeping in a crib, but only this way. What she writes is corroborated by recent empirical studies. These studies have shown that preverbal memories are recoverable as declarative memories if they are reinstated in memory by the slightly older child who has acquired language.[9] Third, Byrne distinguishes between the memories of the senses: visual memories are those she recovers most easily, then tactile memories. Fourth, she wonders at the precision yet limitation of some of her memories: why does she see her grandmother clearly, but never standing or walking?

She also obviously believes (like Proust) that memory is associative. Proust observes, "From the sound of pattering raindrops I recaptured the scent of the lilacs at Combray; from the shifting of the sun's rays on the balcony the pigeons in the Champs-Elysées; from the muffling of sounds in the heat of the morning hours, the cool taste of cherries."[10] Byrne reproduces in her text the associative quality of memory by transitioning from one memory to the next through association. For example:

"But the staircase is not a staircase, it is a broad gravelly drive . . ." (9). In like manner, she skips over years, backwards and forwards, by moving from one image of sand to another (83). She asserts that memory does not yield a logical narrative sequence, but "like a tide on the turn" "sways backwards and forwards over the years" (85). Over time, memory changes earlier associations: "what was contiguous and related no longer appears so" (85). Like the tide, memory creates new patterns. Memory also does not distinguish clearly between what really happened and what she imagined. Thus, she muses that she "remembers" things that could not possibly have happened, for example that she launched a ship.

Even more perplexingly, Byrne's two kinds of memory yield contradictory information. For example, her sense-vision reminds her that she was terrified by the fear of suffocation when she struggled inside her first jersey—so that she never again put on a jersey. Yet her conscious memory tells her that she possessed and wore several jerseys. The author concludes that emotions are tricky: they can masquerade as sense perceptions, fooling the mind into thinking that something happened that did not happen, as well as the reverse.[11] Byrne is evidently aware of psychoanalysis (she speaks of censorship and the "conscious mind" [92]), yet her exploration of memory's tricks is highly empirical and does not read like adopted theory. She never takes recourse to the psychoanalytic concepts of censorship or repression to explain her memories.

Byrne's memories take her into an exploration of her childhood sensibility and thus self-analysis. Her title, "Common or Garden Child," seems like a ploy to defend her book against the accusation that she was not important enough to merit such analysis. It seems like a variant on the appeal to typicality seen in Burnett—a way to raise the protective parasol of self-deprecation. The text does not sustain such modesty, however: the book really is about her, not about an ordinary little girl. Byrne makes no effort to point out the typicality of any of her childhood propensities. Admittedly, she is not a flamboyant personality. She notes that she has a rule-following disposition. She is a straightforward child who takes what is said at face value and thus does not take well to teasing. She was also, apparently, not the most talented or brilliant child of her set, even though she was verbally gifted. She records a change in herself at age ten. Prior to age ten she had been "on velvet" (135): an only child, she had no competition at home, yet plenty of companions, since she attended school starting at the age of five. After age ten things became more complicated. For example, it was hard for her to come to terms with the fact that her best friend was better at nearly everything than she.

One of the most original aspects of the book is that the author traces from early childhood, from the age at which she played at hoops, her conflicted feelings about being a girl. A more accepting author, Anne Treneer, simply notes that boys had iron hoops and hooks whereas girls had wooden hoops and sticks.[12] Byrne resents this disparity, because the iron hoops are easier to control than the wooden ones (10). Two entire chapters are devoted to her childhood conviction that "men are infinitely superior" (41) to "Ladies," who are *dull* (38–39). Thus, men have ideas about what it would be fun to do; they understand how to make things, draw better, give better presents, and have the best ideas about food. "Ladies," in contrast, are always disapproving; they forbid things. She wishes she were a boy, dresses like a boy whenever she can, wants boys' playthings (which to her signify good, real things), and wants to play a boy in the school play. Her praise of men is presented in declarative statements in the present tense and in the most convincing colors. The author's use of free indirect discourse (also in the present tense) shows, however, that this is the child's and not the author's point of view: "Men are the lords of life. . . . My father or my grandfather would let me have a dog, if we could go right away from my mother and grandmother. . . . Men are the nicest people in the world" (52). The reader infers that the author has come around to a modified perspective.

Byrne excels at representing, from the child's point of view, the bumpy transition to early adolescence. Suddenly, "now that you're twelve, thirteen" (167), all kinds of proprieties and behaviors are expected. She seems to be perpetually too old for this yet too young for that. What she does learn, she points out poignantly, is the art of pretense and concealment, that is, not just to be simply and naïvely herself, but to speak and act as people want her to, so as to make getting through the day easier. Concurrently, she experiences considerable tensions with her mother, who appears to be the main perpetrator of the confusions. The fact that her father has died comes up in passing in her thoughts when she is an early adolescent (182). As a radical consequence of this being a book not about events but about recreating the child's point of view and her memories of it, this seemingly major event in her childhood is never treated as such. In the end she represents her mother and herself as reaching complete harmony when they visit the high school she hopes to attend. Her mother had been a teacher in the United States and had given up further education in order to marry her father. Thus, her mother sees in her daughter's desire the fulfillment of her own dream for herself.

Starkie and Byrne both dip their knee at conventions of feminine modesty, only to transgress them in their texts: Starkie with her unrestrained confessional style, Byrne with her deft framing of her childhood desire to be male. Both of these original works are among the most feminist seen to date. As we shall see, the feminism—if not feminism in a political sense, then at least a heightened critical consciousness of gender—apparent in English-language women's childhood autobiographies published during the interwar and the wartime years tends to fade in the immediate postwar period, only to emerge more sharply in French-language works starting in the late 1950s.

The Family Nest and the Challenges beyond It

Another work that plunges into memories is Aline Bernstein's *An Actor's Daughter* (1941), but in an emotional rather than an analytical fashion. Bernstein grew up in glamorous if precarious New York theater circles in the 1880s and 1890s and became a prominent New York set and costume designer. In the autobiography of her childhood and adolescence, she loses herself in scenes of the past. As author, she is supremely indifferent to ages and dates, never bothers with explanations, but is extremely attentive to people and feelings. People—her father, her mother, her mother's beautiful and seductive sister Nana, their many artistic friends and acquaintances—were her world. She was surrounded by love, and she adored and idolized these people in return, who included her in their exciting, artistic, cosmopolitan lives. How could the boring school she was eventually made to attend possibly compete with her father's stage successes, her parents' extravagant parties, the family trip to London, or the intensity of her aunt's loves and despairs that drove her to take solace in the needle? The passionately lived life that surrounded Aline was reality for her. No wonder that in her account of herself she is at pains to describe mystical moments in which her aesthetic sensibility, her realization of the importance of art, music, and beauty, awakens. Her book definitely centers on her, but the very title *An Actor's Daughter* suggests the degree to which other people and her relationships with them are important to her story. According to her biography, she lost her mother at age eleven and her father at age sixteen. Invariably oblivious to dates and to any necessity to clarify things for readers, she does not tell us when she lost her parents, but she does write about their deaths. She closes her story with her father's death, which for her ends her childhood.

Elizabeth Laura Adams, a younger author born in 1909, likewise emphasizes that she grew up in the cocoon of a loving family. The word "love" is prominent in her autobiography of childhood and youth, *Dark Symphony* (1942), as it is in Bernstein's. As in Bernstein's case, family love sheltered her emotionally and initially made her a happy little girl, although, as in Bernstein's case, problems loomed on the horizon. But there the similarities between the two lives and the two works end. Adams grew up in California, not New York; her family was solidly middle class, not artistic; and above all, she was Black and not White. She experienced not just the pain of losing her father when she was fifteen, but that of ongoing racial discrimination. She got a first taste of it in primary school, but it hit her hard later, above all in the Depression years when she tried to find work to support her mother and herself. No matter where she turned, she heard and saw the phrase, "No work for Colored." In writing her autobiography, Adams has a point to make. Whereas Bernstein writes seriously, without irony, and sometimes waxes mystical, Adams's work is carefully constructed to deliver its urgent message about the crippling effects of racial discrimination. Her book is concise, eloquent, and finely tuned, with ironic and humorous touches.

In the first half of her book, Adams paints the picture of her happy childhood in Southern California as the only child of middle-class African American parents. Her parents are not just loving and kind—"No child ever received more love from parents than I"[13]—but in harmonious agreement about all aspects of child-rearing. They are wise: they introduce such fictions as Santa, the Easter Bunny, and the stork, but later explain them for what they are. They are strict and enforce benevolent discipline; when one considers the horrible punishments inflicted on some children, Adams's are on the order of having to stand in the corner or not being allowed to kiss Mother. In short, her parents are exemplary parents. Adams portrays her mother especially as a beautiful, inspiring person. Incidents from Adams's childhood are carefully chosen to establish what a wonderful family she had, by way of contrast with the scenes of vulgarity, strife, and lovelessness she encountered when she worked as a maid in White people's houses during the Depression. She starts to encounter racial prejudice when she begins school. Although she consistently has White school friends, and although her parents tell her to disregard the prejudice and not hate back, an insidious pattern of discrimination begins to haunt her. As an adolescent she is drawn to religion, especially Catholicism. Catholicism appeals to her in particular because of the confessional, which is color-blind. She nearly becomes a Catholic nun.

Adams's work is very much her own personal story. She tells of her love for music and her ambition to be a concert violinist, which she had to give up because of ill-health, of her interest in creative writing, and above all of her quest for Christ, the stated focus of the book. She does not represent herself as a typical American Black girl (and indeed she is not one). What stands out, in historical hindsight, is that, although Adams's message concerns race, she writes a classic individual autobiography and not an autobiography of the group. She does not claim or imply typicality for her story, as later Black autobiographers of childhood and youth will do. Her book also does not set out to raise the consciousness of a Black readership, as Anne Moody's *Coming of Age in Mississippi* and Maya Angelou's *I Know Why the Caged Bird Sings* will in the late 1960s. *Dark Symphony* is not a political book in the same sense. Adams dwells on the suffering racial discrimination causes in its victims, whether these victims are African American, Jewish, Chinese, or other.

In sum: Works published during the World War II years continued the trends that had taken shape during the interwar years. The proportion of female to male authors continued to increase. No new types emerged, but some outstanding works were written that followed previous models. In particular, Enid Starkie wrote in the outspoken vein that was the eye-catching accomplishment in women's childhood autobiography in the interwar years. Like Luhan and Butts, she represents herself as a discontented subject of desire, though as less of a "bad girl" than they and more as a sensitive victim in a large, prominent, not particularly caring family.

The trend toward hybridization in memoirs continued. Memoirs that mixed "my story" with "the story" became the rule. The war itself inspired some authors to write about their childhood memories, whether because they wanted to preserve a record of a happier time or simply because they feared that the war would sweep away the last remnants of life as it once was. The Depression made its mark on one autobiography—Adams's—leaving her jobless-because-Colored. Whereas formerly hardly a work had been written to prove a point (Popp is the exception), Adams writes with an ethical agenda, to convince readers of the evils of racial discrimination.

Writers in the war years had been children in better days, and so the tendency of some to idealize their childhood is not surprising. Others, however, notably Starkie, had been miserable, and let it show. Quite a few writers—Flexner, Posse, Bernstein, Adams, and Byrne—pay touching homage to their mothers, in a fashion reminiscent of Colette. Starkie, on the other hand, speaks of irreconcilable differences with her mother, like Luhan and Butts in the preceding decade.

Psychology is even more pervasive than in the interwar years, and feminism becomes more pronounced. Carr and Byrne joined the sequence of authors who undertook to recreate the child's point of view. Byrne, in her forgotten but fascinating book, not only made an important contribution to that collection, but added a novel twist: her extensive treatment of memory, and her original and perceptive ideas about it, outdid anything that women childhood autobiographers had had to say about that topic before.

CHAPTER FIVE

Women's Childhood Autobiography from the End of the Second World War through the 1960s

1946: Chagall (1895–1944)
1947: Bottome (1882–1963)
1947: P. Lynch (1898–1972)
1948: M. Hamilton (1872–)
1948: Holmes, pseud.
1949: Harding (1902–1971)
1949: Phelps (1867–1950)
1949: Wirth-Stockhausen (1886–1964)
1950: Berend-Corinth (1880–1967)
1950: Wong (1922–2006)
1951: Henrey (1906–2004)
1951: Hilliard, pseud. (1910–1996)
1951/1964: Noël, pseud. (1883–1967)
1952: McCall (1881–1966)
1952: Ogilvie (1859–)
1952: Raverat (1885–1957)
1953: Eyles (1889–1960)
1953: Patchett (1897–1989)
1953: Sone (1919–2011)
1954: Chase (1887–1973)
1954: Herder (1872–1959)
1954: Smith, pseud. (1894–)
1954: Timings (1874–1952)
1955: Burke (1907–1976)
1956: Bardin (1901–)
1956: Sinclair

1956: Thompson (1909–1990)
1957: Howe (c. 1899–)
1957: Irvine (1901–1973)
1957: Lee (1911–1970)
1957: McCarthy (1912–1989)
1957: Slenczynska (1925–)
1958: Baillie (c. 1903–)
1958: Beauvoir (1908–1986)
1958: Bonaparte (1882–1962)
1958: Hale (1908–1988)
1958: Hawker (1910–)
1958: Keppel (1900–1986)
1959: Dunham (1909–2006)
1959: Hatsumi
1959: Havoc (1912?–2012)
1959: Huxley (1907–1997)
1959: Le Franc (1879–1964)
1959: Lutyens (1908–1999)
1959: Sarton (1912–1995)
1959: Shields (1904–1972)
1959: Symons (1909–)
1960: Hitchman (1916–1980)
1960: Holman-Hunt (1913–1993)
1960: Powell (1912–1968)
1960: Rodaway (1918–2012)
1960: Verschoyle (1903–1985)

Women's Childhood Autobiography from the End of WWII through 1960s 187

1961: Dodge
1961: Fen (1899–1983)
1961: Sillar (1869–1968)
1962: Astor (1902–2007)
1962: Maillet (1929–)
1962: Pange (1888–1972)
1963: Franklin (1879–1954)
1963: E. Hamilton (1906–1997)
1963: Lerber (1896–1963)
1963: Malraux (1897–1982)
1963: Sorensen (1912–1991)
1963: Zimmer (1936–)
1964: Adam-Smith (1924–2001)
1964: Avery (1940–)

1964: Marshall
1964: Ziegfeld (1916–2008)
1965: Eakin (1920–1984)
1965: Eaubonne (1920–2005)
1965: Y. Gautier
1965: Heygate
1965–66: Martin (1914–2014)
1966: Bolton (1883–1975)
1966: J. Godden (1906–1984) &
    R. Godden (1907–1998)
1968: Kellner (1908–1998)
1968: Moody (1940–2015)
1969: Angelou (1928–2014)

After the Second World War childhood autobiographies written by women exploded numerically in the English-speaking countries. There were several new developments, but most of these works fell into previously established patterns. In particular, many women jumped on the memoir and semi-memoir bandwagon. Postwar upheavals once again encouraged the commemoration of yesteryear. By this time feminine authorship had come to be taken for granted. Having an interesting story to tell was ample reason to write and publish an autobiography. Women who had lived in exotic places as children or whose childhood had otherwise been unusual picked up the pen to write memoirs. These include Mary Elwyn Patchett, who grew up on a cattle station in the Australian bush and wrote her first book, *Ajax the Warrior* (1953), for a juvenile audience, focusing on her childhood pets; Norah Burke, whose *Jungle Child* (1955) gives the reader a spellbinding peek at growing up in the jungle of the Himalayan foothills, where the author's father worked for the Indian Forest Service, and the family moved from camp to camp on elephants from 1907 to 1918; Bea Howe with *Child in Chile* (1957), fascinating with its account of the 1906 earthquake and her family's trips across the Andes and through the Magellan Straits; Karena Shields's 1959 *The Changing Wind*, an account of growing up on a finca in San Leandro, Mexico, where her father managed a rubber plantation starting around 1910; Elspeth Huxley's bestselling *The Flame Trees of Thika* of the same year, a novelistic account of her family's farming adventure in colonial Kenya; Helen Carmichael Dodge's *My Childhood in the Canadian*

188   Women's Childhood Autobiography from the End of WWII through 1960s

Wilderness (1961), about the life she, her mother, and her numerous siblings led as her lumberman father sought work in one remote forest camp in New Brunswick after the next; and another tale of the Raj by two of Burke's contemporaries, Jon and Rumer Godden, whose *Two Under the Indian Sun* (1966) focuses on the five years the two sisters spent in East Bengal during World War I. The Australian author Miles Franklin, famous for her melodramatic novel (which pretends to be an autobiography) *My Brilliant Career* (1901), wrote a much more down-to-earth autobiography of her actual childhood in *Childhood at Brindabella: My First Ten Years*, published posthumously in 1963, in which she makes Victorian Australia sound like the most wonderful place ever. Another Australian author, Patsy Adam-Smith, wrote *Hear the Train Blow* (1964) about her railway family's life in the bush during the Depression.

Jewish American immigrant autobiographies had been published since the early twentieth century, but in 1950 the Chinese American author Jade Snow Wong (1922–2006) extended childhood and youth autobiography to another American ethnic group with *Fifth Chinese Daughter* (1950).[1] In 1953 the Japanese American Monica Sone (1919–2011) followed suit with *Nisei Daughter*, a family memoir about growing up Japanese American in the interwar years and having to live in internment camps after the bombing of Pearl Harbor.

A spate of late—very late—Victorian retrospectives followed the war. They include Mary I. Ogilvie's *A Scottish Childhood and What Happened After* (1952), written when the author was ninety-three; Eleanor Hallard Sillar's *Edinburgh's Child, Some Memories of Ninety Years* (1961), written by a comparably old Scotswoman; Dorothy McCall's *When That I Was* (1952), about family life in London, conceived to escape a world that had been destroyed for the second time and to acquaint her grandchildren with a vanished way of life; Gwen Raverat's *Period Piece* (1952), a memoir of her childhood in Cambridge and the Darwin family; Caroline Louise Timings's *Letter from the Past: Memories of a Victorian Childhood* (1954), privately published at the behest of her son; and Pauline de Pange's *Comment j'ai vu 1900* (How I saw 1900, 1962), on an aristocratic turn-of-the-century childhood in Paris. Written by younger authors, Sonia Keppel's *Edwardian Daughter* (1958) and Geraldine Symons's *Children in the Close* (1959) are retrospectives of the Edwardian era and World War I, while Elizabeth Heygate takes her story *A Girl at Eton* (1965) from the late Victorian and Edwardian periods into the war years. A few more Anglo-Irish semi-memoirs appeared that evoked the bygone days prior to World War I: Mary Hamilton's gilded memories of growing up on a splendid Irish estate in Victorian days in *Green and Gold* (1949); Elizabeth Hamilton's nostalgic *An Irish Childhood* (1963), in which she remembers her Edwardian childhood; and a more personal Anglo-Irish work that recreates the child's perspective, Moira Verschoyle's *So Long to Wait: An Irish Childhood* (1960), also set in Edwardian days. The lives of well-to-do families in the Victorian and Edwardian periods continued to fascinate even as their servant-studded lifestyle had irrevocably declined. The war years initiated a sharp, continuing decrease in domestic servants as women stepped into better jobs that men had left behind.[2] As Leonora Eyles declared in her autobiography of childhood and youth published in 1953: "The disappearance of household servants has destroyed the English way of life."[3]

North American writers, too, wrote semi-memoirs of the Victorian and Edwardian eras: Orra Parker Phelps's *When I Was a Girl in the Martin Box* (1949) details life on her family's Connecticut farm from the late 1860s on; Mary Ellen Chase's *The White Gate: Adventures in the Imagination of a Child* (1954) is an outstanding, personalized example of a semi-memoir that captures the flavor of life in a large family in rural Maine when "there were no automobiles, almost no telephones, no gasoline engines, no electric lights, almost no bathrooms, or furnaces, or refrigerators, no running water, no boughten bread, no paper towels, no egg beaters, no soap flakes," but "the comfortable knowledge of what one's days would be like, for they were usually very much the same, a sense of security impossible today, and plenty of time."[4] Ariadne Thompson in *The Octagonal Heart* (1956) tells what it was like to grow up in a Greek American family in the years leading up to and following World War I. Esther Kellner's *The Devil and Aunt Serena* (1968) is another such story set in rural Indiana in the same period.

In Germany, Charlotte Herder, in her early 80s, wrote a semi-memoir of her childhood and youth in Prague to 1900, entitled . . . *schaut durch ein farbiges Glas auf die aschfarbene Welt: Kindheit und Jugend im alten Prag* (. . . looks through a colored glass at the ash-colored world: Childhood and youth in old Prague, 1954), for her grandchildren. She included a history of her ancestors, a genealogical table, and many family photos, published it in her family's publishing house in Freiburg, and prefaced the stately volume with an apology for being an amateur writer. In Switzerland, Helene von Lerber published *Liebes altes Pfarrhaus* (Dear old rectory, 1963) about happy family life in an Emmenthal rectory at the turn of the nineteenth to the twentieth century. Also mainly of interest to family—she wrote it for her two daughters—but also to music historians is Julia Wirth-Stockhausen's *Unverlierbare Kindheit* (Unlosable childhood, 1949). This semi-memoir about growing up at the turn of the century in Frankfurt am Main as the youngest child of the singing master Julius Stockhausen focuses outward, yet manages to be extremely personal, inasmuch as the author writes candidly about her feelings, changes of heart, and ultimate ambition to become a librarian now that such a career had become possible for women in Germany. She also frankly analyzes her often conflicted relationships with her parents, siblings, and others.

The Irish children's book author Patricia Lynch follows in the footsteps of previous children's book writers Mary Howitt, Frances Hodgson Burnett, and E. Nesbit in writing her autobiography of childhood, *A Storyteller's Childhood* (1947). This work is the most storified of any woman's childhood autobiography to date: it bears none of the marks of autobiography except for the identity of the protagonist's and the author's names. Lynch's childhood coincidentally resembles Nesbit's, inasmuch as her mother constantly left her here and there in the care of other people. But she does not present this circumstance psychologically, as the source of anxiety that it undoubtedly was, but rather as a story, as a sequence of adventures meant to gain a young audience's attention. Two of Lynch's contemporaries, both popular authors, took the same tack in works written for adults. Bertita Harding, four years younger than Lynch, had an exciting, privileged international childhood in Europe and Mexico and storifies it in *Mosaic in the Fountain* (1949), turning it into something like a polished and witty novel, though she employs real names. Finally, in the same novelistic mode, the prolific popular author "Mrs. Robert Henrey," a French woman who wrote in English for an English audience, writes of her childhood and youth in *The Little Madeleine* (1951). The fortunes and misfortunes of her working-class Parisian family and friends before, during, and after World War I, to which Madeleine herself plays largely the role of witness, make for gripping reading.

In the 1950s, consistent with the turn toward storification, women writers, and above all Americans, started to exploit their childhood memories to literary ends. Typically, such works aimed at an educated adult readership. Focusing on the psychology of young persons, they were written with literary flair. Considering how many of these works started out as pieces published in the *New Yorker*, the idea seems to have been less to engage the general public than to write a *New Yorker*-worthy piece. A prime example of such literary reminiscences is Nancy Hale's *New England Girlhood* (1958). Hale, whose family tree includes Lucy Larcom, collects stories about growing up in Boston that she had largely published elsewhere, mainly in the *New Yorker* (one of the stories appeared there as early as 1936). These artful stories play up nostalgia and are typically constructed so as to have a nostalgia-deflating point. Self-telling is not central here, although the stories capture the nuances of the protagonist's feelings; Hale is plainly not in quest of her self, but in quest of a publishable story. The striptease artist Gypsy Rose Lee started publishing stories in 1943 in the *New Yorker* about her and her sister's extraordinary childhood as child performers. Mary McCarthy followed suit, publishing six of the stories that she would later anthologize, with changes, in *Memories of a Catholic Girlhood* (1957), in the *New Yorker* starting in 1946, and a seventh in *Harper's Bazaar*. In the book version, McCarthy enhanced the autobiographical character of the stories in a variety of ways. She included a photo section; she wrote an introduction "To the Reader" in which she avers that despite some fictionalization this is not a work of fiction, but historical; and she appended commentaries to the stories in which she reflects on what she wrote earlier. In detail and with ostensible candor, she discusses to what extent her account corresponds to what actually happened, pointing out where she fictionalized or might have fictionalized.

Parts of May Sarton's *I Knew a Phoenix: Sketches for an Autobiography* (1959) likewise previously appeared in the *New Yorker*. This poetically written work starts with the story of her parents' lives in Europe; only gradually does it become a personal memoir of her childhood and youth. Virginia Sorensen similarly compiles stories, two of which first appeared in the *New Yorker* and one in *Story*, about her rural Utah childhood and adolescence in *Where Nothing Is Long Ago: Memories of a Mormon Childhood* (1963). Each story is a carefully wrought, multifaceted creation in which the author captures the reverberations of an event that is frequently chosen to be topical (involving, for example, race, attitudes toward women, or violence) in the young girl's consciousness. These very personal stories are presented novelistically, with in medias res beginnings, dialogue, free indirect discourse, and the strategic withholding of information. A sense of Sorensen's childhood generally arises out of the separate stories collectively. Contemporaneously, Reiko Hatsumi published

192 Women's Childhood Autobiography from the End of WWII through 1960s

stories about her childhood in Japan in the *New Yorker* (1956 and 1959) and *Mademoiselle* (1958), stories which she subsequently included in a longer work, *Rain and the Feast of the Stars* (1959). This book is a collection of artistic pieces about change, Westernization, generational conflict, and not wanting to grow up, interwoven with calming and retarding floral and landscape descriptions. Another such carefully tuned work is Violet Powell's outwardly focused autobiography of childhood and youth *Five out of Six* (1960).

Literariness is a hallmark of women's childhood autobiographies written in the two decades following World War II, whether they read like stories or straightforward autobiography. Hale's, McCarthy's, and Sorensen's works occupy a middle ground between autobiography and fiction. Caveats about memory, above all, mark them as autobiographical. In contrast, a work like Canadian (Acadian) author Antonine Maillet's *On a mangé la dune* (We ate the dune, 1962) tips so far into fiction that a subsequent editor took the liberty of republishing it under the rubric "novel." Maillet's work is a third-person recreation of a short, stressful period in an eight- to nine-year-old girl's life in a large family like the author's own; it focuses on important episodes that took place over the course of a year and blurs the line between reality and the girl's fantasy.

Some women pursued the tradition of humorous or entertaining memoirs. Canadian author Jan Hilliard (pseudonym for Hilda Kay Grant) won the Stephen Leacock Memorial Medal for Humor in 1952 for her fictionalized memoir *The Salt-Box* (1951), which is so much in the *Life with Father* style previously imitated by Bertha Damon and Aylene Porter that a contemporary reviewer called it a "life without father"[5]— for Father in this story is lured by the Gold Rush in British Columbia and guiltily visits his five offspring in Nova Scotia at best once a year. Diana Holman-Hunt writes in a similar vein about her two eccentric grandmothers in *My Grandmothers and I* (1960), recreating her child's perspective to concoct a droll, novelistic account—"true in essence, but not in detail"—of her interactions with these and other personalities through that lens.[6] Jill Schary Zimmer, daughter of Hollywood director, screenwriter, and producer Dore Schary, writes humorously of what it was like to grow up in Hollywood in the 1940s and 1950s. Other humorous memoirs include Audrey Marshall's *Fishbones into Butterflies* (1964), Patricia Ziegfeld's *The Ziegfelds' Girl: Confessions of an Abnormally Happy Childhood* (1964), and Robin Eakin's *Aunts Up the Cross* (1965).

Some memoirists made their memoirs more personal, more "auto-biographical," by sticking to an account of their own story (Mary Hamilton), others by viewing the past through the personalizing lens of memory (Bea Howe and Elizabeth Hamilton).

Celebrities started to write autobiographical accounts of their childhood. Gypsy Rose Lee reworked and expanded her *New Yorker* stories into a memoir of her childhood and youth, *Gypsy: A Memoir* (1957), which she published after her mother's death. Her sister June Havoc followed with *Early Havoc* (1959). The child pianist prodigy Ruth Slenczynska published *Forbidden Childhood* in 1957. Each of these women had a bizarre, unusual childhood and youth. All tell of ambitious, driven parents who pushed them into stardom at an early age. Lee and Havoc write entertainingly, Slenczynska accusingly. Among the works written by performers, the dancer Katherine Dunham's *A Touch of Innocence: Memoirs of Childhood* (1959) stands out as a masterpiece. Despite claiming not to be an autobiography, but a family story, and despite her choice of the third person, it is in fact an introspective, highly confessional autobiography from her earliest years to age eighteen, with a great deal of emphasis on her feelings and fears going back to her earliest years, when her White mother was still alive, through a scary period as a preschooler when she lived with her Black father's sister on Chicago's rough South Side, to life in "the Town" where her father settles with a new wife and opens a dry-cleaning business. Somber in tone, her work is extraordinarily literary. Titling her chapters for psychologically important events, she tells a chronological story of an increasingly dismal family life, marred by violence and terrible things said. Without aiming to write an exposé, as Claire Martin will in the next decade, Dunham paints unsparing portraits of the members of her immediate and extended family in a fashion reminiscent of Starkie. She confesses her shame at having such a family and talks about her growing hatred of her father, who makes sexual advances toward a young female relative and then toward herself.

More British working-class women—Holmes, Smith, Sinclair, Hitchman, Rodaway, and Avery—joined the ranks of authors. Postwar social reforms ushered in an era when the hardships of the working-class poor in the earlier twentieth century and the interwar period took on historical interest. Emma Smith, who toward the end of Victoria's reign started out as a "workhouse bastard,"[7] wrote pseudonymously of her wretched pre–World War I childhood in Cornwall in *A Cornish Waif's Story* (1954). Eileen Baillie, writing about the same period, offers in *The Shabby Paradise* (1958) a complementary picture of a London (Poplar) slum, of people "terrifyingly close to the edge of destitution"[8]—albeit from the perspective of her father's vicarage windows. G. V. Holmes (a pseudonym signifying Girls Village Homes) published an affirmative "we"-style memoir, *The Likes of Us* (1948), about what it was like to grow up in Dr. Barnardo's Homes. In *The Bridgeburn Days* (1956), a work more personal and less positive than Holmes's, Lucy Sinclair followed suit with a novelistic exposé of a hardworking and loveless childhood, which some critics think was her own,[9] in a cottage home in the interwar period. Janet Hitchman's bestselling *The King of the Barbareens* (1960) describes her childhood as a World War I orphan in a succession of working-class households and institutions in the 1920s and 1930s, while her case was monitored by the Ministry of Pensions. In the same year her contemporary Angela Rodaway, under the title *A London Childhood* (1960), published a series of poetic, yet soberly factual, self-searchingly personal pieces about growing up in a poor but self-styled "superior" family in North London. The British class structure did not start to be dismantled until after the Second World War. The very young Valerie Avery's account of her gritty working-class childhood during and immediately after World War II, a piece she began in a high school English class and subsequently published under the title *London Morning* (1964), testifies to its persistence. In France, Angélina Bardin, a child abandoned at birth who grew up in a sequence of foster homes and became a farm servant at age thirteen, published an account of her hard life until age seventeen in *Angélina, une fille des champs* (Angelina, a girl of the fields, 1956, written in 1935).

Some women published their memoirs simply because they felt like it, producing works of little interest to anyone except members of their immediate family. Such a work is Lyn Irvine's *So Much Love, So Little Money* (1957). In the following year Beatrice Hawker published a special-interest memoir about growing up Methodist, *Look Back in Love* (1958). Another such work is Yvonne Gautier's *Mon enfance . . . et Elle* (My childhood . . . and her, 1965): published in an edition of one hundred copies, it is a memorial to her beloved mother—the story of a long-suffering woman who took her husband back so as to care for him in his old age after he had divorced her and twice married other women.

Of interest to a wider public are self-focused autobiographies that incorporate personal revelations in the style of Mabel Dodge Luhan, Mary Butts, Laura Goodman Salverson, and Enid Starkie. In the 1950s and 1960s Phyllis Bottome, Leonora Eyles, Simone de Beauvoir, Marie Bonaparte, Mary Lutyens, Elisaveta Fen, Brooke Astor, Clara Malraux, and Françoise d'Eaubonne published impressive autobiographies of this type. Additionally, some authors—Marie Noël, Moira Verschoyle, Marie Le Franc, Clara Malraux—attempted to capture the child's perspective in their works. These latter two types will be discussed in this chapter.

Two ideological trends were on the rise in this period: psychoanalysis and, to a lesser degree, feminism. Both had already been visible in works of the 1930s. The immediate postwar period was the heyday of psychoanalysis, however, and so it is not surprising that psychoanalysis prominently colors the self-focused works. The psychoanalytic climate facilitated a loosening of the female tongue. More women, not just French women, wrote confessionally; more women wrote about sex; sexual abuse became a topic; and more women felt free to criticize their parents in print. Feminism emerges above all in French works written from the late 1950s onward. As Clara Malraux, born in 1897, states with pride in her 1963 autobiography of childhood and youth, it was *her* generation that liberated women, *her* generation that gained women the freedoms they have enjoyed since the end of World War I.[10] After the war, socialism, which preached the emancipation of women through employment, left its mark on some women's writing, in particular Eyles's.

The postwar period saw the rise of one new type of childhood autobiography written by women: the autobiography of abuse. The theme of victimization itself was not new. It goes back to the beginnings of the genre. In mid-nineteenth century, as we have seen, Eliza Farnham wrote in her novelistic *My Early Days* about the "aunt" who adopted and abused her. Athénaïs Michelet wrote in *Mémoires d'une enfant* about how she was the disfavored child in a large family; her mother did not love her. Hannah Lynch's Angela in *Autobiography of a Child* had a childhood that followed the same pattern. The point of the book, which is probably in part fictional, is the victimization of the girl. The protagonist Angela is stylized as a victim who suffers constant punishment, including physical violence. Prior to these, Charlotte Brontë's bestselling novel *Jane Eyre* tells the story of an orphan who suffered physical abuse. There is also the strange case of Gertrude Beasley, whose *My*

First *Thirty Years* (1925), an exposé of her detested family, mentions sexual abuse by her older brothers. Beginning with *A Cornish Waif's Story* (1954), however, we begin to see authentic childhood autobiographies written by women who suffered physical or sexual abuse at the hands of adults and wrote autobiographies in order to tell the public about it. The postwar period also saw childhood autobiographies by women who came from socially disadvantaged groups and wished to tell the public what it was like to grow up as a member of that group. Since the socially disadvantaged are often abused, there is an overlap between these two types. Broadly speaking, the motive for such works is to expose unfavorable conditions. But as we shall see, the abused sometimes feel complicit in their abuse, so that an impulse to confess enters in as well.

This chapter will first look at the autobiographies of abuse, including autobiographies written by women who were socially disadvantaged. Next, it will consider mainstream self-focused autobiographies written by middle-class women. Finally, it will look at autobiographies that capture the child's perspective.

Autobiographies of Abuse

The child of parents who themselves were the children of wealthy parents, the American woman of letters and novelist Mary McCarthy fell on hard times after her mother and father died in the flu epidemic of 1919. She and her siblings suffered physical and emotional abuse at the hands of caregivers who were appointed by her wealthy McCarthy grandparents in Minneapolis; these grandparents installed Mary and her three younger brothers in a separate residence and paid a couple of poorer relations to take care of them. For five years, until her maternal grandparents in Seattle rescued her, Mary, along with her brothers, led the miserable life of abused orphans. If Mary was abused more than her brothers, it was not because she was female, but because she was smart, something (according to her) her Minneapolis relatives could not abide.

McCarthy took her revenge in a couple of stories published in the *New Yorker*, "Yonder Peasant, Who Is He?" (1948) and "A Tin Butterfly" (1951). In 1957 she republished these stories in *Memories of a Catholic Girlhood*, an autobiography in which she takes her story to her final year in high school. In this work, which commentators categorize as a quest narrative, McCarthy anthologized seven of her previously published stories with alterations and added an eighth.[11] She prefaced the book with an opening chapter printed in italics, "To the Reader," in which she gave background and asserted the autobiographical nature of the text despite memory lapses, and she wrote a commentary after each story in the same italics, analyzing it and criticizing it for overstating or fictionalizing here and there. She thereby introduces a novel element of what Isabel Durán calls "meta-autobiography" (commentary on the autobiographical project itself) into an autobiography of childhood,[12] which anticipates comparable moves in postmodern works like Nathalie Sarraute's *Childhood* (1983), where a fictitious interlocutor serves much the same purpose as McCarthy's 1957 voice in *Memories of a Catholic Girlhood*. Once she goes to live with her Seattle grandparents, Mary's story is no longer one of abuse, but that of a gifted, rebellious young woman navigating her way through various parochial and other schools in Seattle and Tacoma. But the two stories "Yonder Peasant, Who Is He?" and "A Tin Butterfly" are abuse stories. They resemble Emily Carr's abuse story in *Growing Pains* (1946), inasmuch as they paint the portrait of a brutal man who oppressed McCarthy when she was young.

McCarthy's tone in these two stories is accusatory rather than self-pitying. In her commentary, she characterizes "Yonder Peasant, Who Is He?" as "an angry indictment of privilege for its treatment of the underprivileged, a single, breathless, voluble speech on the subject of human indifference."[13] She begins by ripping into her grandmother McCarthy, "a cold, grudging, disputatious old woman" (33), a staunch, combative Catholic who ardently hopes for the extirpation of Protestantism. In her home, the children, who had been used to fun and treats when they lived with their parents, are dealt with impatiently, even when they are bedridden with the influenza that killed their parents. Once orphaned, they are shunted off to live with great aunt Margaret and her husband Myers. There, they live poorly: the food is bad, and they are allowed no friendships, no movies, and very little reading. At night their mouths are sealed with adhesive tape to prevent mouth breathing. They are taught no sports. They do not get toys. They only get to play with the toys sent by the Seattle relatives when the latter visit. Mary and one of her brothers repeatedly run away, hoping to get placed in the orphanage asylum.

"A Tin Butterfly" is above all a scathing indictment of Myers, though Mary also paints a negative portrait of her great-aunt Margaret, who like Myers controlled and punished the children. But Myers, unlike his wife, is a meanie. He makes candy, but never gives the children any. He beats them constantly, with "capricious brutality" (65). Mary wins a prize in an essay contest, and her uncle beats her for it, lest she become stuck-up. The story climaxes with the incident referenced in the title: Myers accuses Mary of stealing a Crackerjack butterfly belonging to her little brother. The butterfly is found under the tablecloth at her place. He and Margaret mercilessly whip her, and whip her more because she refuses to confess. She finds out later that Uncle Myers set up the evidence against her: her brother observed him planting the butterfly where it was found. In her commentary, McCarthy, who was well versed in psychoanalysis, casts doubt on her memory of her brother's testimony. In fact, this memory—her memory of her brother's testimony—could be construed as a Freudian screen memory for her desire to revenge herself on Myers. Notwithstanding, the story sticks as an indictment of Myers.

Mary McCarthy had an acid tongue and a literary gift that rivaled those of Luhan, Butts, and Starkie—other well-educated women of means. Subsequent women who took up the pen to write about the abuse they suffered in childhood came from far less privileged backgrounds. In their abuse stories, it mattered more that they were female.

In *A Cornish Waif's Story* (1954), childhood sexual abuse by adults made its first appearance in women's childhood autobiography. Published under the pseudonym Emma Smith, the work tells the life story of a girl born in 1894 who was abandoned in early childhood by her working-class single mother. Whereas some women who grew up in middle-class or wealthy families, such as Martineau, Séverine, Luhan, and Starkie, were more than just intermittently miserable when they were growing up, girls who were orphaned, like Marguerite Audoux, or even left for long periods in boarding schools or boarded with families, like E. Nesbit and Patricia Lynch, were at risk and suffered in entirely different ways. In the foreword to the first edition of *A Cornish Waif's Story*, A. L. Rowse, the author of *A Cornish Childhood* and a historian of Cornwall, writes that the author sent him the manuscript unsolicited in the mail. He has words of high praise for it. In the introduction to the 2010 edition Simon Parker, who found out that Emma Smith's real name was Mabel Lewis, tells a different story. He recounts how he sought out Rowse, and writes: "A 'mass of illiterate rubbish' is how noted Cornish academic and historian A. L. Rowse described the bundle of rough pages brought to him one day by a woman in her sixties, dressed in worn clothes and wearing a head scarf."[14] Rowse told Parker that he had had to rewrite the book. Rowse, according to Parker, also exclaimed, "She was a psychotic bitch. I know all about bitches. The woman was ignorant. She was rubbish."[15]

The fact that Rowse rewrote Lewis's text is of great interest. Trying to piece apart Lewis's story from what Rowse made out of it is guesswork, but Rowse's reworking probably accounts for why the book is cast in a certain mold. It may well have been the Oxford scholar Rowse, and not Mabel Lewis, who had earned her living mainly as a laundress, who gave the "mass of illiterate rubbish" its shape. A working-class childhood autobiography, *A Cornish Waif's Story* adopts many of the conventions of the genre as it was written by middle- and upper-class women, such as the apology and the rendition of early memories. Rowse, who had published his own childhood autobiography, may have thought it prudent to incorporate classic genre conventions in Lewis's. The text contains some surprising literary echoes. One can easily imagine that they were put there by Rowse, who states in his foreword that the text reminded him of *Jane Eyre*. In particular, a basically picaresque series of misadventures is coaxed into something resembling a Bildungsroman. Bildungsroman plots are common in male autobiographies, but in women's childhood autobiographies of that era they are conspicuous for their scarcity. So the Bildungsroman plot with its happy ending is suspect and perhaps attributable to Rowse rather than to Lewis.

Emma Smith's life is narrated in the first person and in chronological order. At the beginning, the narrator proffers an apology, explaining that a sociologist friend suggested that she write her story. After hesitating, she writes, she decided to go ahead with the project because it was a "bit of history" that shows how some sections of the community lived in former times.[16] Her justification for telling her extraordinary story is, therefore, that it is of sociological interest. She brings her story up to the time of writing, but from her marriage in 1921 on she just tells the highlights. Barely over two chapters out of a total of sixteen concern these later years, whereas the first nine chapters are devoted to her childhood prior to the age of twelve.

The text does indeed give the reader a fascinating and horrifying peek into the lives of poor Cornish folk at the start of the twentieth century. Closer inspection reveals, however, that its composition wavers between following a mix of literary models and producing a confession that the author seems to want to make. The literary models, which are mutually compatible, include the Bildungsroman, the Dickensian exposé, and the happy-ending story.

The Bildungsroman model imparts coherence and intelligibility to this autobiography. It injects a sense of becoming, of cause and effect, into what otherwise might look like a haphazard jumble of contingencies. Thus, after a chaotic childhood Emma believes she has found her vocation as a nun, but then, in true Wilhelm Meister fashion, she decides that her vocation is a different one, namely to be a wife and mother — not a banal choice for one who was all but orphaned and on the road to prostitution.

The book recalls Charles Dickens in its exposé character. In his 2010 introduction, Parker immediately invokes Dickens, calling the work "perhaps the most authentic account of late-Victorian child abuse and suffering since Dickens' *A Walk in a Workhouse*."[17] The text itself mentions *Oliver Twist*, and there are strong parallels to *Oliver Twist* in the way a workhouse child is exploited and led if not into outright criminality, then into underworld activities.

Finally, the text seems under pressure to conform to the time-honored novelistic model that brings a life of trials and tribulations to a close with a happy ending. *Oliver Twist* ends happily for Oliver, and so do classic first-person British novels about women that can be seen to serve as models for *A Cornish Waif's Story*'s, such as *Moll Flanders* and *Jane Eyre*. Emma too presents and conceptualizes herself as a victim, yet emphasizes the success she made of herself in the long run as well as positive moments along the way. The 1956 American edition reinforced the happy ending by excising most of the last chapter with its details about her suicide attempt and confinement in a mental hospital.[18]

At the same time, the book is a confession. A confessional impulse is basic to the story, part of its very fabric, and confession is also a key concept for the narrator. Hence this aspect of the text is almost certainly attributable to Smith herself. From the start her story is bound up with illicit sex. She was the child of an unwed mother and was placed in a home for orphaned or unwanted children. From early on she was stigmatized as a "bastard" (20). This victimization through the word of others recalls Jane Eyre, whose aunt stamped her a "liar" when she sent her to a boarding school for orphans. Emma was then sexually abused by men in her foster home from age six until she ran away at age twelve. At that time in her life she thought she would go to hell. She felt less victimized than guilty for her complicity. Although she sought to make a religious confession, and in fact confessed several times, she failed to confess this particular, and to her mind especially grievous, sin until she was sixteen. She writes that the confession she made as a teenager liberated her and brought her peace. Such is the impetus that drives

Women's Childhood Autobiography from the End of WWII through 1960s   201

this book: she makes the impression of wanting, with her book, to make a thoroughgoing final confession.

A working-class background combined with misfortune destined her for victimhood. Her dismal childhood story is this: Her mother, Maud, was one of many children of a Cornish miner who was blinded in an accident. Since the family was poor, Maud was not schooled, but rather had to work in the mines at surface level from an early age. Maud had two children out of wedlock by the same man, who did not marry her. These children were initially raised by Maud's parents, but they also spent much of their time in the Workhouse Union, an institution for the destitute. When Maud eventually married, her husband consented to take Emma's brother Harry, but not Emma ("My man says a boy may be useful later on when he starts earning, but he won't have Emma" [25]). The grandparents moved and could not keep her, so her mother placed her with an old man, an organ grinder, and his wife. This couple took her on to use her as a singer and also because people were likelier to give money to a ragged waif than to two adults. They lived in a filthy, squalid, insect-ridden tenement.

The most distressing part of Emma's story comes when she tells that when she was age six the old man Pratt, the organ grinder, started to abuse her sexually. In describing the abuse Smith gives no detail, but just summarizes, in keeping with pre–World War I decorum: he "undid some of my clothing and behaved in a disgusting way" (31). He continues to perpetrate his "horrible indecencies" (86) every time they are alone. He tells her not to tell. She is also abused by a sword-swallower whom he invites to stay and who is bedded with her on the same pile of rags. She merely explains that "I was still in the medical sense of the word a virgin" (105).

Two patterns emerge in Emma's story. The first is stigmatization. After running away from the Pratts, Emma winds up with her old Sunday school teacher, who finds out that she has been "ruined by a man" (104). The upshot is that she is sent to a convent penitentiary as if she had been a prostitute or woman who had given birth out of wedlock. At age twelve, she is by far the youngest woman there. She insists that being identified as a convent penitentiary inmate "indirectly . . . affected my whole life" (108), because it stigmatized her. The convent entangles her in contradictory restrictions: inmates are not allowed to talk about their past, so she cannot tell what happened to her, yet she is sent away in black clothing that immediately identifies her to the public as an ex-convent penitentiary inmate, hence a prostitute. The black clothing they send her off in repeats the external signposting of the cropped head that earlier marks her as a workhouse child. The convent taboo on speech strangely replicates Pratt's. Her true story remains bottled up inside her. She emphasizes how her past, the sexual abuses, weigh on her.

Another pattern is exploitation. Her family, the Pratts, and her employers when she is placed as a servant at age fifteen all exploit and instrumentalize her. If she cannot be exploited, she is not wanted.

Stigmatization and exploitation persist in Emma's adult mind in a constant tug of war with the opposite explanation that her own waywardness and sinfulness are responsible for her misfortunes. Psychic instability results. As she writes, what helps is confession, for confession brings absolution and hence peace. This book can be understood as an expression of Emma's desire to confess fully and thereby achieve equilibrium. Another way to achieve equilibrium is to have a definite life story, one not subject to doubt and wavering moods. The literary models that find their way into her story go a long way toward making it more definite by turning her into a recognizable type of heroine.

Although she writes discreetly by today's standards (perhaps because of Rowse?), Smith is remarkably candid given the tradition of women's childhood autobiography. Beasley, Luhan, Butts, and Starkie had published words about their mothers that were not nice. Beasley and Luhan put sex on the page. Smith is much less outspoken about sex than these writers, but she openly airs her ambivalent feelings toward her mother. Estranged from her mother, she later, when she herself has a baby, wants to get to know her. They do not hit it off well. Smith also complains about her overly simple gardener husband (though she finds some good words for him too) and declares quite forthrightly, despite the fact that her husband is still living, that she fell in love with someone else, a married man, when they were living in Australia. Open talk about family relationships in a work otherwise so indebted to literary models shows that this type of candor had become acceptable—though, to be sure, Mabel Lewis published her work anonymously and in it refers to herself by a pseudonym.

In the following decade a French Canadian work, published under the author's real name, launched a full-scale attack on an abusive parent: Quebec writer Claire Martin's two-volume story of childhood abuse *Dans un gant de fer*, which came out in French in 1965 and 1966 and was translated into English in 2006 as *In an Iron Glove*. In a 1979 interview Martin stated that she carefully timed the publication of her book. She had been preparing the work for years, but she felt she had to wait until people were ready to hear what she had to say. To her mind, 1959–60 would have been too early. One wonders what precisely made her think the time was ripe in the mid-1960s. Perhaps it took a work like Sylvia Plath's *The Bell Jar* (1963) to set the stage for a shocking autobiography written by a woman. Later would have been too late: "You mustn't arrive last with a book like this. You have to be a bit at the head of the line."[19] Indeed, subsequent decades saw a wave of childhood abuse autobiographies. While Martin's was hardly the first childhood story of abuse (Farnham's Eliza and Hannah Lynch's Angela were subjected to physical violence, and Beasley and the Cornish Waif were abused sexually), what distinguishes Martin's work from its predecessors is her tone of accusation. Like Beasley (but Beasley was not read), Martin writes angrily and sarcastically. Her ire has two targets: her violent and domineering father (who was an old man when she wrote her book) and Roman Catholic convent school. Her agenda is to indict them, along with the Quebec society of her youth that supported their way of doing things: "Despite our remoteness we were at the intersection of every reactionary trend going, situated right in the middle of the most heavily trampled crossroads in the history of bigotry."[20]

She tells her story in the first person and in chronological order starting with her first memory at age two. Part 1, "The Left Cheek," takes her through age twelve, when her mother dies of tuberculosis. Part 2, "The Right Cheek," takes her story up to age twenty. Part 1 is a story of abuse, victimization, and misery, while part 2 shows how she and her six siblings, as they become teenagers, increasingly rebel and band together against their tyrannical father.

First and foremost, the book presents a portrait of her father as temperamentally choleric, violent, and unrestrained. Nearly anything causes him to fly off the handle. He is a bully who slaps, punches, and kicks his wife and his seven children. A big man, he often injures them badly: he breaks his wife's nose on one occasion by throwing her downstairs and breaks her hand on another by hitting it. He often hurts Claire to the point of drawing blood. When she accidentally steps on the dog's foot, he stamps on her foot, tearing out a toenail. She believes that he seeks pretexts to become angry, for he is angry all day long, with peaks. "Anger for him was like morphine for the drug addict," she judges

204 Women's Childhood Autobiography from the End of WWII through 1960s

(123). He accuses the children and then immediately punishes them; there is no room for innocence.

Martin portrays her father as someone who is in every respect a tyrant. He is a know-it-all who brooks no correction. He buys a house in a remote spot and keeps his family isolated. There, everything is forbidden. He gives his children no toys. He offers Claire no lessons, until finally a teacher negotiates piano lessons for her (these are later taken away as a punishment.) The atmosphere at home is stifling and empty, much the way Séverine's Line experienced it. In later life Martin regrets that she did not learn enough music and also did not learn to paint, act, or swim, but only to cook and sew. Her litany goes on and on. Her father is miserly: the house is kept cold, the children barely get the clothes they need, he avoids calling doctors, and when his wife dies he orders a second-class funeral. Yet he pampers himself with expensive outfits and good food, and in general, satisfies his every whim. He enjoys being the center of attention. At one point he even secretly cuts holes in his socks so the children will have to fix them. He is insensitive, deaf to the feelings of others, sure that whatever he does is right. He is religious, and in his self-righteousness assumes that God is on his side.

What does it mean to be a girl in this family? It comes as no surprise that Martin's father is a male supremacist, insulting toward his daughters. "Fundamentally, the only advantage that women have over animals is that they talk" (149), he claims. When his daughters discuss schoolwork, he comments, "I really wonder what good that's going to be to you in serving a man" (150). Quebec society supports this attitude toward women. Advice columns invariably tell women to sacrifice themselves. In Martin's day, no women there went to university. She writes: "We had no right to knowledge, either general or specialized. But yearly maternities, sleepless nights and dreary days, nursing children, washing, cooking, finished off with eclampsia or puerperal fever—no objection to that. Feminine vocation" (299). Her gentle mother, whom she loves and who dies of tuberculosis after bearing seven children, models this self-sacrificial feminine mode of existence.

Last but not least, her father is a prude, always suspicious that his children are indulging in illicit sexual activity. The girls are taught that the slightest provocation will arouse a man to sexual desire.

Despite an initial statement that she has forgiven her father, who at the time of her writing was age ninety, a frail old man and much changed, Martin exercises virtually no narratorial objectivity. She sees

Women's Childhood Autobiography from the End of WWII through 1960s   205

nothing from his perspective. She is out to list all his sins, to judge him, and to damn him. She goes beyond fact in what she imputes to him. For example, he is (for forbidding her maternal grandparents to visit the children) her grandfather's "assassin" (227). She does not hesitate to round out her portrait with hypotheses about what her father probably felt, probably thought. Thus for example, her father does not pay the maid, so she leaves. "As sure as I know him, he must simply have told himself that the maid was not indispensable" (92). We see here a narrator who burns with indignation. This autobiography is driven not just by outrage but by a desire to get even.

All the daughters become boarders first at one, then at another convent school. Brutality and stupidity reign there as well. Their letters are read, their belongings searched. The nuns stress obedience and otherwise teach them little. It is forbidden to mention anything to do with the body. The food is disgusting, in accordance with the image of convent school we get from other writers as well. The girls are subjected to corporal punishment. Writing in the age of psychoanalysis, Martin remarks, "We were totally ignorant of the fact that such violence was a release of frustrated sexuality" (173).

Although the book is more a portrait of Martin's father than of Claire herself, she does discuss the effects of her upbringing on her. The most interesting autobiographical aspect of her work is her assessment of the psychological effect her tyrannical father had on her. Both her father and the convent, she writes, were out to break her spirit, break her pride. But the opposite happens. She merely learns to hate them. She inwardly rejects the authorities, whether at home or at school, and becomes a closet rebel. At the same time, the treatment she receives at home provokes a dominant emotion of shame. At school, Claire is ashamed to admit how badly she is treated at home. The word "shame" occurs very frequently in this account. Among previous authors, Dorothy Whipple frequently experienced embarrassment; the emotion of shame also entered into Sigrid Undset's and Dormer Creston's autobiographies in the form of sexual shame; Gertrude Beasley writes that she was constantly ashamed of her family; Katherine Dunham also experiences shame when her family becomes dysfunctional. Emma Smith suffered public stigmatization. Martin's sense of shame is closest to Smith's and Beasley's. She senses that her mistreatment at her father's hands has the potential to stigmatize her in the world. Experience teaches her that if others find out about her home life, she will be gossiped about and looked down on. So she conceals what goes on. Once, when she comes to school bruised and beaten, she makes up a story about a skating accident. Additionally, for the sake of her classmates she invents a fantasy life for herself so as to have something to talk about. She tells of travels she never took and films she never saw.

In general, Claire becomes quite a liar. Both at home and at school, the atmosphere encourages lying. At home she lies to deceive her tyrannical father. By the time she is a teenager, all the children start to plot against their father, and they dissimulate and cheat rather than rebel. "When you came right down to it, we really only had two preoccupations: to lie to him when he was there, and to disobey him when he wasn't" (221). They secretly make clothes for themselves, and when he is away they invite people and party. Lies spring automatically to their lips when he questions them. In the end the book becomes grimly comical when Claire tells of all the ways in which her growing brothers and sisters outfox her father.

Martin recounts that she found it easier to maintain a false front than to argue or defend herself. After telling about how her father brutally beat her, she reflects: "I could either say nothing, and what had happened would cease to exist, or I could reply that he had hurt me, and he would have thrown himself on me again to teach me better than to judge him. I chose to say nothing. That's the main reason I hated him so, because of that terrified silence he reduced us to, that cowardice he plunged us into, just as deep and as long as he wanted to" (262). The older she gets, the more she thinks she must protect her face and keep him from disfiguring her, or she'll never escape. She thinks of marriage as an escape route and figures she will need to attract a man. Therefore, she prefers to "crawl," so as to avoid beatings. The syndrome she describes is common to prisoners everywhere: faced with a captor she believes is intransigent, she maintains a servile and acquiescent false front, in the belief that all else is hopeless.

As will be seen, Martin's story of the effects of abuse anticipates Maya Angelou's. This woman, like Angelou, actively lies when put on the spot and otherwise does not speak out because she is too terrified and too ashamed to do so. Both women make the impression of wanting to make good their lying and their silence by writing confessional autobiographies. Martin not only accuses her father, but at the same time makes her own confession. She explicitly confesses her fear, her lying, and her failure to rebel. The lurking guilt that characterized Emma

Smith's autobiography finds an echo here. Martin rakes over her life for instances of shameful behavior. Because her father directed so much animus and suspicion toward sexuality, she examines her childhood self for manifestations of sexuality (although she was ignorant of sex until an advanced age) and comes up with two early dreams with latent sexual content. She also confesses something "that's not an easy thing to confess" (296), namely, that at age twenty-five she was a fascist and antisemite. Ultimately, however, Martin accuses others much more than herself.

Janet Hitchman's *The King of the Barbareens* (1960), a childhood autobiography that falls chronologically between *A Cornish Waif's Story* and *Dans un gant de fer*, is not precisely a story of abuse, though it recounts incidents of abuse by grown-ups as well as bullying by other children, but principally the hard-luck story of an orphan who was shunted from one foster home to another. It bears discussion together with *A Cornish Waif's Story* and *Dans un gant de fer* on account of its similar mix of accusatory and self-accusatory tones. Hitchman was a British war orphan who never knew her parents and lived with a succession of mainly working-class women who were willing to take her on in exchange for an allowance paid by the Ministry of Pensions. She takes her story from her earliest memories up to the time of writing, but weights it heavily toward childhood: the first six out of a total of nine chapters concern her preadolescent years, the next two chapters bring her to age sixteen. She conceptualizes her book as an autobiography of childhood, stating as much in the epilogue.[21]

Hitchman's narratorial attitude displays the same tension between self-justification and self-inculpation that we saw in Smith and Martin. Hitchman in fact represents herself much more forthrightly than Smith or Martin as an active agent in her misfortunes. The reader does not have to ferret out a sense of guilt; rather, Hitchman insistently blames a set of givens that, she implies, she hardly could have helped. She was dealt a bad hand, and this set her up for a bad outcome. She was not only orphaned very young, but was unattractive, sickly, difficult, and unruly. Early on she states that she was "born bad-tempered" (27). Her own flaws prove her undoing. She opines ironically, "To be a successful orphan, . . . one must also be beautiful, and have no conscience" (110). The theme of her innate deficiencies serves throughout the book as the explanatory key for her hard childhood and youth. Thus, when she was small she was "given to screaming fits when I couldn't get my own way"

(27); later she was "difficult" (168), "lazy, cheeky, and quarrelsome" (168). Her intrinsic "bad temper and selfishness" (203) repeatedly spoil things for her. This is hardly just her subjective judgment. One foster mother after another hands her back to the Ministry of Pensions, not willing to put up with her, and finally she is expelled from school at Dr. Barnardo's Homes, even though she excelled academically there. To be sure, the life that awaited her as a war orphan and her various caregivers were also at fault. She was destined for domestic service, for which as a bright child she had no appetite. She longed for family. Losing home after home hardened her, making her ever more selfish and determined and less and less the loving, grateful child her caregivers would have liked to see. Hitchman soberly combs through the past—gifted, as she says, with a phenomenal memory (188)—and tells of her various misdeeds. She swung a cat by its tail, she stole, she beat up another girl, and so on. Often she attempts to exculpate herself for specific crimes by giving explanations: she stole because she was given no pocket money; she beat up the girl because she had insulted a poor girl. Yet overall, she sizes herself up as a savage—the "king of the barbareens" of the title—and places a good deal of the blame for her story on herself. This cool appraisal of self and insistent self-blaming are unusual for an autobiography. It is, of course, a way of giving her story a red thread. Like Emma Smith (or her editor), Hitchman avoids letting her story slide into the mere picaresque. Unlike Emma Smith, she accomplishes her task without injecting a Bildungsroman, conversion, or happy-ending storyline into her account. Instead, she establishes a dialectic between social critique and self-critique in such a way as to imply that her story of hard knocks and her mediocre outcome amounted to fate. She is cool and factual and unselfpitying, though she metes out plenty of judgments and expresses plenty of opinions in her adult narrator's voice. It is little wonder that this book achieved the status of a mass-market paperback.

A further example of an autobiography that chronicles abuse comes from the United States. Toward the turbulent end of the 1960s, a young Black civil rights activist, Anne Moody, published her autobiography *Coming of Age in Mississippi* (1968). Moody writes a copious, chronological, four-part account of her childhood, her high school years, her college years, and her subsequent years as a civil rights activist, covering the period from her earliest memories on a Mississippi plantation to the peak of the civil rights movement in 1964, when she was twenty-four.

She wrote her book immediately after those crucial years. Her work is a true autobiography of childhood and youth, conscientiously giving detail, yet certain themes—poverty, lack of education, and above all racial oppression—inevitably rise to the fore. Her work is not centrally about the abuse she personally experiences, but the abuse suffered by the entire African American community of which she is a part, and to which she was witness. Similarly to Smith and Hitchman, she was born into a disadvantaged group, one that was easily exploited and de facto experienced abuse.

Anne, the first in her family to graduate from college, wrote her autobiography, which appeared when she was twenty-eight, for testimonial and documentary reasons: to show what it was about her early life—which closely resembled the early life of many other African American girls in the United States South—that compelled her to become an activist in the civil rights movement, to testify to the justice of that struggle, and to give a personal account of those stirring historical times, the early 1960s, when African Americans fought for their civil rights in the Southern states. Through her personal memoir, Moody gives a picture of Negro life in rural Mississippi. Her own family's story, which stands for many, is one of poverty, hard work, oppression, violence, and belief in religion. She writes in a lively style, sometimes slipping, as narrator, into her Mississippi idiom as well as reproducing it abundantly in passages of dialogue. Anne, whose birth name, Essie Mae, was later accidentally changed on her birth certificate, is smart and peppy, but the cards are stacked against her. She is the oldest of nine children born to her mother, an unskilled plantation worker. After her mother has three children, her father leaves her for another woman. She throws him out and refuses to accept money from him, thereby ensuring poverty for herself and her children. Her mother does acquire a boyfriend whom she eventually marries, but home life is bumpy, and the family remains very poor. It is the Jim Crow South: Essie Mae grows up under conditions of segregation. The family lives in a particularly tough region of rural Mississippi, where the Whites are deeply racist. The Ku Klux Klan keeps the Negroes in line through acts of terror. In general, the Negroes perform manual labor for the Whites for low wages and are afraid of them. Thus Essie Mae, desperately poor, works every day after school from the age of nine, mainly doing childcare and housework for White women. Some of her employers are nicer than others, but if a White woman bosses her around and reminds her of her subordinate place because she is of an inferior race, there is little she can do about it except build up resentment. The older generation of Negroes and in particular her mother are negative role models, constantly cautioning her, out of their profound fearfulness, to be deferential and dissimulate and above all never to speak to Whites about any issue concerning race. She resents her elders' quiescence, even though their fear is amply justified by the lynchings and other forms of violence the Whites perpetrate against the Black community. Moody shows how among the deeply religious Mississippi Negroes hope for the hereafter conspires with fear of the consequences to stifle any notion of taking steps to improve one's lot in the here and now.

Moody gives a rounded picture of her life, not confining herself to stories that illustrate the oppression of African Americans, though there are plenty of these, but also telling stories that have no obvious motivation, such as accounts of her successes in school and her boyfriends in college. Thus the events she recounts do not give the impression of having been selected to illustrate various points, as do, say, Richard Wright's in his pioneering autobiography of childhood and youth *Black Boy*. Her autobiography is emphatically event-oriented. First and foremost, Moody tells what happened. She does not psychologize or analyze other people, philosophize, or even draw conclusions. Indeed, the events speak for themselves. Similarly, regarding herself, she is not introspective; she does not characterize herself or engage in soul-searching. Yet, although she sticks to an account of events, she nevertheless traces the development of her awareness of race, her indignation about racism and the treatment of Blacks in the South, and her trajectory to political activism. She recalls how, already as a small child, she came to wonder about Whites and Blacks—for many Negroes looked White; how she noticed that the Whites oppress and cheat the Blacks in myriad ways; then, as a teenager, how White men sexually exploit Black women. She also recalls her disgust at the way the Blacks kowtow to all this: "I was fifteen years old when I began to hate people. I hated the white men who murdered Emmett Till and I hated all the other whites who were responsible for the countless murders Mrs. Rice had told me about and those I vaguely remembered from childhood. But I also hated Negroes. I hated them for not standing up and doing something about the murders. . . . It was at this stage in my life that I began to look upon Negro men as cowards."[22]

The personal plot in this autobiography shows how Moody rose out of her environment and acquired a different mindset. As a teenager she

Women's Childhood Autobiography from the End of WWII through 1960s 211

becomes intent on attending college. She works and saves money to pay for higher education, then wins a basketball scholarship to a two-year college and a subsequent scholarship to Tougaloo, a four-year college in Jackson. She joins the Movement as a senior college student in the summer of 1963. She writes: "That summer I could feel myself beginning to change. For the first time I began to think something would be done about whites killing, beating, and misusing Negroes. I knew I was going to be a part of whatever happened" (254). She participated in the events in Jackson in the summer of 1963, where she is assailed by the headline news that Medgar Evers had been assassinated. Subsequently she continued to work for the Movement in Mississippi, participating in rallies, demonstrations, sit-ins, and organizing African American communities under dangerous conditions, often suffering arrest and violence and always afraid of reprisals directed at herself or her family back in Centreville. She writes tartly that Martin Luther King "went on and on talking about his dream. I sat there thinking that in Canton we never had time to sleep, much less dream" (307). As for being a woman, it shines through Moody's account that Black women are doubly oppressed, but this is not a feminist work. Race trumps sex in her consciousness of her oppression.

A final abuse story is Maya Angelou's famous autobiography of childhood and youth *I Know Why the Caged Bird Sings* (1969). Like Moody, Angelou was an African American, and like Moody, she wrote a political book with an agenda. She intends with her book to raise consciousness about racial discrimination in the United States, particularly in the South. In her words, Southern Whites are "so prejudiced that a Negro couldn't buy vanilla ice cream."[23] As an autobiography of group identity, her work has much in common with Moody's. But she was twelve years older than Moody, and when she was growing up, challenges to the segregation laws in the Southern states were not yet on the horizon. Her principal literary model was an earlier autobiography of childhood and youth set in the Jim Crow era, Richard Wright's celebrated *Black Boy* (1945). *I Know Why the Caged Bird Sings* shares with *Black Boy* a literary quality that Moody's lacks, and Angelou echoes some of Wright's themes, including a story about a greedy preacher and another about a school graduation ceremony that shows how Black pupils were kept down in school even if they excelled scholastically.

Unlike either Wright's or Moody's work, *I Know Why the Caged Bird Sings* is not just about racial abuse, but about sexual abuse. Angelou tells the shocking story of how she was raped at the age of eight. To quote Kate Douglas: "The most significant development within the autobiographies of childhood written in the 1990s and 2000s has been the rise (and rise) of traumatic autobiographies of childhood."[24] This rise dates to Angelou's publication of *I Know Why the Caged Bird Sings*. Before Angelou published the story of her childhood rape, hardly a woman, besides the Cornish Waif, had published a similar confession. There was nothing new about childhood sexual abuse itself, witness the notorious case of Virginia Woolf. But with the exception of the scandal-defying Gertrude Beasley, women who wrote about their childhood from the middle of the nineteenth to the middle of the twentieth century refrained from publishing such stories.

Angelou's narrative has certain things in common with the Cornish Waif's. Like the Cornish Waif, Angelou felt terrible guilt; she felt she was complicit in her sexual abuse. As with the Cornish Waif, Angelou's motivation to tell the story publicly seems bound up with the injunction of silence imposed on her by the abuser coupled with a subsequent failure to confess. When Angelou's family took the rapist to court, she lied about what had happened. Both adult women identify silence with victimization and guilt, whereas telling the truth, even if it compromises them, promises psychological liberation and even a kind of personal empowerment.

Otherwise, the texts are quite different. The Cornish Waif's account of her abuse is brief and euphemistic, whereas Angelou gives a blow-for-blow account of her abuse from the perspective of the child. The Cornish Waif states that she writes because she believes that her "case" holds sociological interest, whereas Angelou's entire story, including this episode, seems to be written with the purpose of making her readers aware of issues of oppression, vulnerability, and victimhood, especially as they relate to race and sex.

Angelou's story breaks taboos about what can be told, transgressing feminine norms. She details her relationship with the rapist over a period of several months in order to show how she, in eight-year-old innocence, "led him on," and then graphically describes the rape.

Why tell this kind of story in print? Unlike many other critics, I believe that Angelou tells her story with a political rather than with a therapeutic agenda. Her unstated objective is to show on her own example that all girls potentially face a web of sexual exploitation and

Women's Childhood Autobiography from the End of WWII through 1960s   213

seduction—for she had been seduced into believing that her mother's boyfriend loved her.

The key points in the rape story are these: Her mother's boyfriend Mr. Freeman showed physical affection toward her some months before the rape. Marguerite, as she was called at the time, liked this and even thought she might have found her real father at last. Angelou tells the sequence of events leading up to the rape from the perspective of the eight-year-old. The focalization through the child enhances the plausibility of the account. The physical events are given in colloquial detail. At the actual moment of the rape, the narrator steps in and speaks of the overwhelming pain.

After the rape, Freeman tells Marguerite he'll kill her brother if she tells. So she keeps mum, but her family discovers bleeding and infection, forces her to confess, and brings Freeman to trial. In court, she feels under pressure to lie and deny what she believes was her own complicity in the rape. Her testimony causes Freeman to be convicted. He is then temporarily released, whereupon her uncles kill him. She is overwhelmed by lasting guilt for having caused Freeman's death. She stops talking to anyone except her brother, reasoning that if she talks she might cause another person to die.

What is the point of the story? The story of the rape does not engage the subject of race, much less Angelou's principal theme of the oppression of Blacks by Whites. Her rapist is a Black man. She certainly does not suggest that such a domestic rape is typical in Black communities but, rather, presents it as a personal mishap. She draws no explicit moral from it.

I believe, however, that the telling of the rape does bear a message, which is illuminated by the book's title. Angelou is a much more sophisticated, artistic, self-conscious, and independent writer than Emma Smith, the Cornish Waif. She chose her title, "I Know Why the Caged Bird Sings," carefully, as a statement her reader needs to think about. Why does a caged bird sing? Angelou dedicates her book "To . . . all the strong black birds of promise who defy the odds and gods and sing their songs." This dedication suggests that she engages the classic metaphor of bird for artist and that her title is about the power of art, specifically African American art. However, the rape story gives the title another level of meaning. As a child Angelou was a "caged bird" who was bullied and shamed into silence and lying. As a Black and a woman,

214   Women's Childhood Autobiography from the End of WWII through 1960s

the adult author also conceptualizes herself as a caged bird—but as one who sings. In American slang "to sing" means to tell the authorities details of a crime. The Online Slang Dictionary gives an example of usage: "If he gets arrested, he's gonna sing like a canary."[25] *I Know Why the Caged Bird Sings* does have a moral, albeit an implicit one. It demonstrates that keeping silent about the wrongs that one has suffered amounts to complicity with one's victimizer and that lying leads to guilt. Her telling of the rape in her autobiography amounts to making right a wrong (or at least making it more right) by speaking out and speaking truly, by making public what really happened, even though it implicates her. The story of the rape is meant above all to open the eyes of female readers of any race and in a broader sense everyone's.

It is not surprising that orphans, children whose upbringing is not benevolently and carefully supervised, as well as those whose parents are poor, should be targets of abuse. What is new is that women publish their stories, confessing to their shame and anger. It is characteristic of women's writing after World War II that autobiographers do not hesitate to put negativity on the page. Some manage to squeeze humor out of a bad story, while others brim with indignation or anger, but some, as we shall see, just present the loose ends of their unhappy childhood or youth without tying them up, without interpreting them and certainly without any redemptive message. A few women extract some wisdom from the hard time they had in their youth, but that is not universally the case. The message is, rather: "I had a tough time. That's just the way it was. It's *not* funny."

Self-Focused Autobiographies

Self-focused autobiographies of childhood and youth such as we encountered them in the 1930s and early 1940s—works in the style of Luhan, Butts, Salverson, and Starkie—continued after World War II with Phyllis Bottome's *Search for a Soul* (1947), Leonora Eyles's *The Ram Escapes: The Story of a Victorian Childhood* (1953), Marie Bonaparte's *À la mémoire des disparus* (To the memory of those who have disappeared, 1958), Simone de Beauvoir's *Mémoires d'une jeune fille rangée* (*Memoirs of a Dutiful Daughter*, 1958), Mary Lutyens's *To Be Young: Some Chapters of Autobiography* (1959), Brooke Astor's *Patchwork Child* (1962), Clara Malraux's *Apprendre à vivre* (1963), and Françoise d'Eaubonne's *Chienne de jeunesse* (1965). These works start with the writer's earliest memories and take their stories at least up to age sixteen or to some later logical stopping point in young adulthood, such as meeting "the man." Other self-focused autobiographies—Marie Noël's *Petit-jour* (Dawn, 1951) and *Souvenirs du beau mai* (Memories of the beautiful May, 1964), Elisaveta Fen's *A Russian Childhood* (1961), and Moira Verschoyle's *So Long to Wait* (1960)—stop before adolescence.

Eyles, Beauvoir, and Eaubonne adopt the Bildungsroman model: they focus on the formative dialectic of self and circumstances that leads the protagonist to make certain choices, adopt certain resolves, and take certain actions en route to becoming the person she finally becomes. In all cases the road is bumpy. Eyles's and Beauvoir's protagonists disidentify with their upbringing and transcend it by dint of their own efforts, whereas Eaubonne's painfully discovers her homosexuality.

All of the other authors adopt a variety of psychological approaches. Five of them, Bottome, Bonaparte, Lutyens, Astor, and Fen, are primarily interested in their child selves in the context of their relationships. What is important to them is the child's relationships with significant others, with family members or other people the child was close to. These authors strive to understand the other people as well as themselves. They do not represent themselves as "going somewhere"; their stories have no telos; the protagonists transcend nothing; but, it is suggested, they were very much affected by their relationships with other people.

In addition to these authors, Isabel Bolton in *Under Gemini* (1966) poetically evokes the very special relationship she enjoyed with her identical twin sister—to the point that she thought of the two of them as *one* person—until the latter's accidental death at age fourteen. Never was the first person plural used more appropriately in a childhood autobiography than in this work.

Noël and Verschoyle, in contrast, focus on themselves as young children and recreate the way they experienced the world. Finally, Malraux's work is a stylistic mix. Hers is a long, detailed, probing autobiography in the French confessional tradition. But she also recreates the young child's perspective. As a post-Holocaust Jewish writer, she includes historical context, giving detail about what it was like to be Jewish in the early twentieth century. Last but not least, she airs her well-thought-out feminist convictions.

In this set of post–World War II autobiographies, an explicit concern with gender issues is prominent in Eyles, Beauvoir, Malraux, and Eaubonne, present in Fen and Bonaparte, marginal in Bottome, and absent in Noël, Lutyens, and Verschoyle.

Bildungsroman

One form autobiography takes, in an era when more women had real careers, is that of the Bildungsroman. Appropriately, women who had careers availed themselves of this model. As early as 1902, Juliette Adam wrote the story of her childhood and youth in accordance with this dominant masculine model of autobiography, telling how she rose above her origins to become an important, successful, famous person. Gabriele Reuter wrote an eloquent autobiography of childhood and youth that followed the same model, showing how she became a bestselling novelist. If the model did not catch on generally, it is probably because women childhood autobiographers rarely achieved such prominence, or if they did, they did not wish to showcase it. In the 1950s, however, some women of renown turned to autobiography from the vantage point of their successful careers and wrote autobiographies of childhood and youth in the Bildungsroman tradition. Simone de Beauvoir's *Mémoires d'une jeune fille rangée* (1958) is the best-known example. But Leonora Eyles, an English author all but forgotten today but known in her day as a bestselling novelist, author of self-help books, and advice columnist, wrote a work that fell into this genre several years prior to Beauvoir. The French writer Françoise d'Eaubonne followed suit.

The Bildungsroman model emphasizes an outcome. It thus has the potential for streamlining and hence constricting or diminishing an account of childhood. Mathilde Ludendorff's *Statt Heiligenschein oder Hexenzeichen, mein Leben* (Instead of a halo or a witch mark, my life) can serve as an example. She calls her first volume *Kindheit und Jugend* (Childhood and youth, 1932), but the work cannot be considered a childhood autobiography, because she says too little in it about her childhood. The notorious *völkisch* philosopher, a psychiatrist who wrote an autobiography as outspoken as any in the 1930s, squeezes her childhood years into a few teleologically oriented themes. With her sights set on the life story she would eventually write, she makes explicit that she will concentrate on the formative aspects of her childhood, which prove to reduce to two: the praiseworthy "German morality" instilled in her by her parents, and the low blows dealt her by ill-wishing friends and relatives, which had the effect of making her, in the "battle of life" that lay ahead, impervious to what anyone thought of her.[26] In contrast, the postwar works by Eyles, Beauvoir, and Eaubonne all devote ample space to childhood. None of them treat it teleologically.

The title of Leonora Eyles's *The Ram Escapes: The Story of a Victorian Childhood* (1953) is an allusion to the Abraham and Isaac story. Leonora, née Pitcairn, is the ram. Early in life she felt that her father would have sacrificed her to save her little brother, the favored child. The subtitle is misleading, for although this is the story of a late Victorian childhood (Eyles was born in 1889), the charm implied by "Victorian childhood" and borne out by many previous works with similar titles is not the point of this account. This is not a "we" story but, rather, the autobiography of a child who goes from riches when she is tiny literally to rags by the time she is in her teens. It is noteworthy that she styles her life as an "escape" from her Victorian childhood.

Writing in her sixties and a grandmother, Eyles, a socialist journalist and novelist and, as of the 1920s, a famous "agony aunt" or advice columnist, as well as the author of popular titles on sex education, nutrition, and other issues, tells her story up to age eighteen, when, having run away to London from her Staffordshire home, she decides to sail for Australia to become a domestic servant. She writes very much out of her present, adult perspective. She frames the book as her memories and lards her account of her childhood with frequent and extensive narratorial comments on anything she pleases. In particular, she comments on the differences between the period in which she grew up and the time of writing. Having apparently undergone psychoanalysis as an adult, she makes numerous references to "psycho-analysts," and her associative and rambling mode of presentation—within a chronological frame—frequently sounds like an account one might deliver on a psychoanalyst's couch.

"Nonie" (later "Nora") Pitcairn's first memories are of Chicago, where her father, a china manufacturer, went to exhibit china at the 1892 Chicago World's Fair. The family then returns to the Midlands, where her father has his Works. He buys a big, splendid house with a large garden. These are the happy days of Nonie's childhood, the "Victorian childhood" that so many others extolled. Her family has servants and many animals; they take yearly trips to the seaside; she and her sister go to a school for young ladies. All is not completely idyllic, however, because her parents, her saintly mother and her temperamental, tempestuous, and romantic father, are ill-matched. Before she is ten her father starts to drink, and that marks the beginning of the end. He is a violent drunk who shouts and swears and bangs things about, and he damages his heart, kidneys, and liver with drink. The Works start to

218 Women's Childhood Autobiography from the End of WWII through 1960s

suffer. Presently they are shut down, and the family has to leave the house. Her father, who knows little about farming, unwisely buys a farm. Her mother falls ill and dies in 1901, when Nora is at the outset of her teen years. She describes how she is set to watching her mother's corpse to keep the rats off.

Thereafter things go even more speedily downhill for Nora. To the dismay of everyone—her father's family and his children—her father marries his wife's younger sister, who had been living with them. "Aunty" is very young, and Eyles, while she has some sympathy for her in retrospect, dwells on her misdeeds. Over the next few years her father suffers several heart attacks and becomes progressively more of an invalid until his death of cirrhosis and heart disease when Nora is sixteen. Meanwhile, family finances go from bad to worse. At age fourteen Nora is sent to train as a pupil teacher—this is the only way she can get an education without paying fees—and after hours she has to do farm work. She recalls sleeping no more than five hours a night as a teenager. She hates teaching, which makes her panic. At night she writes letters to her dead mother that she destroys in the morning. Clothes are, as they were for Reuter and Starkie, a constant problem: her "evil stepmother" will not spend money on clothes for her, and so she is perpetually dressed in freakish hand-me-downs. When she finally runs away to London, she considers her lack of clothes her undoing: because of her wardrobe, she cannot find a "good job" doing anything resembling what her training qualifies her for.[27]

For all of its remembering and rambling mode of presentation, for all her intimate confessions including accounts of two recurrent dreams, for all her airing of her guilt feelings at managing to enjoy life at all while her father was dying, the implicit justification for this story is not that it is therapeutic for the author to confess all this. Eyles has a social point to make, and it has to do with the reeducation of an initially well-off Victorian child in the school of hard knocks. Eyles's story shows how she got the experience that allows her to express her opinions so authoritatively in the text. For she speaks as an authority: not just with the wisdom of years, but as someone who, as she says, for the past thirty years has answered letters from an average of 10,000 girls a year, plus older women. It tells how she came to her vocation. Plunged into poverty herself as a teenager, she discovered the lives of other poor people and developed a strong desire to save the poor.

Nora runs away from Staffordshire at age eighteen because, distracted by her first boyfriend whom she keeps secret, she fails her matriculation examination for university and because Aunty will not allow her to go to a teacher's training college for which she is qualified. By the restrictive terms of her father's will, Aunty may not remarry and must keep the children together. So Nora, who aspires "to be a great writer" (179), strikes out on her own and never goes back. A naïve girl in a big city, she has the sort of adventures one might expect. She is exhilarated to be on her own, yet desperately poor. For want of proper clothes all she can find is a job addressing envelopes for very little money. She observes: "It took me a long time to realise that people must naturally judge first by appearances. Now I always advise a woman who wants a job to get into debt, beg, borrow or steal clothes far better than she can really afford as her passport to an employer and let him find out her inner qualities afterwards" (161). Finally she is almost sold as a prostitute.

Eyles's personas as novelist, journalist, advice columnist, popular self-help book author, and grandmother all emerge in the style of this memoir. She comments extensively on food, which she considers to have been better in her day: "children growing up to-day have such dull, standardized meals" (28). She contrasts attitudes toward sex in her day with those of today. In her day, she believes, girls thought less about sex: "I think one way in which I and my special friends differed from most young girls of to-day is that I believe we were uninterested in sex" (151). Eyles proleptically refers to her further misadventures after the end of her narrative: in Australia she married a man who was usually drunk. She returned to England at age twenty-four with three children, where, in order to earn a living, she made clothes in a garment factory and typed. But her readers would have known that in the end she realized her ambition to be a writer and followed her drive to save people — poor people. The very existence of her narrator's voice implies that her story of youthful hardships and troubles found a happy ending.

Simone de Beauvoir, almost a generation younger than Eyles, published *Mémoires d'une jeune fille rangée*, the first volume of her four-volume autobiography, in 1958. Born in 1908, Beauvoir was an uncommon woman, but the story of her childhood and youth was a more common one than Eyles's. Her story also featured a teenage rebellion and a decline in her family's wealth that pushed open the door to a career at a time when middle-class women typically did not work, but all this

220   Women's Childhood Autobiography from the End of WWII through 1960s

transpired in much more standard ways than in Eyles's spectacular disaster story. In Beauvoir's early life no one died, no one fell seriously ill, no one remarried, and Simone was never plunged into poverty. The world-famous author of many books, including *The Second Sex* (1949), Beauvoir published the autobiography of her childhood and youth when she was fifty years old. She wrote a woman's version of a Bildungsroman: the story of how she dodged a woman's fate in order to pursue her dream to become an intellectual and a writer. Esther Kleinbord Labovitz discusses Beauvoir's work as precisely that, a Bildungsroman, and Christina Angelfors shows that Beauvoir herself in later life compared this first volume of her memoirs to a "roman d'apprentissage" (i.e., the same thing).[28] Beauvoir begins her story at the beginning of her life, but the crux is her adolescent rebellion against her family's expectations for their daughter and her slow, tortuous wriggle out of the cocoon of the bourgeois lifestyle. She takes her story up to the start of her relationship with Jean-Paul Sartre at age twenty-one.

Simone came from an initially wealthy middle-class Parisian family and grew up happy, well educated, and much doted upon. As of age five she attended a private Catholic school for the daughters of good families, the Cours Désir. She stayed there until she received her *baccalauréat*, whereupon—since she would have to make a living—she was allowed to continue her studies at university level. When she was eleven, her father failed in business. Her good relationship with her family started to deteriorate as of then. The family had to move into a cramped apartment without heat or a bathroom or separate rooms for Simone and her sister. The parents lost their equanimity and good humor. They became despondent and bitter and had no plan B. They came to the conclusion that they could not provide their daughters with a dowry, so they would not be able to marry. "'You girls will never marry,' [her father] often declared. 'You have no dowries; you'll have to work for a living.'"[29] Simone recalls thinking: "I infinitely preferred the prospect of working for a living to that of marriage: at least it offered some hope" (110). As a teenager she did not aspire to become a mother, but rather a famous author. The erstwhile "dutiful daughter" started to think of a woman's life as captivity, whereas a real education, reserved for men, meant freedom. But she was painfully aware that her parents were deeply ambivalent on this score. They fundamentally believed that girls should marry.

In those days, people of my parents' class thought it unseemly for a young lady to pursue a higher education; to train for a profession was a sign of defeat. It goes without saying that my father was a vigorous antifeminist. . . . Before the war, his future had looked rosy; he was expecting to have a brilliant career, to make lucrative investments, and to marry off my sister and me into high society. . . . When he announced: "My dears, you'll never marry; you'll have to work for your livings," there was bitterness in his voice. . . . The war had ruined him, sweeping away all his dreams, destroying his illusions, his self-justifications, and his hopes. . . . He never stopped protesting against his changed condition. (186–87)

So, in pursuing a career, Simone "was growing up to be the living incarnation of his own failure" (187). Her parents vacillate, hoping that her cousin Jacques will marry her without a dowry. They also struggle over which profession she will train for: her father wants her to study law, her mother sees her as a librarian; neither approves of her choice of study, philosophy. Beauvoir formulates her problem thus: "In fact, the sickness I was suffering from was that I had been driven out of the paradise of childhood and had not found a place among men" (241, translation modified).

The reader knows the outcome: Beauvoir, an extraordinarily hardworking individual who at university earned herself the nickname "Castor" (beaver), was ultimately successful in finding her place in a man's world. Yet her autobiography shows what a woman of her generation and social class was up against if she wanted to become someone. Her struggle to get where she got and not cave in to familial pressure in the crucial period when she was an older teenager is the book's real story. This makes her autobiography a female Bildungsroman and her life story a model for women readers.

Although, as Angelfors writes, Beauvoir in this book fuses her own story with another one she wanted to write, the story of her friend Zaza who died at age twenty, *Mémoires d'une jeune fille rangée* is without question a self-focused autobiography in the tradition of Jean-Jacques Rousseau. From the outset the author is at the center of her story and her preoccupations. Rousseauian is the paradise-fall pattern here, which Marilyn Yalom discerns and contrasts with Sartre's anti-Rousseauian representation of his inauthentic childhood in his later *Les Mots* (*The Words*, 1964).[30] As a young child, Beauvoir enjoyed a special, privileged position in her family. She was doted on from birth; until the age of ten she conformed to the image of the child her parents wanted and was as happy as a clam in its shell. Yet the complicated Rousseauian ejection from paradise, in the sense of a loss of innocence on account of being falsely accused of a misdeed, is missing. Her story has more in common with Reuter's and Eyles's than with Rousseau's: her family lost its wealth when she was an early adolescent, and this made her wake up and look around her more than is usual for someone of that age. Her rebellion came with a greater awareness of the world. It is noteworthy that Reuter, Eyles, and Beauvoir, all of whom wrote Bildungsroman-style autobiographies, all had variants on the same story: the family's loss of wealth when the girl was an early adolescent brought a happy childhood to an end. Unlike Reuter and Eyles, Beauvoir does not describe any sudden awakening about her mission in life or sense of identification with people in similar straits—much less feminism, to which she came very late. She became famous as an existentialist and a novelist long before she wrote *The Second Sex*. As in the case of Reuter and Eyles, however, the adverse turn in her family fortunes, combined with her parents' bad reaction to it, led her to reflect, take on agency, and sharpen her sense of purpose.

Françoise d'Eaubonne's story as she tells it in *Chienne de jeunesse* (1965) follows the same pattern: her father loses his job when she is eleven, which brings childhood ("the green paradise") to an end and ushers in "the time of boredom," the title of the second part of this three-part work. Eaubonne had the misfortune to be born in 1920— something that partly explains the title of her autobiography of childhood and youth, in English translation "Dog of a youth." As Doris Lessing, born in 1919, would later point out, European children born in the immediate wake of World War I had a tough time of it.[31] Eaubonne's large Catholic family became impoverished in the Depression. A teenager in the 1930s, she missed out on the fun of the Roaring Twenties. She recalls being bitterly poor, having no money to spend, and being burdened by housework. As a young person she experienced political polarization in France, the rise of fascism, the Spanish Civil War, and the beginning of World War II. She takes her story up to the Liberation in 1944, when she was twenty-five. Another theme of equal if not greater importance is sexuality, specifically her slow, tortured path to her acknowledgement of her homosexuality, despite a certain attraction to men that led to the birth of her daughter. Last but not least, this is the autobiography of one who knew early on that she wanted to be a writer. She wrote her first poem at age seven and started keeping a journal the

Women's Childhood Autobiography from the End of WWII through 1960s · 223

same year. At nine she started a classical tragedy, and at ten she wrote a fifty-page novel. Her ever-renewed commitment to her vocation and her productivity as a poet and novelist are the saving grace of her youth, the chalice that steadies her.

Her highly confessional book is a Bildungsroman-style autobiography that shows some marked similarities to previous autobiographies of childhood and youth by Reuter, Salverson, Eyles, and Beauvoir. Like Reuter and Salverson, she insists on her writerly vocation. Like both of them, she speaks of a moment of revelation:

> 2 September 1935 is an important date in my diary. *My night of ecstasy,* I wrote. I woke up, a feverish spell, paroxysm of tears, but the tears were tears of joy. It seemed to me that the whole world opened to my eyes in a lightning flash like the Red Sea before the Jews, revealing treasures and monsters undiscoverable by human eye; I got up, fetched a pen and ink, did nothing with them; I dropped to the foot of my bed and began furiously hugging the crooks of my arms. It seemed to me that no possession could be compared to the extraordinary privilege of being alive and having to write, of having to compose numerous books. I went to bed still crying, but more softly; the mere contact of the sheets with my skin was a delight. I heard a train whistle in the distance, in the gray of dawn, before sinking into the calmest sleep of my life. The last word that blazed in me was the infinitive that would rule my future: "to write."[32]

The physicality of the self-discovery, the way she embraces herself *as a body,* is unusual.

Eaubonne shares the pattern of early adolescent loss of family fortune with Reuter, Eyles, and Beauvoir. Similarities with Beauvoir, whose work she would have known, are especially pronounced. Here too we see the paradise-fall pattern and the motif of repugnance for marriage and desire to be a writer. But Eaubonne was much more eccentric, hypersensitive, and miserable as a teenager than Beauvoir, and she writes even more confessionally. The ostensible reason for her extraordinarily confessional tone is that she relies heavily on her diary, especially when writing about her teen years. In fact, she cites from it extensively. Her reliance on a text written in her youth gives her autobiography a distinctively emotional, tortured, nonnostalgic quality. The first, childhood part, however, which occupies a quarter of the book and where she had no journal to rely on, is a brilliant, literary, poetic piece of writing. In its style it somewhat resembles Walter Benjamin's *Berlin Childhood around*

1900. In this part too, there is no nostalgia; rather, the writing transmits the sense that Eaubonne was a brilliant but eccentric writer who had an eccentric childhood. Eaubonne recreates a sense of her childhood with a dexterous shaping hand, using adult sophistication and original analogies. She starts with a thoroughly ironic history of her ancestors and a description of her parents: her father was employed in the financial sector, but was a peasant *manqué*, while her mother was an unmaternal, feminist, political revolutionary, a math teacher who regretted having had children. They were leftists but, disillusioned by the war, innocently supported Italian fascism. Eaubonne observes that she was not a rebel because her family was too nonconformist to rebel against (199). She does, however, passionately hate the repressive Catholic school she was sent to after the family moved to Toulouse.

The evidence afforded by the history of women's autobiographies of childhood and youth shows that the young women who rebelled against their families came from solidly middle-class or upper-middle-class backgrounds. In the interwar and war years Séverine, Luhan, Starkie, and to an extent Butts, all of whom came from comfortable or wealthy families, wrote about how they came to disidentify with their upbringing and distance themselves from their parents' bourgeois values. In the 1950s Eyles and Beauvoir told similar stories of rupture under similar conditions. Seemingly, the lifestyle to which their parents had treated them gave them the education and the confidence to revolt against it. To be sure, the new European laws mandating universal schooling loosened families' grip on their daughters' upbringing and contributed to fostering ambitions that went beyond conventional feminine life patterns. Eaubonne, who was younger than the other authors and grew up in more anxious times without family wealth or parental expectations, was as miserable as the girls with conventional middle-class parents, but did not rebel.

Relationships

Three of the five women who focus on the self in relation to others had, unsurprisingly, a background in psychoanalysis or psychology. Phyllis Bottome studied with Alfred Adler, Elisaveta Fen was a child psychologist, and Marie Bonaparte was a patient of Sigmund Freud's and a psychoanalyst herself. While each woman had confirmed and definite psychological opinions of her own, all three were extremely well informed about psychoanalytic theory. For each of them, it was axiomatic that childhood was crucially important. They also shared the conviction that children are inescapably determined at an unconscious level by others' treatment, expectations, and judgments of them. Consequently, one cannot disentangle one's own story from the personalities and actions of other people, in particular one's parents, but also one's siblings, caregivers, and close friends. Bottome and Fen spell out these premises explicitly. Each of these autobiographers sets herself the task of penetrating the cloud cover that lies over childhood and recovering as much as possible from this precious, presumed-to-be-formative stretch of time. Each interrogates her material with the ultimate hope of grasping clues, keys, or patterns.

Phyllis Bottome's *Search for a Soul*, published soon after the war, reflects the influence of psychoanalysis on a woman's childhood autobiography more than any other work thus far except Luhan's. This British writer, a prolific author of novels and stories, also wrote the biography of the psychiatrist Alfred Adler, with whom she had studied in Vienna. She adopts Adler's view that a child by the age of five has chosen its "scheme of life," which becomes "an unconscious permanent pattern."[33] If our childhood pattern is "more or less normal," "we can often remove these early obstructions and self-deceptions for ourselves." But if not, "we shall need the help of a trained psychiatrist" (x). Thus, she attributes extreme importance to childhood as formative and emphasizes that one's first choice is almost certainly wrong and hence must be uncovered and changed. In her book Bottome wants to show how the child she once was became the human being she turned into. Because of her belief in the deterministic force of childhood experiences, her story of herself and her family takes on an aura of fatefulness. The narrative is told from a retrospective point of view with the benefit of hindsight. The narrator, firmly in control, looks back on her naïve younger self from the perspective of wisdom, her eyes having been opened by psychoanalysis, life experience, and age. She takes her story up to age eighteen.

Bottome analyzes her entire family configuration. One of four siblings, she gives a broader account of her family than most of her predecessors, with the exception of Waser and Starkie. Like Luhan, Butts, Salverson, and Starkie, she is highly critical of her parents. She states matter-of-factly: "I shall have to unmask my parents psychologically in the same manner that I unmask myself" (29). She assesses her father, a clergyman, as spoiled by his mother, so that he expected the same treatment from his wife. She sees her hypochondriac mother as driven by fear. In her analysis, when her mother met a man who idolized her, her "starved heart" (13) knew happiness; she wanted him all to herself and demanded his "warm and persistent care" (32). Obviously, despite their charms and their love for each other, her parents were mismatched; neither could provide what the other wanted. Her mother's illness was real enough in its effects on her family, but Bottome repeatedly intimates that her mother was less ill than she imagined and used her illnesses to control her family. The children sided with one parent or the other. Phyllis's domineering paragon of an older sister Wilmett—"a child of . . . magnificent courage and resourcefulness" (143) whom she both admired and hated—plays a role in her childhood as important, as if not more important than, that of her parents. The principal plot of the autobiography is Phyllis's hatred for Wilmett, but it is tempered by a sense of guilt that Wilmett, who sacrificed her own health for her parents, died at an early age of tuberculosis.

Unlike Luhan, Butts, Salverson, and Starkie, Bottome is critical not just of others but of herself. She does not just play the injured innocent, but seeks to discover where she got on wrong tracks and deceived herself. She writes that Adler attributed great significance to one of her actions when she was three years old: she overwatered a tulip she had received as a gift. Again and again in later life, according to him and to her, she repeated this pattern: she imagined a danger, tried to be a savior, and made things worse. At the end of the book, she castigates her youthful self for a lack of self-knowledge. By age eighteen, she writes, "the main task in life had not even been presented to me—I was unable to dis-associate my thoughts from my wishes; and therefore had no moral freedom" (305).

Adopting a chronological organization for her autobiography, Bottome writes in detail and sympathetically of the family fortunes. They moved to a succession of parishes in England and then to the United States. But her mother never liked it there, and her health necessitated a return after a few years. Back in England, her father had a hard time finding a permanent job. Even though the overall presentation is sympathetic, a persistent theme is that the parents let their four children down. The parents were enlightened, but they taught them nothing useful. The girls were expected to earn their living but received no training. The only child to receive a normal education was her little brother. This little boy, with whose care Phyllis was often saddled, was

Women's Childhood Autobiography from the End of WWII through 1960s   227

favored, but his personality was misunderstood. A diffident child, he had the misfortune of being temperamentally completely unlike his exuberant father and was thus subjected to educational demands that proved too much for him. Like Martin, Bottome complains of the narrowness of her upbringing, of the fact that she was not offered the opportunity to learn any skills. She was given no education at all until age seven, when she was taught to read. Subsequently, Bottome complains, she learned nothing except for what was in books. This lack of skills inculcated her with "a dismal sense of inferiority, as regards anything and everything—except books" (51). Her charismatic and much-loved father turned his energy toward his parishioners and had little time for his family, preferring, when he and his wife fell increasingly out of sympathy, to spend his time on the golf links. Her mother blackened his reputation among the children. She overwhelmed Phyllis and Wilmett with "her opinions and illusions" (291). Additionally, her mother gave her a horrific description of sex when she was nine years old, which made her reject her role as woman. It took Phyllis a long time to break loose from her "long slavery to her thoughts and wishes" (292).

Yet Bottome does not paint her upbringing wholly in dark colors, quite the contrary. A happier thread in the story is how Phyllis developed into a novelist. She wrote her first novel at age seventeen and saw it accepted for publication the next year. Bottome's psychoanalytic training seems to have resigned her to the idea that children's upbringing generally falls far short of the ideal. She in no way portrays herself as a victim. She writes in the confessional, revelatory mode of Luhan, writing frankly about her feelings, including her schoolgirl crushes—though as a dutiful child raised in a religious household, she has much less to reveal.

More than any other autobiographer thus far, Bottome posits that one's personal story is inextricably bound up with the story of one's family. Family members become real people here, and her portraits of them, while unsparing, are more balanced than, say, Starkie's. She insists that she quests for the truth. In the 1947 British edition she avers that her study "has only one aim and can have only one merit, that it is as true as I am able to make it."[34] More explicitly: "I have tried in this fragment of an autobiography to write the truth about my own early and mistaken choice of character as well as to portray the influences which no doubt strengthened my choice" (9).

Elisaveta Fen's *A Russian Childhood* (1961) is a psychologically rather than psychoanalytically oriented work. Fen shows that she is versed in

228 Women's Childhood Autobiography from the End of WWII through 1960s

psychoanalytic theory, but, with a long clinical career as a child psychologist in England behind her, she likes to invoke her own opinions. Especially in her first chapters, which are devoted to her closest relatives and herself, she aims to understand the people close to her as well as her own younger self.

Following classic models, Fen takes her story from her first memories up to age eleven, when she is sent to boarding school. Within this overarching chronological framework, she adopts a traditional form of organization, arranging her work by topic. First she focuses on portraits of family members, then on localities and customs, so that rather than present a chronological account, she writes about "the people" and "the way things were" generally, though these pieces are frequently punctuated by accounts of specific episodes.

The portraits she paints of people are probing and not at all cheerily positive. She analyzes her brother, her sister, and her parents quite mercilessly. In this respect her work has much in common with Bottome's. In particular, Fen paints a portrait of her four-year-older brother as someone who basically liked to hurt her. Her father, she concludes, was a cold personality who barely noticed her. Moreover, he preferred her brother. His obliviousness to her caused her to seek recognition from other men. Her eight-year-older sister was sweet but painfully unconfident. Her mother, to whom she was devoted, earns the best portrait, though she experienced her mother as someone who constantly held the children in check "for their good," lest they do themselves harm. Yet Fen recalls that when she suffered from night terrors, she would call her mother: "A touch of her hand on my forehead was enough to make me feel safe again. She held it there for a moment or two, to see whether I was running a temperature, then stroked my hair, rearranged my pillow, my bedclothes, and gently covered me up. The magic touch made the hot pillow cool again; the reassuring presence turned the threatening shapes looming in the semi-darkness into the familiar cupboards and chairs."[35] When her mother is too busy to pay attention to her, she doubts her love, and on an occasion when her mother criticizes her "demonstrations" (69) of affection toward a piano player, she's shattered. She pays a great deal of attention to her own emotional reactions. Sentences like these abound: "My first reaction to this discovery was distress, and only later indignation and resentment" (17). "It was a blend of torment and delight" (55). "Ravished, entranced, I gazed . . ." (56). "I should not have been more hurt, humiliated or surprised" (70).

"The feeling of humiliating helplessness was paramount . . . fear was added to humiliation" (72). She herself comes across as an adventurous, impulsive, not particularly obedient, yet eager to please and to be thought well of, imaginative and poetically talented upper-class daughter. She recalls joys, passions, fears, humiliations, helplessness, dreams, fantasies, transgressions, and epiphanic moments of awareness in which she comes to understand herself and her powers better. When a boy courts her, for example, she figures out that she has the power to withhold love. She notes children's tendency to think certain thoughts obsessively, against their will, hence not to be in control of their thoughts. A theme that she explores in particular is her own rejection of feminine roles (which to her signify powerlessness) and her imaginative identification with males—reminiscent of Muriel Byrne. She is drawn to daredevil "boy" activities and fantasizes about being a hero.

Fen's later chapters are different in tone. Like Bottome, she rounds out her intensely personal account with descriptions of the places, people, and customs of her childhood—memoir-style material that might be seen to appeal to a general readership. She seems intent on preserving the memory of a Russia that no longer exists. It is noteworthy that Fen, as a psychologist, does not express any blanket doubt in memory, but rather gives her opinion on the hallmark of a genuine memory: its triviality (10). Fen, born in 1899, grew up with father, mother, two siblings, and many servants as the daughter of a provincial governor in pre-Revolutionary White Russia; thus, her memories of growing up are largely idyllic. Striking a note that would have been relevant when she wrote her memoir, she recalls animosity between the townspeople and the large Jewish population of the town. That is nearly the only negative detail in her account of the way things were in her childhood. These chapters, which are not overtly nostalgic but manage nonetheless to present the past as wonderful and special, recall the memoirs of the dispossessed Anglo-Irish writers. Fen makes concessions to an English readership, explaining, for example, that Russians celebrated name days rather than birthdays.

The remaining three writers of the 1950s and early 1960s who focused on themselves in the context of their early relationships—Marie Bonaparte, Brooke Astor, and Mary Lutyens—are upper-class women who had unusual, if not exotic, childhoods.

Marie Bonaparte, great grandniece of Napoleon, Princess of Greece and Denmark, patient, disciple, translator, and protector of Sigmund

230   Women's Childhood Autobiography from the End of WWII through 1960s

Freud, Freudian analyst and founder of the French Institute of Psychoanalysis, wrote one of the most engaging and longest of childhood autobiographies. *Derrière les vitres closes* (Behind closed windows) forms the first volume of her two-volume autobiography of childhood and youth *À la Mémoire des disparus* (1958). Turning to autobiography in her seventies, Bonaparte states that she writes her story in order to push back death and forgottenness a little. As a Freudian and a psychoanalyst, she is fascinated by childhood and eager to recapture all that she can recollect of her own. Her memory seems prodigious, and her extensive recreations of her child's perspective in free indirect discourse or interior monologue augment the impression that she is someone for whom the world of childhood is very close. She was the privileged only child of an heiress who died when she was an infant and an officer who was Napoleon's great-nephew. But hers was a "sad childhood."[36] A fragile child in poor health, she was watched over by her grandmother, a governess, a nurse, and various other adults. She was never permitted to do most things that children do, including play with other children. "I was kept like a hothouse flower" (171). "Hothouse plant" is a phrase that she uses repeatedly to describe the way she was brought up. Her cloistered existence and her longing for freedom are leitmotifs in her story.

Bonaparte ends her 439-page volume with her first communion at age twelve. She stands out among childhood autobiographers for the amount of attention she devotes to early childhood. She creates a telling psychological portrait of the little girl she once was. Paris in the 1880s as experienced in an upper-class lifestyle forms the backdrop of her narrative. Marie ("Mimi") appears as an unusually reflective and sensitive child, who sympathetically projects her feelings about freedom and loss into the animals, plants, and other things around her. Relationships with others—loves, jealousies, hatreds—are an important subject, though as an only child who spends much of her time alone, she relates to significant others such as her dead mother and her adored but largely absent father mainly through fantasies. She recounts these fantasies in abundant detail, often in free indirect discourse. Rumors swirl in the hothouse, feeding her fantasies. Freudian doctrine shimmers up throughout this account: the meaning of death for children, the desire for the mother's breast, the symbolic significance of planting with the nose, of a train-like bogey that haunts her dreams, of "la mer" ("the sea")—a pun on *mère*, mother, of various encodings of her attraction to her father. The theme of the deceptiveness of adults, seen in Burnett and many

Women's Childhood Autobiography from the End of WWII through 1960s   231

other writers, is articulated here as well, initially apropos of the lies she is told about where babies come from. Actual analysis by Freud later brought back Bonaparte's unconscious memories, notably the key memory of how Mimi's nurse and her lover repeatedly had sex in her bedroom when she was tiny, which, she thinks, had a profound effect on the development of her thinking later in childhood. Another theme, albeit one that only flickers up from time to time, is the disadvantages with which society burdens women: their lack of agency, the double standard. But mainly she complains about her confinement and lack of freedom, which of course are byproducts of her femininity as well as her fragile health.

Some echoes of Bonaparte are found in the American Brooke Astor's *Patchwork Child* (1962). Astor too was a wealthy woman who looked back on her careful upbringing as an only child. As with Bonaparte, her sex determined her upbringing: she was raised to become a successful woman of her social class, which meant making a good marriage. Astor was not born with quite the silver spoon in her mouth that Bonaparte was, but became wealthy through marriage. She was the daughter of a US marine officer, who eventually became the commandant of the Marine Corps, and his socialite wife. Her parents were not precisely rich, but they were sufficiently well off always to have had servants in Washington, DC, as well as in the other parts of the globe to which they constantly traveled. Brooke spent many of her childhood years in exotic parts of the world including China. Yet her mother raised her very conservatively. As an only child she was mainly in the company of grown-ups. She attended the best schools in Washington, but her mother had no intention of sending her, as a girl, to college. Astor takes her story to age sixteen, when she married her first husband.

Astor both starts and ends her book with her all-important family. She makes the impression of having grown up in a protective shell of parents, grandparents, family friends, and nursemaids. Although she does not adopt the analytical approach seen in Bottome, Fen, and Bonaparte, she writes a self-focused (and particularly charming) childhood autobiography, in which she constructs a portrait of herself with lavish, convincing confessional content. Like Eaubonne, she relies on her diary, which perhaps accounts for her astonishingly good memory. She is adept at capturing telling details, many of which have to do with the incomprehensible adult world. Thus, she learns a terrible lesson when she innocently repeats her mother's snide comment about a neighbor's house to the neighbor herself and has to take the heat. She wonders why grown-ups only seem to want to talk about dull things, like "Are your hands clean" and "Did you meet any little friends on your walk,"[37] whereas she cannot extract any information from them on more interesting subjects. She eventually comes to a momentous insight about herself and her family: she realizes that her parents are two different people rather than a monolithic unit and also that each parent and grandparent has entirely different aspirations for her. Her mother wants her to be pretty and the life of the party; her father wants her to be more into sports; her grandmother, who had once owned slaves, wants her to be a Southern Lady. Buffeted by these conflicting desires for her future, she herself longs to be dressed just like everybody else (a veteran theme in women's childhood autobiographies) and resists having to grow up at all. At age thirteen she completely rejects the concept of sexual relations between men and women. This does not prevent her, starting at age fourteen, from fantasizing about being a femme fatale, the belle of the ball, even though (as the narrator points out) her looks give her little basis for such dreams. The other developmental story she tells is that of her literary interests. She writes stories, plays, and poems from a young age and wants to be a writer. In school, at age thirteen, she has a set of friends with like interests; and as in Una Hunt's 1914 story, they invent a private language. In real life, she married three times. Her last husband was a multimillionaire, and she became a philanthropist as well as a socialite. She also published a couple of novels.

Mary Lutyens's *To Be Young: Some Chapters of Autobiography* (1959) is likewise devoid of psychoanalytic theory, but like Bottome's *Search for a Soul*, it chronicles a mistaken early choice. Lutyens's story stretches the imagination in its account of the author's obsessive, unchanging childhood passion for a young man and dazzles in its tale of the exotic international life led by foremost theosophists in the British Empire. Lutyens, a generation younger than Bottome, writes a highly confessional, almost incredible story of her unshakable and obsessive love for an Indian youth ten years older than she, from early childhood (age three to six) until his death when she was seventeen. Mary's mother, Lady Emily Lutyens, was a committed theosophist who took this South Indian Brahmin, Nitya, and his brother Krishna, who was destined by the movement to become a World Teacher, under her wing in Britain.

Lutyens follows a painstaking chronological course from her early childhood to Nitya's death by tuberculosis, which leaves her chastened and self-questioning. The story starts in Britain, but later her mother takes her to India, where the family has strong ties: her grandfather, Robert Bulwer-Lytton, was viceroy of India, and her father, an architect, one of the builders of the new Indian capital. Subsequently, despite paternal protests, her mother takes her to learn from the spiritual teacher Bishop Leadbeater in Australia. Lutyens's work is a true autobiography, since she puts herself at the center of her unusual and exotic story. Reminiscent of Una Hunt, she includes an account of her imaginary friend, a hero whom she constructs out of books she has read, so that she has her own private world until she is thirteen and her imagination (so she says) leaves her. Central here, however, is the suspense story of her love for Nitya: the reader wonders how it will turn out.

Living throughout her childhood in proximity to theosophic circles, Mary nearly becomes a theosophist herself. During her Indian sojourn she turns against the "world of men" (the British world) and embraces "the extreme simplicity of Indian life," while despising the Raj.[38] So she decides to become a disciple of theosophy, a belief that espouses the doctrine of reincarnation and karma, involves serving the Masters (in her case, her Master will be one living in Tibet), and encourages religious tolerance. She too records a momentous insight: at age sixteen, she finally confesses her love to Nitya, whereupon she realizes that her spiritual aspirations are fraudulent; actually she only wants Nitya. Is her love for Nitya ever requited? Seemingly yes, and she is ecstatic, but then seemingly no. Nitya prefers to be nursed in his final months by a wonderful, generous American woman rather than by Mary. Nitya's untimely death leaves his love for Mary an open question for her to wonder about. The book ends on this inconclusive note. Lutyens's narrative challenges the reader to consider what is involved in letting go of a lasting emotional investment that led to nothing—if ever one really does.

The Child's Perspective

In the post–World War II period Marie Le Franc, Marie Noël, Charlotte Berend-Corinth, and Moira Verschoyle continued the type of the psychological self-study initiated by Joan Arden in 1913 and perpetuated in the 1930s and 1940s by Agnes Miegel, Anna Schieber, Sigrid Undset, Francesca Allinson, Dormer Creston, Emmy Ball-Hennings, Emily Carr, and Muriel St. Clare Byrne, in which the author recreates the perceptions and feelings of her childhood self. Clara Malraux also set herself this same agenda at the outset of her longer, more complex autobiography

234 Women's Childhood Autobiography from the End of WWII through 1960s

of childhood and youth. This type of project would seem by its very nature to demand an excellent memory. The Canadian author Le Franc confounds expectations. One of the oldest authors in the group, she wrote *Enfance marine* (Marine childhood, 1959) in her extreme old age to conjure her childhood perceptions in Brittany, which date to the 1880s. She insists, however, that she can remember very little—but she is all the more sure that the place had a formative influence on her. The French poet Marie Noël's *Petit-jour* (1951), to which she added *Souvenirs du beau mai* in 1964 and that also revives perceptions that date to the 1880s, is more true to type. At a point when she believes she is nearing the end of her life, Noël poetically and poignantly revives her recollections of her early childhood spent in Burgundy, mainly Auxerre. She calls her child self by her real name (Marie) and her family by her real family name (Rouget). She goes back to the dawn "where there still are monsters and not yet any paths,"[39] a phrase she comes back to as she thinks about how little time remains to her on earth, and focuses especially on her memories of very early childhood. As a narrator, she melts into these memories, reliving them, and evokes with great skill the sometimes barely describable feelings of a child who was strikingly prone to negative emotions. They include a fear of abandonment and an obsession with things going away, disappearing, or dying. She persistently feels that someone is missing, someone who is there just for her; she hates it when her mother leaves, sure that she won't return; she dislikes guests; and she hates it when other children come to play, for they just bring noise, torment, and disasters. In spite of this preoccupation with loss, she experiences a desire to be stolen by a fairground animal demonstrator and is gripped by a "mysterious and terrible emotion" (102) when she later hears the melody she associates with him. Noël received a strict Catholic upbringing and tells of her fascination with and rebellion against religion, building up to the momentous, superb occasion of her First Communion at age twelve, described in *Souvenirs du beau mai*. She supplies some explanatory commentary, but mainly she presents relived memories in the style of Joan Arden.

In *Als ich ein Kind war* (When I was a child, 1950), the painter Charlotte Berend-Corinth (1880–1967) also revives memories dating to the 1880s. She looks back on her Berlin childhood over a chasm of over fifty years, during which half-century she married the artist Lovis Corinth, became a widow, and, as a Jew, left Germany in the Nazi period, finally to land in California. Her story spans her earliest memories up to her entry into art academy at age sixteen, not in the form of a consecutive narrative but—in a style familiar from such earlier German authors as Helene Adelmann, Clara Blüthgen, and Sophie Reuschle—of short pieces, each with its own title. She puts these pieces in approximate chronological order and, underscoring her autobiographical intention by using real names, states at the end that what she has written is what she actually remembers of her childhood. Most of the pieces involve dramatic episodes, high emotions, or consistent states of affairs. They thus approximate the way a person typically remembers the distant past. She does not frame her stories as memories, however, but recounts them with plenty of memory-defying detail and dialogue, as if she were right there, living those events as a child. Regarding self-presentation, she projects the self-image of a highly imaginative, exceptionally suggestible, indeed gullible child—who is therefore called "dumb." Clear distinctions between fantasy and reality elude her child self: she is repeatedly visited by angels, believes that the action on stage in a Tom Thumb performance is real, is persuaded by her older sister that there's a bear under the bathtub, and so forth.

The narrator in this book is more intrusive than in most works that recreate the child perspective. She alternates between sympathy (she repeatedly mentions that in many ways no one understood her until her husband came along) and irony (at her naïveté, in not realizing, for example, that her favorite hen has been served up for lunch, or that she should not repeat certain things grown-ups say). Her comments on her parents are clearly the fruit of retrospective analysis: she loved her mother but stresses matter-of-factly that she was hardworking, conscientious, assiduous, and perfectionistic, but not fun, whereas she simply adored her good-looking, charming, luxury-loving father. Her father loved her as well: she recounts a drama in which he desperately searched for his lost child at night in Marienbad and finally rescued her from an outdoor toilet for men into which she had accidentally locked herself. A recurrent theme is Charlotte's love of drawing, which blossoms into a desire to study at the art academy and become a painter, something her upper-middle-class parents had not at all envisaged. She does not, however, allude to her later accomplishments as a painter, nor to the fact that her father committed suicide for embezzlement a few years after her narrative ends.

Moira Verschoyle, in her fifties at the time of writing, is another author who has no problems with memory. Her *So Long to Wait: An Irish*

236   Women's Childhood Autobiography from the End of WWII through 1960s

Childhood (1960) is an extraordinary, detailed exercise in self-knowledge that rings authentic, particularly in regard to what she has to say about the psychology of only children. Complementing the work of Mary Frances McHugh, Enid Starkie, Elizabeth Bowen, Mary Hamilton, and Elizabeth Hamilton, Verschoyle's childhood autobiography is another testimonial to the life of the Anglo-Irish in Ireland. Moira grows up in well-to-do circumstances in Limerick, across the river from County Clare. Her father is a younger son who progressively becomes poorer, lives off an increasing "overdraft,"[40] and tends in Anglo-Irish fashion to live nostalgically in the past. Moira is not really an only child, but her brother and sister are so much older that she is raised as if she were one. She is her mother's pampered pet. Verschoyle confines herself to the life of her mind up to age eight or nine, when life was a "long, aimless procession of days" (134).

Like Laura Goodman Salverson previously, Verschoyle orients and entices the reader with an in medias res third-person opening before shifting to first-person narration for the remainder of the book. Verschoyle uses this opening to introduce the personality of the child. She reconstructs the thoughts of the very young child on an occasion when she has been sent to bed early for naughtiness. Moira had been overconfident and thoughtless. She impulsively picked her mother's greenhouse flowers without asking permission so as to give them to a poor woman, but then let the pony eat them, forgetting her original purpose. It is her frequent behavior pattern. She marches to a different drummer from the grown-ups. She communicates herself poorly to them and in turn doesn't understand their point of view—though as her mother's darling she is always sure of her ultimate sympathy. Like Sigrid Undset, Verschoyle is good at rendering the instability and shifts of a child's perspective. Just as she forgets about the poor woman when she sees the pony, Moira's thoughts in bed wander. She slips into fearful imaginings about the dark; she screams and screams. But then when the grown-ups come, "a curious pride made her feign sleep" (6). Repeatedly we see Moira like this: impulsive, inexplicably forgetful, self-centered, and proud.

In the more "natural" first-person remainder of the book, Verschoyle continues to take the child's perspective, using a spectrum of techniques including dialogue. Moira was a willful and egocentric child, but Verschoyle manages to write about herself without narratorial irony. She generally avoids commentary, but sometimes explains and draws conclusions about the child's actions and feelings in a basically sympathetic,

Women's Childhood Autobiography from the End of WWII through 1960s   237

yet neutral tone. Thus she comments, for example, "Children have no weapons except rudeness with which to counter mockery" (102); or "Children with brothers and sisters of their own age seem to have a tribal sense and a solidarity which a child by itself misses" (136). The grown-up point of view is represented in two other ways: by the child's mother, who makes every effort to be sympathetic to her willful little girl but sometimes fails, and by the selection of the stories, which seem to have been chosen to reveal the child's personality and way of thinking. For example, there is a terrible story about a dog. The neighbor, with whom her family is not on entirely amicable terms, encourages her to adopt one of his puppies. She senses that this will be forbidden and does so secretly, collecting and training the frightened, pathetic little dog every day in places where her parents cannot see her. But then her father surprises her by riding up while she is walking the dog. She quickly stuffs it through a hedge. As ill luck will have it, she cannot get back to it that day; her anxiety mounts; worry makes her sick. Finally, in desperation, the next day she pays a servant to find it and is utterly relieved to find out that the puppy is back with the neighbor. Verschoyle paints her relief in vivid colors: suddenly, food tastes good to her, and she can enjoy baths. But then, inexplicably, she doesn't follow up; she doesn't return to see the dog for two weeks; she just doesn't feel like it. The reader is left to wonder why. Perhaps there was too much high drama from which she instinctively needed to distance herself. Her negligence is badly repaid. At the end of that time she sees the dog's drowned body in the river.

Some of the psychology of only children that we have seen in other writers, such as Luhan and Byrne, recurs here. Moira craves friends, wants to play with other children, wants to "belong." Like many other little girls, she wants to be dressed exactly like every other little girl. The child is, however, blind to adult psychology and also to the feelings of other children, even if she has had those feelings herself. Thus, she longs for friends; but when she gets one, she is intolerant of having her little sister tag along. "My own solitude hadn't taught me to be kind to the lonely" (137), she writes. Moira has a strong will to power, reminiscent of Judith Gautier. She hates losing face or anything that diminishes her power and status. Like many other writers' childhood selves, she hates grown-ups making fun of her, and she also hates it if they discuss her with each other. Such things can drive her to fury, and in her fury she can go to considerable lengths. For instance, she commits a minor misdeed, digging up her mother's plants to help the cat find a toilet. Because her mother's friend is there and suspects her, she lies about it. She gets a beating. This makes herself so furious that as an act of rebellion against the grown-ups, she displays herself naked in the window to the gardener's boy. All in all, this is a persuasive psychological portrait of a little girl from within.

A Stylistic Mix

Clara Malraux's *Apprendre à vivre* (1963) is a self-focused, self-analytical autobiography of childhood and youth in the French confessional tradition. It neither adopts the Bildungsroman template, like Eyles, Beauvoir, and Eaubonne, nor is it centrally concerned with relationships, like Bottome, Fen, and Lutyens, but is the introspective, psychologically searching story of herself. In the extensive initial portion of the text, Malraux follows the "child's perspective" model in seeking to recreate the way she saw things as a child. Subsequently, her work becomes a classic confessional autobiography of childhood and youth. She also contributes to Jewish social history and writes a feminist work.

Clara Malraux (1897–1982), née Goldschmidt, was a prominent French writer and intellectual who was notorious for her acrimonious relationship with her ex-husband, the famous writer and later statesman André Malraux. Like Beauvoir, she chose to write a multivolume autobiography. The first volume of her six-volume *Le Bruit de nos pas* (The sound of our steps, 1963–79), *Apprendre à vivre* (Learning to live, 1963), appeared when she was in her sixties. It covers her life through her early twenties, up to the point in 1921 when she met her future husband André. It is not the volume the public had waited for. People were much more interested to see what Clara would reveal about her eventful and chaotic adult life and her prominent ex-husband's. Clara's life of adventures entered the public spotlight when she and André were arrested for art theft in Cambodia in 1924. But public expectations notwithstanding, *Apprendre à vivre* is a major work in its own right.

In her text, Clara painstakingly quests for herself: not just for her past self, but for the truth about herself. She strives to reconstruct her earlier moods and beliefs by way of mercilessly analyzing her earlier self at each developmental twist and turn. Seemingly, she commits to paper everything she remembers of the past. Length seems not to matter. This makes for an extremely detailed account. The very abundance of detail underscores the impression that she composed the work in a sincere "tell it all" spirit. So does her revelation of her childhood fantasies and her immature teenage ideas, which she critiques in a dispassionate, distanced way. Last but not least, she also criticizes her present temptation to frame herself in a set of particular terms and give her life story too much of a plot.[41] Hers is a Rousseauistic autobiography, except that Clara is more self-conscious, more self-questioning, and far less self-justifying than Rousseau.

At the outset, Malraux joins the ranks of those who earnestly attempted to find their way back into their childhood world in order to recreate their thoughts and feelings as children. She seeks poetic language adequate to conveying the child's delicate, fluctuating, subverbal perceptions and feelings. She starts the book by projecting herself into the small-child perspective. She reconstructs, in the present tense, how she loved to touch things. She avers that her early memories are fragmentary—a statement that for any sophisticated author by this point in time had become de rigueur—and likens them poetically to floating jellyfish. The instability of things (is it a staircase or a dragon's mouth?) for a small child is a theme. Life lived more in the unreal than in the real is another. The fluidity of childhood perception and the rampant power of fantasy over the child's mind are themes already encountered in such writers as Hunt, Farjeon, Fen, and Verschoyle. Similarly to Hunt and Ebner-Eschenbach, Malraux states that she led various fantasy lives, alternating between different identities. She details her fantasies: she had an imaginary double and imaginary vassals.

When Clara starts writing about herself as a teenager, however, less than halfway through the volume, her narrative abandons the mode of recreating the perceptions of her younger self. It settles into more traditional patterns, giving portraits of family members and people she knew, imparting significant lessons about life that she learned, recounting episodes from wartime, and the like, all from a retrospective point of view. This change in style implicitly supports what other autobiographers have said about how the quality of their memories of childhood changes around age seven to nine. As Verschoyle wrote, at that point her life got a direction; as Hannah Lynch claimed, after age seven, life became a story. Psychological studies corroborate that adults have more memories from the period between the ages of seven and ten than from earlier years and that starting at age ten, a twenty-year "reminiscence bump" begins.[42]

Malraux's is patently a childhood autobiography written in the age of psychoanalysis. Malraux reconstructs, indeed dredges up, her childhood

240   Women's Childhood Autobiography from the End of WWII through 1960s

as if for a psychoanalyst. At one point, she even reproduces what she tells her psychoanalyst in a psychoanalytic session and gives the psychoanalyst's responses. The text contains ongoing allusions to the psychoanalytically saturated climate in which she wrote. She analyzes her relations with her mother and her mother's relations with *her* mother and pays attention to her childhood sexuality before the "latency period" (127). Yet despite her familiarity with and acceptance of the discourse of psychoanalysis, what stands out most about her investigation of her early life and early memories is that she appears sincerely and carefully to be trying to get at the truth of the way things were, a project for which psychoanalysis does not always serve her as a useful tool. There are many aspects to her self-representation that she does not assimilate to psychoanalytic postulates, and she sometimes disagrees with them, challenging, for example, the notion that blindness is terrifying because it symbolizes castration. To her mind blindness is terrifying in and of itself.

One of the fruits of her self-analysis is the insight that she conceived of herself as one who was elected, who had a duty toward others to save them. Like the similarly psychoanalytically influenced Bottome, Malraux acknowledges a sense of mission that was implanted in her early on: she wants to be a savior. Yet she also acknowledges that for her, hesitation and a penchant for amusement always counterbalanced conviction and passion, so that she often stopped three-quarters of the way to her goal, tired or distracted by other people (158). She does not hesitate to confess memories that are embarrassing. Thus, she says that she was a child who cried at the drop of a hat; she would force herself to faint so as to get out of going to school; she was an obsessive collector of pebbles and was badly stricken when the grown-ups inadvertently threw her collection out. Sexuality is treated openly and confessionally. She writes of her attraction to her girl friend when all the men were off at war, of her feelings about masturbation, and of her stupid and immature rejection of her boyfriend Jean's caresses.

As behooves a writer of her era, Malraux keeps up a commentary on memory. For example, she acknowledges that her memories of her father, who died when she was thirteen, are surely supplemented by the accounts of others. A reference to memories as magic lantern slides (53) makes clear that Proust is in her thoughts. Yet she expresses very little doubt about her memories. Regardless of whether she remembers her past states of mind or events, the richness of detail with which she remembers is astonishing. Few people remember this well—which is

Women's Childhood Autobiography from the End of WWII through 1960s 241

not to say that Malraux is not among the few who do. She replays the events surrounding her father's death, her first kiss, her friendship with her friend Jean that does not lead to a sexual relationship, and the beginning of her affair with André Malraux as if she had movies and not memories in her brain. Were they burned in her mind, or is she, as an adult, fantasizing? She makes no apologies for possibly misremembering when she recounts these sequences of events.

Clara, who was Jewish, had a protected upper-bourgeois childhood, and also an unusual one, since she shuttled every year with her German-born parents, who had opted to become French, and her two brothers between Paris and Magdeburg, where her maternal grandparents lived. In the process she learned both French and German. Her family was well off and happy, and she speaks well of her parents. The first volume of her autobiography of childhood and youth spans the belle époque, World War I, and the immediate postwar period. Though her work is a true, self-focused autobiography and not a memoir, she nonetheless gives an interesting retrospective of the customs and mood of the day, including how her family experienced the war. A constant theme is what it meant to be Jewish in that era. She remembers how she was discriminated against as a Jew both in France and Germany. It is not a surprising train of thought for one who narrowly escaped being deported to Auschwitz in 1944.[43]

There is a distinct feminist tone in this autobiography, more pronounced than in any other work to date, with the exception of Salverson's. Though Simone de Beauvoir had published her groundbreaking feminist work *The Second Sex* in 1949, the feminist tone in Malraux's childhood autobiography is considerably sharper than in Beauvoir's *Mémoires d'une jeune fille rangée*. Clara was a longtime feminist. In the 1920s, after she broke with her well-to-do family for a life of adventure with André, she was a rebel on many fronts: she became a leftist, took up opium smoking, and believed in sexual freedom for women and practiced it herself.[44] Her stormy marriage with André Malraux, who increasingly sidelined her and then left her for another woman, deepened her feminist convictions. She started expressing her views in print in the late 1930s after André left her. After the war she translated Virginia Woolf's *A Room of One's Own* into French (published in 1951). In her childhood autobiography she closely examines what it meant to be female when she was growing up. Thus, she concedes that her mother was certainly a happy married woman. Yet, her mother seems to have spent most of her time waiting for her husband. And when her husband dies, she is in no position to make something new of her life and finally commits suicide. Thus, Clara does not see her mother as a model. Her feminist sentiments color her account of her girlhood perception of women as Chinese coolies weighted down by the double burden of maternity and conjugality. She also remarks that when she was a girl, she came to despise other girls for being too acquiescent. Yet Clara too succumbed to social expectations to a degree. Although she was literarily gifted, and although she felt her vocation was to be a writer, during her marriage to André Malraux she would fall into the role of the wife who did not write.

In sum: The first two decades after World War II brought a democratization and significant numerical increase in women's childhood autobiographies. In a climate where female authorship was taken for granted, the genre flourished. More women wrote. In particular, many women published semi-memoirs and outwardly focused autobiographies. In the personally focused works, psychological approaches continued to dominate. Some women started to exploit their childhood literarily, writing brilliant pieces for such venues as the *New Yorker*. Fictionalization, prominent in the history of women's childhood autobiography thus far, is now employed chiefly for artistic ends, not for concealment. Other women, such as Eyles and Beauvoir, wrote Bildungsroman-style autobiographies from the height of their successful careers. At the same time, more women from poor and disadvantaged backgrounds took to the pen. Abuse stories started to appear in print, written both by women whose backgrounds had put them at risk and by middle-class women. In general, however, with the exception of Moody and her description of coming of age in Mississippi, women autobiographers told their own individual stories for their own sake and did not represent themselves as typifying a group.

Two trends are evident. First and most obviously, authors keep in step with the times, molding the genre as appropriate to a new generation of women, some of whom had Bildungsroman-worthy lives.

Second, authors aim at novelty, toward exceeding rather than conforming to previous generic norms. The push toward newness is seen in the heightened literariness and in the stories that focus on abuse and hardship. In seeming paradox, despite this keeping in step with the times and this push toward the new, there is in this period an overall trend toward blending and hence toward homogeneity. New works entered a competitive field. Autobiography and memoirs of childhood, or childhood and youth, had caught on. The public had an appetite for autobiography, and many were published. It was no longer enough to be bold or candid to attract public notice, though these things helped. If written by a non-celebrity, but even if written by a celebrity, a work did well to offer thematic novelty and stylistic flair. To judge from patterns among the many works, authors seem to try to touch as many bases as possible: to tell an interesting and unusual story, include a convincing personal element, and produce an engaging, well-written narrative. The result is a blending, in particular of memoir and personal autobiography into semi-memoir, which remained the most discreet of the options, but also of memoir-like features such as thematic novelty into personal autobiography. The many works that were produced in the 1950s and 1960s seem more cut from a template—resemble one another more—than works written in previous periods.

Not only do the many women who tell their stories because they have a good story routinely round out their memoirs with accounts of their thoughts and feelings, but some of the most deeply introspective and self-analytical autobiographies, Marie Bonaparte's, Brooke Astor's, and Mary Lutyens's—autobiographies that were not written just for the sake of the story—were authored by women whose childhoods were unusual enough to have merited a memoir with no self-analysis. Thus Bonaparte was an aristocratic Parisian "hothouse flower" whose family groomed her for a royal marriage; Brooke Astor was an American who spent a large portion of her childhood in Hawaii, Panama, and China; and the upper-class British Mary Lutyens led the exotic life of a daughter of a leading theosophist. Their works, all very original, participate by coincidence in the blending of types that other writers adopt by design.

Not differently from previous periods, narrators range from intrusive and opinionated to effaced. All of the Bildungsroman-style works and abuse stories feature strong narrators. In the field of relational autobiographies, Bonaparte especially but also Astor and Lutyens inject retrospective commentary into their recollections of childhood, while the Adler disciple Bottome and the child psychologist Fen approach their childhood from a purely retrospective, analytical point of view. At the opposite end of the spectrum, Noël, Berend-Corinth, Verschoyle, and Malraux are intent on recapturing the mentality of the child, not on analyzing it. These latter four writers make significant new contributions to the collection of insights established by earlier women who wrote with the same purpose: Arden, Hunt, Miegel, Schieber, Undset, Allinson, Creston, Ball-Hennings, Carr, and Byrne. Their works are masterpieces of introspection and do not duplicate anything published previously. Whereas Berend-Corinth and Malraux write mainly of the child's imaginings and fantasies, Verschoyle emphasizes, in addition, her emotions and passions and writes discerningly of the kinds of things that triggered them. Noël tries to recover her very earliest memories and comes up with a fascinating pattern of possessiveness, fear of loss, and self-protection from the time when the birth of her brother deprived her of her nurse until approximately age six.

What became of the new boldness of the interwar and war years? It is still there. Yet there is a distinct difference between the outspoken works written in the 1930s and 1940s and comparable works published in the postwar period. The women who published in the 1930s and early 1940s—Luhan, Butts, Salverson, Starkie—expressed a lot of anger, mainly out of rebelliousness against their background, regardless of what it was, and against society generally. They recall their discontent as children and their desire for the good things they imagined life had to offer: education, excitement, freedom. As adult narrators, they sympathize with their child selves, even if they style themselves as "bad girls," and underwrite their early discontent. While they write in a polished style, they express themselves with the candidness and lack of restraint of people who have had a few drinks at the bar.

None of these women who published in the interwar years had been affected by a war or any other unusually adverse conditions as children, though Salverson's childhood had not been easy. The rebels who wrote after World War II had seen much more trouble. Beauvoir's and Hitchman's early lives had been impacted by World War I, McCarthy's by the 1918 influenza epidemic, Eaubonne's by the Depression. These women had had tough childhoods, and they emphasize how hard things had been for them. They also write in a less unbuttoned, more planned and reflective way than the women who wrote in the 1930s and early 1940s. Beauvoir writes in measured tones, Hitchman builds in a continuous self-analysis, McCarthy scrutinizes her earlier texts in a retrospective critique, Eaubonne assiduously consults her diary to reconstruct her feelings. The other writers who produce introspective self-analyses do so in a comparatively balanced way. Bottome, Fen, Bonaparte, Astor, and Berend-Corinth examine their closest relatives and their family

Women's Childhood Autobiography from the End of WWII through 1960s 245

relationships carefully. Bottome and Fen are quite critical of family members, whereas Bonaparte, Astor, and Berend-Corinth are not, but even the critical writers do not lash out at their relatives after the fashion of Luhan, Butts, or Starkie. Bottome's "truthful" analysis of her mother is not complimentary, but she makes the impression of trying to understand what made her mother tick rather than heaping scorn on what she represented.

Anger in postwar childhood autobiography generally has specific targets. Authors pursue their targets precisely and deliberately. We see the rise of the sharply accusatory memoir in Mary McCarthy, Ruth Slenczynska, and Claire Martin. These autobiographies have real-world agendas: the women want to get even with the people who oppressed and tortured them when they were young. Works with agendas, written to accomplish a particular purpose, become more common than they had been previously. Moody too has an obvious design on her readership: to expose conditions for African Americans in Mississippi.

Negativity is part of many childhood autobiographies in the postwar period. One senses that the roots of the contemporary "misery memoir" lie here. In part this negativity can be traced to a changing demographic. Before the post–World War II period, most of the women who wrote childhood autobiographies came from the middle and upper classes. Those who came from disadvantaged backgrounds, like Popp and Audoux, had predictably bad stories to tell. In the post–World War II period, thanks to improved standards of education, more women clambered out of their disadvantaged backgrounds to write about them. Additionally, the wars and the Depression brought reversals of fortune to middle-class families. Quite a few women write about losing a parent. The death of the father, which left the mother to scramble as the breadwinner, had always upturned children's lives: it changed the lives of Sand, Larcom, Burnett, Popp, Reuter, and Adams. In the post–World War II period, single mothers, such as those of the Cornish Waif, Gypsy Rose Lee and her sister June Havoc, Yvonne Gautier, and Anne Moody, continued to struggle financially, with significant consequences for their daughters. The death of a mother had a different effect: girls tended to experience it as a disaster. We saw previously how Eleanor Hallowell Abbott abruptly changed her tone from humorous to serious and confessional when she wrote about her unhappy life with her father and stepmother after her mother died. In the post–World War II period, Eyles's, Dunham's, and Martin's early years were darkened by their mothers' deaths. Not only did the mother's death rob the girl of the adult to whom she was most closely attached, leaving an affective hole, but it resulted in a dysfunctional family life. These girls' fathers seemed unable to cope with the challenges of raising a family.

Finally, whereas the death of a parent had always been an eminently mentionable fact in childhood autobiography, in the post–World War II period new topics come onto the table. Women start to avail themselves of the genre to tell how they were abused as children. Eaubonne writes of the anguish her homosexuality caused her. Intimate confession had long since become acceptable. Now writers feel free to write about their pain and suffering, regardless of its cause. What this adds up to, in terms of women's self-presentation, is a new willingness to tell a dark personal story.

The childhood autobiographies by Astor and Beauvoir show how gendered the upbringing of upper-middle-class girls born in the early twentieth century continued to be: how they were raised for what at the time was perceived to be a woman's ideal destiny, namely a good marriage. In women's childhood autobiographies published between 1945 and 1969, feminist rebellion is seen above all in French writers— Beauvoir, Malraux, and to a lesser extent Bonaparte—and in the French Canadian writer Claire Martin. These writers are critical of women's "ideal destiny" and of what they perceived life actually to hold in store for women: a lack of self-determination, subservience to a husband, a life centered on the body, drudgery or empty waiting depending on their social class, deficiencies in psychic and physical well-being. Beauvoir, who purposely never married, additionally shows how as a teenager she struggled against the feminine fate in order to earn herself a spot in the public world of men.

Conclusion

Organizing women's childhood autobiography by type is not difficult. Any narrative involves a teller or narrator (in autobiography, the persona adopted by the author), a narrated world (the subject matter), and an implied reader or narratee (the audience the narrator seems to be writing for). In a given childhood autobiography, each of these aspects can be located at a point on a sliding scale—it being understood that authors are not obliged to be consistent, but can shift gears whenever and however often they please in the course of a single work. A narrator can be more or less effaced or intrusive. An intrusive narrator can be more or less analytical, opinionated, or judgmental. Narrators frequently adopt tones, such as sympathy, pathos, irony, or humor. In terms of the narrated world, self-writing about childhood ranges from other- to self-oriented: points on this sliding scale from other to self are memoirs, semi-memoirs, outwardly focused autobiographies, re-creations of childhood interiority, and confession. By "memoir" I mean a work that presents an account of the time, the place, and/or the family. A "semi-memoir" likewise tells the story of the time, the place, and/or the family, but includes a subjective element, telling how the protagonist felt about outward events and perhaps part of the protagonist's own story. An outwardly focused autobiography is *this* woman's story, even though she focuses on outward events. A re-creation of childhood interiority turns the lens inward to focus on the mind of the child and seeks to render the child's perspective, for example by focalizing the narrative through the child. The confession also turns the lens inward, but focalizes the account through the narrator, who divulges intimate truths about her past self. The implied reader is a construct extrapolated from the author's themes

248 Conclusion

and style of writing as well as any overt statements she makes about her intended readership and can range from her family to the general public, from male to female, and from members of the author's social group to people outside it.

A bird's-eye view of the history of women's published childhood autobiographies from 1845 onward tells us that the dominant narrator type is intrusive, opinionated, and sympathetic. The most popular of the subgenres is the hybrid: the semi-memoir. Most of the time the implied reader is the general public. But some work or works occupy every point on each scale. Moreover, things change over time.

Self-writing for publication complicates the already complex project of self-reflection and remembering implied by autobiographical writing. It is, broadly speaking, the difference between deciding what you think and deciding what you think you can say. Self-reflection is, of course, influenced by culturally determined notions and values, which offer models for self-understanding that can govern the lived life itself. Thus, one can conceptualize oneself as and act like a "rebel," a "savior," or a "victim" — to name some of the personae women adopt in their childhood autobiographies. Writing for publication, in contrast, does not just mean presenting the fruits of one's reflection to the public, but entails fresh considerations. Unless one is a celebrity or public figure, the more the book is just about "me," the less justifiable it seems. For who cares about this "me"? If one is not a celebrity or a public figure or otherwise extraordinary, but just an ordinary person, one's story in and of itself is not interesting to the broader public. Something more needs to be included. The popularity of the various subtypes of childhood autobiography can in large part be accounted for as effects of the author's intention to publish. They can be thought of as ways of making the work not just "about me" — or if it is "about me," justifying its being so. The most obvious and widespread of the variants that deflect a work away from self-focus is the memoir, which paints an informative picture of the time and place; the semi-memoir enhances the memoir by adding a personal note without compromising the memoir's advantages. Shrinking the centrality of the "me" by focusing on the group, as in the "we" stories, or writing a relational autobiography that devotes significant space to accounts of other people are other routes that avoid a seemingly egocentric self-focus. The claim of typicality also justifies telling one's life story and lends it greater interest. Writing to make a

Conclusion

theoretical point—say, about identity, truth, memory, or language—became fashionable in the poststructuralist period and can also serve as a justification for publishing an autobiography.

All of these are ways of saying, "This book is not just about me, but about something more interesting." Yet there are other ways to appear not to be writing just about oneself—methods to which childhood autobiography is well suited, since an adult is looking back on the child she once was. It is both easy and natural for the author to adopt a stance of distance from such a protagonist. This distance is underscored if she assumes a position of wisdom or poses as a detached scientific investigator in commenting on—to paraphrase Burnett—"the one she knew the best of all." Adopting an ironic or a humorous tone also works as a distancing device.

In contrast, recreating the child's perspective dispenses with the interplay of narrator's and character's points of view. The narrator deemphasizes her ownership of the protagonist and avoids evaluating her, but instead functions as a simple rememberer who loses herself in reliving the child's experience of the world.

But let's say one truly wants to write "just about me." This is where the convention of confession is useful. A confession appeals to the truth as something hidden. Revealing things that are normally hidden, not talked about, or even secret sparks interest. The truth is all the more interesting if what is revealed is transgressive, but even if not, the very act of unveiling, even if performed by an ordinary person, of emerging from under wraps, lures the public to read. Opting for confession also allows, though it does not mandate, identification with one's past self and sympathy with its issues: one thinks of Michelet's desire for a doll, Starkie's revulsion at having to kiss the ground beneath her governess's feet, Verschoyle's guilt at being responsible for her puppy's death, Malraux's revelation of how upset she was when the grownups threw out her pebble collection, or Martin's fear and hatred of her father. Beyond revealing the subject, confession necessarily implicates the author as being more or less daring, depending on what she reveals.

Publishing one's story requires gumption; but it cannot be overemphasized that the intention to publish exercises a strong shaping force on what gets written.

Beyond these considerations, in the course of 150 years not just the social fabric and the material conditions of women's lives, but Western beliefs about truth, memory, and identity—as well as about childhood and femininity—changed. These changes in the cornerstones of autobiography had a profound effect on what was written.

To summarize the genre history: women began publishing this type of work in both France and England around the middle of the nineteenth century—several decades later than men. In each country, they wrote in a completely different fashion. In England women initially published books about their childhood for young audiences: how things were then, and what can be learned from it. In France, following Jean-Jacques Rousseau (or more precisely, following George Sand), women wrote confessionally. Nevertheless, until approximately 1900, examples are sparse across the board. The years before World War I produced some interesting experiments, with a few women attempting to recreate the inner life of the child.

Why did women turn to the genre of childhood autobiography at all? That very turn appears to have been gendered. Standards of decorum governed women's behavior including women's writing. Women's adult lives were refractory material. Women mainly had personal and domestic lives. Discretion forbade trumpeting one's personal life in print, and women's domestic lives counted as unremarkable. If a woman had a public life, modesty demanded that she not flaunt that in print either. In the Victorian era, a woman could write about herself as a child with far less awkwardness than about herself as an adult. Before Sigmund Freud told the world otherwise, childhood was considered to be an innocent, presexual period of life. A telling example is Sand's copious account of her childhood in her *Histoire de ma vie* (*Story of My Life*), versus her glaring omission of her adult affairs. Sand lost her brother in early childhood, but many other nineteenth-century women grew up with siblings, and another charm of childhood autobiography for such writers was that they could focus on the activities of the group rather than on the self.

Regarding other people, autobiographers have generally been conscious that they ought to balance truth with discretion. In this respect too, childhood autobiography offered a haven for decorum. Other people meant first and foremost parents. Before World War I children were expected to respect their parents, and parents could be dealt with in a few admiring words. If that distorted the truth too much, childhood lay far enough in the past for one to be able to hold one's tongue until one's parents were dead, as did Athénaïs Michelet in criticizing her mother.

Another factor in women's turn to childhood autobiography was that, in the age of large families, women, as the designated caregivers of children, were held to have a special "in" in matters of childhood. The entire female sex was strongly associated with children. This "natural" partnership between women and children fostered a climate in which women writers could succeed as children's book authors and in which women wrote childhood autobiography—related phenomena.

After World War I many women published memoirs about their Victorian childhoods, emphasizing milieu and customs rather than self. But the 1930s saw a significant upswing in confessional autobiographies, especially where one does not expect to see them: in the English-speaking countries. The postwar sea change in women's lives, together with the rise of feminism, psychoanalysis, and socialism, can be held responsible. All of a sudden women stopped writing apologies for being so bold as to write about themselves and started breaking all kinds of taboos. They started writing about sex and mercilessly criticizing their parents in print. The period from the mid-1930s until the end of World War II is a first golden age of women's childhood autobiography. It saw a conjunction of a steep rise in production, mainly within the "safe" memoir mode (which, however, became increasingly hybrid), and the publication of startlingly outspoken works written by a few intrepid authors.

In the interwar years the genre jelled into two major types: memoir (including semi-memoirs) and confessional autobiography. In the 1930s the *New Yorker* started publishing childhood memoirs, indicating that they were becoming chic. After World War II many women turned to the genre. A great many opted for the "safe" alternative: the memoir, where the justification for writing is having had an interesting childhood, perhaps spent in some exotic foreign place. Even in such memoirs, however, authors started to put more and more of themselves into their largely outwardly focused work. Other authors embraced the confessional mode. Whether in confessional autobiographies or in memoirs, post–World War II authors were pervasively attentive to psychology. The genre took on a momentum that involved, on the one hand, borrowing from and blending the old and, on the other, pushing at the horizon of expectation to create something innovative that ideally would click with the new age. More working-class and minority women turned to the genre, and certain new themes arose, notably abuse. This period also saw a trend toward literariness. Quite a few women exploited their childhoods to literary ends.

Feminist tones, which would color nearly every work written from 1969 on, entered women's childhood autobiography as early as the 1890s and became prevalent in the 1930s.

As Philippe Lejeune, Timothy Dow Adams, Paul John Eakin, and others have pointed out, telling the truth is among the most familiar rules of autobiography.[1] Leigh Gilmore has argued that the social authority of autobiography springs from "its relation to culturally dominant discourses of truth telling."[2] By consequence, too, the outward appearance of truth telling changes historically according to changing conceptions of truth. Thus in the 1930s, psychoanalytic insights started to sound true.

Changes in ideas about memory have also affected what has counted as true. Autobiography relies on memory. Autobiographers have always realized that their memory was faulty, but before Freud announced that the powerful mental mechanism of repression made memory thoroughly unreliable—in fact, tantamount to fabrication—people generally believed that if they were sure they remembered something correctly, it happened that way. Psychoanalysis dealt this confidence in memory a huge blow. Autobiographers and readers alike started to view memory with skepticism. Beginning with Sir Frederic Bartlett's *Remembering* (1932), modern psychological research declared memory "constructive." More recently, neuroscience has established that each time a memory is retrieved, the process of reconsolidation changes it. Today, just about everyone believes that "truth" mediated by individual memory is very likely not true. How to remember anything accurately? Impossible. A raised eyebrow greets people claiming to do so. Today, people believe that memory fails us in a variety of ways: present interests dictate what is remembered, yet we can be deeply affected by things we cannot remember, such as events in early childhood.

In quest of the truth, some childhood autobiographers, such as Lunt, Carbery, Erbach-Schönberg, Eaubonne, and Astor, made a point of consulting diaries. Others, like McCarthy, consulted with relatives in an effort to find out what really happened. But another strategy that writers have employed is to climb to the high ground of subjectivity and write about things that are unfalsifiable—the child's feelings and imaginings. Childhood autobiography, as an island where factual accuracy is not in high demand and imperfect recollection expected, has tended to weather the wave of memory skepticism that swept the second half of the twentieth century. Much of childhood cannot easily be fact-checked—should it occur to anyone to do so—and the inner life of the child cannot be verified at all.

Memory skepticism had the effect of relaxing the truth standards for autobiography by increasing tolerance for the use of fictional techniques. Since everyone knows that we remember fuzzily, readers grant autobiographers latitude in the presentation of their fuzzy truths, including the adoption of techniques that make the fuzzy look sharp. A case in point is tolerance for dialogue that no one could possibly remember. Ben Yagoda has an excellent discussion of readers' tolerance for fictionalization in *Memoir: A History*.[3] G. Thomas Couser criticizes what he calls the "hi-def memoir" for moving too far in the direction of fiction.[4]

Most critics insist on a distinction between autobiography and fiction along a simple fault line: an autobiography makes a commitment to veracity, whereas fiction does not. By consequence of this basic definition, the autobiographer and the novelist are differently situated in the real world. An autobiographer, who signs off on her work as a factual account, is answerable for what she writes in a way in which a novelist is not. She runs real risks. If she deviates from fact, she risks accusations of lying or misrepresentation and conceivably even a libel suit. She can badly hurt the feelings of relatives and friends, who can see themselves as harmfully exposed to the public if there is no cushioning declaration that the characters are invented. Michel Foucault famously wrote that the "author function" arose out of a desire to punish.[5] Autobiography can be dangerous for the autobiographer, so it is no wonder that writers often fail to declare their work as autobiography.

Whereas authors can have much to gain by blurring the distinction between autobiography and fiction, readers and critics like to know what's what. How to tell if a work is autobiography or fiction? Lejeune asserted that autobiography and fiction could not be distinguished on formal grounds and proposed a formula for assigning a work to one category or the other, based on the idea that the writer of an "autobiography" extends a "pact" to the reader and signals that the story will be true by giving the narrator and the protagonist his own name as it appears on the title page. Useful though this yardstick is, in reality the distinction between autobiography and fiction is not binary. Authors are ingenious in finding ways to fudge it. The history of women's childhood autobiography shows that not every author of a true story signs her name to her work. Narrators are frequently not named. Protagonists can bear confusing names and nicknames. Thus, Caroline Rémy disguises herself anagrammatically as Line Myre; Dormer Creston (a pseudonym for Dorothy Julia Baynes) calls her child protagonist "Dolly." Such strategies are reminiscent of the bat in the fable who, anxious to avoid trouble, says it is a mouse or a bird depending on who is asking.

Lejeune is right that there are no hard and fast formal grounds for distinguishing autobiography from fiction. Historically, autobiographers have availed themselves of fictional techniques, even as fiction has mimicked autobiography.[6] The history of women's childhood autobiography corroborates the often made assertion that increasingly throughout the twentieth century fictional techniques have invaded autobiography, including ones that have no business being there, like omniscience and telepathy. But autobiography also has conventions of its own, such as the justification and the thematization of memory. Fiction can borrow these conventions if it wants to ape autobiography. Thus Miles Franklin in her novel *My Brilliant Career* (1901) mimics conventions of autobiography at the outset, including the justification and the presentation of her first memory, and assures the reader that her "autobiography" has no plot, because there are no plots in life. All this is hocus-pocus, because her work is, in fact, a highly melodramatic fiction with plenty of plot. In short, adopting techniques associated with the other genre is both a temptation and another way of fudging, and it can go both ways: autobiographers often like to leave up in the air whether their work is fiction, and novelists sometimes want to make their inventions sound like real stories.

In women's childhood autobiography's unending negotiation between truth and fiction, different things have been at stake at different times. In the pre–World War I days, when women believed that publishing their own story could make them look self-aggrandizing, fictionalization, in the sense of making autobiographical works look like novels, largely served as protective coloring. Telling one's story as if it were a novel was a way of distancing oneself from it, of attenuating the connection of identity between author and subject. Burnett's story of the Small Person, told in a light and humorous fashion, made it almost seem as if the author were writing yet another children's book and not an autobiography. Changing real names and adopting fictional trappings were also helpful devices if one wanted to criticize other people—if one's purpose was, say, to trash one's parents, like Lynch and Séverine. Dubbing an autobiographical work a *novel* was another way of hiding

(Kovalevskaya, Delarue-Mardrus), though it could also point to artistic aspirations, as in the case of Audoux. None of the early English child-perspective stories (Arden, Allinson, Creston) call themselves autobiographies, but this may have to do with the authors' sense that an "autobiography" was the story of a life and that bestowing the appellation on passages from the mind of the child would be a misnomer. The German authors of child-perspective narratives in the 1930s are more forthright.

When women stopped prefacing their autobiographies with apologies, namely in the interwar years, fictionalization for the sake of modesty went by the board. Writers fictionalized for different reasons. Sigrid Undset's choice of the third person gave her greater artistic liberty. Mary McCarthy's discussions in her *Memories of a Catholic Girlhood* of what she may or may not have fabricated in her *New Yorker* stories testify to the extent to which the truth can collide with the composition of a good story. Later, Doris Lessing would complain that it hampered her to have to cleave to fact; she claimed that fiction can, paradoxically, create a better picture of the real.[7] Readers like good stories, too. A lot of fictionalizing for the sake of interest and readability came to be accepted. As Eakin writes, "We tolerate a huge amount of fiction these days in works we accept nonetheless as somehow factual accounts of their authors' lives; we don't bat an eye."[8]

In a climate where fiction—up to a point—is tolerated in autobiography, labels, which were never a foolproof guide, are often bestowed for pragmatic reasons. In the course of the 1960s, the fact that "memoir" and "autobiography" sold better than fiction influenced the decision to call a work a memoir. According to Yagoda, the cofounder of Random House Bennett Cerf declared in the late 1960s that in the 1920s when he started in the publishing business "fiction outsold nonfiction four-to-one. Now the ratio is absolutely reversed, and nonfiction outsells fiction four-to-one."[9] Maxine Hong Kingston had thought of *The Woman Warrior* as fiction; her publisher persuaded her to call it memoir. Critics cite the case of James Frey, who unsuccessfully tried to market *A Million Little Pieces* (2005) as a novel, then successfully marketed it as a memoir and was lionized by Oprah Winfrey until Frey was found out to have invented large parts of the story. As Couser puts it, "There is no such thing as bad publicity, and Frey could cry all the way to the bank."[10]

Another point of rapprochement between autobiography and fiction is the appeal to typicality. Appeals to typicality have been a major strategy in novels and autobiographies alike. Both novelists and autobiographers have traded heavily in typicality in order to draw readers in. ("This is not just my story, but that of many!") Typicality keeps bobbing up as an explicit or implicit justification for publishing a childhood autobiography. But like so many other features of the genre, its value changes over the years. Initially, the appeal to typicality was a self-deprecating move (Larcom) or a justifying move (Antin) or a combination of both (Burnett, Nesbit). Later it became a standard justifying move. Molly Hughes, Enid Starkie, and even the Cornish Waif suggest that the stories of their childhoods are representative for the period and the milieu in which they grew up. Uttley implies that the way she experienced the physical world is typical for children; Byrne calls herself a "common or garden child." Other kinds of appeals—an author's hope that her autobiography will be helpful to the reader (for example, Sand and Waser)—also engage the notion of typicality by suggesting that one's own story has potential parallels in the lives of other people. Typicality can be invoked to further a cause: the implied typicality of Popp's miserable youth is meant to further the cause of socialism. Starting in the late 1960s, the autobiography of the group (Moody and Angelou, and later many others) asserts typicality in order to target important social issues.

The autobiography of the group is a type of autobiography that has a real-world agenda. It has been asserted that autobiography generally is distinguished from fiction by precisely this criterion: having a real-world agenda. H. Porter Abbott observes that the autobiographer is "present in the text, pushing and shoving the facts, coloring events, in short, doing something for himself."[11] True enough. Couser further claims that "memoir seeks to exert *leverage* (force) on reality in a way that fiction typically does not."[12] Measuring childhood autobiographies written by women against this latter idea, it can be said that some, but not all, works measure up. Many do not have an apparent design on the audience, but appear to have been written out of a desire to make something—or to make something of oneself. Obvious exceptions include writers such as Adelheid Popp, who wants us to know about the terrible conditions of the Austrian working class; Agnes Harder, who wishes to impress on us the wholesomeness of German provincial life; Anne Moody and Maya Angelou, who want us to know what Blacks had to suffer in the American South; or Claire Martin, who writes an exposé of conditions for women in Quebec. Martin writes with the additional agenda of getting even with her tyrannical father. But a great many women appear, to judge from the effort they put into their work, to have written primarily with literary aspirations—to be creators. They did not have any kind of political agenda or other design on the reader. Examples show, too, that there can be a considerable bifurcation between an author's stated agenda and the agenda that her book reveals. Thus, Starkie and the Cornish Waif allegedly write to inform the reader about what life was like when they were children, but Starkie attacks her family, while the Cornish Waif seems motivated by a desire to confess. More than a few writers say that they are going to do X, but in fact do Y.

What does women's writing about childhood tell us about gender? Obviously, it tells us first and foremost about the adult writers and their public self-performance. Every autobiography, for that matter every book, indeed every utterance, negotiates with varied success between sayability (or publishability), appeal, and persuasiveness on the one hand, and impulse, speaking from the heart, speaking one's mind on the other. It must be remembered that women from the start were, in writing autobiography, pushing back against a massive set of preconceptions about women, while also to some extent accommodating them. Here it is useful to cite Jill Ker Conway, who emphasizes that in writing the way they did, women autobiographers were following socially prescribed roles. She writes: "Nineteenth- and early-twentieth-century women had great difficulty making themselves subjects and objects of their own stories."[13] In women's childhood autobiography, the "we" mode, prominent in the nineteenth and early twentieth centuries, can count as a variant of the tone that in Conway's view dominates women's autobiography as of mid-nineteenth century. Conway ascribes this tone, which according to her arises out of the belief that women are emotional creatures close to nature who lack agency and whose telos is marriage and domesticity, to the "romantic image" to which women were expected to conform. The tone itself means concealing agency, stylizing oneself as passive, concentrating on inner life, and appearing as "disembodied."[14] Women's childhood autobiographies suggest, however, that the thematic and stylistic characteristics that Conway bundles under the rubric of "romantic image" should be unbundled. The female narrators of childhood autobiographies in the nineteenth and early twentieth centuries usually do, with a few exceptions, adopt a tone of modesty in presenting their stories to the public. But this pervasive characteristic is generally not accompanied by any reluctance to foreground the child self and her agency, except in the "we" stories, much less by any implication that the female child's telos is marriage and domesticity. Female children, it seems, were not expected to conform to the "romantic image," or, to the extent that they were expected to do so, adult women autobiographers exploded the idea that they did. In general, including in the pre–World War I period, the child protagonists of childhood autobiographies show a great deal of agency. Women writers in this period show an interest in the inner life of the child, but this does not carry the implication that the child had no outer life. Their attempts to recreate the child's perspective come across as an enterprising form of psychological inquiry, not as conformity to a socially dictated feminine "package."

Women's turn to childhood autobiography shows enterprise and agency right from the start, or in other words, in the nineteenth and early twentieth centuries. Before World War I, childhood autobiography as a genre beckoned to women because it treated a topic on which they could presume to write authoritatively. Women's authority in matters of the nursery was, given separate spheres, as difficult to challenge as women's authority in running a household. Moreover, as a form of self-writing, the topic—childhood—was relatively uncontroversial, so that talking about one's own childhood appeared reasonably consonant with feminine modesty. But women's evident reach for excellence within this genre was itself a form of pushing back.

Women's childhood autobiography tells us not just about the adult authors, but also about how girls grew up in that era and how the authors as little girls once felt and thought. Childhood innocence may have served as an umbrella, but the writers do not parrot this or any other cliché about children. Rather, they write out of their experience and their reflection on it. They may adopt a "feminine" tone of self-deprecation or irony, but this is window dressing, easily seen through, which does not affect the power of what they reveal. Early women's childhood autobiography tells us, for example, how a little girl raised in a privileged context can develop an inflated sense of self-worth and even bend the grown-ups to her imperious will (Judith Gautier, Adam, Ebner-Eschenbach); but also how, in a large family, a child can be left out of the group and experience loneliness and misery (Michelet, Lynch). We hear how a little girl becomes a leader (Judith Gautier, Lynch), how a girl found her vocation (Larcom, Burnett, Barton), how little girls ran away from home, either in desperation (Lynch) or in pursuit of an ambition (Gilder), and how a girl could be extremely ambitious (Antin). We hear

Conclusion

of the tedium of sewing (Michelet, Larcom, Creevey) as well as knitting (Braun, Adelmann, Schumacher, Lenk) and the rigors of convent school (Judith Gautier, Audoux), but also, in great detail, of girls' imaginings, games, and pastimes (Burnett, Hunt), which in some cases involved fantasy worlds (L'vova, Ebner-Eschenbach, Hunt). We find out that mothers were loved (Sand, Burnett, Nesbit), hated (Michelet, Lynch), and sought (Farnham, Audoux, Bischoff)—and in each case, why. Authors tell us of their childhood fears and their passions for things and animals (Arden, Nesbit), as well as their indignation at the deceptiveness of adults (Burnett).

Romanticism accorded great importance to childhood. Psychoanalysis retheorized it and accorded it even greater importance. By the 1920s everybody knew that early childhood was formative. Few women state this as clearly as Phyllis Bottome, who, citing her mentor Alfred Adler, believed that one becomes the person one is by the age of five. The presumed, unquestioned importance of childhood encouraged women's continued attention to it. In the post-Freudian climate, it tells us something about women that they do not follow or corroborate psychoanalytic doctrines on femininity, such as, for example, the portentous penis envy that Freud ascribed to young girls. Not even Mabel Dodge Luhan, a devotee of Freud's, credits her young self with penis envy. In the interwar years, women write back at being pushed into a corner by this kind of disempowering interpretation. If an avant-garde of childhood autobiographers in these years reject the kinds of behaviors their elders demanded of them and the lives envisioned for them, and in particular refuse the yoke of traditional femininity, it is, as they present it, not because something is wrong with them, but because many things are wrong with the world. Their childhood autobiographies, particularly those in which anger boils up, form a reply and a counterweight to the pigeonholes in which patriarchal society sought to confine women. Even where they had won the right to vote, women had to struggle against patriarchal attitudes in the interwar years, and to judge from their autobiographies of childhood and youth, as well as from what they became, some took up the challenge. In distinction to Conway, who writes, "by the midtwentieth century we see new, more confident narrative styles emerging,"[15] I date the advent of the "more confident narrative styles" to the 1930s—not the 1950s.

In the interwar years, women childhood autobiographers start to credit their young selves with a longing for life and excitement, together with a desire for greater freedom. It is a theme that never goes away. It is a major facet of a general dissatisfaction with one's lot, some of which has to do with being a girl instead of a boy. We hear repeatedly that boys get a better education, better toys, and much more freedom, all of which prepares them for a more "real" life. In contrast, the emphasis in girls' upbringing falls on outward appearance and deportment—on externalities. We hear repeatedly that girls are judged by and taught early on to mind their looks and their manners. From the outset, as seen in Michelet, women childhood autobiographers, inasmuch as they attend to gender, show ambivalence about being a girl. Very few think, like Molly Hughes, that it is good to be a girl. While many authors refrain from commenting on the desirability of being one sex rather than the other, no women childhood autobiographer in any period celebrates being female as better than being male.

One of the great accomplishments of women's childhood autobiographies from the beginnings through the present day is to provide a rich collection of insights into childhood. From the first works onward we learn about children both as objects and as subjects. The things the works show about the child as object are mainly things most people know already: children are malleable, easily influenced, easily deceivable, and easily exploited. Women childhood autobiographers supply many specific instances of their malleability, impressionability, deception, and exploitation at the hands of adults. Where the child is an object, biological sex matters. Girls have been trained to conform to roles that society deems appropriate for girls. The Cornish Waif's stepfather did not want to adopt a "useless" girl—whereupon, as a girl, she was sexually abused by her foster father. All children are at risk for sexual exploitation, but girls are particularly so.

Women's childhood autobiographies also contain a plethora of fascinating insights into children as subjects. Their illumination of the inner life of the child, the authors' reconstructions of the way they thought and felt as children, is a stellar accomplishment of the genre. Again, authors are not reiterating clichés, but writing out of their own experience. There is a great deal of variation from child to child, but over the course of a century and a quarter, patterns become visible. It is emphasized again and again that children are emotional, passionate beings. Fear is an important part of early childhood: many writers recall being afraid of many things, real or imaginary, for much of the time. Some—Blüthgen, Undset, Deland, Schieber, Pagés—write about the horror they felt at their first encounter with death. Some—Judith Gautier, L'vova, Noël—write of an early passionate attachment to a caregiver. Many describe emotional attachments to various adults and friends in later childhood. There is one thing about which one can generalize absolutely: the girls across the board prefer the warm, loving adult who makes them feel like a special person, whether this person is male or female, parent, grandparent, or other caregiver. They dislike strict, disciplinarian, or cold people who are in charge of them. Children can be jealous, mainly of siblings; angry, mainly at unjust punishment; and burn with hatred toward grown-ups who abuse their power. Verschoyle explicitly makes self-centeredness and blindness toward the feelings of others part of the picture.

As for children's consciousness, Undset and Verschoyle make a point of demonstrating the idiosyncratic rhythms and instability of children's thought, while Schieber, Noël, and Undset additionally show how small children have an entirely different sense from adults of what is important and unimportant. As Noël says, in the small child's world there are "monsters and not yet any paths." Small children have not figured things out; they have not developed routines; they jump to wild conclusions. Undset tells us how small physical details loom large for them. To judge from the great many authors who tell us about their imaginative life as children, imagination governs children's mental life. Often, the authors tell us, they invented scenarios that they quickly abandoned for the next creation. But some girls led fantasy lives parallel to their real lives, like L'vova, Ebner-Eschenbach, and Malraux, while Hunt expanded hers into an entire world. Hunt, Posse, and Lutyens had imaginary companions. Children are capable of losing themselves in their fantasies, and, as Schieber, Noël, and Verschoyle show, they can also lack certainty in distinguishing the real from the unreal, especially when they are gripped by fear. Fen recalls that she went through a phase when she was unable to exercise control over her own thoughts. She was horrified to find herself thinking "bad" things against her will. Compared to other aspects of women's childhood autobiography, authors' insights into child psychology do not change much over time. Subsequent authors add incrementally to the overall picture, while finding new, ingenious ways in the verbal medium to represent the mental life of children. A case in point is Arundhati Roy, who, in *The God of Small Things* (1997), demonstrates her seven-year-old alter ego's nimble imagination by deforming grown-ups' phrases according to the way the child understands them—a brilliant stylistic innovation.

One can consider the Bildungsroman plot, the paradise-fall pattern, and the epiphany concerning vocation to be tropes of the "childhood and youth" story, to which some women autobiographers recur. An autobiographer who uses these classic patterns can be suspected of adapting her experience to conform to them rather than describing it as it happened. Are there similar tropes of the "just childhood" story? Not in the same way. Instead, a huge amount of evidence accumulates around a few general conclusions. What arises out of the autobiographies collectively, the common denominator for evocations of childhood, is that children live in a different world from adults. They have a different sense of reality, different priorities, and a different sense of time. They lack a fixed sense of self. They do not understand the world of adults and only gradually and painfully learn to conform to the various basically incomprehensible rules of the adult world. Conversely, adults regularly lose track of things that are truly important for children—such as, for example, the importance of being dressed like everybody else in the peer group. All this is so believable and attested to by so many different and individual pieces of evidence that it is wholly unlikely that authors are not in fact describing their own experience.

In the 1970s women's childhood autobiography experienced a boom. The last three decades of the twentieth century saw an explosion in the numbers of women's childhood autobiographies published. A feminist outlook, whether acknowledged or not, became pervasive. So did the influence of psychoanalysis, again whether authors acknowledged it or not. Outspokenness, especially in matters pertaining to sexuality, increased. Mother-daughter relationships, whether tempered by feminist kindness, blazing with fury, or problematized as a mixed blessing, continued as a theme in most works. In addition, major new trends appeared. They include autobiography in which the individual represents herself as the member of a social class, ethnicity, or other group; inventive literary experiments that reflect poststructuralist skepticism about self-writing and identity; and the use of the child perspective as a device to make a political point. The autobiography of the group, seen in the late 1960s with Anne Moody's *Coming of Age in Mississippi* and Maya Angelou's *I Know Why the Caged Bird Sings*, became widespread. For example, Maxine Hong Kingston in *The Woman Warrior* (1976) speaks as the Chinese American child of Chinese immigrant parents and inspired further childhood autobiographies of the same type. Nazi-era and Holocaust childhood autobiographies in which authors consider their experiences representative for Germans or Jews of their generation proliferated in the 1970s and 1980s; one of the earliest was Christa Wolf's reconstruction in *Patterns of Childhood* (1976), which Wolf presents as the story of the fictitious Nelly Jordan, of how a German child was sucked into Nazi ideology. Regarding literary experiments, Maxine Hong Kingston stands out for introducing a brilliant formal innovation: in *The Woman Warrior* she presents not her child self but the conflicting stories with which her Chinese American listening ear was bombarded. Nathalie Sarraute in *Childhood* (1983) published another such formal tour de force, presenting her childhood memories in the form of a dialogue with an interlocutor; the memories appear to be arising spontaneously in Sarraute's mind even as the initially skeptical interlocutor counters her with argumentative comments. Finally, in the 1980s women worldwide started to turn to the genre of childhood autobiography for diverse, not always strictly autobiographical reasons. Writers such as the Moroccan Fatima Mernissi in *Dreams of Trespass* (1994), the Iranian Marjane Satrapi in *Persepolis* (2000–2003) and *Embroideries* (2003), and the Indian Arundhati Roy in her novel *The God of Small Things* (1997) use the child perspective as a device, a filter with which to illuminate an account of the milieu in which they grew up. The purpose is political: the point is to show how a messy state of affairs, how life in a particular culture, appeared to a child's naïve eyes.

As women from different cultures continue to turn to the genre, it will be interesting to see what shapes it takes in the future. Will women employ it as innovatively and creatively as they have in the past? Will they bring fresh revelations about childhood? Will they deepen our understanding of girls and young women, even as they tell us about the kinds of lives they lead in different parts of the world?

Notes

Introduction

1. The reasons for women's historical reticence specifically with regard to writing and publishing autobiography have been thoroughly explored and explained by Sidonie Smith, *A Poetics of Women's Autobiography* (Bloomington: Indiana University Press, 1987).

2. Richard N. Coe, "The Autobiography of Childhood and Adolescence: A Bibliography of Primary Sources in the Major Languages of European Origin," in *Reminiscences of Childhood: An Approach to a Comparative Mythology*, Proceedings of the Leeds Philosophical and Literary Society, Literary and Historical Section, vol. 19, part 6, 68–95 (Leeds Philosophical and Literary Society Ltd., 1984).

3. Jeffrey E. Long, *Remembered Childhoods: A Guide to Autobiography and Memoirs of Childhood and Youth* (Westport, CT: Libraries Unlimited, 2007).

4. Joy Hooton, *Stories of Herself When Young: Autobiographies of Childhood by Australian Women* (Melbourne: Oxford, 1990).

5. Gudrun Wedel, *Autobiographien von Frauen: Ein Lexikon* (Cologne: Böhlau, 2010).

6. Each bibliographer operates with a somewhat different conception of the topic. Coe, Hooton, Long, and Wedel all list autobiographies of childhood and youth, but none are concerned, as I am, with how much attention is paid to childhood versus adolescence and young adulthood. None differentiate between self-focused autobiographies and outwardly focused memoirs, though these two distinct types, albeit they can intersect, exist. Indeed, Long calls all his titles "memoirs," and Wedel calls all hers "Erinnerungen" (recollections). Long and Wedel find the distinction between autobiography and autobiographical novel (often a hard call) important, as I do; Long excludes autobiographical novels, whereas Wedel includes them but identifies them as such. In contrast, Coe and Hooton include autobiographical novels.

266 Notes to Pages 6–12

7. E. H. Gombrich, *Norm and Form: Studies in the Art of the Renaissance* (London: Phaidon, 1978), 88.

8. Marianne Hirsch, *The Mother/Daughter Plot: Narrative, Psychoanalysis, Feminism* (Bloomington: Indiana University Press, 1989).

9. Sidonie Smith and Julia Watson, *Reading Autobiography: A Guide for Interpreting Life Narratives*, 2nd ed. (Minneapolis: University of Minnesota Press, 2010), present a very useful catalogue of "Sixty Genres of Life Narrative" that critics have proposed, with commentary. "Confession" is a key term for me, since Rousseau's *Confessions* started a trend in women's childhood autobiography; Rita Felski in "On Confession," in Felski, *Beyond Feminist Aesthetics* (Cambridge, MA: Harvard University Press, 1989), 86–121, examines in an illuminating fashion the convergence of confession with other phenomena I trace, the appeal to typicality and group identity, in women's autobiography influenced by contemporary feminism. "Memoir" is another key term for me, but I use it in its older sense, not in accordance with its current usage as an umbrella term for life writing. "Relational autobiography," a concept that has received so much attention that it has been almost redefined, is a term I use sparingly and simply, without gender implications.

10. Susanna Egan, *Mirror Talk: Genres of Crisis in Contemporary Autobiography* (Chapel Hill: University of North Carolina Press, 1999), 14.

11. *Conversations with Maxine Hong Kingston*, ed. Paul Skenazy and Tera Martin (Jackson: University Press of Mississippi, 1998), 216.

12. Smith and Watson cite postcolonial works that publish autobiography as fiction to turn it into "testimony," to voice stories that oppressed people cannot voice directly. Sidonie Smith and Julia Watson, "The Trouble with Autobiography: Cautionary Notes for Narrative Theorists," in *A Companion to Narrative Theory*, ed. James Phelan and Peter J. Rabinowitz (Malden, MA: Blackwell, 2005), 356–71, here 361–64.

13. E.g., G. Thomas Couser, *Memoir: An Introduction* (Oxford: Oxford University Press, 2012), 8.

14. Werner Brettschneider, *"Kindheitsmuster": Kindheit als Thema autobiographischer Dichtung* (Berlin: Erich Schmidt Verlag, 1982); Richard N. Coe, *When the Grass Was Taller: Autobiography and the Experience of Childhood* (New Haven, CT: Yale University Press, 1984); Philippe Lejeune, *Le récit d'enfance en question* (Nanterre: Université de Paris X, 1988); Roman Reisinger, *Die Autobiographie der Kindheit in der französischen Literatur* (Tübingen: Stauffenburg Verlag, 2000); Debbie Pinfold, *The Child's View of the Third Reich in German Literature: The Eye among the Blind* (Oxford: Oxford University Press, 2001); Rocío G. Davis, *Begin Here: Reading Asian North American Autobiographies of Childhood* (Honolulu: University of Hawai'i Press, 2007); Katrin Lange, *Selbstfragmente: Autobiographien der Kindheit* (Würzburg: Königshausen und Neumann, 2008); Kate Douglas, *Contesting Childhood: Autobiography, Trauma, and Memory* (New Brunswick, NJ: Rutgers University Press, 2010).

Notes to Pages 12–16   267

15. Valerie Sanders, *The Private Lives of Victorian Women: Autobiography in Nineteenth-Century England* (New York: Harvester Wheatsheaf, 1989).

16. Valerie Sanders, ed., *Records of Girlhood: An Anthology of Nineteenth-Century Women's Childhoods* (Aldershot, Hampshire: Ashgate, 2000), and Valerie Sanders, ed., *Records of Girlhood*, vol. 2, *An Anthology of Nineteenth-Century Women's Childhoods* (Farnham, Surrey: Ashgate, 2012). Further references to these works will be given in the text.

17. Joy Hooton, *Stories of Herself When Young: Autobiographies of Childhood by Australian Women* (Melbourne: Oxford University Press, 1990).

18. Jill Ker Conway, *When Memory Speaks: Reflections on Autobiography* (New York: Alfred A. Knopf, 1998), 16.

19. Conway, *When Memory Speaks*, 16.

20. Conway, *When Memory Speaks*, 3.

21. Sanders, *Records of Girlhood* (2000, 4–5), makes similar points, adding, "Childhood can easily be made entertaining and impersonal, and with so many subjects regarded as taboo for women writers, it was one of relatively few areas freely available to them, a legitimate domestic theme with distinct educational potential" (5).

22. Coe, *When the Grass Was Taller*, 9.

23. Hooton, *Stories of Herself When Young*, notices Australian women's propensity to shift the focus from themselves to others and elevates it to the hallmark of distinctive feminine tradition of autobiographical writing in Australia. She finds that the common denominator of Australian women's childhood narratives is relatedness: "The most common and consistent characteristic of women's autobiographies is the characteristic that Carol Gilligan defines in her study of female development in *In a Different Voice*, that is, definition of the self in a context of relationship and judgment of the self in terms of ability to care" (91). Hooton accepts psychologist and sociologist Nancy Chodorow's theory that girls and boys, on account of their pre-Oedipal relationships with their mothers, develop different paradigms of selfhood based in connectedness (girls) and individuation (boys) (86). I would not make a similar assertion for women's childhood autobiography generally. The French women are self-foregrounding from the start. Lange, *Selbstfragmente*, draws attention to "a striking decentering of the self" (53) in nineteenth-century German childhood autobiography generally; most of her examples are male. A recent study on relational autobiography, Anne Rüggemeier, *Die relationale Autobiographie* (Trier: Wissenschaftlicher Verlag Trier, 2014), does not connect relationality in autobiography to gender, but rather believes that a "new genre" of relational autobiography arose especially as of the 1970s in the English-speaking countries and that it is based in a relational identity concept (7), which began with William James (47) and subsequently pervaded twentieth-century psychology, sociology, philosophy, and psychoanalysis, and which undermined the idea of autonomous identity. Obviously, Rüggemeier's theory does not account for feminine traditions of self-decentered autobiographical writing, such as family history, but undeniably,

268   Notes to Pages 16–29

some important women childhood autobiographers in the post–World War II period whose self-performance is relational came from backgrounds in psychology or psychoanalysis.

24. Couser, *Memoir*; see especially his first chapter, 15–32.

25. Bernd Neumann, *Identität und Rollenzwang: Zur Theorie der Autobiographie* (Frankfurt: Athenäum, 1970), 10; Smith and Watson, *Reading Autobiography*, 274. Smith and Watson note, "In contemporary parlance *autobiography* and *memoir* are used interchangeably. But distinctions are relevant" (274).

26. Couser, *Memoir*, 51.

27. Rosemary Lloyd, *The Land of Lost Content: Children and Childhood in Nineteenth-Century French Literature* (Oxford: Clarendon Press, 1992), viii. As an example of a writer who uses the term "enfant" for unmarried sixteen- or seventeen-year-olds she mentions George Sand (129–30).

28. Simone de Beauvoir, *The Second Sex*, trans. H. M. Parshley (New York: Vintage, 1989), chapters on "Childhood" and "The Young Girl," 267–370; on loss of confidence due to changes in the body in particular, e.g., 332. *Shortchanging Girls, Shortchanging America* (Washington, DC: American Association of University Women, 1991), 3–17.

29. For a more in-depth discussion of the concept of genre and genre criticism, see chapter 2 of Lorna Martens, *The Diary Novel* (Cambridge: Cambridge University Press, 1985).

30. Egan discusses the influence of an audience on self-writing and of alterity on self-perception in *Mirror Talk*, 2.

Chapter 1. Beginnings

1. Mary Howitt, *My Own Story: or, The Autobiography of a Child* (London: Thomas Tegg, 1845), 8.

2. George Sand, *Story of My Life. The Autobiography of George Sand*, a group translation edited by Thelma Jurgrau (Albany: SUNY Press, 1991), 73–76.

3. Her mother died on November 13, 1864; Athénaïs started writing her childhood memoirs ten months later. Jules Michelet, *Journal*, vol. 3, ed. Claude Digeon (Paris: Gallimard, 1976), 268, 343.

4. J. Michelet, *Journal*, vol. 3, 353, 388, 390, 403.

5. Athénaïs Michelet, *Mémoires d'une enfant*, ed. Pierre Enckell (n.p.: Mercure de France, 2004), 96.

6. Enid Starkie, *A Lady's Child* (London: Faber and Faber, 1941), 27; Doris Lessing, *Under My Skin* (New York: Harper Perennial, 1995), 114.

7. E.g., J. Michelet, *Journal*, 3:409; Paul Viallaneix, introduction to *Journal*, by J. Michelet, 2:xxviii; Pierre Enckell, introduction to *Mémoires d'une enfant*, by A. Michelet, 12.

8. J. Michelet, *Journal*, 3:413.

9. Enckell, introduction to *Mémoires d'une enfant*, by A. Michelet, 14.

10. Madame A. Daudet, "L'Enfance d'une Parisienne," in *Oeuvres de Madame A. Daudet 1878–1889* (Paris: Alphonse Lemerre, 1892), 28. Unless noted otherwise, all translations in this book are mine.

Notes to Pages 30–41

11. All details on her biography are from Anne Hogenhuis-Seliverstoff, *Juliette Adam 1836–1936: L'Instigatrice* (Paris: L'Harmattan, 2001).

12. On the masculine model, see Sanders, *Private Lives*, 53–54, and Hooton, *Stories of Herself*, 83–84, 93–94.

13. Judith Gautier, *Le Collier des jours: Souvenirs de ma vie* (Saint-Cyr-sur-Loire: Pirot, 1994), 189. Further references will be given in the text.

14. Arnold Bennett, introduction, n.p., and John N. Raphael, afterword, 92, to Marguerite Audoux, *Marie Claire*, trans. John N. Raphael (Breinigsville, PA: Dodo Press, 2010).

15. Angela Kershaw, "Proletarian Women, Proletarian Writing: The Case of Marguerite Audoux," in *A "Belle Epoque"? Women in French Society and Culture, 1890–1914* (New York: Berghahn, 2006), 253–68, here 253.

16. Kershaw, "Proletarian Women," 254.

17. Bernard-Marie Garreau, *Marguerite Audoux: La couturière des lettres* (n.p.: Tallandier, 1991), shows that Audoux's Mother Superior placed her in 1876 with a tailor and only the following year, in 1877, with a farmer, whereas the book elides the first placement (31–36); the farmer did not die, but was evicted from his farm (55–56); Marie-Claire's lover Henri's mother was in real life not a widow, but married (69); Henri Dejoulx, the person on whom Audoux modeled Marie-Claire's lover Henri Deslois, married someone else only in 1886, not soon after Audoux's return to the convent in 1881 (72, 74).

18. Linda H. Peterson, *Traditions of Victorian Women's Autobiography: The Poetics and Politics of Life Writing* (Charlottesville: University Press of Virginia, 1999), 3.

19. Peterson, *Traditions*, 18.

20. Peterson, *Traditions*, 20, 26.

21. Valerie Sanders, ed., *Records of Girlhood: An Anthology of Nineteenth-Century Women's Childhoods* (Aldershot, Hampshire: Ashgate, 2000), 78.

22. Sanders, *Records of Girlhood* (2000), 36.

23. Howitt, *My Own Story*, 8.

24. "Mary Howitt," in Sanders, *Records of Girlhood* (2000), 90–102.

25. Eliza W. Farnham, *My Early Days* (New York: Thatcher & Hutchinson, 1859), x.

26. Philippe Lejeune, *On Autobiography*, ed. Paul John Eakin, trans. Katherine Leary (Minneapolis: University of Minnesota Press, 1989), 11–14.

27. *Eliza Woodson, or, The Early Days of One of the World's Workers: A Story of American Life* (New York: A. J. Davis, 1864), iii.

28. Lucy Larcom, *A New England Girlhood* (n.p., n.d.), 92. Further references to this edition will be given in the text.

29. Shirley Marchalonis, *The Worlds of Lucy Larcom, 1824–1893* (Athens: University of Georgia Press, 1989), 246.

30. Margaret Fuller's poetic introductory chapter for an "autobiographical romance," written in 1840 and available to the public posthumously in *The Memoirs of Margaret Fuller Ossoli* (1852), is an exception: this slim, unfinished sketch is about the growth of the poet's mind. But Fuller's was a closet childhood autobiography, not meant for public consumption.

31. Shirley Marchalonis, "Lucy Larcom," *American Women Prose Writers: 1820–1870*, ed. Sharon M. Harris (Farmington Hills, MI: Gale Group, 2000), 246–52, here 251.

32. Jane Marcus, "Invincible Mediocrity: The Private Selves of Public Women," in *The Private Self: Theory and Practice of Women's Autobiographical Writings*, ed. Shari Benstock (London: Routledge, 1988), 114–46, here 114.

33. Marchalonis, "Lucy Larcom," 251.

34. Rose Norman, "New England Girlhoods," *Legacy: A Journal of American Women Writers* 8, no. 2 (1991): 104–17, here 109–10; Carol Holly, "Nineteenth-Century Autobiographies of Affiliation: The Case of Catharine Sedgwick and Lucy Larcom," in *American Autobiography: Retrospect and Prospect* (Madison: University of Wisconsin Press, 1991), 216–34, here 224; Amy Kort, "Lucy Larcom's Double-Exposure: Strategic Obscurity in *A New England Girlhood*," *American Literary Realism* 31 (1998): 25–40, here 26; Marchalonis, "Lucy Larcom," 251; Karen L. Kilcup, "Lucy Larcom, 1824–1893," in *American Writers: A Collection of Literary Biographies*, Supplement XIII: *Edward Abbey to William J. Smith*, ed. Jay Parini (New York: Scribner's, 2003), 137–57, here 148.

35. Jessica Lewis, "'Poetry Experienced': Lucy Larcom's Poetic Dwelling in *A New England Girlhood*," *Legacy* 18, no. 2 (2001): 182–92, here 188.

36. Lewis, "Poetry Experienced," 189.

37. Ida Gandy, *A Wiltshire Childhood* (London: Allen and Unwin, 1929), 20.

38. Clara Barton, *The Story of My Childhood* (New York: Baker & Taylor, 1907), 12. Further references will be given in the text.

39. Caroline A. Stickney Creevey, *A Daughter of the Puritans: An Autobiography* (New York: G. P. Putnam's Sons, 1916), 271, 270.

40. Frances Hodgson Burnett, *The One I Knew the Best of All* (New York: Charles Scribner's Sons, 1893), vii. Further references to this edition will be given in the text.

41. Sally Shuttleworth, "Inventing a Discipline: Autobiography and the Science of Child Study in the 1890s," *Comparative Critical Studies* 2, no. 2 (2005): 143–63, here 155.

42. http://www.forgottenfutures.com/game/ff8/nesbit.htm; Julia Briggs, *A Woman of Passion: The Life of E. Nesbit, 1858–1924* (London: Hutchinson, 1987), 4.

43. Briggs, *A Woman of Passion*, xiv, 185.

44. E. Nesbit, *Long Ago When I Was Young* (London: Macdonald, 1987), 27. Further references will be given in the text.

45. *The Bookman* 9 (1899): 297. For a detailed account of the controversy surrounding the work when it was first published, see Faith Binckes and Kathryn Laing, "Irish Autobiographical Fiction and Hannah Lynch's *Autobiography of a Child*," *English Literature in Transition, 1880–1920* 55, no. 2 (2012): 195–218.

46. Faith Binckes, "Lynch, Hannah (1859–1904)," in *Oxford Dictionary of National Biography*, online ed., 2004, https://doi.org/10.1093/ref:odnb/55794.

47. Hannah Lynch, *Autobiography of a Child* (New York: Dodd, Mead & Co., 1899), 175. Further references will be given in the text.

48. See John Wilson Foster, *Irish Novels 1890–1940* (Oxford: Oxford University Press, 2008), 278–79.

49. According to Faith Binckes and Kathryn Laing, *Hannah Lynch (1859–1904): Irish Writer, Cosmopolitan, New Woman* (Cork: Cork University Press, 2019), 8–9, Hannah was the fourth of four daughters by her mother's first marriage and never knew her father, but only her stepfather, with whom her mother had four more daughters.

50. Binckes, "Lynch, Hannah (1859–1904)." The online resource *Orlando: Women's Writing in the British Isles from the Beginnings to the Present* (http://orlando.cambridge.org/) also gives Lynch ten sisters.

51. "Anna Teresa Calderwood Cantwell," https://www.findagrave.com/memorial/188664904/anna-teresa-cantwell (accessed October 15, 2021).

52. Penny Brown, *The Captured World: The Child and Childhood in Nineteenth-Century Women's Writing in England* (New York: St. Martin's, 1993), mentions other instances of literariness, e.g., her description of Angela's crippled brother Stevie "is partially informed by literary stereotypes of the dying child" (134), while her casting of herself as an unhappy outcast "has clear echoes of Romantic and sentimental literature" (135).

53. According to Peterson, *Traditions*, 93, there were multiple "autobiography" types that could have served Brontë as models. She argues that Brontë initially draws on the tradition of spiritual autobiography, but later indirectly invokes, through the missionary aspirations of Jane's cousin and suitor St. John Rivers, the type of the woman's missionary memoir that had started to appear in the 1830s and 1840s.

54. Hester Marsden-Smedley, "Ivy . . . Friend of the Family," *Twentieth Century Literature* 25, no. 2, Ivy Compton-Burnett Issue (Summer 1979): 173–82, here 175.

55. Dawn Potter, "The Poems of Milly Jourdain," May 23, 2013, http://dlpotter.blogspot.fr/2013/05/the-poems-of-milly-jourdain.html.

56. Joan Arden, *A Childhood* (Cambridge: Bowes and Bowes, 1913), vii. Further references will be given in the text.

57. Cf. Christiane Maria Binder's discussion of "a child's perception and self-perception" (287) in British Victorian women's autobiographies in *From Innocence to Experience: (Re-)Constructions of Childhood in Victorian Women's Autobiography* (Trier: Wissenschaftlicher Verlag Trier, 2014), 287–92. Binder examines the works anthologized in Valerie Sanders's *Records of Girlhood* (2000) and finds that they frequently testify to an interest in the child's inner life, yet "see this phase with new (adult, retrospective, conscious, critical) eyes" (288). In short, the narrators comment.

58. Una Hunt, *Una Mary: The Inner Life of a Child* (New York: Charles Scribner's Sons, 1914), vii. Further references will be given in the text.

59. Mary Antin, *The Promised Land* (Boston: Houghton Mifflin, 1912), xiii. Further references to this edition will be given in the text.

272   Notes to Pages 66–79

60. Ben Yagoda, *Memoir: A History* (New York: Riverhead Books, 2009), 158–59.

61. Beatrice Mall-Grob, *Fiktion des Anfangs: Literarische Kindheitsmodelle bei Jean Paul und Adalbert Stifter* (Stuttgart: Metzler, 1999), 61.

62. Karl A. Schleunes, "Enlightenment, Reform, Reaction: The Schooling Revolution in Prussia," *Central European History* 12, no. 4 (December 1979): 315–42, here 317.

63. Margarete Lenk, *Aus meiner Kindheit: Jugenderinnerungen* (Zwickau i. Sa.: Johannes Hermann, 1910), 3.

64. *Als unsre großen Dichter noch kleine Jungen waren* (Leipzig: Franz Moeser Nachf., 1911).

65. Hedwig Dohm, "Kindheitserinnerungen einer alten Berlinerin," in *Als unsre großen Dichterinnen noch kleine Mädchen waren*, ed. Ida Boy-Ed (Leipzig: Franz Moeser Nachf., 1912), 42.

66. Sophie Reuschle, *Kinderzeit* (Leipzig: Matthes, 1921), 90.

67. Marie von Ebner-Eschenbach, *Autobiographische Schriften*, vol. 1, ed. Christa-Maria Schmidt (Tübingen: Niemeyer, 1989), 92.

68. Andrew Baruch Wachtel, *The Battle for Childhood: Creation of a Russian Myth* (Stanford, CA: Stanford University Press, 1990), 15, 82, 86.

69. Introduction to Sofya Kovalevskaya, *A Russian Childhood*, trans., ed., and introd. Beatrice Stillman (New York: Springer-Verlag, 1978), 33, 37.

70. Wachtel, *Battle*, 88–90.

71. Kovalevskaya, *Russian Childhood*, 208.

72. Kovalevskaya, *Russian Childhood*, 108.

73. Elizaveta L'vova, "From the Distant Past: Fragments from Childhood Memories," in *Russia through Women's Eyes: Autobiographies from Tsarist Russia*, ed. Toby W. Clyman and Judith Vowles (New Haven, CT: Yale University Press, 1996), 282–310, here 301.

74. Valerie Sanders, *The Private Lives of Victorian Women*, notes that eighteenth-century women autobiographers often sounded much like Daniel Defoe's Moll Flanders (39) but that "Victorian women lost no time in fumigating the eighteenth-century tradition" (47). Philippe Lejeune, "L'autobiographie et l'aveu sexuel," *Revue de la littérature comparée* 325 (January–March 2008): 37–51, here 44, speaks of the "triumph of puritanism" in France from the end of the eighteenth century to the beginning of the twentieth. Mme Roland, writing in 1793, says candidly, though euphemistically, that she was sexually assaulted by her father's pupil before her first communion, i.e., before age eleven, and also mentions the awakening of her sexual feelings at age fourteen; but her first editor omitted these particular passages in her *Mémoires particuliers*, even though she intended these memoirs for publication. The censored passages first appeared in editions of 1864. See Anne Coudreuse, "La mémoire littéraire dans quelques *Mémoires* de la Révolution," *Itinéraires* 2 (2011): 23–27.

Chapter 2. The Interwar Years: Memoirs and Semi-Memoirs

1. Jennifer E. Milligan, *The Forgotten Generation: French Women Writers of the Inter-War Period* (Oxford: Berg, 1996), 87.

Notes to Pages 79–103   273

2. Jean-Philippe Vauchel, "La Représentation de l'enfance dans la littérature narrative de la France de l'entre-deux-guerres," PhD diss., University of Lille III, 2000, 29.

3. Mary Butts, *The Crystal Cabinet: My Childhood at Salterns* (Boston: Beacon Press, 1988), foreword by Camilla Bagg, afterword by Barbara Wagstaff, 45.

4. Mary MacCarthy, *A Nineteenth-Century Childhood* (London: William Heinemann, 1924), 2. Further references will be given in the text.

5. Annabel Huth Jackson, *A Victorian Childhood* (London: Methuen, 1932), 83. Further references will be given in the text.

6. Mary Frances McHugh, *Thalassa: A Story of Childhood by the Western Wave* (London: Macmillan, 1931), 201. Further references will be given in the text.

7. Mrs. [Adela] Orpen, *Memories of the Old Emigrant Days in Kansas, 1862–1865, Also of a Visit to Paris in 1867* (Edinburgh: William Blackwood & Sons, 1926), 57.

8. Joanna Richardson, *Colette* (London: Methuen, 1983), 90.

9. M. [Mary] Vivian Hughes, *A London Family, 1870–1900. A Trilogy.* (London: Geoffrey Cumberledge, Oxford University Press, 1946), 3. Further references will be given in the text.

10. Molly Hughes, *A London Child of the 1870s*, with a new preface by Adam Gopnik (London: Persephone Books, 2008), x.

11. Wanda Icus-Rothe, *Sonne der Heimat: Meine Jugend auf den Höhen des Hunsrücks* (Berlin: Deutsches Verlagshaus Bong, 1921), 304.

12. Sophie Reuschle, *Kinderzeit* (Leipzig: Matthes, 1921), 64.

13. Fürstin Marie zu Erbach-Schönberg, Prinzessin von Battenberg, *Entscheidende Jahre: 1859—1866—1870: Aus meiner Kindheit und Mädchenzeit* (Braunschweig: Hellmuth Wollermann Verlagsbuchhandlung, 1921), 3. Further references will be given in the text.

14. Agnes Harder, *Die kleine Stadt: Aus meinen Kindertagen* (Königsberg: Gräfe und Unzer, 1927), 43. Further references will be given in the text.

15. Eleanor Margaret Acland, *Good-Bye for the Present: The Story of Two Childhoods* (New York: Macmillan, 1935), 15–16. Further references will be given in the text.

16. *Destiny Obscure: Autobiographies of Childhood, Education and Family from the 1820s to the 1920s*, ed. and introd. John Burnett (London: Allen Lane, 1982), 36.

17. Eleanor Farjeon, *A Nursery in the Nineties* (London: Oxford University Press, 1960), 529. Further references to this edition will be given in the text.

18. Gwen Matheson and V. E. Lang, "Nellie McClung: 'Not a Nice Woman,'" in *Women in the Canadian Mosaic*, ed. Gwen Matheson, 1–20 (Toronto: Peter Martin Associates, 1976).

19. Nellie L. McClung, *Clearing in the West: My Own Story* (Toronto: Thomas Allen, 1935), 25. Further references will be given in the text.

20. Helen Woodward, *Three Flights Up* (New York: Dodd, Mead & Company, 1935), 37. Further references will be given in the text.

21. Alison Uttley, *Ambush of Young Days* (London: Faber & Faber, 1937), 10. Further references will be given in the text.

274 Notes to Pages 106–138

22. Eleanor Hallowell Abbott, *Being Little in Cambridge When Everyone Else Was Big* (New York: Appleton-Century, 1936), 97. Further references will be given in the text.

23. Louise Weiss, *Souvenirs d'une enfance républicaine* (Paris: Denoël, 1937), 229.

Chapter 3. The Interwar Years:
The Golden Age of Psychological Self-Portraiture

1. Séverine (Caroline [Rémy] Guebhard), *Line (1855–1867)* (Paris: Crès, 1921), 267. Further references will be given in the text.

2. Willa Z. Silverman, "Mythic Representations of Napoleon in the Life and Works of Gyp," in *Correspondances: Studies in Literature, History, and the Arts in Nineteenth-Century France*, ed. Keith Busby (Amsterdam: Rodopi, 1992), 203–12, here 203.

3. Gyp, *Souvenirs d'une petite fille*, 2 vols. (Paris: Calmann-Lévy, 1927–28), 1:127. Further references will be given in the text.

4. Gabriele Reuter, *Vom Kinde zum Menschen: Die Geschichte meiner Jugend* (Berlin: S. Fischer Verlag, 1921), 190. Further references will be given in the text.

5. Bert Almon, *This Stubborn Self: Texas Autobiographies* (Fort Worth: Texas Christian University Press, 2002), 113.

6. Almon, *The Stubborn Self*, 116–20.

7. Mary Helen Specht, "The Disappearance of Gertrude Beasley," *Texas Observer*, May 17, 2011, https://www.texasobserver.org/the-disappearance-of-gertrude-beasley/.

8. Dorothy Whipple, *The Other Day: An Autobiography* (London: Michael Joseph, 1936), 104. Further references will be given in the text.

9. Lois Palken Rudnick, *Mabel Dodge Luhan: New Woman, New Worlds* (Albuquerque: University of New Mexico Press, 1984), 256.

10. Rudnick, *Mabel Dodge Luhan*, 256, 356, 257.

11. Mabel Dodge Luhan, *Intimate Memories: Background* (London: Martin Secker, 1933), 18. Further references will be given in the text.

12. Mary Butts, *The Crystal Cabinet: My Childhood at Salterns* (Boston: Beacon Press, 1988), foreword by Camilla Bagg, afterword by Barbara Wagstaff, 280. The first edition is Mary Butts, *The Crystal Cabinet: My Childhood at Salterns* (London: Methuen & Co Ltd., 1937). Hereafter, the first edition will be cited in the text.

13. Butts, *Crystal Cabinet* (1988), iii.

14. Butts, *Crystal Cabinet* (1988), v.

15. The dazzling critical piece "Our Children" appears only in the 1988 edition.

16. Butts, *Crystal Cabinet* (1988), 265.

17. Laura Goodman Salverson, *Confessions of an Immigrant's Daughter* (Toronto: University of Toronto Press, 1981), 115. Further references to this edition will be given in the text.

18. Stich cites Nellie McClung, *The Stream Runs Fast* (Toronto: Allen, 1945), 145, as the source of this quotation.

19. Dorrit Cohn, *Transparent Minds: Narrative Modes for Presenting Consciousness in Fiction* (Princeton, NJ: Princeton University Press, 1978), 21–140.

20. Sigrid Undset, *The Longest Years*, trans. Arthur G. Chater (New York: Knopf, 1935), 7. Further references will be given in the text.

21. Mark L. Howe, Mary L. Courage, and Carole Peterson, "How Can I Remember When 'I' Wasn't There: Long-Term Retention of Traumatic Experiences and Emergence of the Cognitive Self," in *The Recovered Memory/False Memory Debate*, ed. Kathy Pedzek and William P. Banks (San Diego: Academic Press, 1996), 121–49, here 125–26.

22. Nathalie Sarraute, *L'Ère du soupçon* (Paris: Gallimard, 1956), 7–8.

23. Doris Lessing, *Under My Skin* (New York: Harper Perennial, 1995), 18.

24. Francesca Allinson, *A Childhood* (London: Published by Leonard & Virginia Woolf at the Hogarth Press, 1937).

25. Dormer Creston, *Enter A Child* (London: MacMillan, 1939), vii. Further references will be given in the text.

26. "Conversation Piece: Childhood in a Stately Home," review of *Enter a Child*, by Dormer Creston, *TLS*, October 14, 1939, 594.

27. Anna Schieber, *Doch immer behalten die Quellen das Wort: Erinnerungen aus dem ersten Jahrsiebent* (Heilbronn: Eugen Salzer, 1932), 65, 95. The title is a quotation from Eduard Mörike's poem "Um Mitternacht" ("At Midnight").

28. Bärbel Reetz, *Emmy Ball-Hennings: Leben im Vielleicht. Eine Biographie* (Frankfurt am Main: Suhrkamp, 2001), 35–37.

29. Emmy Ball-Hennings, *Das flüchtige Spiel: Wege und Umwege einer Frau* (Einsiedeln/Cologne: Benziger, 1940), 9.

30. Emmy Ball-Hennings, *Blume und Flamme* (Frankfurt am Main: Suhrkamp, 1987), 16. Further references to this edition will be given in the text.

31. Reetz, *Emmy Ball-Hennings*, 38. Reetz further suggests that Ball-Hennings displaces her "longing for the only true church" onto the childhood of her alter ego Helga (312).

32. Margaret Wade Deland, *If This Be I, As I Suppose It Be* (New York: D. Appleton-Century Co., 1935), 6. Further references will be given in the text.

33. James Humphry III notes that "Mrs. Deland was a member of both the Boston Society for Psychic Research and the English Society for Psychical Research"; "The Works of Margaret Deland," *Colby Library Quarterly* 2, no. 8 (November 1948): 134–40, here 136–37.

34. Maria Waser, *Sinnbild des Lebens* (Frauenfeld: Huber, 1963), 124. Further references to this edition will be given in the text.

35. Norah Burke, *Jungle Child* (New York: Norton, 1955), 145.

36. Philippe Lejeune, "L'autobiographie et l'aveu sexuel," *Revue de la littérature comparée* 325 (January–March 2008): 37–51, here 45.

37. Jill Ker Conway, *When Memory Speaks: Reflections on Autobiography* (New York: Alfred A. Knopf, 1998), 43.

276   Notes to Pages 166–192

Chapter 4. Women's Childhood Autobiography during World War II

1. Amelie Posse-Brázdová, *In the Beginning Was the Light*, trans. Grenville Grove (New York: Dutton, 1942), 11. Further references will be given in the text.

2. Kathleen Cannell, *Jam Yesterday* (New York: William Morrow, 1945), 1.

3. Helen Thomas Flexner, *A Quaker Childhood* (New Haven, CT: Yale University Press, 1940), preface, unnumbered. Further references to this edition will be given in the text.

4. Joanna Richardson, *Enid Starkie* (London: John Murray, 1973), 128.

5. Enid Starkie, *A Lady's Child* (London: Faber and Faber, 1941), 11. Further references will be given in the text.

6. Richardson, *Enid Starkie*, 134, 135–36.

7. Richardson, *Enid Starkie*, 179.

8. M. St. Clare Byrne, *Common or Garden Child: A Not-unfaithful Record* (London: Faber and Faber, 1942), 7. Further references will be given in the text.

9. Patricia Bauer, *Remembering the Times of Our Lives: Memory in Infancy and Beyond* (New York: Psychology Press, 2007), 321–23.

10. Marcel Proust, *In Search of Lost Time*, vol. 5, *The Captive* and *The Fugitive*, trans. C. K. Scott Moncrieff and Terence Kilmartin, rev. D. J. Enright (New York: Modern Library, 2003), 645.

11. Byrne, *Common or Garden Child*, both 92. In the reverse case, emotion masquerades as reason; see also 106–7, 147.

12. Anne Treneer, *School House in the Wind: A Trilogy* (Exeter: University of Exeter Press, 1998), 126.

13. Elizabeth Laura Adams, *Dark Symphony* (London: Sheed & Ward, 1943), 55.

Chapter 5. Women's Childhood Autobiography from the End of the Second World War through the 1960s

1. Rocío G. Davis, *Begin Here: Reading Asian North American Autobiographies of Childhood* (Honolulu: University of Hawai'i Press, 2007), which addresses issues of the adaptation of European and American models by minority ethnic groups (her focus is Asian North American childhood autobiographies), comments extensively on Wong, 114–22.

2. "The statistics leave no doubt that domestic service went into irreversible decline during the 1940s." Paul Addison, "Domestic Dramas," review of *Servants: A Downstairs View of Twentieth-Century Britain*, by Lucy Lethbridge, *TLS*, May 10, 2013, 7.

3. Leonora Eyles, *The Ram Escapes: The Story of a Victorian Childhood* (London: Peter Nevill, 1953), 31.

4. Mary Ellen Chase, *The White Gate: Adventures in the Imagination of a Child* (New York: Norton, 1954), 33–34.

5. Ann F. Wolfe, "Personal History Notes," *Saturday Review*, May 12, 1951, 21.

Notes to Pages 192–200

6. Diana Holman-Hunt, *My Grandmothers and I* (New York: Norton, 1961), v.

7. Emma Smith [pseud.], *A Cornish Waif's Story: An Autobiography* (London: Odhams Press, 1954), 15.

8. Eileen Baillie, *The Shabby Paradise: The Autobiography of a Decade* (London: Hutchinson, 1958), 38.

9. N. M. R., "Bleak House," review of *The Bridgeburn Days*, by Lucy Sinclair, *Manchester Guardian*, April 3, 1956; Marghanita Laski, "Institution Child," review of *The Bridgeburn Days*, by Lucy Sinclair, *Observer*, April 8, 1956, 12; Laura Tisdall, "'That Was What Life in Bridgeburn Had Made Her': Reading the Autobiographies of Children in Institutional Care in England, 1918–46," *Twentieth Century British History* 24, no. 3 (September 2013): 351–75, here 351–52.

10. Clara Malraux, *Apprendre à vivre* (Paris: Grasset, 1963), 247.

11. Martha F. Lifson, "Allegory of the Secret: Mary McCarthy," *Biography* 4, no. 3 (1981): 249–67; Paul John Eakin, *Fictions in Autobiography: Studies in the Art of Self-Invention* (Princeton, NJ: Princeton University Press, 1985), 3–55; Isabel Durán, "From Memories of Childhood to Intellectual Memoirs, or from Mary McCarthy to 'Mary McCarthy,'" in *Writing Lives: American Biography and Autobiography*, ed. Hans Bak and Hans Krabbendam (Amsterdam: VU University Press, 1998), 89–96, here 89.

12. Durán, "From Memories," 95.

13. Mary McCarthy, *Memories of a Catholic Girlhood* (New York: Harcourt Brace, 1985), 49. Further references to this edition will be given in the text.

14. Emma Smith, *A Cornish Waif's Story: An Autobiography*, introduction by Simon Parker, foreword by A. L. Rowse (Redruth: Truran, 2010), vii.

15. Smith, *Cornish Waif's Story* (2010), viii.

16. Emma Smith [pseud.], *A Cornish Waif's Story: An Autobiography* (London: Odhams Press, 1954), 11. Further references to this edition will be given in the text.

17. Smith, *Cornish Waif's Story* (2010), vii.

18. Heather Milton, "Novel Expectations: The Unsuccessful Production of the Modern Subject through Victorian Narrative in *A Cornish Waif's Story: An Autobiography*," *a/b: Auto/Biography Studies* 22 (2007): 270–88, here 271. Milton notes how even the 1954 edition buys into "the persistent fantasy of security, upward mobility, and self-determination promoted by Victorian narratives" (284)—models that work for Oliver Twist and Jane Eyre because they are born middle class, but are much more problematic in the case of Emma Smith, who "remains a subordinate member of the working class" (285). Regenia Gagnier had previously argued that Victorian working-class autobiographers, including Emma Smith, tended to grasp at an inappropriate bourgeois model of autobiography, with ineffective results. Regenia Gagnier, "The Literary Standard, Working-Class Autobiography, and Gender," in *Women, Autobiography, Theory: A Reader*, ed. Sidonie Smith and Julia Watson (Madison: University of Wisconsin Press, 1998), 264–75.

19. Françoise Iqbal and Gilles Dorion, "Claire Martin: Une interview," *Canadian Literature* 82 (1979): 59–77, here 76.

20. Claire Martin, *In an Iron Glove: An Autobiography*, trans. Philip Stratford, introduction by Patricia Smart (Ottawa: University of Ottawa Press, 2006), 7. Further references to this edition will be given in the text. The work was originally published as Claire Martin, *Dans un gant de fer* (Montréal: Le Cercle du livre de France), part 1, *La joue gauche*, 1965; part 2, *La joue droite*, 1966.

21. Janet Hitchman, *The King of the Barbareens* (Harmondsworth: Penguin, 1972), 216. Further references to this edition will be given in the text.

22. Anne Moody, *Coming of Age in Mississippi* (New York: Dell [Laurel], 1976), 129. Further references to this edition will be given in the text.

23. Maya Angelou, *I Know Why the Caged Bird Sings* (New York: Bantam Books, 1988), 40.

24. Kate Douglas, *Contesting Childhood* (New Brunswick, NJ: Rutgers University Press, 2010), 171.

25. *Online Slang Dictionary*, s.v. "sing," http://onlineslangdictionary.com/meaning-definition-of/sing (accessed September 26, 2020).

26. Mathilde Ludendorff, *Statt Heiligenschein oder Hexenzeichen, mein Leben*, vol. 1, *Kindheit und Jugend* (Munich: Ludendorffs Volkswarte-Verlag, n.d.), 53, 90. Ludendorff also allows herself stories with entertainment value: "From this rich time I can, of course, select only a few things for mention, which win their right to a place in this book on account of their humorous content or because they had an influence on my soul and thereby also on my later work" (65).

27. Leonora Eyles, *The Ram Escapes: The Story of a Victorian Childhood* (London: Peter Nevill, 1953), 161. Further references will be given in the text.

28. Esther Kleinbord Labovitz, "Simone de Beauvoir: Memoirs of a Dutiful Daughter," chapter 2 in *The Myth of the Heroine: The Female Bildungsroman in the Twentieth Century* (New York: Lang, 1986), 73–143; Christina Angelfors, "*Mémoires d'une jeune fille rangée* de Simone de Beauvoir: Autobiographie ou fiction?," in *Résonances de la recherche: Festskrift till Sigbrit Swahn*, ed. Utgiven Av et al. (Stockholm: Uppsala, 1999), 13–20, here 16.

29. Simone de Beauvoir, *Memoirs of a Dutiful Daughter*, trans. James Kirkup (Cleveland: The World Publishing Company, 1959), 110. Further references to this translation will be given in the text.

30. Marilyn Yalom, "Sartre, Beauvoir, and the Autobiographical Tradition," *Simone de Beauvoir Studies* 8, no. 8 (1991): 75–81.

31. Doris Lessing, *Under My Skin* (New York: Harper Perennial, 1995), 8–10.

32. Françoise d'Eaubonne, *Chienne de jeunesse* (Paris: Julliard, 1965), 133. Further references will be given in the text.

33. Phyllis Bottome, *Search for a Soul* (New York: Reynal and Hitchcock, 1948), x. There are differences between this and the British edition of 1947. Further references to this edition will be given in the text.

34. Phyllis Bottome, *Search for a Soul* (London: Faber and Faber, n.d.), 9.

Notes to Pages 228–255 279

35. Elisaveta Fen, *A Russian Childhood* (London: Methuen, 1961), 51. Further references will be given in the text.

36. Marie Bonaparte, *À la Mémoire des disparus I (Derrière les vitres closes)* (Paris: Presses Universitaires de France, 1958), 85. Further references will be given in the text.

37. Brooke Astor, *Patchwork Child* (New York: Harper & Row, 1962), 42.

38. Mary Lutyens, *To Be Young: Some Chapters of Autobiography* (London: Rupert Hart-Davis, 1959), 104, 100.

39. Marie Noël [pseud.], *Petit-jour et souvenirs du beau mai* (Paris: Stock, 1969), 13. Further references will be given in the text.

40. Moira Verschoyle, *So Long to Wait: An Irish Childhood* (London: Geoffrey Bles, 1960), 163. Further references will be given in the text.

41. Clara Malraux, *Apprendre à vivre* (Paris: Grasset, 1963), 235. Further references will be given in the text.

42. Patricia Bauer, *Remembering the Times of Our Lives: Memory in Infancy and Beyond* (New York: Psychology Press, 2007), 33, 313.

43. Isabelle de Courtivron, *Clara Malraux, une femme dans le siècle* (n.p.: Éditions de l'Olivier, 1992), 188.

44. Courtivron, *Clara Malraux*, 97.

Conclusion

1. Philippe Lejeune, *On Autobiography*, ed. Paul John Eakin, trans. Katherine Leary (Minneapolis: University of Minnesota Press, 1989), 22; Timothy Dow Adams, *Telling Lies in Modern American Autobiography* (Chapel Hill: University of North Carolina Press, 1990), 9; Paul John Eakin, "Breaking Rules: The Consequences of Self-Narration," *Biography* 24, no. 1 (2001): 113–27, here 115.

2. Leigh Gilmore, *Autobiographics: A Feminist Theory of Women's Self-Representation* (Ithaca, NY: Cornell University Press, 1994), 14.

3. Ben Yagoda, *Memoir: A History* (New York: Riverhead Books, 2009), 264–66.

4. G. Thomas Couser, *Memoir: An Introduction* (Oxford: Oxford University Press, 2012), 72ff.

5. Michel Foucault, "What Is an Author?," in David H. Richter, *The Critical Tradition: Classic Texts and Contemporary Trends* (Boston: Bedford/St. Martin's, 2007), 904–14, here 908.

6. Couser, *Memoir* devotes chapter 3 to a discussion of this issue.

7. Doris Lessing, "Describing This Beautiful and Nasty Planet," interview with Earl G. Ingersoll, July 9, 1993, in *Doris Lessing: Conversations*, ed. Earl G. Ingersoll (Princeton, NJ: Ontario Review Press, 1994), 228–40, here 236.

8. Paul John Eakin, *Living Autobiographically: How We Create Identity in Narrative* (Ithaca, NY: Cornell University Press, 2008), 63.

9. Yagoda, *Memoir*, 239.

10. Couser, *Memoir*, 87.

11. H. Porter Abbott, "Autobiography, Autography, Fiction: Groundwork for a Taxonomy of Textual Categories," *New Literary History* 19, no. 3 (1988): 597–615, here 601.

12. Couser, *Memoir*, 170.

13. Jill Ker Conway, *When Memory Speaks: Reflections on Autobiography* (New York: Alfred A. Knopf, 1998), 88.

14. Conway, *When Memory Speaks*, 43.

15. Conway, *When Memory Speaks*, 88.

Bibliography of Women's
Childhood Autobiographies to 1969

Abbott, Eleanor Hallowell. *Being Little in Cambridge When Everyone Else Was Big*. New York: Appleton-Century, 1936.

Acland, Eleanor Margaret. *Good-Bye for the Present: The Story of Two Childhoods*. New York: Macmillan, 1935.

Adam-Smith, Patsy. *Hear the Train Blow*. Sydney: Ure Smith, 1964.

Adam, Madame (Juliette Lamber). *Le Roman de mon enfance et de ma jeunesse*. Paris: Alphonse Lemerre, 1902. Engl. tr.: Mme Edmond Adam (Juliette Lamber). *The Romance of My Childhood and Youth*. New York: D. Appleton & Co., 1902.

Adams, Elizabeth Laura. *Dark Symphony*. New York: Sheed & Ward, 1942.

Adelmann, Helene. *Aus meiner Kinderzeit*. Berlin: R. Appelius, n.d. [1892].

Allinson, Francesca. *A Childhood*. London: Published by Leonard & Virginia Woolf at the Hogarth Press, 1937.

Angelou, Maya. *I Know Why the Caged Bird Sings*. New York: Random House, 1969.

Antin, Mary. *The Promised Land*. Boston: Houghton Mifflin Co., 1912.

Arden, Joan. *A Childhood*. Cambridge: Bowes & Bowes, 1913.

Astor, Brooke. *Patchwork Child*. New York: Harper & Row, 1962.

Audoux, Marguerite. *Marie Claire*. Paris: Fasquelle, 1910. Engl. tr.: *Marie Claire*. Translated by John N. Raphael. Breinigsville, PA: Dodo Press, 2010.

Avery, Valerie. *London Morning*. London: William Kimber, 1964.

Baillie, Eileen. *The Shabby Paradise: The Autobiography of a Decade*. London: Hutchinson, 1958.

Ball-Hennings, Emmy. *Blume und Flamme: Geschichte einer Jugend*. Einsiedeln/Cologne: Benzinger, 1938.

Bardin, Angélina. *Angélina, une fille des champs*. Paris: André Bonne, 1956.

Barton, Clara. *The Story of My Childhood*. New York: Baker & Taylor, 1907.

Beasley, Gertrude. *My First Thirty Years*. Paris: Contact Editions, Three Mountains Press, 1925.

Beauvoir, Simone de. *Mémoires d'une jeune fille rangée*. Paris: Gallimard, 1958. Engl. tr.: *Memoirs of a Dutiful Daughter*. Translated by James Kirkup. Cleveland: The World Publishing Company, 1959.

Berend-Corinth, Charlotte. *Als ich ein Kind war*. Hamburg-Bergedorf: Stromverlag, 1950.

Bernstein, Aline. *An Actor's Daughter*. New York: Alfred A. Knopf, 1941.

Bischoff, Charitas. *Augenblicksbilder aus einem Jugendleben*. Leipzig: H. G. Wallmann, 1905.

Bixby-Smith, Sarah. *Adobe Days: A Book of California Memories*. Cedar Rapids, IA: Torch Press, 1925.

Blüthgen, Clara. *Aus der Jugendzeit: Frühe Erinnerungen*. Berlin-Lichterfelde: Verlag von Edwin Runge, n.d. [1919].

Bolton, Isabel. *Under Gemini: A Memoir*. New York: Harcourt, Brace & World, 1966.

Bonaparte, Marie. *À la Mémoire des disparus I (Derrière les vitres closes)*. Paris: Presses Universitaires de France, 1958.

Bottome, Phyllis. *Search for a Soul*. London: Faber and Faber, 1947.

Bowen, Elizabeth. *Seven Winters*. Dublin: Cuala Press, 1942.

Boy-Ed, Ida, ed. *Als unsre großen Dichterinnen noch kleine Mädchen waren*. Leipzig: Franz Moeser Nachf., 1912.

Braun, Isabella. *Aus der Jugendzeit*. Stuttgart: Otto Risch, 1871.

Burke, Norah. *Jungle Child*. New York: Norton, 1955.

Burnett, Frances Hodgson. *The One I Knew the Best of All: A Memory of the Mind of a Child*. New York: Charles Scribner's Sons, 1893.

Butts, Mary. *The Crystal Cabinet: My Childhood at Salterns*. London: Methuen & Co Ltd., 1937.

Byrne, M. St. Clare. *Common or Garden Child: A Not-unfaithful Record*. London: Faber and Faber, 1942.

Campbell, Ellen. *An Australian Childhood*. London: Blackie, 1892?

Cannell, Kathleen. *Jam Yesterday*. New York: William Morrow & Company, 1945.

Carbery, Mary. *Happy World: The Story of a Victorian Childhood*. London: Longmans, Green and Co., 1941.

Carr, Emily. *The Book of Small*. Toronto: Oxford University Press, 1942.

Chagall, Bella. *Brenendike likht.* New York: Folks-Farlag, 1945. Engl. tr.: *Burning Lights.* Translated by Norbert Guterman. New York: Schocken Books, 1946.

Chase, Mary Ellen. *The White Gate: Adventures in the Imagination of a Child.* New York: W. W. Norton, 1954.

Cohen, Rose. *Out of the Shadow.* New York: George H. Doran Company, 1918.

Colette. *La Maison de Claudine.* Paris: J. Ferenczi et fils, 1922. Engl. tr.: *My Mother's House and Sido.* Translated by Enid McCleod and Una Troubridge. New York: Farrar, Straus & Young, 1953.

Coyle, Kathleen. *The Magical Realm.* New York: Dutton, 1943.

Creevey, Caroline A. Stickney. *A Daughter of the Puritans: An Autobiography.* New York: G. P. Putnam's Sons, 1916.

Creston, Dormer [Dorothy Julia Baynes]. *Enter A Child.* London: MacMillan, 1939.

Crowell, Evelyn Miller. *Texas Childhood.* Dallas, TX: Kaleidograph Press, 1941.

Damon, Bertha. *Grandma Called It Carnal.* New York: Simon and Schuster, 1938.

Daudet, Madame Alphonse. *L'Enfance d'une parisienne.* Paris: Charavay Frères, n.d. [1883].

Deland, Margaret Wade. *If This Be I, As I Suppose It Be.* New York: D. Appleton-Century Co., 1935.

Dodge, Helen Carmichael. *My Childhood in the Canadian Wilderness.* New York: Vantage Press, 1961.

Dohm, Hedwig. "Kindheitserinnerungen einer alten Berlinerin." In *Als unsre großen Dichterinnen noch kleine Mädchen waren,* edited by Ida Boy-Ed, 17–57. Leipzig: Franz Moeser Nachf., 1912.

Dunham, Katherine. *A Touch of Innocence: Memoirs of Childhood.* New York: Harcourt, Brace and World, 1959.

Eakin, Robin. *Aunts Up the Cross.* London: Anthony Blond, 1965.

Eaubonne, Françoise d'. *Chienne de jeunesse.* Paris: René Julliard, 1965.

Ebner-Eschenbach, Marie von. *Meine Kinderjahre.* Berlin: Paetel, 1906.

Eyles, Leonora. *The Ram Escapes: The Story of a Victorian Childhood.* London: Peter Nevill, 1953.

Farjeon, Eleanor. *A Nursery in the Nineties.* London: Victor Gollancz Ltd., 1935.

Farnham, Eliza W. *My Early Days.* New York: Thatcher & Hutchinson, 1859.

Fen, Elisaveta. *A Russian Childhood.* London: Methuen & Co Ltd., 1961.

Flexner, Helen Thomas. *A Quaker Childhood.* New Haven, CT: Yale University Press, 1940.

Franklin, Miles. *Childhood at Brindabella: My First Ten Years.* Sydney: Angus and Robertson, 1963.

Gandy, Ida. *A Wiltshire Childhood.* London: Allen & Unwin, 1929.

Gautier, Judith. *Le Collier des jours (Souvenirs de ma vie).* Paris: Félix Juven, n.d. [1902].

Gautier, Yvonne. *Mon Enfance . . . et Elle. Souvenirs.* Paris: Editions de la Revue Moderne, 1965.

Gilder, Jeannette. *Autobiography of a Tomboy.* New York: Doubleday, Page, 1901.

Godden, Jon, and Rumer Godden. *Two Under the Indian Sun.* New York: Knopf/Viking, 1966.

Gyp. *Souvenirs d'une petite fille.* 2 vols. Paris: Calmann-Lévy, 1927–28.

Hale, Nancy. *A New England Girlhood.* Boston: Little, Brown and Company, 1958.

Hamilton, Elizabeth. *An Irish Childhood.* London: Chatto and Windus, 1963.

Hamilton, Mary. *Green and Gold.* London: Allan Wingate, 1948.

Harder, Agnes. *Die kleine Stadt: Aus meinen Kindertagen.* Königsberg: Gräfe und Unzer, 1927.

Harding, Bertita. *Mosaic in the Fountain.* Philadelphia: Lippincott, 1949.

Hatsumi, Reiko. *Rain and the Feast of the Stars.* Boston: Houghton Mifflin, 1959.

Havoc, June. *Early Havoc.* New York: Simon and Schuster, 1959.

Hawker, Beatrice. *Look Back in Love.* London: Longmans, Green, 1958.

Henrey, Mrs. Robert. *The Little Madeleine.* London: Dent, 1951.

Herder, Charlotte. *. . . schaut durch ein farbiges Glas auf die aschfarbene Welt: Kindheit und Jugend im alten Prag.* Freiburg im Breisgau: Verlag Herder, 1954.

Heygate, Elizabeth. *A Girl at Eton.* London: Rupert Hart-Davis, 1965.

Hilliard, Jan. [pseud.]. *The Salt-Box.* New York: Norton, 1951.

Hitchman, Janet. *The King of the Barbareens.* London: Putnam, 1960.

Holman-Hunt, Diana. *My Grandmothers and I.* London: Hamish Hamilton, 1960.

Holmes, G. V. [pseud.]. *The Likes of Us.* London: F. Muller, 1948.

Howe, Bea. *Child in Chile.* London: Andre Deutsch, 1957.

Howitt, Mary. *My Own Story: or, The Autobiography of a Child.* London: Thomas Tegg, 1845.

Bibliography of Women's Childhood Autobiographies to 1969

Hughes, M. [Mary] V. [Vivian]. *A London Child of the Seventies*. London: Oxford University Press, 1934.

Hughes, Mrs. F. *My Childhood in Australia: A Story for My Children*. London: Digby, Long & Co., 1891?

Hunt, Una. *Una Mary: The Inner Life of a Child*. New York: Charles Scribner's Sons, 1914.

Huxley, Elspeth. *The Flame Trees of Thika: Memories of an African Childhood*. London: Chatto & Windus, 1959.

Icus-Rothe, Wanda. *Sonne der Heimat: Meine Jugend auf den Höhen des Hunsrücks*. Berlin: Deutsches Verlagshaus Bong, 1921.

Irvine, Lyn. *So Much Love, So Little Money*. London: Faber and Faber, 1957.

Ishimoto, Baroness Shidzué. *East Way, West Way: A Modern Japanese Girlhood*. New York: Farrar & Rinehart, 1936.

Jackson, Annabel Huth, née Grant Duff. *A Victorian Childhood*. London: Methuen, 1932.

Kellner, Esther. *The Devil and Aunt Serena*. Indianapolis: Bobbs-Merrill, 1968.

Keppel, Sonia. *Edwardian Daughter*. London: Hamilton, 1958.

Kovalevsky, Sonja. *Ur ryska lifvet: Systrarna Rajevski*. Stockholm: Hæggström, 1889. Engl. tr.: Sofya Kovalevskaya. *A Russian Childhood*. Translated, edited, and introduced by Beatrice Stillman. New York: Springer Verlag, 1978.

Lagerlöf, Selma. *Mårbacka*. Stockholm: A. Bonnier, [1922]. Engl. tr.: Selma Lagerlof. *Marbacka*. Translated by Velma Swanston Howard. New York: Doubleday, Page & Co., 1924.

Larcom, Lucy. *A New England Girlhood, Outlined from Memory*. Boston: Houghton, Mifflin, 1889.

Lee, Gypsy Rose. *Gypsy: A Memoir*. New York: Harper & Brothers, 1957.

Le Franc, Marie. *Enfance marine*. Montréal: Fides, 1959.

Lenk, Margarete. *Aus meiner Kindheit: Jugenderinnerungen*. Zwickau i. Sa.: Johannes Herrmann, 1910.

Lerber, Helene von. *Liebes altes Pfarrhaus: Kindheitserinnerungen*. St. Gallen: Vadian-Verlag, 1963.

Lubbock, Sybil Marjorie. *The Child in the Crystal*. London: J. Cape, [1939].

Luhan, Mabel Dodge. *Intimate Memories: Background*. London: Martin Secker, 1933.

Lunt, Cornelia Gray. *Sketches of Childhood and Girlhood: Chicago, 1847–1864*. Evanston, IL: privately printed, 1925.

Lutyens, Mary. *To Be Young: Some Chapters of Autobiography*. London: Rupert Hart-Davis, 1959.

L'vova, Elizaveta. "Davno minuvshee: Otryvki iz vospominanii detstva." *Russkii vestnik*, 1901, 10:399–416; 11:76–89. Engl. tr.: "From the Distant Past: Fragments from Childhood Memories." In *Russia through Women's Eyes: Autobiographies from Tsarist Russia*, edited by Toby W. Clyman and Judith Vowles, 282–310. New Haven, CT: Yale University Press, 1996.

Lynch, Hannah. *Autobiography of a Child*. New York: Dodd, Mead & Co., 1899.

Lynch, Patricia. *A Storyteller's Childhood*. London: Dent, 1947.

MacCarthy, Mary Josepha. *A Nineteenth-Century Childhood*. London: William Heinemann Ltd., 1924.

Maillet, Antonine. *On a mangé la dune*. Montréal: Beauchemin, 1962.

Malraux, Clara. *Le Bruit de nos pas*. Vol. 1, *Apprendre à vivre*. Paris: Grasset, 1963.

Marie, Fürstin zu Erbach-Schönberg, Prinzessin von Battenberg. *Entscheidende Jahre: 1859—1866—1870: Aus meiner Kindheit und Mädchenzeit*. Braunschweig: Hellmuth Wollermann Verlagsbuchhandlung, 1921.

Marshall, Audrey. *Fishbones into Butterflies: A Kind of Remembering*. London: Chatto & Windus, 1964.

Martin, Claire. *Dans un gant de fer*. Montréal: Le Cercle du livre de France. Part 1, *La joue gauche*, 1965; Part 2, *La joue droite*, 1966. Engl. tr.: *In an Iron Glove: An Autobiography*. Translated by Philip Stratford. Toronto: Ryerson Press, 1968.

McBride, Mary Margaret. *How Dear to My Heart*. New York: Macmillan, 1940.

McCall, Dorothy. *When That I Was*. London: Faber and Faber, 1952.

McCarthy, Mary. *Memories of a Catholic Girlhood*. New York: Harcourt, Brace, and Co., 1957.

McClung, Nellie L. *Clearing in the West: My Own Story*. Toronto: Thomas Allen, 1935.

McHugh, Mary Frances. *Thalassa: A Story of Childhood by the Western Wave*. London: Macmillan, 1931.

Michelet, Mme J. [Athénaïs Michelet]. *Mémoires d'une enfant*. Paris: L. Hachette et Cie, 1867 [appeared November 1866].

Miegel, Agnes. *Kinderland: Heimat und Jugenderinnerungen*. Leipzig: Hermann Eichblatt, 1930.

Moody, Anne. *Coming of Age in Mississippi*. New York: Dial Press, 1968.

Neilson, Elisabeth. *The House I Knew: Memories of Youth*. Boston: Houghton Mifflin, 1941.

Nesbit, E. *Long Ago When I Was Young*. London: Ronald Whiting and Wheaton, 1966. First published serially under the title *My School-Days* in *The Girl's Own Paper* (October 1896 to September 1897).

Noailles, Anna de. *Le livre de ma vie*. Paris: Hachette, 1932.

Noël, Marie. *Petit-jour: Souvenirs d'enfance*. Paris: Librairie Stock, Delamain et Boutelleau, 1951.

Noël, Marie. [pseud.]. *Petit-jour et souvenirs du beau mai*. Paris: Stock, 1964.

Ogilvie, Mary I. *A Scottish Childhood and What Happened After*. Oxford: George Ronald, 1952.

Orpen, Mrs. [Adela]. *Memories of the Old Emigrant Days in Kansas, 1862–1865, Also of a Visit to Paris in 1867*. Edinburgh: William Blackwood & Sons, 1926.

Pagés, Helene. *Die klingende Kette*. Freiburg im Breisgau: Herder, 1936.

Pange, Comtesse Jean de [Pauline de Broglie Pange]. *Comment j'ai vu 1900*. Paris: Grasset, 1962.

Patchett, Mary Elwyn. *Ajax the Warrior*. London: Lutterworth Press, 1953.

Phelps, Orra Parker. *When I Was a Girl in the Martin Box*. New York: Island Press, 1949.

Phillips, Margaret Mann. *Within the City Wall: A Memoir of Childhood*. Cambridge: Cambridge University Press, 1943.

[Popp, Adelheid]. *Die Jugendgeschichte einer Arbeiterin*. Munich: Reinhardt Verlag, 1909. Engl. tr.: Adelheid Popp. *The Autobiography of a Working Woman*. Translated by E. C. Harvey. Westport, CT: Hyperion Press, 1913.

Porter, Alyene. *Papa Was a Preacher*. New York: Abingdon-Cokesbury Press, 1944.

Posse, Amelie. *I begynnelsen var ljuset*. Stockholm: Natur och Kultur, 1940. Engl. tr.: Amelie Posse-Brázdová. *In the Beginning Was the Light*. Translated by Grenville Grove. New York: Dutton, 1942.

Powell, Violet. *Five out of Six: An Autobiography*. London: Heinemann, 1960.

Raverat, Gwen. *Period Piece: A Cambridge Childhood*. London: Faber and Faber, 1952.

Reuschle, Sophie. *Kinderzeit*. Leipzig: Matthes, 1921.

Reuter, Gabriele. *Vom Kinde zum Menschen: Die Geschichte meiner Jugend*. Berlin: S. Fischer Verlag, 1921.

Rodaway, Angela. *A London Childhood*. London: B. T. Batsford, 1960.

Ross, Marie Marchand. *Child of Icaria*. New York: City Printing Company, 1938.

Salverson, Laura Goodman. *Confessions of an Immigrant's Daughter*. London: Faber and Faber, 1939.

Sand, George. *Histoire de ma vie*. Paris: V. Lecou, 1854–1855. Engl. tr.: *Story of My Life: The Autobiography of George Sand*. A group translation edited by Thelma Jurgrau. Albany: SUNY Press, 1991.

Sarton, May. *I Knew a Phoenix: Sketches for an Autobiography*. New York: Rinehart and Co., 1959.

Schieber, Anna. *Doch immer behalten die Quellen das Wort: Erinnerungen aus dem ersten Jahrsiebent*. Heilbronn: Eugen Salzer, 1932.

Schumacher, Tony. *Was ich als Kind erlebt*. Stuttgart: Deutsche Verlags-Anstalt, 1901.

Seidel, Ina. *Meine Kindheit und Jugend: Ursprung, Erbteil und Weg*. Stuttgart: Deutsche Verlagsanstalt, 1935.

Séverine [Caroline (Rémy) Guebhard]. *Line (1855–1867)*. Paris: Crès, 1921.

Shields, Karena. *The Changing Wind*. New York: Crowell, 1959.

Sillar, Eleanor Hallard. *Edinburgh's Child, Some Memories of Ninety Years*. Edinburgh: Oliver and Boyd, 1961.

Sinclair, Lucy. *The Bridgeburn Days*. London: Victor Gollancz Ltd., 1956.

Skariatina, Irina. *Little Era in Old Russia*. Indianapolis: Bobbs Merrill, 1934.

Slenczynska, Ruth, and Louis Brancolli. *Forbidden Childhood*. Garden City, NY: Doubleday, 1957.

[Smith, Emma (pseud.)]. *A Cornish Waif's Story: An Autobiography*. Long Acre, London: Odhams Press Ltd., 1954.

Sone, Monica. *Nisei Daughter*. Boston: Little, Brown, 1953.

Sorensen, Virginia. *Where Nothing Is Long Ago: Memories of a Mormon Childhood*. New York: Harcourt, Brace & World, 1963.

Soskice, Juliet M. *Chapters from Childhood: Reminiscences of an Artist's Granddaughter*. London: Selwyn & Blount, Ltd., 1921.

Starkie, Enid. *A Lady's Child*. London: Faber and Faber, 1941.

Stern, E. G. *My Mother and I*. New York: Macmillan, 1917.

Symons, Geraldine. *Children in the Close*. London: B. T. Batsford, 1959.

Thirkell, Angela. *Three Houses*. London: Oxford University Press, H. Milford, 1931.

Thompson, Ariadne. *The Octagonal Heart*. Indianapolis: Bobbs-Merrill, 1956.

Bibliography of Women's Childhood Autobiographies to 1969

Timings, C. L. *Letter from the Past: Memories of a Victorian Childhood*. London: Andrew Melrose, 1954.

Treneer, Anne. *School House in the Wind*. London: Cape, 1944.

Undset, Sigrid. *Elleve Aar*. Oslo: H. Aschehoug & Co. (W. Nygaard), 1934. Engl. tr.: *The Longest Years*. Translated from the Norwegian by Arthur G. Chater. New York: Knopf, 1935.

Uttley, Alison. *Ambush of Young Days*. London: Faber and Faber, 1937.

Verschoyle, Moira. *So Long to Wait: An Irish Childhood*. London: Geoffrey Bles, 1960.

Waser, Maria. *Sinnbild des Lebens*. Stuttgart: Deutsche Verlags-Anstalt, 1936.

Weinhandl, Margarete. *Und deine Wälder rauschen fort: Kindheit in Untersteier*. Graz: Leykam-Verlag, 1942.

Weiss, Louise. *Souvenirs d'une enfance républicaine*. Paris: Denoël, 1937.

Whipple, Dorothy. *The Other Day: An Autobiography*. London: Michael Joseph, Ltd., 1936.

Wirth-Stockhausen, Julia. *Unverlierbare Kindheit*. Stuttgart: Engelhornverlag Adolf Spemann, 1949.

Wong, Jade Snow. *Fifth Chinese Daughter*. New York: Harper, 1950.

Woodward, Helen. *Three Flights Up*. New York: Dodd, Mead & Company, 1935.

Woodward, Kathleen. *Jipping Street*. London: Longmans, Green and Company, 1928.

Ziegfeld, Patricia. *The Ziegfelds' Girl: Confessions of an Abnormally Happy Childhood*. Boston: Little Brown, 1964.

Zimmer, Jill Schary. *With a Cast of Thousands: A Hollywood Childhood*. New York: Stein and Day, 1963.

Index

Abbott, Eleanor Hallowell, 78, 103, 105–7, 109; humor in, 105–7, 126, 172, 245

Abbott, H. Porter, 256, 280n11

abuse: stories of, 40, 55–56, 170, 195–214; emergence of as topic, 214, 242, 246, 251; sexual, as topic, 76, 195–96, 212, 272n74; sexual, in childhood autobiography, 124, 193, 198, 200–202, 211–14, 260

Acland, Eleanor Margaret, 10, 78, 85, 92–95, 104, 163; memory, 95, 104; narrator in, 99; religion in, 95; third-person narration in, 93, 145; "we" style in, 46, 94, 98

Adam, Edmond, 29, 31

Adam, Juliette Lamber, 18, 22, 29–31, 36, 127, 258; autobiography of famous person type, 30, 120, 216; self-portraiture in, 29, 127

Adams, Elizabeth Laura, 166, 170, 183–85, 245

Adams, Timothy Dow, 252, 279n1

Adam-Smith, Patsy, 187–88

Addison, Paul, 276n2

Adelmann, Helene, 22, 67–69, 71, 88, 235, 259

Adler, Alfred, 224–26, 243, 259

African American childhoods, 183–84, 193, 208–14

Agoult, Marie d', 29

Alcott, Louisa May, 151

Allinson, Francesca, 79, 110, 149, 151–53, 163, 170; child's vision in, 112, 144, 233, 244, 255; epiphany in, 137, 152; narrator in, 144

Almon, Bert, 124, 274n5

Als unsre großen Dichter noch kleine Jungen waren, 71, 272n64

Als unsre großen Dichterinnen noch kleine Mädchen waren, 71, 272n65

ambition: fostered in girls by education, 224; of girls, before World War I, 29, 66, 72; of girls, in interwar and World War II years, 108, 120, 128, 173; of girls, after World War II, 184, 190, 219–21; of parents, for their daughters, 193, 221. *See also* vocation, as theme

amnesia, childhood, 179. *See also* memory: early memories, interest in; memory: first memory

Angelfors, Christina, 220–21, 278n28

Angelou, Maya, 3, 184, 187, 206, 211–14; agenda in, 211, 213–14, 256; typicality in, 256–62

Anglo-Irish childhoods, 84, 103–4, 171–75, 188–89, 236

Antin, Mary, 22, 65–66, 71, 101, 256, 258

292 Index

Arden, Joan, 22, 59–61, 104, 151–53, 259; child's vision in, 75–76, 80, 111, 127, 144, 233, 244, 255; compared to Una Hunt, 62; memory in, 59–60, 234

Astor, Brooke, 187, 214, 231–32, 243, 246, 252; confessional mode in, 195; relational focus in, 215, 229, 244–45

Audoux, Marguerite, 22, 34–36, 59, 76, 245, 259; fictionalization in, 35, 75, 255, 269n17; as orphan, 35, 40, 198

autobiographical pact, 40, 253

autobiography: defined vs. memoir, 15–16; history of term, 36–37. *See also* autobiography, conventions of

autobiography, conventions of: justification, 254, 256; thematization of memory, 146, 192, 254; plotlessness, 11, 254; detail, 148; agenda, 256–57. *See also* autobiographical pact; novelistic techniques in autobiography

Avery, Valerie, 187, 193–94

Bagg, Camilla, 134

Baillie, Eileen, 186, 194

Ball, Hugo, 155

Ball-Hennings, Emmy, 110, 112, 155–57, 162; child's vision in, 144, 233, 244

Balzac, Honoré de, 136

Bardin, Angélina, 186, 194

Barrès, Maurice, 116

Barrès, Philippe, 116

Bartlett, Sir Frederic, 252

Barton, Clara, 22, 46–48, 75, 258

Baudelaire, Charles, 171

Bauer, Patricia, 276n9

Baynes, Dorothy Julia. *See* Creston, Dormer

Beasley, Gertrude, 110, 124–25, 128, 164–65; candidness in, 141; confessional mode in, 127; feminism in, 125, 127, 140; on her mother, 124,

202; sex in, 124, 127, 150, 195–96, 202–3, 212; shame in, 124, 205

Beauvoir, Simone de, 17–18, 186, 219–24, 238, 241, 244; autobiography of famous person type, 120; Bildungsroman model in, 214–16, 220–21, 242; confessional mode in, 195; feminism in, 241, 246; compared to Gabriele Reuter, 120, 123; and Rousseau, 221–22; *The Second Sex*, 17, 220, 222, 241, 268n28; compared to Louise Weiss, 107–8,

Bebel, August, 72

Benjamin, Walter, 28, 63, 132, 223

Bennett, Arnold, 34, 269n14

Berend-Corinth, Charlotte, 186, 233–35, 243–45

Bernstein, Aline, 166, 170, 182–83, 185

Bildungsroman, autobiography modeled on: before World War I, 76; in interwar years, 79; after World War II, 242–43; as trope of childhood and youth story, 262; women's childhood autobiographies that adopt Bildungsroman model, 119–23, 119, 215–24

Binckes, Faith, 270n45, 270n46, 271n49

Binder, Christiane Maria, 271n57

Bischoff, Charitas, 22, 67, 69–70, 75, 259

Bixby-Smith, Sarah, 78, 84

Blake, William, 135

Blüthgen, Clara, 71, 78, 89, 235, 260

boarding school, as theme, 53, 59–60, 83–84, 91, 137; childhood autobiographers sent to, 95, 115, 132, 228

Bolton, Isabel, 187, 215

Bonaparte, Marie, 18, 186, 229–31, 243; confessional mode in, 195; deceptiveness of adults in, 50, 230; feminism in, 246; relational focus in, 215, 244–45; psychoanalysis in, 224, 231; self-focus in, 214

Index

Bonaparte, Napoleon, 116

books, theme of reading in childhood, 22; in specific authors, 29, 50–51, 61, 94, 96, 104, 115, 140, 143, 148, 151, 177

Bottome, Phyllis, 186, 224–29; confessional mode in, 111, 195; relational focus in, 215, 227, 238, 244–45; psychoanalytic influence on, 224–25, 231–32, 240, 243, 259; self-focus in, 214

Bowen, Elizabeth, 166, 173, 236,

Boy-Ed, Ida, 273n65

Braun, Isabella, 22, 24, 67–68, 71, 259

Brettschneider, Werner, 12, 266n14

Briggs, Julia, 270n42

Brill, A. A., 129

Brontë, Charlotte, 39–40, 195, 271n53. *See also Jane Eyre*

brothers, theme of: brother favored, 201, 217, 226–27, 228; freedom of, 27, 68; good relationship with, 87, 97, 121, 197–98, 213; sexist attitude of, 27, 174; tormented by, 27, 83, 124, 228

Brown, Catherine Madox, 82

Brown, Ford Madox, 82

Brown, Penny, 271n52

bullying, theme of, 53, 57, 87, 153, 207; by adult in family, 203, 213

Bulwer-Lytton, Robert, 233

Burke, Norah, 162, 186–87

Burne-Jones, Edward, 82

Burnett, Frances Hodgson, 22, 48–52, 61, 104, 245; compared to Eleanor Acland, 94; children's book author, 23, 190; deceptiveness of adults in, 50, 115, 229, 259; imagination in, 49, 259; humorous, 74, 143, 254; compared to Una Hunt, 62; memory in, 49–50, 62, 73, 94; on her mother, 51–52, 259; psychological study, 62, 150, 249; storytelling in, 58, 75, 99; third-person narration in, 48–49, 74, 93, 113, 145; typicality in, 49, 180, 256; vocation in, 49, 100, 120, 127, 143, 258

Burnett, John, 95, 273n16

Butts, Mary, 80, 106, 110, 134–37, 165, 184; analytical, 131; candidness in, 137, 141, 153; confessional mode in, 111, 127–28, 170, 195; critical of family, 136–37, 139, 225, 245; feminism in, 140; indiscretion in, 172–73; on her mother, 136, 185, 202; narrator in, 135, 144, 198; rebelliousness in, 224, 244–45; self-focus in, 135, 214; self-profiling, 131, 138; theme of sex in, 175

Byrne, M. St. Clare, 149, 166, 178–82, 185; child's vision in, 170, 233, 244; feminism in, 182; male identification in, 181–82, 229; on memory, 105, 170, 178–80; as only child, 237; typicality in, 256

Campbell, Ellen, 22–23, 58, 75

candor, in women's childhood autobiographies: in interwar years, 128, 133, 137, 141, 153; in war years, 172–73, 175, 177; after World War II, 191, 202; rise of in interwar years, 79, 110–11

Cannell, Kathleen, 166–68

Carbery, Mary, 166–67, 252

caregivers, women as children's, 14, 21, 251

Carr, Emily, 166–67, 169–70, 185, 197, 233, 244

Cerf, Bennett, 255

Chagall, Bella, 186

Chase, Mary Ellen, 186, 189

child perspective, adoption of, 247, 249; as device, 262–63; and interest in inner life of child, 258; and use of term "autobiography," 255; in women's childhood autobiographies before World War I, 35–36, 52,

child perspective (*continued*)
59–61; in women's childhood autobiographies in interwar years, 142,
144–57, 163; in women's childhood
autobiographies in World War II
years, 170, 178–82; in women's
childhood autobiographies after
World War II, 233–39. *See also*
child's vision, recreation of; free
indirect discourse, use of in childhood autobiographies; interior
monologue, use of in childhood
autobiographies

children's book writers, as childhood
autobiographers, 8, 74–75, 250;
before World War I, 23–24, 38–39,
41, 48, 52, 67–70; in interwar years,
95, 89, 103, 154; after World War II,
187, 190

child study movement, 50, 111, 163

child's vision, recreation of, 59–61,
75–76, 80, 144–57, 178–79, 233–39.
See also child perspective, adoption
of; inner life of child

Chodorow, Nancy, 267n23

clothes, theme of: clothes as problem,
63–64, 122, 139, 176, 204, 218–19;
importance of wearing the same
clothes as other little girls, 64, 149,
176, 232, 237, 262

Coe, Richard N.: "Autobiography of
Childhood and Adolescence," 4–5,
79, 265n2, 265n6; concept of "childhood," 8, 15; *When the Grass Was
Taller*, 8, 12, 14, 266n14

Cohen, Rose, 22, 66, 101

Cohn, Dorrit, 146, 275n19

Colette, 78, 85–86, 163, 186

confession: aspects of confessional
childhood autobiography in interwar years, 164–65; aspects of
confessional childhood autobiography after World War II, 246; childhood autobiographies written in

confessional style before World
War I, 24–36, 39, 47, 66, 73–74;
childhood autobiographies written
in confessional style in interwar
years, 83, 96, 106–7, 111–12, 127–28,
120–24, 127–43, 155–56; childhood
autobiographies written in confessional style in World War II years,
170–77, 182; childhood autobiographies written in confessional style
after World War II, 193, 199–202,
206–7, 212–15, 218, 223, 227, 231–
33, 238–41; French tradition of confessional autobiography, 23, 74,
112–13, 127–28, 176; history of in
women's childhood autobiography, 250–51; increase in confessional childhood autobiography in
interwar years, 127, 163–65; as
mode of autobiography, 65, 81,
247, 249; psychoanalytic influence
on confessional style, 195; as term,
7, 266n9

convent school, theme of, 31, 33–34,
54, 56–58, 119, 126, 203, 205–6

Conway, Jill Ker, 14, 164–65, 257, 259,
267n18

Corinth, Lovis, 234

Cornish Waif's Story, A, 40, 196, 245,
256–57, 260. *See also* Smith, Emma

Coudreuse, Anne, 272n74

Courage, Mary L., 275n21

Courtivron, Isabelle de, 279n43

Couser, G. Thomas, 16, 253, 255–56,
266n13

Coyle, Kathleen, 166, 171

Creevey, Caroline A. Stickney, 22,
47–48, 95, 259

Creston, Dormer, 110, 151–54, 164,
205, 254; child's vision in, 112, 144,
170, 233, 244, 255; epiphany in, 137,
153; fictionalization in, 144, 164,
254; narrator in, 144

Crowell, Evelyn Miller, 166, 168

Index

Damon, Bertha, 78, 103, 105–6, 172, 192
Darwin, Charles, 80
Daudet, Julia, 22, 28–29, 49–50, 59–60, 74
Davidson, Angus, 134–35
Davis, Rocío G., 12, 15, 266n21, 276n1
Day, Clarence, 105
death: of both parents, 170, 183, 196, 218; of father, 25, 28, 41, 50–51, 58, 72, 87–88, 93, 98, 120, 122–23, 134, 136–37, 144, 150, 168, 173, 181, 183, 240–41, 245; of mother, 35, 106, 169, 203–4, 230, 245–46; as theme, 52, 64, 89, 150, 154, 159, 234
deceptiveness of adults, theme of, 50–51, 115, 230–31, 259
Deland, Margaret Wade, 110, 112, 131, 158–60, 260, 275n33
Delarue-Mardrus, Lucie, 58–59, 75, 145, 255
Dickens, Charles, 100, 200
Dillard, Annie, 3
discretion: in autobiography, 11; in women's childhood autobiography, 38, 74, 77, 172, 202, 243, 250
Dodge, Helen Carmichael, 187–88
Dohm, Hedwig, 22, 71
dolls, theme of, 22, 28, 102, 115; desire for, 27; disliked, 139, 155; types of play with, 50–51, 65, 133
Dorion, Gilles, 278n19
Dostoyevsky, Fydor, 73
Douglas, Kate, 12, 15, 212, 266n14
Dunham, Katherine, 186, 193, 205, 245
Durán, Isabel, 197, 277n11
Duras, Marguerite, 3

Eakin, Paul John: "Breaking Rules," 252, 279n1; *Fictions in Autobiography*, 277n11; *Living Autobiographically*, 255, 279n8
Eakin, Robin, 187, 192
Eaubonne, Françoise d', 187, 195, 214–16, 222–24, 244, 252; Bildungsroman

model in, 215–16, 238; diary in, 223, 231, 244; homosexuality in, 215, 246
Ebner-Eschenbach, Marie von, 22, 71–72, 74, 258; fantasy life in, 72, 239, 259, 261
Egan, Susanna, 9, 20, 266n10, 268n30
Eliot, George, 97
Enckell, Pierre, 28, 268n7
epiphany. *See* illumination, sudden
etiquette. *See* social skills, theme of learning acceptable one
Evers, Medgar, 211
exposés, 72, 124, 193–96, 199–200, 203–5, 256
Eyles, Leonora, 123, 186, 189, 214–20, 222, 224; Bildungsroman model in, 215–16, 222–23, 238, 242; clothes problem in, 122; confessional mode in, 111, 195; death of mother, 218, 245; narrator in, 218–19; compared to Gabriele Reuter, 120; self-focus in, 214; socialism in, 195

fakes. *See* hoaxes
family history, women's childhood autobiography as, 8, 15–16, 267n23; before World War I, 24, 26, 41, 46, 65–67, 69; in interwar years, 81–82, 84–85, 92, 95–98, 100–101, 138–39; in World War II years, 167–69, 171–72; after World War II, 188–89
famous women, childhood autobiographies of, 10; before World War I, 24, 29–30, 46, 216; in interwar years, 98, 119–21, 128–29, 216; after World War II, 216–17, 220, 229–39. *See also* novelists, as childhood autobiographers; performers, childhood autobiographies of
Farjeon, Benjamin, 96
Farjeon, Eleanor, 78, 92, 95–99, 109, 173; fantasy life, 97, 177, 239; semi-memoir type, 95, 169

Farnham, Eliza W., 22, 39–40, 75, 195, 203, 259
faux pas, theme of, 66, 231–32. *See also* social skills, theme of learning acceptable ones
fear, as theme, 39, 53, 61, 124, 129, 151–53, 193, 229, 259–61; of abandonment, 234; of being an adopted child, 97; of dark, 53, 236; of father, 206, 249; of impending catastrophe, 93; as instilled by mother, 136; quest for origin of, 148; of suffocation, 180; of Whites, 210
Felski, Rita, 266n9
feminism: first-wave, 162, 251; history of in women's childhood autobiography, 3, 6, 75, 127, 182, 185, 195, 246, 252; in specific women's childhood autobiographies before World War I, 53–54, 72; in specific women's childhood autobiographies in interwar years, 84, 98, 101–2, 107–8, 125, 127, 137–38, 140; in specific women's childhood autobiographies in World War II years, 169, 174, 182; in specific women's childhood autobiographies after World War II, 204, 222, 215, 238, 241–42
Fen, Elisaveta, 186, 227–29, 239, 261; analytical approach in, 227–28, 231, 243; confessional mode in, 195; relational approach in, 215, 224–25, 238, 244–45
fictionalization: as practice in childhood autobiography, 11–12, 20, 242, 253–55; in specific childhood autobiographies, 35, 62, 74–75, 88, 146–47, 153, 164, 192; as theme, 191, 197. *See also* novelistic techniques in autobiography
fiction-autobiography blends, 11; in women's childhood autobiographies, 40, 58, 111–12, 144, 151–52, 192. *See also* fictionalization

Flaubert, Gustave, 36, 136, 171
Flexner, Helen Thomas, 166–69, 185
Ford, Ford Madox, 82
Foster, John Wilson, 271n48
Foucault, Michel, 253, 279n5
Frame, Janet, 3
France, Anatole, 29, 32
Franklin, Miles, 187–88, 254
free indirect discourse, use of in childhood autobiographies: before World War I, 70; in interwar years, 99, 109, 153, 155, 157; in World War II years, 179, 181; after World War II, 191, 230
Freud, Sigmund, 83, 111, 165; on childhood, 250; and Luhan, 128–29; and Marie Bonaparte, 224, 229–31; on memory, 54, 94, 164, 198, 252; and sex, 143, 164, 175; on women, 6, 259
Frey, James, 255
Fröbel, Friedrich Wilhelm August, 67
Fuller, Margaret, 269n30

Gagnier, Regenia, 277n18
Gambetta, Léon, 29
Gandy, Ida, 78, 99, 103–4, 163; "we" style in, 46, 82, 94, 98
Garreau, Bernard-Marie, 35, 269n17
Gautier, Judith, 22, 31–36, 43, 259, 261; self-portrait in, 29, 31, 50, 127; as strong personality, 29, 31, 237, 258
Gautier, Théophile, 31
Gautier, Yvonne, 187, 194, 245
gender: childhood autobiography and, 12–15, 20–21, 44, 76–77, 216, 250–51, 257–60; differential treatment of, as theme before World War I, 27, 49, 51, 65, 68; differential treatment of, as theme in 1920s, 83–85, 115, 119, 122–23; differential treatment of, as theme in 1930s, 88, 106, 108, 126, 136; differential

treatment of, as theme in 1940s, 169, 174, 181–82, 226–27; differential treatment of, as theme in 1950s, 201, 217, 220–21, 231, 246; differential treatment of, as theme in 1960s, 204, 228–29, 242, 246. *See also* higher education, theme of; schooling, theme off

Gide, André, 164, 171, 176

Gilder, Jeannette, 22, 58, 75, 258

Gilligan, Carol, 267n23

Gilmore, Leigh, 252, 279n2

girlhood, aspects of: authors' comparisons with boyhood, 27, 65, 88, 115, 181, 260; experienced as confining, 27, 115–16, 174, 204; lack of education, 83, 176, 204, 227; emphasis on observing proprieties, 112–13, 118–19, 181; parents want boy, 117, 201; negative stereotyping of girls, 174, 200, 204. *See also* brothers, theme off; gender: differential treatment of; higher education, theme of; schooling, theme of

Godden, Jon, 187–88

Godden, Rumer, 187–88

Goethe, Johann Wolfgang von, 121

Goldman, Emma, 125

Goltz, Bogumil, 103

Gombrich, E. H., 6

Gopnik, Adam, 88

Grahame, Kenneth, 43

Grant Duff, Mountstuart, 83

Greenwood, Grace, 23, 41

Grisi, Carlotta, 31, 33

Grisi, Ernesta, 31

group identity, autobiography of, 196, 209, 211, 262–63, 266n9

growing up, theme of resistance to, 192, 232

Guebhard, Caroline (Rémy). *See* Séverine

Gyp, 110, 112–13, 116–19, 122

Hale, Nancy, 186, 191–92

Hamilton, Elizabeth, 103, 187, 189, 193, 236

Hamilton, Mary, 103, 186, 189, 193, 236

Harder, Agnes, 78, 91, 256

Harding, Bertita, 186, 190

Hatsumi, Reiko, 186, 191–92

Havoc, June, 186, 193, 245

Hawker, Beatrice, 186, 194

Henrey, Mrs. Robert, 186, 190

Herder, Charlotte, 186, 189

Heygate, Elizabeth, 187, 188

higher education, theme of, 108, 169, 173, 209–11, 220–21; denied, 204, 219, 231

Hilliard, Jan, 186, 192

Hirsch, Marianne, 266n8

Hitchman, Janet, 186, 193–94, 207–9, 244

Hitler, Adolf, 91, 93, 154, 162

hoaxes, 85

Hogenhuis-Seliverstoff, Anne, 269n11

Holly, Carol, 270n34

Holman-Hunt, Diana, 186, 192

Holmes, G. V., 186–87, 193

Hooton, Joy, 5, 13, 265n4, 265n6, 267n23

Howe, Bea, 105, 186–87, 193

Howe, Mark L., 275n21

Howitt, Mary, 8, 22–23, 38–39, 41, 75, 190; "we" style in, 38, 68

Hughes, Mary Vivian, 78, 87–88, 95, 99, 104, 163; on being a girl, 88, 260; social history in, 87, 92; typicality in, 171, 256; "we" style in, 46, 87

Hughes, Molly. *See* Hughes, Mary Vivian

Hughes, Mrs. F., 22–23, 39, 75, 104

humor, 58, 126, 163, 249; in specific authors, 51, 58–59, 103, 105–7, 126, 192, 278n26. *See also* tone, importance of

Humphry, James, III, 275n33

298 Index

Hunt, Una, 22, 62–65; child's vision in, 80, 244; imaginary companion in, 63, 168, 233; imaginary self in, 62–63, 239; imaginary world in, 63, 74, 261; inner life of childhood in, 62, 76; narrator in, 62, 153; private language in, 65, 232; religiousness in, 64, 156
Huxley, Elspeth, 186–87

Icus-Rothe, Wanda, 78, 88–90, 102, 163
Iehl, Jules. *See* Yell, Michel
illumination, sudden, 64, 137, 152–53, 168, 229; concerning vocation, 123, 143, 223, 262
imaginary friend, 63, 168, 233, 261
imaginary second self, 62–64, 74, 239
imaginary world, 63, 72, 74, 233
indiscretion. *See* candor, in women's childhood autobiographies
inner life of child: interest in, 76, 112, 258, 271n57; representation of, 62–65, 74, 76, 250, 260–61. *See also* child perspective, adoption of; child's vision, recreation of
interior monologue, use of in childhood autobiographies, 121, 230
Iqbal, Françoise, 278n19
irony, 81, 163, 249; in specific authors, 57–58, 66, 82, 112–13, 126, 152, 157, 224, 235. *See also* tone, importance of
Irvine, Lyn, 186, 194
Ishimoto, Baroness Shidzué, 110, 125

Jackson, Annabel Huth, 78, 83–85, 87–88
Jacobs, Harriet, 18
James, William, 125, 267n23
Jameson, Anna, 37
Jane Eyre, 37, 58, 75, 199, 200. *See also* Brontë, Charlotte
Jean Paul, 67

Jewish childhoods, 65–66, 101–2, 108, 215, 234–35, 238–42
journalists, as childhood autobiographers, 53, 58, 107, 112, 216–17
Jung, Carl, 83

Keller, Helen, 18
Kellner, Esther, 187, 189
Kemble, Fanny, 18
Keppel, Sonia, 186, 188
Kershaw, Angela, 269n15
Kilcup, Karen L., 270n34
Kincaid, Jamaica, 3
King, Martin Luther, Jr., 211
Kingston, Maxine Hong, 3, 11, 158, 255, 262–63
Kipling, Rudyard, 83
knitting, as theme, 26, 68, 70–71, 77, 80, 259
Kort, Amy, 270n34
Kovalevskaya, Sofya, 22, 73–75, 255
Kovalevsky, Sonja. *See* Kovalevskaya, Sofya

labels. *See* victimization: of girls by disparaging discourse
Labovitz, Esther Kleinbord, 220, 278n28
Lagerlöf, Selma, 78, 81, 145
Laing, Kathryn, 54, 270n45, 271n49
Lang, V. E., 273n18
Lange, Katrin, 12, 266n14, 267n23
language acquisition, role of in child development, theme of, 50, 117, 159–60
Larcom, Lucy, 22, 40–51, 104; death of father, 41, 245; focus on milieu, 26, 75; modesty of, 41, 70; and Nancy Hale, 191; narrator in, 45; religiousness of, 41, 44–45, 95, 156; sewing in, 41, 259; typicality in, 44, 256; vocation in, 43, 100, 258; "we" style in, 43, 61, 94, 98; on women, 45, 76

Index

large family: era of, 14–15, 43, 251; unhappy childhood in, 25–27, 56, 71, 124, 174, 195, 203, 258. *See also* "we" style

Laski, Marghanita, 277n9

Lawrence, D. H., 129

Leadbeater, Charles Webster (Bishop), 233

Leduc, Violette, 18

Lee, Gypsy Rose, 186, 191, 193, 245

Le Franc, Marie, 186, 195, 233–34

Lejeune, Philippe: "L'autobiographie et l'aveu sexuel," 164–65, 272n74; "Le récit d'enfance en question," 12, 266n14; *On Autobiography*, 40, 252–54, 269n26

Lenk, Margarete, 22, 67, 70–71, 75, 259

Lerber, Helene von, 187, 189

lesbianism, as theme, 215, 222, 246

Lessing, Doris, 10; "Describing This Beautiful and Nasty Planet," 255, 279n7; *Under My Skin*, 27, 149, 268n6

Lessing, Gotthold Ephraim, 72

Lethbridge, Lucy, 276n2

Lewis, Jessica, 44–45, 270n35

Lewis, Mabel. *See* Smith, Emma

Lifson, Martha F., 277n11

literariness in women's childhood autobiographies, 190–92, 242, 252

literary experimentation in women's childhood autobiographies, 262–63

Lloyd, Rosemary, 17, 268n27

Long, Jeffrey E., 5, 12, 265n3, 265n6

Loti, Pierre, 32, 76, 86, 103

Lowell, Jean, 85

Lubbock, Sybil Marjorie, 78, 103, 163

Ludendorff, Mathilde, 216, 278n26

Luhan, Mabel Dodge, 18, 106, 110–11, 127–35, 163, 165; analytical, 131; as "bad girl," 184; candidness of, 137, 141, 172–73, 175; confessional mode in, 127, 133, 170, 195, 227; critical of parents, 129, 185, 202, 225, 245;

narrator in, 129–30, 144, 161, 198; as only child, 237; and psychoanalysis, 130, 158, 259; rebelliousness in, 132, 224, 244–45; self-focused, 131, 214; self-profiling, 138–39; theme of sex in, 130, 132, 150, 175, 202

Lunt, Cornelia Gray, 78–79, 95, 109, 252; family audience in, 10, 85, 92

Lutyens, Lady Emily, 232

Lutyens, Mary, 186, 195, 229, 232–33, 243; confessional mode in, 195, 232; imaginary companion in, 168, 233, 261; relational focus in, 215, 238; self-focus in, 214, 233

L'vova, Elizaveta, 22, 73–74, 259, 261

Lynch, Hannah, 22, 40, 53–59, 109, 258; feminism in, 54, 75; fictionalization in, 57–58, 75; life, 54, 271n49, 271n50, 271n52; on memory, 29, 54, 239; as middle child, 56; on her mother, 55, 71, 254, 259; victimization in, 31, 56, 74, 195; violence in, 55–56, 203

Lynch, Patricia, 186, 190, 198

MacCarthy, Mary Josepha, 78, 82–84, 99

Maillet, Antonine, 187, 192

Mall-Grob, Beatrice, 272n61

Malraux, André, 238, 241

Malraux, Clara, 18, 187, 238–42, 249; child's vision in, 195, 233–34, 238–39, 243–44; confessional mode in, 195, 215, 238; fantasy life in, 239, 261; feminism in, 246; self-focus in, 214, 238

Marchalonis, Shirley: "Lucy Larcom," 43, 270n31; *The Worlds of Lucy Larcom*, 269n29

Marcus, Jane, 42, 270n32

Marie, Fürstin zu Erbach-Schönberg, 78, 90–91, 163, 252

Marsden-Smedley, Hester, 271n54

Marshall, Audrey, 187, 192

Martens, Lorna, 268n29
Martin, Claire, 187, 193, 202–7, 227, 249; accusation in, 203–5, 245; agenda in, 203, 256–57; confession in, 206–7; death of mother in, 204, 245; feminism in, 204, 246
Martineau, Harriet, 18, 37, 39, 198
Matheson, Gwen, 273n18
McBride, Mary Margaret, 166–67
McCall, Dorothy, 186, 188
McCarthy, Mary, 186, 196–98, 244, 252; accusation in, 197–98, 245; fictionalization in, 191–92, 197, 255
McClung, Nellie L., 78, 85, 92, 98–103, 163; feminism in, 46, 98, 100; and Laura Goodman Salverson, 137–38, 140–42; as narrator, 99; vocation in, 100; "we" style in, 46, 99–100
McHugh, Mary Frances, 78, 84, 89, 163, 236
memoir, defined vs. autobiography, 15–16, 247; domestic memoir, 37–38, 74; as term, 256, 266n9, 268n25; women's childhood memoirs before World War I, 65–69, 71–72, 74–75; women's childhood memoirs in interwar years, 79–91, 103–5, 108–10, 118, 163, 251; women's childhood memoirs in World War II years, 167; women's childhood memoirs after World War II, 187, 192–94, 229, 245. See also semi-memoir; "we" style
memory: and autobiography, 11, 146, 192, 252–54; in childhood autobiography, as theme, 22, 185; childhood presented as, 28, 49, 59–60, 74, 158, 160–61, 178, 193, 234; comments about, in childhood autobiographies, 25, 30, 52, 72, 116, 146, 171, 192, 197, 208, 234–35, 239–41; early memories, interest in, 28–29, 33, 50, 54, 73, 94, 100, 104, 117–18, 161, 179, 199, 234, 239; first memory, 26,

69, 91, 124, 141–42, 146, 179, 203; history of study of, 49; history of theory of, 250, 252–53; modern scientific findings on, 147, 160, 179, 239, 275n21; Proustian treatment of, 94, 105, 178–80, 240; psychoanalytic influence on, 198, 231; in representation of child's vision, 234; theorized in childhood autobiographies, 28, 33, 49–50, 73, 94–95, 158–61, 170, 178–80, 229. See also amnesia, childhood; screen memory
mentality of child. See inner life of child
Mernissi, Fatima, 3, 263
Mialaret, Athénaïs. See Michelet, Athénaïs
Michelet, Athénaïs, 8–9, 22, 25–28, 32, 36, 260, 268n3; on her brothers, 27, 176; confessional mode in, 127; on her doll, 27, 50, 249; as middle child, 26, 56, 195; misery in, 27, 56, 258; on her mother, 25–28, 55, 130, 195, 250, 259; narrator in, 26, 28; sewing in, 40–41, 259
Michelet, Jules, 25, 28, 268n3
Miegel, Agnes, 112; child's vision in, 112, 144, 154, 233, 244
Milligan, Jennifer E., 79, 272n1
Milton, Heather, 277n18
Mirabeau, Sibylle Gabrielle Marie Antoinette de Riquetti de, comtesse de Martel de Janville. See Gyp
modesty: expected of women, 74, 76, 106, 250; narrative attitude of in women's childhood autobiographies, 42–47, 51, 70–71, 99, 163, 257; reproved for lack of, 66. See also sex, theme of: avoidance of topic of
Moll Flanders, 136, 200, 272n74
Moody, Anne, 184, 187, 208–11; agenda in, 245, 256; typicality in, 209, 242, 256, 262
Mörike, Eduard, 275n27

mother-daughter relationship: change in, over time, 25, 140, 182; mother-daughter conflict, 26–27, 30, 55, 135–36, 173–74, 202. *See also* mothers

mothers: absent, 25, 30, 53, 70, 190, 202; impractical, helpless, 51–52; loving, caring, 53, 86, 169, 204, 228; manipulative, 226–27; practical, hardworking, 139, 235; strict, cold, punitive, loveless, 27, 30, 55, 70–71, 73, 91, 130; tributes paid to, 51–53, 86, 101, 108, 155, 169, 185, 194. *See also* parents, girls' preference for one over the other

Murray, Gilbert, 59

Neilson, Elisabeth, 166–67
Nesbit, E., 22, 52–53, 168, 198; fear in, 53, 61; memory in, 52, 60, 85; on her mother, 53, 259; storytelling in, 58, 75, 190; typicality in, 52, 256
Neumann, Bernd, 16, 268n25
New Yorker, The, 105, 196, 255; role of in publishing childhood autobiography, 190–93, 242, 251
Noailles, Anna de, 110, 125
Noël, Marie, 186, 215, 261; child's vision in, 195, 233–34, 243–44, 261
Norman, Rose, 270n34
nostalgia, 43; in men's childhood autobiographies, 14, 32, 76; in women's childhood autobiographies before World War I, 29, 52, 60, 70–71; in women's childhood autobiographies in interwar years, 80–82, 84–90, 96, 109; in women's childhood autobiographies after World War II, 189, 191. *See also* tone, importance of
Novalis, 67
novelistic techniques in autobiography, 254; in specific childhood autobiographies, 35, 40, 57, 74–75,

96, 121, 141–42, 146, 191–92, 200. *See also* child perspective, adoption of; free indirect discourse, use of in childhood autobiographies; interior monologue, use of in childhood autobiographies; fictionalization; literariness in women's childhood autobiography; storytelling style, in childhood autobiography; third-person narration in childhood autobiographies

novelists, as childhood autobiographers: before World War I, 24, 31, 53, 72; in interwar years, 82, 85, 92, 98, 116, 119–20, 126, 134, 143, 145–46, 154, 158; after World War II, 191, 196, 216, 222, 224–25, 232. *See also* children's book writers, as childhood autobiographers

Ogilvie, Mary I., 186, 188
only child, women who grew up as, 69, 116, 118, 130–31, 136, 180, 183, 230–31, 236
Orpen, Adela, 78, 84–85, 99
orphan, women who grew up as, 35, 39–40, 194, 196–97, 200, 207–8

Pagés, Helene, 78, 102–3, 163, 260
Pange, Pauline, 187–88
paradise-fall pattern, 76, 88–91, 103, 221–23, 262
parents, girls' preference for one over the other: criteria, 139, 261; in specific women's childhood autobiographies, 26–28, 136, 139, 170, 181, 194, 203–4, 235
Parker, Simon, 198, 200
Patchett, Mary Elwyn, 186–87
pathos, 113–14, 116. *See also* tone, importance of
performers, childhood autobiographies of, 155, 193
Peterson, Carole, 275n21

302 Index

Peterson, Linda H., 36–37, 269n18, 271n53
Phelps, Orra Parker, 186, 189
Phillips, Margaret Mann, 166, 171
Pinfold, Debbie, 12, 266n14
Plath, Sylvia, 203
poets, as childhood autobiographers: before World War I, 28, 41, 43, 52, 59; in interwar years, 92, 142, 154–55, 158; after World War II, 191, 215, 223, 234
political agenda in women's childhood autobiographies, 72–73, 75, 184, 208–14, 262–63
Popp, Adelheid, 22, 34, 72–73, 75; agenda in, 72, 75, 85, 256; death of father, 245; typicality in, 256
Porter, Alyene, 105, 166, 192
Posse-Brázdová, Amelie, 166–68, 185, 261
Potter, Dawn, 271n55
poverty, childhood experience of: before World War II, 35–36, 66–67, 69–70, 72, 101, 122–24; after World War II, 193–202, 208–10, 217–19, 222–24
Powell, Violet, 186, 192
Preyer, Wilhelm, 67
privacy, desire for, 41–42, 117
private language, theme of, 65, 232
Proust, Marcel, 76, 86, 94; on childhood, 103; on memory, 94, 105, 178–79, 240, 276n10
psychoanalysis: and concept of childhood, 8, 111, 131, 164; historical reception of, 127; impact of, on childhood autobiography, 20, 111, 164–65, 195, 251–52, 259, 262; influence of in specific women's childhood autobiographies, in interwar years, 83, 111, 128–31, 143, 158–59; in World War II years, 175, 180; after World War II, 198, 205, 217, 224–27, 229–31, 239–40.

See also Adler, Alfred; Freud, Sigmund
psychological approaches: before World War I, 8; turn to in interwar years, 80, 92, 162–63; pervasiveness of in World War II years, 185; dominance of after World War II, 242, 251
psychology, authors attentive to: before World War I, 25, 29, 35, 50, 53–55; in interwar years, 101–2, 110–62; in World War II years, 170, 178; after World War II, 193, 205, 215, 224–42
publication: effect of intention to publish, 4, 42, 248–49
punishment, theme of, 40, 91, 115, 133, 183; corporal, 56, 88, 150, 195, 197, 204–5; humiliating, 176–77

Quinby, Lee, 16

race, theme of, 183–84, 191, 210–14
Raine, Kathleen, 3
rape, theme of, 124, 212–14
Raphael, John N., 269n14
Raverat, Gwen, 186, 188
rebelliousness, 83, 162, 224, 244, 246; in specific authors before World War I, 31, 56–58; in specific authors in interwar and World War II years, 113, 118, 127, 132, 139–40, 165, 176; in specific authors after World War II, 197, 205, 218–22, 238, 241
Reetz, Bärbel, 155, 157, 275n28, 275n31
Reisinger, Roman, 12, 266n14
relationships, focus on, 16, 267n23; in specific women's childhood autobiographies, 101–2, 182–83, 215, 224–33, 244–45
religion, theme of: harm caused by, 141, 209–10; importance of, 41,

43–45, 64, 156–57, 160, 184; problems with, 72, 80, 93, 95, 106, 115
Rémy, Caroline, 113, 254. *See also* Séverine
Reuschle, Sophie, 71, 78, 89–90, 235
Reuter, Gabriele, 110, 119–24, 137–43, 163, 222–23; autobiography of famous person type, 120, 216; Bildungsroman model in, 119–21; clothes problem in, 122, 218; confessional mode in, 112, 123–24, 128, 138; death of father, 122, 245; epiphany in, 123, 137, 143, 152; feminism in, 138; vocation in, 120, 123, 143, 223
revelation. *See* illumination, sudden
Richards, Laura E., 46
Richardson, Henry Handel, 18
Richardson, Joanna: *Colette*, 273n8; *Enid Starkie*, 173, 276n4
Rilke, Rainer Maria, 132
Rimbaud, Arthur, 171
Rodaway, Angela, 186, 193–94
Roland, Madame, 272n74
Romanticism, 7–8, 14, 103, 259; German Romanticism, 67, 121
Ross, Marie Marchand, 78, 85
Rossetti, Christina, 82
Rousseau, Jean-Jacques, 36, 67; autobiographical tradition of, 8, 23–24, 74, 138, 221–22, 239, 250, 266n9; on childhood, 76, 103
Rowse, A. L., 198–99, 202
Roy, Arundhati, 261, 263
Rudnick, Lois Palken, 274n9
Rüggemeier, Anne, 267n23
Russell, Bertrand, 125

Salverson, Laura Goodman, 110, 137–43, 165, 173, 226; candidness in, 141; confessional mode in, 111, 127–28, 137–43, 195; epiphany in, 137, 143; feminism in, 138, 140–41, 241; and Nellie McClung, 137–38;

on her mother, 139; narrator in, 139–40, 144; on her parents, 139, 225; rebelliousness in, 139, 142, 244; self-focus in, 214; self-profiling, 138; third person opening in, 142, 236; vocation in, 143, 223
Sand, George, 8, 22, 23–25, 36, 50, 268n27; autobiography of famous person type, 120; confessional mode in, 127, 250; death of father, 25, 245; and Judith Gautier, 31; and Juliette Adam, 29; on her mother, 25, 51, 86, 259; self-focus in, 128; typicality in, 256
Sanders, Valerie: *Private Lives of Victorian Women*, 12, 267n15, 272n74; *Records of Girlhood*, 12–13, 37–38, 267n16, 267n21
Sanger, Margaret, 125
Sapir, Edward, 160
Sarraute, Nathalie: *Childhood (Enfance)*, 13, 197, 263; tropisms, 148
Sarton, May, 186, 191
Sartre, Jean-Paul, 220–21
satire, 51, 82, 126. *See also* tone, importance of
Satrapi, Marjane, 3, 263
Schary, Dore, 192
Schieber, Anna, 71, 110, 154–55, 260; child's vision in, 112, 144, 154, 233, 244, 261
Schleunes, Karl A., 272n62
schooling, theme of, 65–66, 82–83, 87–88, 137, 176–77
Schumacher, Tony, 22, 24, 67, 69, 71, 259
screen memory, 54, 198. *See also* Freud, Sigmund: on memory
secret passion, topic of, 122, 223–33
Sedgwick, Catharine, 41
Seidel, Ina, 78, 80, 92–93, 95, 163
self-delusion, theme of, 226–27, 233
self-focused childhood autobiographies, 15; critical attention to, 15,

304 Index

self-focused childhood
  autobiographies (*continued*)
  265n6; French tradition of, 23,
  267n23; self-focused women's childhood autobiographies before World
  War I, 24–37, 53, 65–66, 70, 73–74;
  self-focused women's childhood
  autobiographies in interwar years,
  110–66; self-focused women's childhood autobiographies during World
  War II, 170–84; self-focused women's
  childhood autobiographies after
  World War II, 195, 214–42
self-image, 9, 248; as "bad girl," 131,
  136, 184, 244; as rebel, 31, 56–58,
  132, 139–40, 142, 197, 219–20; as
  savage, 159, 208; as savior, 226, 240;
  as victim, 6, 31, 53–57, 113, 173,
  184, 195–98, 200–204, 248. *See also*
  self-presentation
self-portrait, 29–34, 79, 89, 95–96,
  100–101, 110–65, 230–31. *See also*
  self-presentation
self-presentation, 4, 18–19, 110, 257–
  58; authoritative, 132, 218, 225;
  humorous, 51, 58, 106, 109, 143;
  modest, 43, 47, 51, 66, 70–71, 76, 163,
  180, 250; as similar to other children, 44, 49, 52, 104, 154; as typical
  of social group, 211, 242; as unique
  individual, 59, 75, 115. *See also* self-
  portrait; tone, importance of
semi-memoir: defined, 16, 92, 247, 249;
  as most popular type overall, 248;
  women's semi-memoirs of childhood in interwar years, 85, 93–103,
  107–9, 163, 251; women's semi-
  memoirs of childhood in World
  War II years, 167–70, 184–85;
  women's semi-memoirs of childhood after World War II, 187–90,
  242–43
Séverine (Caroline Rémy Guebhard),
  50, 110, 112–16, 121, 165, 198;

on being a girl, 115, 119, 174;
  deceptiveness of adults in, 115;
  fictionalization in, 164; narrator in,
  113–14, 115–16; on her parents, 113,
  116, 154, 254; rebelliousness in,
  113, 224; stifling home life in, 113,
  116, 128, 131, 204; third-person
  narration in, 113–14, 145
sewing, as theme, 26, 41, 65, 80, 148,
  259
sex, theme of: in interwar years, 111,
  124, 127–28, 132, 135–36, 143–44,
  148, 150–51, 164–65; in World War
  II years, 175–76, 202; after World
  War II, 195, 200–202, 204–5, 207,
  219, 222, 227, 231–32, 240–41,
  262; avoidance of topic of, 76. *See
  also* abuse: sexual, in childhood
  autobiography
shame, 39, 70, 126, 154, 213–14; at
  burning father's books, 136; at
  family, 124, 193, 205; at having
  been abused, 206; sexual, 151, 205,
  207
Sherwood, Mary Martha, 37
Shields, Karena, 186–87
Shuttleworth, Sally, 270n41
Sillar, Eleanor Hallard, 187–88
Silverman, Willa Z., 274n2
Sinclair, Lucy, 50, 186, 193–94
Skariatina, Irina, 78, 81
Slenczynska, Ruth, 186, 193, 245
Smith, Emma ("Cornish Waif"), 186,
  193–94, 198–203, 205–9, 212–13. *See
  also Cornish Waif's Story, A*
Smith, Sidonie: *A Poetics of Women's
  Autobiography*, 265n1; *Reading Auto-
  biography*, 16, 266n9, 268n25; "The
  Trouble with Autobiography," 11,
  266n12
social history, contribution to in
  women's childhood autobiogra-
  phies: before World War I, 65–66,
  69; in interwar years, 84, 87–88,

92–95, 98–99, 101–3; after World War II, 199, 238
socialism, 102, 164, 195, 251; socialist authors, 72–73, 112, 125, 217
social skills, theme of learning acceptable ones, 34, 51, 77, 112–13, 118–19, 181. *See also* faux pas, theme of
Sone, Monica, 186, 188
Sorensen, Virginia, 187, 191–92
Soskice, Juliet M., 78, 82, 163
Specht, Mary Helen, 274n7
Starkie, Enid, 27, 166, 170–78, 226, 236, 249; clothes problem in, 122, 218; confessional mode in, 111, 170, 176, 182, 195; critical of family, 174–75, 193, 225, 227, 245, 257; feminism in, 174; indiscretion in, 172–73; misery in, 173, 176–77, 185, 198; on her mother, 174, 202; outspokenness in, 184–85; rebelliousness in, 244–45; self-focus in, 214; theme of sex in, 175–76; typicality in, 172, 256
stealing, theme of, 43, 48, 50, 131, 198, 208
Stendhal, 8, 136
stereotyping, 14, 42; of African Americans, 183; of bastards, 193, 200; through clothing, 201–2; of girls, 68, 174, 200, 204; of women, 108, 131
Stern, E. G., 22, 66
Stich, K. P., 141
Stillman, Beatrice, 272n69
Stockhausen, Julius, 190
storytelling style, in childhood autobiography, 38–39, 49, 52, 57–58, 68–69, 75, 99, 126, 142, 190
Symons, Geraldine, 186, 188

teasing, theme of, 38, 149, 180
third-person narration in childhood autobiographies, 48–49, 81, 93, 113–14, 145–46, 158, 192, 255; in opening segment of childhood autobiographies, 98, 141–42, 236
Thirkell, Angela, 78, 82, 163
Thompson, Ariadne, 186, 189
Thoreau, Henry David, 105
Timings, C. L., 186, 188
Tisdall, Laura, 277n9
Tolstoy, Leo, 73
tone, importance of, 20, 247. *See also* humor; irony; nostalgia; pathos; satire
Tonna, Charlotte Elizabeth, 37
toys, theme of, 61, 94, 197, 204, 260
trauma, 6–7, 24, 33, 57, 212
Treneer, Anne, 166, 168, 181
truth, in autobiography, 11, 252–54
Turner, J. M. W., 107
twins, stories of, 215
typicality, assertion of, 248, 255–56, 266n9; by specific authors, 44, 49, 52, 65, 145, 152, 171–72, 180. *See also* group identity, autobiography of; self-presentation: as similar to other children; self-presentation: as typical of social group

Undset, Sigrid, 110, 144–51; child's vision in, 112, 144, 148–49, 155, 163, 233, 236, 244, 261; on death, 150, 260; fictionalization in, 145–47, 164; on memory, 146–47; narrator in, 144, 147; sex in, 132, 148, 150–51, 175, 205; third-person narration in, 145–47, 255
Uttley, Alison, 78, 103–5, 168, 256

Vallès, Jules, 76
Vauchel, Jean-Philippe, 79, 273n2
Verschoyle, Moira, 186, 215, 235–39, 249; child's vision in, 189, 195, 233, 236, 239, 243–44, 261; as only child, 237
Viallaneix, Paul, 268n7

Index

victimization: examples of, 31, 39–40, 53–57, 113–16, 173–74; of girls by disparaging discourse, 174, 200, 204; theme of, 6, 195–96, 212, 214. *See also* abuse; self-image

Villinger, Hermine, 71

violence, theme of, 191, 193, 203–6, 208–11; by adults against children, 27, 40, 55–58, 117, 170, 195–98; as punishment, 56, 88, 150, 198, 203–5, 238

vocation, as theme, 22, 258, 262; help humanity, 100; help poor people, 218; nurse, 47; philosopher, 221; poet, 43; teacher, 41, 100, 102; wife and mother, 200; writer, 24, 49–51, 96, 120, 123, 140, 143, 222–23, 232, 242

Wachtel, Andrew Baruch, 73, 272n68

Wagstaff, Barbara, 134

Waser, Maria, 110, 112, 158, 160–62, 225, 256

Watson, Julia: *Reading Autobiography*, 16, 266n9, 268n25; "The Trouble with Autobiography," 11, 266n12

wealth, childhood experience of, 83, 107–8, 129–37, 217, 220, 229–32

Wedel, Gudrun, 5, 265n5, 265n6

Weinhandl, Margarete, 166–67

Weiss, Louise, 78, 80, 107–9, 118

"we" style, 257–58; women's childhood autobiographies in "we" style before World War I, 38, 40–46, 68–69; women's childhood autobiographies in "we" style in interwar years, 82, 87, 90, 94–95, 98–101, 105; women's childhood autobiographies in "we" style after World War II, 194

Whipple, Dorothy, 110, 125–26, 172, 205

Whorf, Benjamin Lee, 160

Wieland, Christoph Martin, 121

Winfrey, Oprah, 255

Wirth-Stockhausen, Julia, 186, 190

Wolf, Christa, 3, 263

Wolfe, Ann F., 276n5

Wong, Jade Snow, 186, 188

Woodward, Helen, 78, 92, 101–2, 163

Woodward, Kathleen, 78, 84

Woolf, Virginia, 152, 212, 241

words. *See* victimization: of girls by disparaging discourse

Wordsworth, William, 44, 76, 137, 163; on childhood, 8, 19, 76, 103, 105; and childhood autobiography, 81

working-class authors: before World War I, 34–36, 66, 72–73, 75; in interwar years, 84, 101; after World War II, 193–94, 198–201, 207, 251, 277n18

Wright, Richard, 210–11

writers, as childhood autobiographers, 9–10. *See also* children's book writers, as childhood autobiographers; novelists, as childhood autobiographers; poets, as childhood autobiographers

Yagoda, Ben, 253, 255, 272n60

Yalom, Marilyn, 221, 278n30

Yell, Michel (Jules Iehl), 34

Ziegfeld, Patricia, 187, 192

Zimmer, Jill Schary, 187, 192

Zweig, Stefan, 80

Wisconsin Studies in Autobiography

William L. Andrews,

Series Editor

The Examined Self: Benjamin Franklin, Henry Adams, Henry James
Robert F. Sayre

Spiritual Autobiography in Early America
Daniel B. Shea

The Education of a WASP
Lois Mark Stalvey

Forbidden Family: A Wartime Memoir of the Philippines, 1941–1945
Margaret Sams
Edited with an introduction by Lynn Z. Bloom

Journeys in New Worlds: Early American Women's Narratives
Edited by William L. Andrews, Sargent Bush, Jr.,
Annette Kolodny, Amy Schrager Lang, and
Daniel B. Shea

The Living of Charlotte Perkins Gilman: An Autobiography
Charlotte Perkins Gilman
Introduction by Ann J. Lane

*Mark Twain's Own Autobiography: The Chapters from the
"North American Review"*
Mark Twain
Edited by Michael J. Kiskis

American Autobiography: Retrospect and Prospect
Edited by Paul John Eakin

The Diary of Caroline Seabury, 1854–1863
Caroline Seabury
Edited with an introduction by Suzanne L. Bunkers

*A Woman's Civil War: A Diary with
Reminiscences of the War, from March 1862*
CORNELIA PEAKE MCDONALD
Edited with an introduction by MINROSE C. GWIN

My Lord, What a Morning
MARIAN ANDERSON
Introduction by NELLIE Y. MCKAY

American Women's Autobiography: Fea(s)ts of Memory
Edited with an introduction by MARGO CULLEY

Livin' the Blues: Memoirs of a Black Journalist and Poet
FRANK MARSHALL DAVIS
Edited with an introduction by JOHN EDGAR TIDWELL

Authority and Alliance in the Letters of Henry Adams
JOANNE JACOBSON

The Zea Mexican Diary: 7 September 1926–7 September 1986
KAMAU BRATHWAITE

*My History, Not Yours: The Formation of
Mexican American Autobiography*
GENARO M. PADILLA

Witnessing Slavery: The Development of Ante-bellum Slave Narratives
FRANCES SMITH FOSTER

Native American Autobiography: An Anthology
Edited by ARNOLD KRUPAT

American Lives: An Anthology of Autobiographical Writing
Edited by ROBERT F. SAYRE

*Intensely Family: The Inheritance of
Family Shame and the Autobiographies of Henry James*
CAROL HOLLY

People of the Book: Thirty Scholars Reflect on Their Jewish Identity
Edited by JEFFREY RUBIN-DORSKY and
SHELLEY FISHER FISHKIN

Recovering Bodies: Illness, Disability, and Life Writing
G. THOMAS COUSER

My Generation: Collective Autobiography and Identity Politics
JOHN DOWNTON HAZLETT

*Jumping the Line: The Adventures and
Misadventures of an American Radical*
WILLIAM HERRICK

Women, Autobiography, Theory: A Reader
Edited by SIDONIE SMITH and JULIA WATSON

The Making of a Chicano Militant: Lessons from Cristal
JOSÉ ANGEL GUTIÉRREZ

Rosa: The Life of an Italian Immigrant
MARIE HALL ETS

*Illumination and Night Glare:
The Unfinished Autobiography of Carson McCullers*
CARSON MCCULLERS
Edited with an introduction by CARLOS L. DEWS

Who Am I? An Autobiography of Emotion, Mind, and Spirit
YI-FU TUAN

The Life and Adventures of Henry Bibb: An American Slave
HENRY BIBB
With a new introduction by CHARLES J. HEGLAR

Diaries of Girls and Women: A Midwestern American Sampler
Edited by SUZANNE L. BUNKERS

The Autobiographical Documentary in America
JIM LANE

Caribbean Autobiography: Cultural Identity and Self-Representation
SANDRA POUCHET PAQUET

*How I Became a Human Being:
A Disabled Man's Quest for Independence*
MARK O'BRIEN, with GILLIAN KENDALL

*Campaigns of Curiosity: Journalistic
Adventures of an American Girl in Late Victorian London*
ELIZABETH L. BANKS
Introduction by MARY SUZANNE SCHRIBER and ABBEY L. ZINK

The Text Is Myself: Women's Life Writing and Catastrophe
MIRIAM FUCHS

Harriet Tubman: The Life and the Life Stories
JEAN M. HUMEZ

Voices Made Flesh: Performing Women's Autobiography
Edited by LYNN C. MILLER, JACQUELINE TAYLOR, and
M. HEATHER CARVER

The Woman in Battle: The Civil War Narrative of
Loreta Janeta Velazquez, Cuban Woman and Confederate Soldier
LORETA JANETA VELAZQUEZ
Introduction by JESSE ALEMÁN

Maverick Autobiographies:
Women Writers and the American West, 1900–1936
CATHRYN HALVERSON

The Blind African Slave:
Or Memoirs of Boyrereau Brinch, Nicknamed Jeffrey Brace
JEFFREY BRACE as told to BENJAMIN F. PRENTISS, Esq.
Edited and with an introduction by KARI J. WINTER

The Secret of M. Dulong: A Memoir
COLETTE INEZ

Before They Could Vote:
American Women's Autobiographical Writing, 1819–1919
Edited by SIDONIE SMITH and JULIA WATSON

Writing Desire: Sixty Years of Gay Autobiography
BERTRAM J. COHLER

Autobiography and Decolonization:
Modernity, Masculinity, and the Nation-State
PHILIP HOLDEN

When "I" Was Born: Women's Autobiography in Modern China
JING M. WANG

Conjoined Twins in Black and White:
The Lives of Millie-Christine McKoy and Daisy and Violet Hilton
Edited by LINDA FROST

Four Russian Serf Narrative
Translated, edited, and with an introduction by John MacKay

*Mark Twain's Own Autobiography: The Chapters from the
"North American Review,"* second edition
Mark Twain
Edited by Michael J. Kiskis

Graphic Subjects: Critical Essays on Autobiography and Graphic Novels
Edited by Michael A. Chaney

A Muslim American Slave: The Life of Omar Ibn Said
Omar Ibn Said
Translated from the Arabic, edited,
and with an introduction by Ala Alryyes

Sister: An African American Life in Search of Justice
Sylvia Bell White and Jody LePage

Identity Technologies: Constructing the Self Online
Edited by Anna Poletti and Julie Rak

*Masked: The Life of Anna Leonowens,
Schoolmistress at the Court of Siam*
Alfred Habegger

We Shall Bear Witness: Life Narratives and Human Rights
Edited by Meg Jensen and Margaretta Jolly

Dear World: Contemporary Uses of the Diary
Kylie Cardell

*Words of Witness: Black Women's Autobiography
in the Post-"Brown" Era*
Angela A. Ards

*A Mysterious Life and Calling:
From Slavery to Ministry in South Carolina*
Reverend Mrs. Charlotte S. Riley
Edited with an introduction by Crystal J. Lucky

American Autobiography after 9/11
Megan Brown

Reading African American Autobiography:
Twenty-First-Century Contexts and Criticism
Edited by ERIC D. LAMORE

Whispers of Cruel Wrongs: The Correspondence
of Louisa Jacobs and Her Circle,1879–1911
Edited by MARY MAILLARD

Such Anxious Hours: Wisconsin Women's Voices from the Civil War
Edited by JO ANN DALY CARR

The Divided States: Unraveling National Identities
in the Twenty-First Century
Edited by LAURA J. BEARD and RICIA ANNE CHANSKY

As Told by Herself: Women's Childhood Autobiography, 1845–1969
LORNA MARTENS